Open Source Messaging
Application Development:
Building and Extending Gaim

SEAN EGAN

Apress®

Lead Editor: Jason Gilmore
Technical Reviewer: Nathan Walp
Editorial Board: Steve Anglin, Dan Appleman, Ewan Buckingham, Gary Cornell, Tony Davis, Jason Gilmore,
    Jonathan Hassell, Chris Mills, Dominic Shakeshaft, Jim Sumser
Associate Publisher: Grace Wong
Project Manager: Beth Christmas
Copy Edit Manager: Nicole LeClerc
Copy Editor: Candace English
Production Manager: Kari Brooks-Copony
Production Editor: Kelly Winquist
Compositor: Susan Glinert and Wordstop Technologies Pvt. Ltd., Chennai
Proofreader: Linda Seifert
Indexer: Broccoli Information Services
Artist: Kinetic Publishing Services, LLC
Cover Designer: Kurt Krames
Manufacturing Manager: Tom Debolski

Distributed to the book trade in the United States by Springer-Verlag New York, Inc., 233 Spring Street, 6th Floor, New York, NY 10013, and outside the United States by Springer-Verlag GmbH & Co. KG, Tiergartenstr. 17, 69112 Heidelberg, Germany.

In the United States: phone 1-800-SPRINGER, fax 201-348-4505, e-mail orders@springer-ny.com, or visit http://www.springer-ny.com. Outside the United States: fax +49 6221 345229, e-mail orders@spriger.de, or visit http://springer.de.

For information on translations, please contact Apress directly at 2560 Ninth Street, Suite 219, Berkeley, CA 94710. Phone 510-549-5930, fax 510-549-5939, e-mail info@apress.com, or visit http://www.apress.com.

The information in this book is distributed on an "as is" basis, without warranty. Although every precaution has been taken in the preparation of this work, neither the author(s) nor Apress shall have any liability to any person or entity with respect to any loss or damage caused or alleged to be caused directly or indirectly by the information contained in this work.

The source code for this book is available to readers at http://www.apress.com in the Downloads section.

For Dad

Contents at a Glance

Contents

About the Author

 **SEAN EGAN** maintains the Gaim project, `http://gaim.sourceforge.net`. He is a major contributor to the project, managing a team of 10 core developers, and reviewing and incorporating patches from over 200 contributors. A Long Island, NY native, Sean has a bachelor's degree in computer science from Binghamton Universtiy.

Sean has been involved in Gaim development for five years and learned most of what he knows about software development from his experience with the project.

About the Technical Reviewer

NATHAN WALP is a software engineer at Recognition Research, Inc. in Blacksburg, VA. He has more than five years experience writing software, and has been working on Gaim since 2001; he is responsible for Jabber support, among many other things.

Acknowledgments

I'd like to thank my friends and family for their support while I was writing this book, especially my parents Doug and Lynn, and my sister Erin.

I'd like to thank everyone at Apress for their support and patience with me, especially those I worked with directly: Beth Christmas, Jason Gilmore, Candace English, Julie Miller, and Kelly Winquist.

Mostly, I'd like to thank everyone who's contributed to Gaim, making this book possible; especially Nathan Walp (who is also the technical reviewer for this book), Mark Spencer, Jim Duchek, Rob Flynn, Syd Logan, Eric Warmenhoven, Adam Fritzler, Benjamin Miller, Decklin Foster, Mark Doliner, Luke Schierer, Ethan Blanton, Etan Reisner, Tim Ringenbach, Daniel Atallah, Robert McQueen, Christian Hammond, Herman Bloggs, Stu Tomlinson, Gary Kramlich, Ka-Hing Cheung, Kevin Stange, and Felipe Contreras.

Introduction

I discovered Gaim in the AOL Instant Messenger (AIM) user profile of a friend about five years ago. I didn't know a lot about Linux then. I knew that it was a free implementation of UNIX with publicly available source code, but my previous experiences with UNIX comprised staring at a shell prompt, trying to type cryptic commands into a "DOS-like" console. Likewise, I assumed that Linux was primitive compared to the high-tech, state-of-the-art Windows 98 I was using that day when I read my friend's profile.

"Visit the Gaim Web page," it invited me. I followed the link and found my preconceptions were wrong. On what I had seen as a platform solely for Web servers and corporate mainframes, I could perform such everyday tasks as chatting with my friends. I expected nothing but text commands, but I found Web browsers, e-mail clients, and games—all with windows to scroll and buttons to click. Linux no longer looked like DOS; it was an actively developed desktop operating system. Wanting to contribute to that development process, I quickly downloaded the Gaim source code and started coding.

At the time, though, I had just started learning how to use my operating system and didn't know any C (the language Gaim is written in). This didn't stop me; I quickly taught myself all the skills necessary to write this hugely popular desktop application, using Gaim as an example. Today, I'm the lead developer of the Gaim project, and I work closely with a group of developers to maintain and enhance the most popular open source instant messaging application on the planet.

About Gaim

Gaim is a modular instant messaging client that supports a wide variety of IM protocols, including AIM, ICQ, MSN, Yahoo!, and Jabber. Although it was originally written for Linux, it now runs on most popular operating systems, including Windows and Mac OS X. Although exact user statistics are impossible to obtain, its users number in the hundreds of thousands, if not over a million. It's so popular because, in addition to functionality available in other clients, it offers many unique features and is infinitely extensible through a powerful plug-in API. Most importantly in the context of this book is that Gaim is free and open source software.

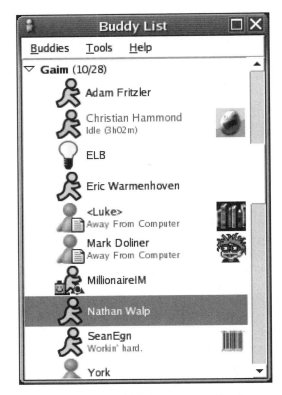

Figure 1. *A screenshot of the Gaim application*

"Free software" and "open source software" are terms that differ slightly in semantics but describe essentially the same thing. When downloading Gaim, you are offered the source code. Having unfettered access to the source code is quite valuable for understanding how Gaim works, and is necessary should you wish to make any modifications. The only major provision is that you grant this same right to modify your changes. This way, Gaim benefits from hundreds of talented developers around the world, offering their contributions back to the community. Because Gaim is built entirely with open source tools, involving yourself in its development is easy, and it makes an excellent example to learn from.

About This Book

This book will help you to learn the same important programming skills I learned using Gaim as an example. I'll explore the various techniques and technologies used by Gaim, and after reading this book you will be able to use what you've learned to create your own networked, cross-platform desktop application.

This book introduces GTK+, the library used to create Gaim's graphical user interface. You will understand the principles behind it, and will know enough of its API to make changes to Gaim's GUI and to develop interfaces for your own applications.

This book will also introduce network programming. You will learn what sockets are and how to use them to make your applications communicate over the Internet. I'll also introduce you to a concept known as *reverse engineering*, showing you how to capture and interpret network traffic so that your application can speak otherwise-closed, proprietary protocols.

I'll examine different ways to make sure that your applications are accessible to everyone, regardless of what kind of computer they're running on (portability) and what languages your users speak (internationalization). I'll also discuss some of the important differences between platforms, and you will learn about how computers store text. We will look at the gettext system, which allows your application to be translated to other languages.

Throughout, I'll examine useful coding techniques implemented within Gaim to make programming in C and managing a large project easier. A per-chapter breakdown of the material covered in this book follows.

Chapter 1: Getting Started

In Chapter 1, you'll install a build environment containing all the software and libraries you'll need to build Gaim and other desktop programs. I'll also introduce you to using Gaim, sharing some little known, undocumented features.

Chapter 2: The Open Source Development Process

As an open source application, Gaim is developed with processes unfamiliar to many people. However, the open source development process is very powerful and is gaining in popularity. This chapter will explain how the process works and how you can become part of it.

Chapter 3: Development Tools

Chapter 3 will introduce you to the development tools used in the development of Gaim and other open source (and proprietary) software. I will explain how to use editors, the GCC compiler, make, GNU Autotools, CVS, and SourceForge.net so that you will be able to contribute to Gaim as well as start your own projects from scratch.

Chapter 4: Programming Gaim

In this chapter, I will discuss the powerful programming techniques used throughout Gaim's source code. I will discuss object-oriented programming and how it is implemented in C by Gaim and the GTK+ library. I will discuss important data structures used by Gaim, and finally I will cover the Gaim plug-in API, allowing you to write plug-ins to extend Gaim's features.

Chapter 5: GTK+ Basics

This chapter will introduce GTK+, the library used to create Gaim's graphical user interface. You will learn how to create your own dialogs with commonly used widgets; how to attach callback functions, called when the user interacts with your program; and how to manipulate existing interfaces. I will walk you through the development of a plug-in and explain each decision made in creating the plug-in as I make it.

Chapter 6: Advanced GTK+

Now that you're equipped with a basic of understanding of GTK+, I will explore its internal workings more thoroughly. You will learn how to create your own GUI objects, or *widgets*, by following a sample plug-in that radically changes Gaim's File Transfer dialog with three such custom objects.

Chapter 7: Sockets

In Chapter 7, I'll introduce sockets, the programmatic interface to the Internet. You will learn some basic principles of networking, and how to communicate over a network. I will explain how to hook your networking code to GTK+'s GLib library to integrate it into GTK+'s main loop and ensure cross-platform compatibility.

Chapter 8: Protocol Plug-Ins

After learning how to communicate over the Internet, you will learn about various protocols, including IM protocols. You will learn how to intercept and interpret Internet traffic used by IM clients—a process called reverse engineering. I will then teach you how to add a new protocol to Gaim as a protocol plug-in. I will review how Gaim and the plug-in communicate events between each other.

Chapter 9: Internationalization

In this chapter, you will learn how to write programs that speakers of any language can use. I will review the gettext system for providing translation of your program at runtime. I will explain the concept of text encodings, why they are significant, and how to write code that understands them.

Chapter 10: Portability

Chapter 10 will address *portability*; that is, making your program run on as many systems as possible, regardless of hardware or operating system. I will discuss major differences you need to concern yourself with and how to use the portability functions of GTK+.

Prerequisites

I mentioned that when I started working on Gaim I was a complete amateur who didn't even know the language it's programmed in. As such, I don't expect you to be very experienced either. You'll learn as we go.

However, I won't be introducing basic concepts of C, the language used to build Gaim. Therefore,you should possess at least a rudimentary understanding of the language, and have a basic knowledge of underlying principles of computer programming. Although I learned C by example, there are other books that will do a better job of teaching you This book will focus on higher-level aspects of the development process. However, you can most likely get by with knowing C++, Java, or another language with a C-like syntax, as I will elaborate on more-difficult or obscure techniques.

Because Gaim is created entirely with free software, everything you need is freely available for download on the Internet. In Chapter 1, you will install the tools you'll need for developing Gaim and your own applications.

With a basic understanding of programming and a few free tools, you should be able to follow this book and to write large programs like Gaim on your own.

Summary

Gaim has many advantages over other clients, but its major asset is that it's open source. Because of this, anyone with an idea and the ability to code can make it a better program. Also, it acts as a teaching tool—a real-life, practical example of a large codebase from which you can learn to write similar code. This book will use Gaim's example to teach you exactly that. I am also available to answer any questions you may have. To e-mail or IM me, see my contact information at `http://gaim.sourceforge.net/contactinfo.php`.

CHAPTER 1

Getting Started

The Internet has unquestionably changed how we communicate. People who 15 years ago sent letters by post and made long-distance phone calls are now achieving the same results—faster and cheaper—with e-mail and instant messaging. Hundreds of thousands of people do so every day with Gaim, a multi-protocol, cross-platform, open source instant messaging (IM) client.

IM is the combination of two technologies: *messaging* and *presence notification. Messaging* allows one to send short messages to another IM user in real time. *Presence notification* is the technology behind the "buddy list." An IM user sends the IM server a list of other users and receives from the server notifications whenever his "buddies" change status or availability. Although both technologies have been available in some form since the advent of computer networking, it wasn't until 1996 that they were first combined in the still-popular ICQ (http:// www.icq.com/).

Because IM is still a relatively young phenomenon, it can be extremely exciting to participate in the development of related technologies. Because it is free and open source, Gaim is an excellent way to involve yourself in IM software development. In this chapter, I will present an overview of instant messaging and Gaim. I will then instruct you in creating a build environment suitable for building Gaim and any other networked, cross-platform, desktop application. It will be from this environment that you work with the examples used throughout this book, and by expanding on this environment you will be able to build your own applications.

History of IM

ICQ was released in November 1996 by the Israeli company Mirabilis. Being the first system to combine messaging and presence notification, it achieved instant popularity. Within six months, it dominated as the world's largest Internet communications network, a position it would hold until 1997 when America Online entered the market with their AOL Instant Messenger (AIM) service (http://www.aim.com/).

AIM was immediately popular because it allowed its users to communicate for free with the over 10 million users of the AOL service. In June of 1998, AOL announced its intentions to purchase Mirabilis and has since been the predominant IM provider in the United States.

In other countries, where speaking to AOL users wasn't a priority, relative latecomers Yahoo! Messenger (http://messenger.yahoo.com/) and Microsoft's MSN Messenger (http:// messenger.msn.com/) gained a foothold. Although AIM still retains about half the market share,

Yahoo! and MSN are growing rapidly with tens of millions of users each. Unfortunately for IM users, each of these services is disconnected; an AIM user can only IM other AIM users.

Because IM lacks a single standard protocol like e-mail's SMTP to ensure its standardization, it remains in the control of corporations looking after their own interests. There are various attempts to remedy the situation (a noteworthy one being Jabber, to be discussed in more detail in Chapter 8), but many users resort to running more than one IM program simultaneously. Although this is now an influential reason for the popularity of multi-protocol IM clients, Gaim was originally created to solve a different problem.

History of Gaim

In 1998, Mark Spencer, a college student at Auburn University, wanted to use the AIM service from his Linux computer. Unfortunately, at that time AOL did not make a Linux version of its client. Mark also wanted to learn GTK+ (http://www.gtk.org/), a multi-platform toolkit used for creating graphical user interfaces. Naturally, he did what anyone would do: he wrote an AIM client in GTK+.

Note I'll spend a fair amount of time throughout this book introducing GTK+ and its many features.

The first version of Gaim, released in December 1998 and shown in Figure 1-1, was simple and lacking in features, but it attracted other developers to the project.

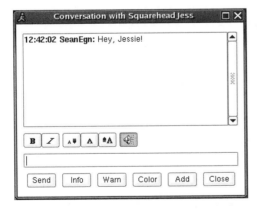

Figure 1-1. *A screenshot of the first release of Gaim from December 1998*

Gaim continued to grow for almost two years as a Linux-based AIM client, until 2000 when protocol plug-ins were introduced.

A *protocol plug-in* (or PRPL—pronounced "purple") is a special type of Gaim plug-in that originally allowed Gaim to work on services besides AIM. Today, they are used for every protocol supported by Gaim as part of its modular design. I will discuss protocol plug-ins in depth in Chapter 8.

In 2002, Herman Bloggs wrote a Gaim plug-in that would interact with his TiVo DVR. Potential users of his plug-in complained that they couldn't use Herman's plug-in because Gaim did not run on Windows. Herman responded by porting Gaim to Windows. Today, about half of Gaim's users use the Windows port; the other half use any of the wide variety of other systems supported by Gaim.

Setting Up Your Build Environment

Most people who use Gaim use a binary package. A binary package is the fastest way to start using Gaim, because the software has already been built for your machine. Because of this, we provide binary packages for a wide assortment of different platforms on our Web page at `http://gaim.sourceforge.net/downloads.php`. What differentiates free, open source software from proprietary software, though, is that as an open source project, Gaim also provides source packages. Source packages allow you to make changes to the code and compile the changes into your own binary packages. Because you will be working with Gaim's code throughout this book, it's important that you know how to make changes and compile Gaim on your own machine.

Gaim can be compiled on most computers, regardless of architecture or operating system, but the specifics in doing so may vary from system to system. Gaim runs on a wide number of popular systems, including Linux, Windows, Mac OS X, and UNIX. I will focus here on the most popular platforms. Because Gaim was originally intended for Linux, compilation depends on many UNIX tools. Fortunately for Windows users, a project called Cygwin exists to provide these tools on Windows. If you are not using Windows, you can skip to the section "Library Dependencies."

■**Tip** The most up-to-date Windows build instructions are available at `http://gaim.sourceforge.net/win32/build.php`.

Cygwin

The heart of Cygwin lies in its libraries, which include UNIX system calls not available to the Windows API. This allows Windows programs linked against Cygwin to make system calls that will work just as they would on UNIX. Although Gaim isn't linked against the Cygwin libraries, the tools used to build it are. They can be downloaded for free from `http://www.cygwin.com`. At this Web page you will see an Install or Update Now! link to an installation executable. Download and execute this application.

Installation Type

After a copyright notice, the first page in the installation wizard, seen in Figure 1-2, asks you to choose an installation type. Choose Download from Internet. This will download Cygwin packages and install them automatically.

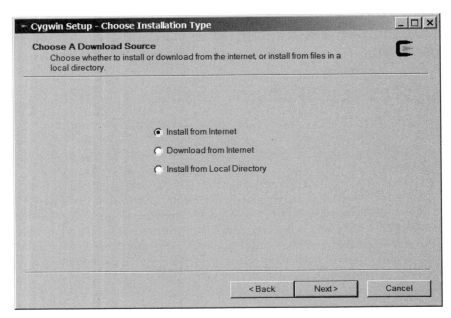

Figure 1-2. *Cygwin's Choose Installation Type dialog*

Installation Options

The next screen, shown in Figure 1-3, will ask you where to install Cygwin. You can accept the default or change it to whatever you want as long as you remember the location; you will need it later to install library dependencies. It will also ask for the default text type. Choose UNIX (see Figure 1-3).

■**Note** The ASCII (American Standard Code for Information Interchange) standard for representing text includes numerous control codes to represent cursor movement. Most of these are remnants of previous technologies since made obsolete, but two relating to creating new lines are still relevant. Characters 10 and 13 are line feed and carriage return, respectively. The difference originates from how typewriters work; line feed moves the cursor down one row but remains in the same column, and carriage return returns the cursor to the beginning of the row. While Windows uses both characters to represent a new line, UNIX uses only line feed.

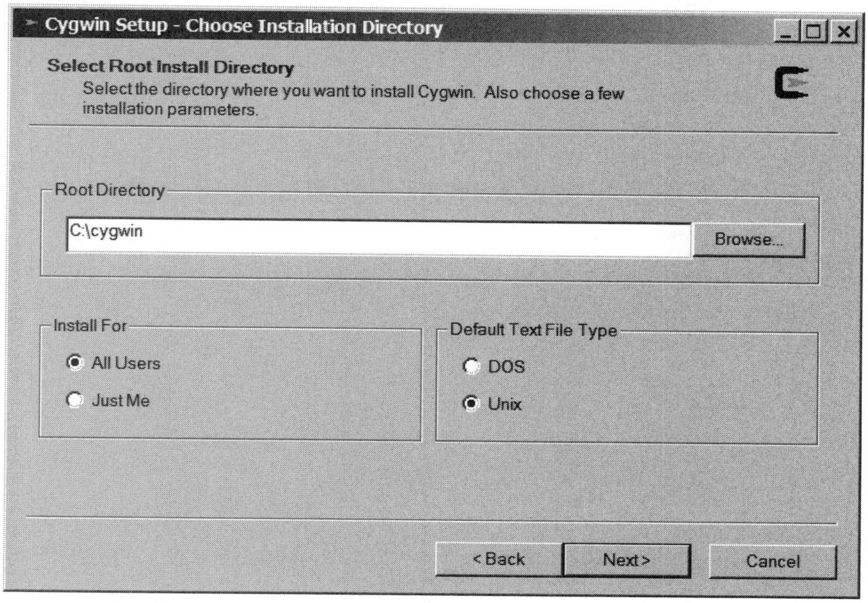

Figure 1-3. *Cygwin's installation options dialog*

Local Package Directory

After choosing where Cygwin will be installed, you will be asked for a directory to which the installer will download packages before installing them via the dialog shown in Figure 1-4. You can change this from the default, if you wish. You won't need this directory for anything else in the build process, so it's not important that you remember where you installed it.

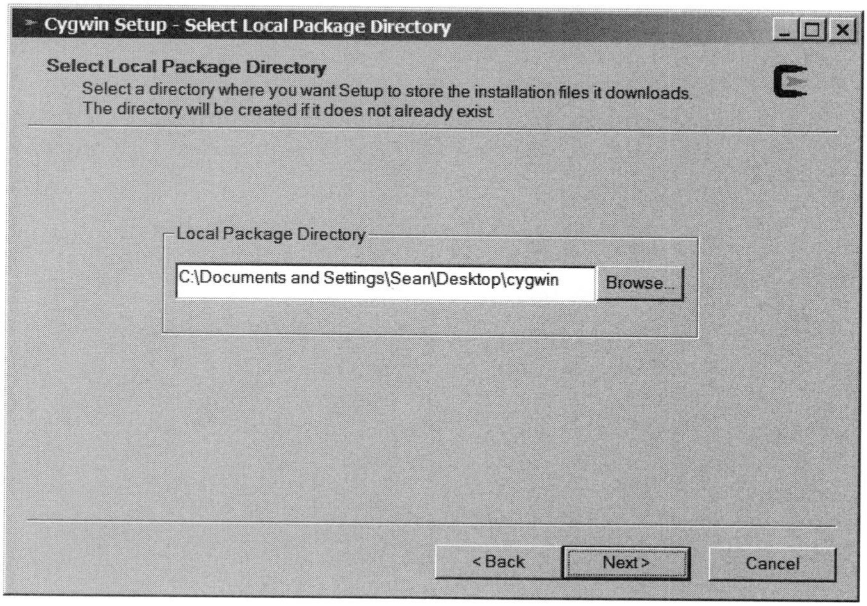

Figure 1-4. *Cygwin's Local Package Directory dialog*

Connection Type

The next page in the wizard, shown in Figure 1-5, asks for your proxy settings. On some network configurations, a computer may not be able to connect directly to the Internet. Instead, the computer's Internet traffic is relayed through another computer, known as a proxy. If your network uses a proxy, enter the appropriate settings. If not, use Direct Connection. If you're unsure what to use, consult your system administrator or Internet service provider.

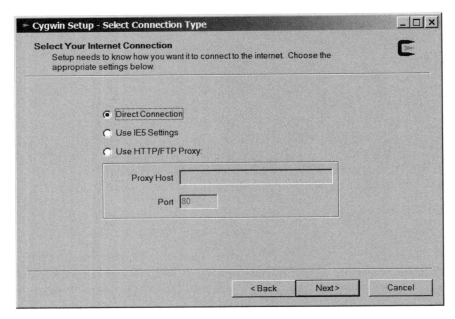

Figure 1-5. *Cygwin's Connection Type dialog*

Mirror Selection

You will next be asked to choose a download site. Because Cygwin is free software, it is mirrored all over the globe. Choose a download site near you from the list shown in Figure 1-6, and click Next to choose which packages you want to install.

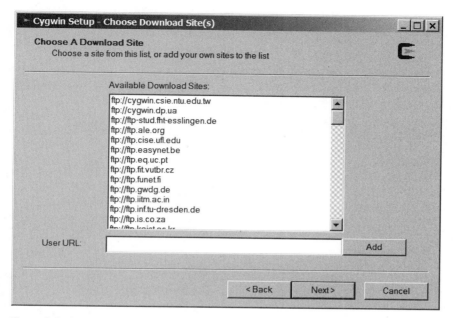

Figure 1-6. *Cygwin's mirror selection dialog*

Package Selection

The default Cygwin install will install enough tools for a usable UNIX command shell, but will not install certain packages you need to compile Gaim. From the dialog shown in Figure 1-7, click the plus sign next to Devel in the list to expand that category. Scroll down until you see CVS. Gaim's central source repository is accessed using a system called CVS. CVS will be discussed later in this chapter. Click the word Skip and it will change to install the latest version of make.

Make is a tool to determine from a makefile which source files need to be compiled. This is especially useful for a large program such as Gaim; changing one source file will not cause others to be recompiled. Choose to install it from the Devel category.

The server the Gaim project uses for CVS employs a protocol called SSH, which stands for "secure shell." You can download OpenSSH from the Net category.

The final package that Gaim requires is in the Archive category, three categories above Devel. Unzip is a utility to extract `.zip` archives. You will use this when installing Gaim's library dependencies. Click to install it, and then hit Next to start the installation, or you can browse some of the other UNIX tools offered by Cygwin. Of special interest may be the Editors category.

Gaim's source code can be edited with any editor. If you have a favorite, you can use that. However, if you don't have an editor, try one offered by Cygwin. The most popular editors for most UNIX developers, Vim and Emacs, are both included. However, these both have a steep learning curve, so you may feel more comfortable using something else.

Note Vim and XEmacs (my preferred variety of Emacs) both have native Windows ports found at `http://www.vim.org/` and `http://www.xemacs.org`, respectively. I will discuss these and a few other alternatives in Chapter 3.

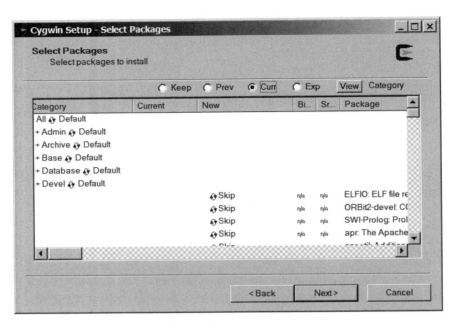

Figure 1-7. *Cygwin's Select Packages dialog*

Creating Icons

When the installation is finished, it will ask you to put an icon in the Start menu or Desktop. Doing either of these will give you a convenient way to access your Cygwin prompt. Upon running Cygwin, you will see a shell prompt. If you are unfamiliar with UNIX, now is a good time to review some commands you'll need to learn.

Using Cygwin

After activating the Cygwin icon, you probably see something like this:

```
Sean@Donatello ~
$
```

This is the default Cygwin prompt. The first line tells you who and where you are. Your username appears before the @ symbol, and your computer's host name appears after it. The final element on this line is your current directory.

The character ~ is UNIX shorthand for "my home directory." Whereas Windows uses a multi-rooted file system, in UNIX everything resides in a single root directory called / and pronounced "root." Your home directory has the same name as your user account and is located in /home. Therefore, if your username were sean, your home directory would be /home/sean.

Cygwin will use the directory it installed to as the / directory. Within, it has created a typical UNIX file hierarchy. Therefore, if your username is sean and you installed Cygwin to c:\cygwin, your home directory will be at /home/sean in Cygwin and C:\cygwin\home\sean in Windows. This will be important later when you install library dependencies.

Your library dependencies will be installed to ~/win32-dev. To create this directory from Cygwin use the mkdir (which stands for "make directory") command:

```
%>mkdir ~/win32-dev
```

Now you can change to this new directory with cd (which stands for "change directory"):

```
%>cd ~/win32-dev
```

You will notice that your prompt now shows you're in ~/win32-dev.

MinGW

To provide a UNIX-like environment in Windows, Cygwin offers the utilities you've just installed, such as CVS, make, and SSH. Because Gaim is designed to be built on UNIX, it uses Cygwin to provide this environment in Windows. Cygwin also offers a set of libraries to allow other UNIX programs to run within Cygwin's UNIX-like environment, but Gaim does not use these libraries. Cygwin is required only when building Gaim, not when running it. Although linking against Cygwin's libraries would allow Gaim to make UNIX system calls on Windows, it is preferable to make it a native Windows application, not requiring compatibility .dlls (dynamically linked libraries) like Cygwin's.

A .dll is a library of functions available to a program at runtime. Because they are accessed at runtime, programs using them will not need to be recompiled when the .dll changes. For a library like Cygwin, this is important to facilitate easy library upgrades. Cygwin's .dlls, however, would restrict the degree to which Gaim could utilize Windows calls. Gaim would be confined to running within Cygwin's UNIX-like environment rather than having access to the system as a whole. It is preferable to make Gaim a Windows-native application. To accomplish this, it uses MinGW, a collection of tools, header files, and libraries that will allow you to create Windows-native binaries.

Installing MinGW

MinGW is available at http://www.mingw.org. From the main MinGW Web page, click Download to reach the file list. MinGW is composed of many packages, such as compilers for various languages, a debugger, Windows system headers, and other utilities. Fortunately, the MinGW package will install all the packages required to compile Gaim. This package is available as an installer .exe file. Download and run it from the Current section of the file list.

The MinGW installer will prompt you for the installation directory. You can keep the default, or you can change it to whatever you'd like. Be sure, though, to remember where you installed it, as you need to configure Cygwin to use MinGW.

Configuring Cygwin

Because you will be invoking the MinGW compiler from the Cygwin shell, you must tell Cygwin where to find the compiler. This is done by setting the PATH environment variable, which is a list of directories Cygwin will search in for binaries, separated by colons.

In Cygwin's UNIX-like file system, your multi-rooted file system is located at /cygdrive. If MinGW is installed to c:\mingw in Windows, Cygwin will find it at /cydrive/c/mingw. If it's at d:\development\mingw, tell Cygwin to search /cygdrive/d/development/mingw.

To set the PATH variable, type PATH= followed by a colon-delimited list of directories. The compiler and related utilities will be located in the bin subdirectory of your MinGW installation directory, so if MinGW is installed to c:\mingw, run PATH=/cygdrive/c/mingw/bin. To avoid destroying the current PATH, include it when setting your new PATH. The Cygwin shell will replace $PATH with the contents of PATH, so doing PATH=/cygdrive/c/mingw/bin:$PATH will prepend /cygdrive/c/mingw/bin to the current PATH.

Tip The shell used by Cygwin, named Bash, includes a feature called tab completion. By pressing the tab key, it will attempt to complete the file name you are currently entering. If multiple files match what you've entered, it will print a list of the possibilities. If you're having difficulty navigating the Cygwin file system, type PATH=/cygdrive/ and press the Tab key. Cygwin will show you a list of your drives or further complete your command. Finish typing the directory you want, and press Tab again. You can do this until you've completed the entire path.

To avoid resetting your path whenever you use Cygwin, you can set it in a script called ~/.bash_profile, which is run every time Cygwin starts. To append the command to ~/.bash_profile, open it in any editor and add the command to set PATH to the end of it.

Library Dependencies

Gaim makes use of several free libraries to handle its user interface, cryptography code, and embedded scripting, among other tasks. If you use Linux or another UNIX-like operating system, you should consult your distribution's documentation about how to find and install these libraries and their corresponding development packages.

Tip Using Mac OS X? Because OS X is a UNIX operating system, it's possible to get Gaim to compile and run on it. I recommend using Fink, a port of the Debian project's APT system, to install these libraries and the software you need. Fink can be found at http://fink.sourceforge.net.

Windows users will find these libraries—and the most up-to-date build instructions—at http://gaim.sourceforge.net/win32/build.php. You should download the files linked from there to ~/win32-dev (which you created earlier) and extract them from that directory.

The files linked to from http://gaim.sourceforge.net/win32/build.php are of two different archive types. Files ending with a .tar.gz extension are called tarballs. These files are archives of several files joined together with the tar utility and then compressed with gzip. You can extract these with the following command:

```
tar xvzf filename.tar.gz
```

Several options are used in conjunction with the `tar` utility, namely `xvzf`. The `x` option tells `tar` to perform an extract operation, rather than create a new `tar` archive. The `v` option represents verbosity, telling `tar` to print its status to the screen each time it extracts a file. The `z` option tells `tar` that this is a tarball that needs to be decompressed with `gzip`, as opposed to an uncompressed archive. Finally, the `f` option tells `tar` to take its input from a file, as opposed to from the console or a pipe.

The other type of archive you'll see is `zip`, which you are probably already familiar with. These can be extracted with the `unzip` utility:

```
unzip filename.zip
```

All the libraries Gaim depends on are also free, open source software, available on the Internet in either `.zip` or `.tar.gz` format. In the sections following, I have explained briefly which libraries you need, what they are used for, and where you can download them.

GTK+

GTK+ is a cross-platform widget toolkit used by Gaim and many other projects for creating graphical user interfaces. GTK+ will be covered in depth in Chapters 5 and 6. The GTK+ homepage is at `http://www.gtk.org/`.

GtkSpell

One of Gaim's unique features is its inline, automatic spell checking, provided by GtkSpell. GtkSpell was written by Evan Martin and uses a library called aspell to detect misspelled words, which it then highlights in Gaim conversation windows, as seen in Figure 1-8. Like all the libraries in the section, you will find GtkSpell linked from `http://gaim.sourceforge.net/win32/build.php`.

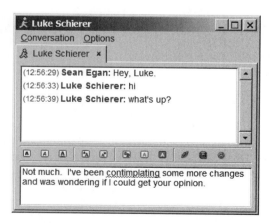

Figure 1-8. *Spell-checking in Gaim by GtkSpell*

Mozilla NSS

Certain parts of Gaim—most notably its support for MSN Messenger—require cryptographic functions found in the NSS library, part of the Mozilla project. In turn, NSS requires NSPR, a library that provides platform-independent methods of accessing common operating system functions such as file I/O, threading, memory management, and networking.

Mozilla uses NSPR for platform independence, or portability; Gaim uses the portability functions provided by the GLib library, which is part of GTK+. I will discuss using GTK+ to ensure portability in Chapter 10.

■**Note** If you have Mozilla or a Mozilla-based Web browser (such as Firefox), you already have the NSS and NSPR libraries. You probably do not, however, have the necessary header files to create your own applications using NSS. Download and extract the development packages from `http://gaim.sourceforge.net/win32/build.php`. They'll install everything required to build applications with NSS's cryptographic functions.

Perl and Tcl

Gaim has the capability to support embedded scripting languages and currently includes two: Perl and Tcl. These embedded script interpreters allow Gaim plug-ins to be written in scripting languages. Scripts have several advantages over compiled binary plug-ins—the most prevalent being that development can usually occur much more rapidly. For Windows users, Tcl can be found as a tarball linked from `http://gaim.sourceforge.net/win32/build.php`. For Perl, though, you will use ActivePerl.

ActivePerl is a distribution of Perl for Windows available from ActiveState. Visit `http://www.activestate.com/` and follow the instructions there to install ActivePerl 5.8 to `C:\Perl`. You will then need to download the required headers and library files from `http://gaim.sourceforge.net/win32/build.php` and extract them to the `~/win32-dev` directory.

Getting Gaim

You can download the latest release of Gaim's source code as a tarball from `http://gaim.sourceforge.net/downloads.php`. If you are using Windows, download the source tarball to your Cygwin home directory (not to `~/win32-dev`). Users of Linux and other UNIX-like operating systems can download it wherever they'd like. Extract it as you did the library dependencies mentioned previously; to `tar xvzf gaim-VERSION.tar.gz` (where `VERSION` is the version of Gaim you've downloaded). You will now have a `gaim-VERSION` directory, suitable for compiling the latest release from source. If, however, you are interested in participating in Gaim development, it's better to use CVS.

CVS is a system that keeps a single repository of Gaim source. Because Gaim development is highly active, working on source from the latest release could mean you are modifying outdated code. To ensure you're working with the latest code, use Gaim's anonymous CVS server.

■**Caution** Although CVS always contains the latest features and fixes, it also always contains the latest bugs. It is not uncommon for serious bugs to make their way into CVS before they are identified and fixed. Also, Gaim shares a CVS server with thousands of other projects; checking out Gaim from CVS uses server resources that could be better used by people attempting to help develop any of these thousands of projects. Therefore, I strongly discourage using Gaim's CVS repository unless you're contributing to Gaim development.

Before you can check out Gaim source, the CVS server requires you to log in. To do this, run the following command:

```
cvs -:pserver:anonymous@cvs.sourceforge.net:/cvsroot/gaim login
```

It will ask you for a password. There is none; just hit Enter.
Now you can check out Gaim from CVS:

```
cvs -d:pserver:anonymous@cvs.sourceforge.net:/cvsroot/gaim checkout gaim
```

You will now have a `gaim` subdirectory in the directory where you ran the command. I will explain how to use some of CVS's more useful features in Chapter 3.

Configuring Gaim

Because Windows installations are nearly identical, a single set of makefiles (which instruct make how to build Gaim) will work on all Windows systems. Windows users can, therefore, skip this section. Linux and UNIX users, however, need custom makefiles.

These makefiles will be generated by a shell script in the root of the Gaim source tree called `configure` (this script won't exist if you've just checked out from CVS. Run `./autogen.sh` to generate it). This script is created by the GNU Autotools system.

Autotools allows an application developer to specify certain parameters to check for and alter the compiler commands as appropriate. For instance, when you run the `configure` script, it will check for the location of the GTK+ library, and will instruct the compiler where to find it. I will explain how to use autotools in your own projects in Chapter 3. Run the following command from the root of the source tree to configure Gaim:

```
./configure
```

The configuration process should finish without any further intervention. When `configure` is finished, it should print a list of the compile-time options it will use. If `configure` fails, it will tell you why; it's usually due to missing dependencies. Review the above section "Library Dependencies" to be sure you've installed development packages for each of them.

Tip In many systems, the current directory (represented as a single dot) is not included in the PATH. To run a program in the current directory, it's necessary to run it as `./program`. Some users add "." to their PATH: (`export PATH=$PATH:.`); however this is considered by many to be a security risk. Typically, ordinary users cannot add programs to the directories specified in PATH, but adding the current directory makes it easier to accidentally run malicious programs purposed to compromise your computer. Picture someone creating a program that deletes all your files, and naming it the same as a common UNIX utility, suppose `ls`, in your home directory. If the impostor program is found before the real `ls`, you're in a lot of trouble. If you come from a DOS background, you may be more comfortable including "." in your PATH, but do so at your own risk.

Compiling Gaim

As I mentioned earlier, Gaim uses the make utility to manage compilation. If you successfully executed `configure`, you now have files called `Makefile` in every directory of the source tree; Windows users have prebuilt makefiles called `Makefile.mingw`.

To compile Gaim, execute the following command from within the Gaim directory:

```
%>make
```

If you are using Windows, you will need to tell make to use the Windows `Makefile.mingw` file with the `-f` argument:

```
%>make -f Makefile.mingw
```

You will see make calling the commands to build Gaim. When compilation finishes, you will return to a shell prompt. Next, run the following command to install Gaim:

```
make install
```

If you're using Windows, execute the following to install Gaim:

```
make -f Makefile.mingw install
```

In Windows, it will install to a `win32-install-dir` directory in your source tree. On UNIX-like systems, it will most likely install to the appropriate location for your machine—probably a place included in your PATH.

Note On most UNIX-like systems, `make install` will require root access. Whereas regular users are prevented from installing software by the UNIX security model, the root user is not. To become a root user before running `make install`, run `su` and provide the root password. If you do not know the root password on the machine you are using, use the `--prefix` argument to `configure`. This will cause make to install it to the directory you specify, rather than the system default. `configure --prefix ~` will cause make to install Gaim to your home directory.

You can now run Gaim from where it's installed by running `gaim` if it installed to your `PATH`, or, if using Windows, by running `/win32-install-dir/gaim`.

Using Gaim

Now that you're running Gaim, you probably want to use it. Although we aim to have its user interface be as intuitive as possible, the following section will overview some of Gaim's features and how to use them.

Adding a New Account

If this is your first time using Gaim, running Gaim will show you the Add Account dialog, shown in Figure 1-9. It asks you to create a new account to use with Gaim.

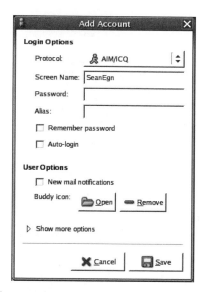

Figure 1-9. *Gaim's Add Account dialog*

The Protocol drop-down menu lists all the available protocols. Choose one with which you have an account.

■**Note** After AOL purchased Mirabilis, it converted the ICQ service to use the same protocol as AIM, called OSCAR. Because the two services use the same protocol, they share a single entry in the protocol drop-down list. I will discuss OSCAR in Chapter 8.

Enter your screen name and, if you want Gaim to remember your password, click the Remember Password check box and enter your password in the Password text box. Be aware, though, that your password will be stored in plain text in a file in your home directory. If you are using a computer shared by people who might access that file, you may not want to save your password there; Gaim will prompt you for it when you attempt to connect. Although your screen name and password are the only required information to connect to an IM service, other options can be set here too.

Depending on the protocol, you'll be prompted about whether you want to be notified of new e-mail to an e-mail account associated with your account, or for a buddy icon. A buddy icon is a small image that others will see in their conversation window when talking to you.

■**Tip** In addition to using the Open button to choose an icon from a file chooser, you can drag an image file from any graphical file manager into this window to set your buddy icon.

Clicking Show More Options will reveal additional options you most likely won't need to change. These can include, depending on your protocol, the Internet address of the server to which you want to connect and text encodings to use in non-English conversations (I'll explain text encodings in Chapter 9). You'll also find proxy settings, which you should set as appropriate. When you finish configuring your account, hit Save to return to the Accounts dialog.

Accounts

The Accounts dialog, shown in Figure 1-10, is Gaim's main interface for managing accounts. You will see a list of currently configured accounts with buttons to delete or edit them and to add a new account.

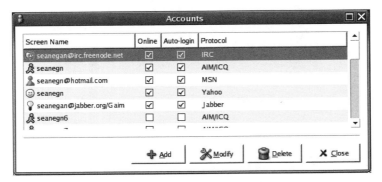

Figure 1-10. *Gaim's account manager*

If you would like to use another account simultaneously (on a different protocol, perhaps) hit Add, and follow the instructions from the "Adding a New Account" section of this chapter. The list itself contains check boxes to connect or disconnect an account in the Online column. Click the check box next to your newly created accounts to sign them on.

Buddy List

Once your account connects to the IM server, you will see the Gaim buddy list, shown in Figure 1-11. On most popular IM services (including AIM, ICQ, Jabber, MSN, and Yahoo!), your buddy list will be automatically downloaded from the IM server, and you will see the buddies from each connection you've made merged into a single list interface. Each entry provides basic information about status, and more information can usually be seen in the tooltip window by hovering your mouse cursor over an entry. If you have used any IM client before, you probably recognize this interface, but Gaim has its own idiosyncrasies you may need to adjust to.

Figure 1-11. *Gaim's buddy list*

One such idiosyncrasy is known as contacts. *Contacts* are a transparent grouping of IM buddies representing a single person. That is, if you have my AIM, ICQ, and Jabber screen names on your buddy list, you can combine them as a single contact, which will occupy only a single space in your buddy list. This is done as transparently as possible; the contact will appear in your list as a single buddy. In fact, all the entries in your list currently are actually contacts, though they may contain only one buddy each.

To consolidate two or more buddies into a contact, right-click one of the buddy list entry and choose Expand from the context menu. This will show the contact as a nested subtree of the buddy list containing one buddy, as seen in Figure 1-12. Simply drag other buddies into this subtree.

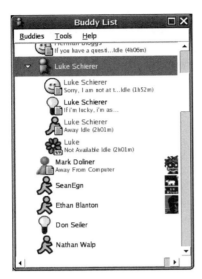

Figure 1-12. *An expanded contact in Gaim's buddy list*

You may also find that each entry in your buddy list is too large for your taste; whereas most IM clients offer a single line of text for each entry, Gaim provides two. The Gaim developers believe that by doing this, we are able to provide the user with important information that would be invisible using a smaller list. Most importantly, the user's buddy icon is included to the right of the entry, if applicable. Because an image is far easier to recognize than text, having buddy icons here makes it easier to locate a single buddy in a large, crowded list. If you would still prefer to have a single line per buddy, you can turn off this feature from the Buddy List section of the preferences.

Preferences

The application's preferences are located in the Tools menu of the buddy list, and are shown in Figure 1-13. From here, you can configure Gaim to better fit your personal tastes.

Gaim attempts to follow a UI design philosophy that embraces minimizing the number of user preferences. The thought is that the software should do one thing extremely well and, if written correctly, should not need the user to make decisions for it. I will discuss principles of UI design further in Chapter 5.

Because of this, you will not be overwhelmed by preferences, and the preferences you are trying to change should be easy to find. Browse the various panes to discover the options available to you.

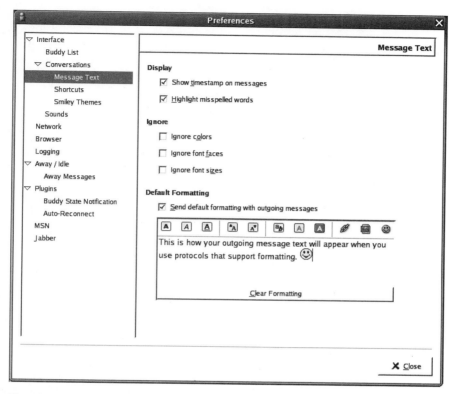

Figure 1-13. *Gaim's Preferences dialog*

Conversations

Double-clicking a buddy in your buddy list will open a conversation window with that buddy (see Figure 1-14). Alternatively, you can open a new conversation from the dialog at Buddies ➤ New Instant Message.

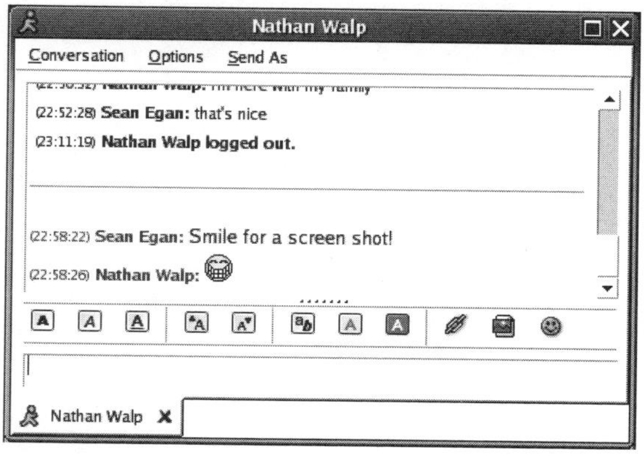

Figure 1-14. *A Gaim conversation*

The IM window is divided vertically into two panes. In the bottom pane, you compose your message; in the top pane, the conversation history is displayed. Anyone familiar with other IM clients should be familiar with this interface. Above the message composition box, you will see a formatting toolbar which you can use to edit the text formatting of your message. At the top of the window, you will find a menu from which you can access several common operations. You will also notice a single tab on the IM window.

Gaim uses tabbed conversation windows. A window can be populated with many conversations, which you can switch between using the tabs at the top (or wherever you've configured them to appear) of the conversation windows. Conversations can also be moved. You can drag a tab to another spot in the window, or out of the window to form a new conversation window, to which other conversations can be added.

New conversations are added to conversation windows in a manner prescribed by the New Conversation Placement options found in the Conversations page of the preferences.

Tools

The buddy list also contains a Tools menu, which contains other features. In addition to the Preferences dialog, you will find options to set your away status, protocol-specific account options such as your user information or cell phone forwarding, and a list of current file transfers. One feature originated in Gaim (but now adopted by other clients) is the Buddy Pounce, as shown in Figure 1-15.

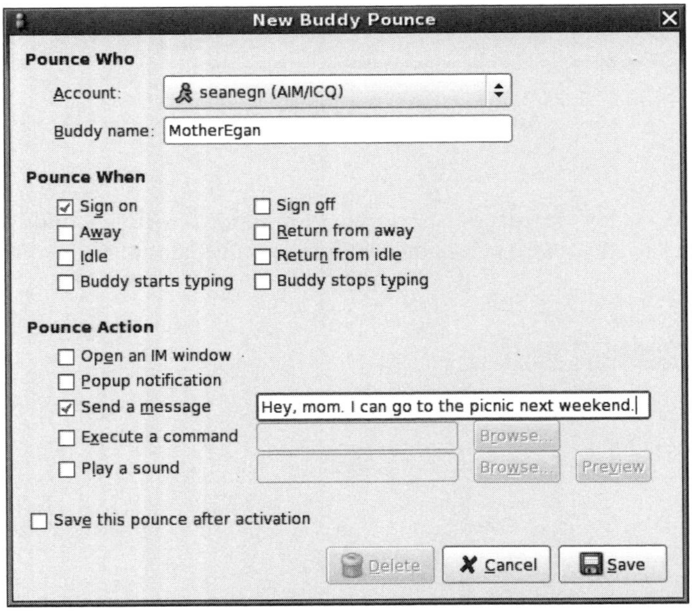

Figure 1-15. *Gaim's Buddy Pounce dialog*

A Buddy Pounce is an action caused by your buddy doing some action of his own. For example, I want to send my mother a message about the family picnic. She's not currently online, and I'm about to go out for the night. I can set up a Buddy Pounce to send a message to her when she signs on, without my intervention.

After opening the Buddy Pounce dialog, I can type my mother's screen name in the appropriate text field, or I can drag my mother's buddy list entry into the Buddy Pounce dialog. I choose the appropriate settings; in the example in Figure 1-15, I set Pounce When as Sign On, Pounce Action as Send Message, and filled in the text box next to it. I hit Save to store the pounce, and when my mother signs on, she'll receive that message.

Summary

From a developer's perspective, Gaim is exciting because it provides a platform for working with still emergent, yet already very relevant, instant messaging technology. By installing a build environment and familiarizing yourself with the Gaim application, you've prepared yourself not only for compiling and modifying Gaim, but for developing your own cross-platform applications. In the next chapter, I'll provide some insight into the open source development process. I'll explain important principles surrounding it and how to make your small hobby project grow as actively developed and widely used as Gaim.

CHAPTER 2

The Open Source Development Process

Contributing to open source development is extremely rewarding. With just a few hours' work, anybody, regardless of age or location, can contribute code appreciated by millions of people around the world. Leading an open source project is perhaps even more rewarding; open source projects, for the most part, run themselves. However, successful open source leaders are often heralded as software luminaries when in actuality most of the hard work is done by hundreds of other contributors.

I'm often asked how one can get started in open source development. This chapter will answer that question. Open source is a strange world to those used to development in a corporate environment, or in school, or even just as a hobby. In this chapter, I'll open the doors to this world, explaining how things work within it and how you can become an open source citizen in good standing.

Open Source versus Free Software

Throughout this book, I use the terms "free software" and "open source software" nearly interchangeably. However, the two terms have subtly different meanings you should be aware of.

The free software movement was started by Richard Stallman to ensure that computer users are not enslaved to the wills of software developers. It emphasizes that computer users should have the freedom to fully use, study, modify, and distribute the software they use. Proprietary software is seen as inferior because it has overly restrictive licenses, which prohibit the user from using the software in certain ways, modifying it, distributing it, or fully understanding how it works. The source code for free software is provided merely because it's impossible to study how the program works or modify it to meet your own needs without it.

The open source movement sprung out of the free software movement. Some free software developers sought to see free software more widely used, especially in the corporate world where the word "free" was often interpreted to refer to price rather than freedom. Companies were reluctant to adopt free software on the precept that because it was free, it was also worthless. The open source movement adopted a new name and a new set of principles to make it more palatable to businesses.

Open source emphasizes the quality of the software generated when everyone has access to the source code. It attempts a less philosophic and more pragmatic look at source code. Free software makes source available merely because otherwise users are unable to exercise their freedom to study and modify the software; source acts as a means to those ends. Open source puts all the emphasis on having source code available because it generates better programs. Open source sees proprietary software as inferior not because it restricts users' rights, but because it was developed with an inferior development technique.

Because open source attempts to attract a huge diversity of programmers, the community is marked by a similar diversity in opinions and philosophy. Whereas I side more with the philosophical importance of free software, many disregard this and are more interested in the quality of software produced. Still others think that both camps have their niches and free software and proprietary software can coexist nicely. Whatever the case, though, all open source developers share the ultimate goal of creating excellent software, and motivations rarely conflict. Regardless of philosophy, the term "open source software" remains more prominently used because its meaning is less ambiguous in English than "free software."

■**Note** Other languages use different words to describe the two different meanings of "free." You may often see the words *libre* and *gratis* borrowed in English writing to avoid ambiguity. The words refer to freedom and cost, respectively.

When I use "free," I refer to philosophical reasons Gaim is available to everyone. When I use "open source," I refer to the development process that results in high-quality software. In this chapter, I will focus solely on the open source development process. If you are interested in learning more about the free software philosophy, visit the Free Software Foundation at http://www.fsf.org.

Why the Open Source Development Process Works

What characterizes the open source development process is a large number of people with only very loose organization reviewing and contributing to the source code. This is contrasted with traditional proprietary methods, which are characterized by greatly restricted access to source code. Typically proprietary developers have access to only the specific source code they're writing and only very few people are able to enhance or fix a specific piece of code.

The advantages of having a larger team of developers are obvious, but how is a large, unorganized group of people from all over the world able to coordinate and create a single cohesive project? What motivates open source developers to spend their spare time fixing other people's bugs? Do these benefits apply to all types of software? This section will answer these questions as they pertain to Gaim (and to many other open source projects).

Organization

Open source is typically marked by loose organization. While some open source projects pride themselves on strict organization, founding nonprofit organizations with boards of directors devoted to development of the project (GNOME and Mozilla, for instance, have the GNOME Foundation and Mozilla Foundation, respectively), most are just a confederation of hackers in which some have a bit more influence than others. In Gaim, developers fall into a few different levels. They are shown in pyramid form in Figure 2-1.

Note The word *hacker* originally referred to a talented programmer who finds great enjoyment in solving difficult problems. More recently it's been used to describe people who break computer security systems. When open-source developers use it, they almost always use the first meaning.

Figure 2-1. *The four levels of influence in the world of Gaim development*

Itch Scratchers

At the bottom are one-time patch writers. These are people who scratch a particular itch by writing a single patch and aren't heard from again (until they have another itch to scratch). The patches are typically things like bug fixes, slight UI changes, and the like. Itch scratchers aren't typically subscribed to mailing lists and don't typically hang out on our Internet Relay Chat (IRC) channel with other developers. As such, the other developers rarely get to know these people personally. Gaim has had about 200 developers who have each written relatively few, usually unrelated patches.

Crazy Patch Writers

When someone starts submitting patches frequently, we call him a "crazy patch writer." This very Gaim-specific term is a playfully irreverent title given to developers who earn a considerable amount of respect through their contributions. Other projects may give these contributors a more serious-sounding title, but most projects have this classification in some form. Unlike one-time itch scratchers, who write patches just to make their own experience better, crazy patch writers typically strive to be part of the core Gaim team. They want their opinions to be considered highly in design decisions. They want to earn the seal of approval that says they're trusted to contribute to Gaim development without their work being heavily scrutinized. The patches crazy patch writers write are grander in nature than those from itch scratchers, but they also contribute bug fixes and other minor changes. These patches often add entirely new features. To do this, crazy patch writers hang out on IRC and subscribe to mailing lists to benefit from the guidance of other developers. More-experienced developers help crazy patch writers learn to navigate the Gaim code and understand the higher-level philosophies dictating Gaim development. Crazy patch writers are credited in the Gaim About box.

Crazy patch writers usually specialize in one or two particular areas of Gaim, generally those in which he's most interested. When I was a crazy patch writer, I was known for writing a large number of patches to the IRC plug-in, and later to GtkIMHtml, the interface element that displays rich-formatted text.

Developers

After a while, when the Gaim developers are satisfied that they can trust a crazy patch writer to write high-quality code that conforms to Gaim's overall vision, they are promoted to "developer." Developers are given the power to commit their code to the central Gaim source repository without it first being reviewed by another developer.

With this privilege comes the responsibility to review patches, bugs, and feature requests. When a crazy patch writer is promoted to developer, he usually assumes responsibility over his specialty. For instance, Tim "Marv" Ringenbach specialized in writing Yahoo! patches as a crazy patch writer, and as a developer he reviews Yahoo! patches, bugs, feature requests, technical support issues, and the like.

Lead Developer

Lastly, you'll find the lead developer at the top of the pyramid. Leaders run their own projects however they choose. As lead developer of Gaim, I have my own experiences, and for me, leading Gaim developers is a very hands-off affair; each of them (including myself) owns his a part of the code and properly maintains it and enhances it as necessary. Therefore, the best way to lead the developers is to get out of their way and make their jobs easier. Most of my additional responsibilities are clerical; I administer the mailing lists and CVS and promote crazy patch writers to developers, for instance. Other lead developers, however, may take less or more control depending on their personal leadership style. The lead developer also has the final say in the project's overall design. Because each project's equivalents of crazy patch writers are promoted only when they have a good understanding of the design, it's rarely necessary to dictate "This is the way we will do this." Personally, I typically do this only for very important features, and then only after a long debate weighing the opinions of all the developers.

This is probably the most important job of an open source leader. Without a single strong, unifying vision, open source software suffers. The peril of allowing a huge number of disparate developers to contribute is that the software quickly fills up with features and options with only very limited use to very few people. This makes the program less useful for everyone else, who will have a harder time locating and using the features and options they actually need to use.

Therefore, Gaim, like many other open source projects, follows the design dictated by the lead developer, which other people understand and implement their own way. For instance, I decided that Gaim will follow the human interface guidelines of the GNOME desktop (a popular

Linux desktop environment I'll discuss more in Chapter 5) despite not being a GNOME project and having many users who do not use GNOME. After a debate with other Gaim developers, we finally came to the consensus that the benefits of following GNOME's usability guidelines benefited Gaim more than hurt it. Therefore, other developers all write their GUI code to conform to the GNOME guidelines.

The developers, of course, aren't paid to work on Gaim, so what inspires them to follow my design? What inspires them to work on Gaim doing boring, tedious tasks like fixing bugs? Open source developers typically have much different motivation than developers of proprietary software.

Motivations of Open Source Developers

I've given a couple of presentations about open source to business students and they've generally been much more interesting for me than the ones I've given to computer science students. Business students are fascinated that so many people are willing to create such high-quality software without being paid for it. Even when they understand that hackers really *enjoy* the work, they realize that open source developers are still turning down the potential to get paid for doing something they already enjoy.

Again, though, the diversity of open source developers leads to a wide diversity of motivations. Developers work on open source software to hone their skills, to gain experience, to pad their résumés, and to gain respect in the community. Some, in fact, even do it for money either through employment, contract work, or a project that pays open source developers, such as Google's Summer of Code (http://code.google.com/summerofcode.html). However, in my opinion the most important motivation—what inspires developers even to consider starting in open source—is fun. Hackers really enjoy figuring out the best way to solve problems in software, and open source is a good way to do this; I thoroughly enjoy working on Gaim. Of course, writing code would be just as fun if Gaim were proprietary for-pay software. What, then, makes open source more appealing to hobbyists looking to have fun?

Fun

Working on Gaim isn't fun just because it involves working on code, but also because it involves collaboratively working on a very large piece of code used by hundreds of thousands of people alongside hundreds of other developers. This sort of experience is nearly impossible with proprietary software. Anyone can download Gaim's source code and start working on it and have their work committed for everyone to use within a day, but there's no way to just start working on Microsoft Word for fun. The only way to work on proprietary software for fun is to start your own project.

However, if you start your own proprietary project, it takes a lot of effort to get it as large-scale as something like Gaim. The potential developers of a proprietary project are only yourself and a small number of people you trust with the source code. When you start an open source project, every single user is potentially a developer. The larger your project becomes in terms of users, the more developers it gets. This in turn makes the project grow, fueling a cycle of open source project growth.

This is the main reason open source development is able to attract so many people: working on an open source project is the only way you can work on a real-world heavily used program without applying for a job somewhere. Naturally, the same motivations that cause a developer to start working on open source cause him to continue working on it and promote up the ranks towards "lead developer." However, other motivations exist that specifically motivate developers to promote through the ranks. The most prominent of these is ego.

Ego

Everyone likes to feel important, and open source developers are no different. Ego is often a significant factor in motivating developers to devote effort to one particular project rather than spread their efforts among many. Developers motivated by ego (and I would venture that all open source developers are inspired by ego to some extent) seek recognition in the open source community.

The same lack of barriers that encourages new developers also allows developers to easily increase their influence. Proprietary software projects are often marked by strict organization; it can be difficult to get promoted by those above you. The only real power a developer in open source has is granted by the respect of his peers. By convincing those peers of his talents, he earns the respect of the community and is seen as a more "important" figure.

Experience

Many open source developers participate for the experience earned. This is particularly true for students (who have little other opportunity to gain real-world experience) and those between jobs (who want to keep their skills up-to-date with the latest technologies). Indeed, a respected position on a prominent open source project does look good on a résumé.

By including substantial open source experience on your résumé, you show potential employers that you enjoy programming and that you've earned the respect of your peers as a strong programmer. You also demonstrate that you possess highly specialized skills in fields rapidly emerging with the growth of Linux and other open source software. Educating yourself about these important new technologies, or any technology for that matter, is another strong motivation for open source development.

Education

Because you have access to the source code, open source projects make excellent educational experiences. If you need to better understand any concept in information technology, from how an operating system scheduler works to how best to implement an instant messaging protocol, it's very likely that you will find a good example to learn from in open source software.

In fact, this concept is the very basis of this book. By examining how Gaim's code works, you will gain a better understanding of it. Further, open source invites you to contribute to the software, making whatever changes best suit your needs. Actively contributing to an open source project educates you even further by experience. Because it's such a powerful educational tool, learning about programming from the software you use is one of the fundamental rights of the free software philosophy.

Free Software Philosophy

Some developers are motivated by a belief that, by advocating the creation and use of free software, they're actually using their talents to make the world a better place. Among other motivations, this inspires a number of Gaim developers, myself included.

Because of this (and perhaps equally important because of a strong respect for the copyright law that powers open source), we're far stricter about ensuring software freedom than some other projects. For instance, the popular OpenSSL project is probably the most popular encryption implementation in the world. However, one specific clause in its license prevents us from using it in good faith.

OpenSSL's license says that any project that uses the library must mention OpenSSL in any advertising it does. Other than this, developers are free to use OpenSSL however they wish, but because Gaim developers care about the users' right to advertise Gaim without mentioning OpenSSL (and perhaps even more so about the developers' own right license Gaim under the General Public License, GPL), we use alternate encryption libraries instead. Nobody actually expects the developers of OpenSSL to sue developers who advertise their products without mentioning the OpenSSL developers, but Gaim's strict adherence to the letter of the law—even among those who don't particularly care about a user's right to freely advertise—represents a respect for the GPL and what it represents. Many other projects use OpenSSL regardless. Technically, these projects are not free software.

Because we're so pedantic about ensuring freedom, Gaim prefers developers whose beliefs are in sync with the free software movement. But when everyone is free to contribute code, how is it that Gaim can select certain developers over others? In the next section I will explain how by its nature, the open source project weeds out developers whose beliefs are out of phase with the maintainers'.

How the Open Source Development Process Works

As I stated earlier, Gaim essentially manages itself. The nature of open source software results in like minds working together. Hence, most of the Gaim developers tend to have very similar views not only on code issues, but on unrelated issues such as politics. Gaim, like most open source projects, operates as a *meritocracy*.

Meritocracy

A meritocracy is an organization in which power is distributed according to ability rather than anything else. Gaim's lead developer has no power other than that afforded by the other developers. It's only through their respect for this individual's ability to run the project that he or she can act as lead developer. For instance, even though I control the Gaim Web page and other developer resources, the nature of free software allows the other developers to "fork" the code, starting their own project to replace Gaim if they were extremely dissatisfied with me.

Likewise, new developers can be promoted only by earning the respect of the other Gaim developers. This is what causes developers of open source projects to be so like-minded. It's the goal of new developers to have their patches accepted into Gaim. If the new developer has the same mindset as the existing developers, more of his patches will be accepted. This will encourage him to write more patches and eventually be promoted to crazy patch writer, and then developer.

A strict meritocracy, like all forms of leadership, has both positive and negative points. It's useful for open source projects because it enforces a single unified vision that all developers are trusted to be in sync with.

If the new developer has fundamental differences of opinion with the existing developers, patches that reflect his opinion will be rejected by developers who disagree with him. Likewise, developers that write poor-quality code will have their patches rejected. These developers will often be discouraged and lose interest in working on Gaim. This way, the only people left working on Gaim are those with appropriate skill and mindsets similar to the existing developers. However, this same exclusion is also a curse. While meritocracies exist to most efficiently enforce project goals, they often appear as elitist cliques, impenetrable to outsiders.

Talented new contributors are almost always welcome to an open source project. Unfortunately, the meritocracy that discourages poor programmers and unsuitable differences in opinion also discourages new talent eager to learn, and perfectly valid alternate perspectives.

Involving yourself in an open source project is difficult; you must gain a strong working knowledge of the project's potentially huge codebase and be able to extend it, sometimes without the aid of any documentation at all. Often, the existing developers are the only ones who can possibly help you, and if they seem out of reach or unwilling to accept your efforts, the difficulty of contributing to open source is greatly amplified.

When encountering the meritocracy of an open source project, remember that, despite their efforts to stay on track with a single vision, contributions are always welcome. If a patch you submit is rejected, find out why and revise it until it's accepted. As you work on contributions, you'll eventually come to understand what's expected of developers. With hard work and persistence, you'll become part of the meritocracy.

Cathedral and the Bazaar

In 1997, Eric Raymond wrote an essay called *The Cathedral and the Bazaar* in which he makes perhaps the best known case for why open source development works. He describes what distinguishes open source techniques from more-traditional development processes. This essay is noted for influencing Netscape to release the Mozilla browser under an open source license. You can read the essay at http://www.catb.org/~esr/writings/cathedral-bazaar/.

Raymond likens traditional development processes to cathedrals: impressive feats of architecture, created by a small team of carefully organized developers. Prior to the emergence of Linux, it was believed this was the only way to efficiently create large programs.

However, as Raymond observed Linux development, he noticed a different style that he likens to a bazaar. An enormous group of people all work on their own code that gets assimilated into a single codebase. There's little organization or detailed design. When I use the term "open source," I refer specifically to this bazaar-like process.

Raymond notes that a few important things a leader must do to make open source development work. First, the original author needs to do enough work himself to produce something other developers can use. Other developers won't be interested in working on a project until they have something to play with. Mark Spencer, Gaim's original author, worked on it alone for months before he was able to attract other developers.

Also, a maintainer needn't necessarily be great at program design himself, argues Raymond, but he must be able to recognize good design from others. All of the Gaim developers are able look at a submitted patch and immediately recognize if it's well designed. By accepting only well-designed patches, the developers ensure that Gaim's code remains of high quality.

Given these two preconditions, Raymond says, new developers will start working on your project, finding and fixing bugs, writing enhancements, writing documentation, creating artwork, and doing all sorts of other helpful things. These community contributions will aid in pushing your project from its infancy into a mature open source application.

However, in practice the larger, more popular projects rarely follow the ideals discussed in *The Cathedral and the Bazaar* exactly as described. Many such projects, including Linux, Mozilla, and Gaim, are developed by a relatively small number of people in close coordination, rather than a huge bazaar of unorganized strangers. However, this certainly doesn't prevent you from participating! The following section explains how to get started in open source development.

Contributing to Open Source Development

Many people are truly interested in involving themselves in open source development, but are unsure how to do it. How can you infiltrate a large meritocracy, working on a huge project with hundreds of thousands of lines of source code completely foreign to you? The key, which I'll elaborate on in this section, is to start small.

Getting Started

It's perhaps a bit ambitious to take on a huge task on an open source project as your first contribution. Until you're thoroughly familiar with the code and with the developers, you'll not be aware of the best way to attempt the project. You can ask the developers to give you pointers and hints, which they will usually gladly do. But most likely, you'll eventually come to the conclusion that perhaps you've bitten off more than you can chew.

Instead, you're much better starting off with a smaller project, localized to one specific aspect of the project. My first contribution to the Gaim project was to add a single function to its embedded Perl script interpreter. It was just a few lines of code, but it served to introduce me to Gaim, as well as to the developers who reviewed and accepted my patch.

Choosing a Project

Perhaps the most important choice in starting open source development is what project to contribute to. I chose Gaim because I really enjoy working with emergent instant messaging technology. Your first project should be something you use regularly and would be interested in extending in some way. At the time I made my submission, I was fascinated with writing Perl scripts to automate certain IM tasks. I decided it would be cool to have a dynamic user profile on AIM, but the Perl plug-in lacked the ability to change this. I soon realized this would be my first contribution.

I have worked on other open source projects in minor capacities as well, likewise because I've had a specific itch to scratch. In one instance, I discovered a bug that quickly leaked all my system memory. In another instance, I wanted to be able to drag songs from my MP3 player's playlist to a Gaim conversation window to send them to a friend.

Most people who ask me how to get started in open source development don't have an itch to scratch. They have free time they would like to donate to the project, but don't particularly have anything they personally would like to see implemented.

Gaim doesn't maintain a list of jobs that need to be done, but other projects do. If you don't have a particular itch to scratch, perhaps one of these projects would be well suited for you. Some projects recently have even introduced "bounties." They offer a list of projects they would like to see done and then pay you a certain amount when you complete one. This would be a strong motivation to start your efforts on a given project.

Writing Your First Patch

Once you have a project in mind, you have to decide what to write. In most cases, this is easy. If you have an itch to scratch, scratch your itch. If you're trying to claim an open source bounty, work on that project. However, if you've determined what project you want to work on but don't have a specific goal, it can be difficult to decide what to do.

Many projects have a TODO file distributed with the source code. Gaim does, but it's unmaintained, hasn't been updated in years, and should probably be removed. Gaim has no list of tasks we need done; you'll need to discover your own.

Many open source developers claim that fixing bugs is the best way to get started on a project. Although Gaim doesn't have a list of features and enhancements to work on, we have a *huge* list of reported bugs. These developers claim that it's easy to go through that list and fix bugs as an introduction to the project. From my experience, though, there are better ways to introduce yourself to a project.

Some bugs are caused by trivial human programming errors that are easy to detect and fix without understanding the context of the code. It's entirely plausible to see the error in `free(string); function1(string);` without bothering to learn what the `string` variable or `function1()` function are. Unless you make a purposeful effort to learn about this, a new programmer will gain little experience fixing this type of bug.

Most other bugs are caused by unexpected interaction between completely different parts of the program. This means that to fix bugs, you will often first need a complete understanding of how each component is expected to interact. I find that it's difficult to have a real grasp of this without prior experience working on the code. Therefore, new developers are often unable to fix bugs as effectively as they can add new features. Attempting to track down difficult bugs in unfamiliar code can lead to frustration. Many developers thrive on the challenge of figuring out puzzles like this. If you are one of these, perhaps fixing bugs is an appropriate introductory task. At the very least, you'll quickly become the best friend of other developers who find bug fixing tedious, such as myself. But I prefer to implement fun new features as a way to begin familiarizing yourself with the code. These features should be localized to one particular part of the application, so you need only learn about that one component and not the bigger, more complicated, picture of how each component interacts with others.

Probably the best way to know what features the developers want is to get to know them personally. Remember, being accepted as part of the development community requires you get along with the other developers personally. If you're looking for a task to work on in Gaim, hang out in the Gaim IRC channel and subscribe to the mailing lists. You may not get a good answer if you ask a developer directly what you should do, but just by watching the discussions, you will quickly discover things that developers want done. Pick a small task localized to one area and implement it. Feel free to ask the developers for hints and tips along the way. It will help them get to know you.

Submitting Your Work

All projects have a designated way to submit patches. You should find that way somewhere in the project's documentation. Usually, you are requested to submit it to an issue tracker, a database containing all the bugs, patches, feature requests, etc. for the project. This makes it easy for the developers to manage user contributions. If you attempt to send a patch any other way; it will probably just get lost and forgotten about.

However, as I've said, befriending the developers is important if you intend to enter their organization. If you asked a developer for help on your patch, you should write him a brief thank-you letter along the lines of the following:

> *Hi. Thank you for helping me to write my patch to implement Super Cool Feature in Gaim. I completed my patch and it seems to work great! When you get a chance, I'd appreciate it if you would please review it at* `http://Link_To_Patch` *and offer some feedback. Thanks again!*

This is sure to leave a good impression on the developer who reviews your patch. If I were to receive a letter like this, I would certainly give the patch more attention than others, being sure to offer constructive feedback to ensure the new developer understands what the Gaim developers look for.

It may take a few revisions for your patch to get accepted; if this is your first patch for the project, this is normal. It will take a while to get a good grasp of how the code is designed, what style is expected, and other issues. With each revision you make, you learn more about what the project wants from you.

Climbing the Ranks

As you learn what the project wants from you, you will be able to write patches more easily. With each small, localized patch you write, you learn about another aspect of the program. Eventually, you'll have contributed enough small, localized patches that you'll understand how most of the application's parts work and how they interrelate. You'll have a full understanding of the project's preferred coding style, and the other developers will probably recognize you and your work.

At this point, you are probably qualified to take on a larger project, affecting multiple parts of the application. You've also likely paid enough attention to mailing lists and IRC to know what large tasks need to be completed. To be promoted to crazy patch writer in Gaim, you will typically need to start writing patches of this scale.

Small, straightforward patches—the kind that new developers typically submit—are easily reviewed. Gaim developers can often decide whether to accept or reject them in a single glance. Once promoted to crazy patch writer, your large patches will be heavily scrutinized by the developers who review your patches to ensure their quality is good. Once the developers are able to consistently commit your work without making any modifications, they can trust you to commit your work yourself. It is typically when this happens that you will be promoted to developer.

The final promotion in Gaim is to lead developer. Open source projects typically have only one lead developer, and when he decides to move on to something else (in Gaim, we typically refer to this as "retiring"), it is his responsibility to choose his successor. Naturally, the aspects usually considered are seniority, ability, talent, commitment, and personality. It's important to choose a successor you're confident can do a good job managing an open source project.

Managing Your Own Open Source Project

Managing an open source project is an extremely rewarding experience. Despite there being very little additional work for a lead developer over a developer, I receive a lot more recognition. Whenever Gaim needs a single human representative, be it for magazine, newspaper, or radio interviews, I'm usually the person contacted first. Additionally, despite Gaim essentially managing itself, being the lead developer of a popular project implies to people that you're an exceptionally talented leader. This isn't really true; there's very little that an open source maintainer needs do to be successful. I'll discuss these requirements in this section.

Becoming a Maintainer

In his follow-up to *The Cathedral and the Bazaar*, an essay titled *Homesteading the Noosphere* (also found at http://www.catb.org/~esr/writings/cathedral-bazaar/), Eric Raymond identifies the three possible ways to become the maintainer of an open source project: starting a project of your own, forking an existing project, and inheriting an existing project.

Starting Your Own Project

The most obvious way to maintain an open source project is to start one yourself. I've personally never done this, and as 80% of projects at SourceForge.net (the leading host of open source projects) never make it out of beta, it seems that starting a successful project is not easy.

The problem with starting your own project is that there are increasingly fewer things that need to be written as free software. There's little point in starting a new IM client from scratch when you can just modify Gaim to meet your needs.

If you have an original idea (of which plenty exist), though, you should, of course, work on it. Remember that you will need to work on it alone until you get to a stage where it's usable and interesting for other hackers to play with. Then code submissions will come in on their own. It could take a while to get to this stage, although if you are passionate about your idea, investing your efforts should not be an issue.

For a large number of applications, though, starting from scratch is not a good idea. The open source process encourages code reuse and provides a rich repository of code you can start from; you shouldn't duplicate effort when possible. There is almost always some other project that can serve as a starting point for your project. If the developers of that project don't agree with the direction you have in mind, though, you are granted the freedom to start a new project based on the existing code. A new project based on an existing one is called a *fork*.

Forking an Existing Project

Just as starting a new project that duplicates features of an existing project is frowned upon in open source, forking an existing project must be done carefully to avoid criticism by other developers. Open source developers hate duplicated effort and, by nature, having two disjointed versions of the same application requires both sides to duplicate each other's efforts.

There are valid reasons for forking existing projects, namely fundamentally differing visions. However, in order to maintain good standing, it's best to submit the changes you make back to the original project in the form of patches. Oftentimes, this is implausible as the two projects diverge further away from each other, but when done, both projects benefit from the efforts of the other.

There are several notable cases of successful forks in open source, but by and large they fail. Gaim has been forked numerous times for various reasons, but ultimately, it's been realized that work is best concentrated on one version of Gaim's code and the forks quickly fall into inactivity. One notable example of a successful Gaim fork is the Gaim-vv project at `http://gaim-vv.sourceforge.net/`. This project adds voice and video features to a forked version of Gaim, but as it's developed by Gaim developers and intended to be merged back into Gaim eventually, it doesn't technically meet the definition of a fork.

Inheriting an Existing Project

The final way to maintain your own project is to inherit an existing project from a past maintainer. This is how I came to be in charge of Gaim.

This is probably the most difficult way to take charge of a project; it requires that the original author (or successor to the original author) lose interest in working on the project. Most people enjoy leading high-profile, popular projects, so it's difficult ever to get that opportunity. Gaim, however, has changed hands relatively frequently. In the seven years since it was created, I am the fourth maintainer. Further, you need to rise to the top of the project's hierarchy to be considered for succession, a challenge in its own right.

More likely, you will be able to find an abandoned project to take over. As mentioned earlier this section, SourceForge.net is full of abandoned projects. These projects were never able to reach a critical mass and the authors eventually gave up on them. You can e-mail the maintainers of those projects and ask to take over; in most cases, they'll gladly hand over the project.

Management Techniques

As I've been saying throughout this chapter, once you have control over an open source project, maintaining it is easy. Your main tasks are to make it easier for other developers to work, to encourage them to work, and to dictate overall goals for the project.

As lead developer of Gaim, I make the work of other developers easier by administering the infrastructure provided by SourceForge.net. This includes delegating certain administration to other developers who may need it. Open source is characterized by lots of delegation like this. Each developer of an open source project has certain parts that he "owns." Responsibility for it is delegated to him; he reviews patches and bug reports about it, and he typically has the final say on how it is implemented. Being delegated complete responsibility like that is itself an encouraging factor to open source developers.

The motivations discussed earlier in this chapter are usually enough to drive development. A lead developer rarely needs to motivate the rest of the team. Promising new developers, though, can often be encouraged to work on specific tasks. They are already motivated to work, but seek direction in how to apply their efforts. I mentioned that new developers wishing to become part of the meritocracy should listen to the developers for patch ideas. I have received code written by aspiring new developers by requesting they take on certain projects.

The most important responsibility of an open source leader is to enforce a single unified vision for the development team to follow. Because a leader has only the power afforded by the respect of peers, if the prescribed vision is really terrible, nobody will listen and developers will work on other projects instead. Therefore, a good open source leader should take the opinions of all the developers under consideration and then make a judgment based on that. A leader has to be able to defend his decisions, so it's very important to be a good debater and to be able to express your opinions well. It is very rare to see a successful open source leader who writes poorly and unconvincingly.

Summary

The open source process is a really important development process that's revolutionizing the software world because it allows any ol' freshman with a computer at a public university to go on to become a prominent, well-respected leader in the software industry. Offering the source code to the entire world invites everyone to help make an open source project successful.

Another important benefit of available source code is that developers can read other people's code to discover the best way to solve certain problems. Throughout this book, you will do just that: learn important open source techniques from Gaim's source code. In the next chapter, I will introduce the tools you will use in the development of Gaim and other applications.

CHAPTER 3
■ ■ ■

Development Tools

The knowledge presented in this book will teach you how to create your own desktop applications using open source technologies. That knowledge, however, is useless without the development tools needed to put it to use. The open source tools introduced in this chapter are among those most commonly used for software development.

Chapter 1 guided you through the process of installing most of the software that will be explained here. If you are a UNIX user, they were most likely already installed; Windows users installed the software using Cygwin. In this chapter, I will explain how to use it.

Editors

It would be pretty difficult to write effective code without some sort of editing application. Capable editors not only provide a workspace for writing code, but also a variety of tools useful for quickly and efficiently managing it. There is a huge variety of editors out there, and if you have one you're already comfortable with, you can go on using that. However, some editors are simply less suitable for writing code than others. For instance, most people can be far more productive with vi or Emacs than with Nano or Windows Notepad.

There are two major type editors in the UNIX world: Emacs and vi. Most other editors borrow features from one or both of these. The two are very different, and a large part of UNIX humor is the so-called "religious war" between advocates of each. Emacs is applauded for its power and versatility and criticized for being large and slow. vi is liked for being small and fast, but is criticized for its confusing user interface.

Both vi and Emacs, however, are very well suited for editing code, and most UNIX users may have a preference for one over the other but are familiar with both. A few things make these editors considerably better suited for writing code than other editors:

- Both editors support *syntax highlighting*, which colors bits of code depending on their syntactical function. For instance, comments may be orange and variable names blue.

- Both editors understand commonly used indentation styles. After hitting the Enter key, the cursor will probably have appropriately indented the next line.

- Both editors have easily accessible keyboard shortcuts for things particularly useful to coders. Simpler editors require to you select text to delete it; code editors provide special commands for deleting the current line, deleting the current word, and deleting from the cursor to the end of the line, for instance.

- Both editors can be integrated with the GNU build system, to be discussed throughout this chapter.

- Gaim developers will make fun of you if you use an editor like Pico.

Personally, I use an Emacs editor (specifically XEmacs) for most of my coding, and a vi editor (specifically Vim) for smaller jobs, such as fixing a syntax error if my compile failed. I appreciate Emacs's more familiar user interface (especially the way it handles editing multiple files), but don't like to wait for it to load when I need to change only one line of code.

I'll skim the surface of both editors here and provide enough information to give you a passable knowledge of how to use each.

Emacs

Emacs is my preferred editor for working on large projects due to its more familiar interface. In Emacs, commands are entered by using combinations of the Ctrl, Alt, and other ordinary keys; the way commands are entered is the most notable difference between Emacs and vi. This way is probably most familiar to you, as most editors use it. If you didn't install Emacs from Cygwin, you can download a native Windows version from http://www.xemacs.org.

Features

I mentioned that Emacs handles multiple files better, which I think makes it better for larger projects. The version of Emacs I use, XEmacs, displays files in a tabbed interface, shown in Figure 3-1, which I find makes it easier to switch between two open files than the vi approach.

Also seen in Figure 3-1 is the game Tetris, which is part of Emacs and a source of criticisms that it's too "bloated." Emacs has always had a powerful Lisp plug-in architecture, and over time many plug-ins have been developed. From within Emacs you can use a virtual psychiatrist, a calendar, a mail reader, and even an AIM client.

Emacs was one of the first programs to come out of the GNU project, so it's well integrated with the GNU development tools. You can compile and debug your applications from within Emacs. Despite the powerful features it contains, though, I tend to use it only for simple editing.

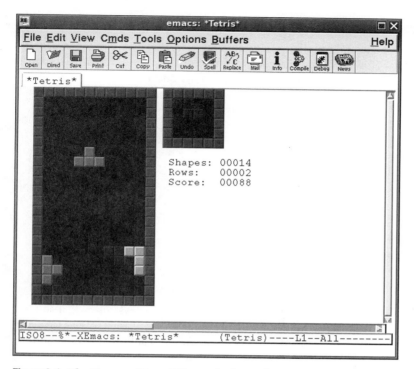

Figure 3-1. *The Emacs editors (XEmacs is shown here) are often considered "bloated" due to features like this Tetris game.*

Usage

Every keystroke in Emacs is a command. For most of these keystrokes, the command is `self-insert-command`. This is the command that causes Emacs to insert a character into the current document. When you type the letter I, the `self-insert-command` is called and an I is inserted into the document. For other commands, though, Emacs makes heavy use of two modifier keys called Control and Meta.

These two keys are typically abbreviated C and M, so when you read `C-x`, this means "hold down Control, and press the A key." Most PC users have a Control key on their keyboard, but not a Meta key. On these machines, the Meta key usually maps to the Alt key, so `M-f` means "hold down Alt, and press F."

Some commands require more than one keystroke. The first keystroke is called a *prefix command*, and waits for a second keystroke. Functions with the same prefix command are typically similar in function. For instance, `C-h` is used by commands that provide help. Try `C-h i` (which is different from `C-h C-i`) to read the Emacs manual.

Common Commands

XEmacs also includes a menu and a toolbar, so it's not necessary that you remember all of its many cryptic commands. However, many people prefer to keep their hands on the keyboard at all times and prefer a keyboard command to a menu or toolbar button.

The C-x prefix command includes most of the functions for managing various files and documents. Table 3-1 shows some of the more useful commands.

Table 3-1. *Emacs Commands for Manipulating Files*

Command	Description
C-x C-f	Opens a file for editing
C-x C-s	Saves a file
C-x C-k	Closes a file
C-x C-c	Exits Emacs

Once you have your file loaded, you can simply type into it; each keystroke will insert its character. Usually you can also navigate the document with your keyboard's arrow keys. However, when coding it's often useful to have finer control over navigation. Table 3-2 provides some useful commands for getting from one place in your file to another.

Table 3-2. *Emacs Commands for Navigating Within a File*

Command	Description
C-f	Moves forward one character
C-b	Moves backward one character
M-f	Moves forward one word
M-b	Moves backward one word
C-a	Moves to the beginning of the line
C-e	Moves to the end of the line
C-p	Moves up one line
C-n	Moves down one line
M-<	Moves to the beginning of the file
M->	Moves to the end of the file
C-M-a	Moves to the beginning of the current function
C-M-e	Moves to the end of the current function

Of course, often you don't know precisely where within a file the code you're looking for is useful. Other times, you need to replace all instances of one string with another, perhaps to rename a variable or function. For these tasks, you should use Emacs's search and replace features.

Emacs features *incremental search*, which means that as you type the phrase you're searching for, Emacs goes to the first instance of what you've written already. This is good because you'll rarely need to type the entire phrase you're searching for. Emacs will locate it based on the first few characters. Table 3-3 shows Emacs's search and replace functions.

Table 3-3. *Emacs Commands for Searching for and Replacing Text*

Command	Description
C-s	Incremental search.
M-% (Alt-Shift-5)	Find and replace; Emacs will prompt for the text to search for and the text to replace it with.

Lastly, once you've found text, you may need to delete it or move it. Depending on how your Emacs is configured, you should be able to use the Backspace and Delete keys as you would expect them to work, but just as Emacs offers commands to navigate based on lines and words, it also allows you to delete elements larger than a character.

When you delete something this way, it gets saved to Emacs's equivalent of a clipboard. You can then paste the deleted text somewhere else in the text. Emacs offers no other special commands for copying and pasting. In fact, to copy text, I just delete it and then immediately paste it. Depending on your system, Emacs may integrate with the native clipboard. Table 3-4 shows the commands used to delete text.

■**Tip** The standard way to copy text to the X Window System is to select it. Any selected text is implicitly in the clipboard. Then use the middle mouse button (often the scroll wheel) to paste.

Table 3-4. *Emacs Commands for Deleting, Copying, and Pasting Text*

Command	Description
M-d	Deletes from the cursor to the end of the current word
M-DEL	Deletes from the beginning of the current word to the cursor
C-k	Deletes from the cursor to the end of the current line
C-u C-0 C-k	Deletes from the beginning of the current line to the cursor
C-y	Pastes previously deleted text at the cursor

These functions merely scratch the surface of what Emacs is capable of, but they make up nearly 100% of what I use it for. You can read Emacs's own help documentation via C-h i.

vi

When I have only one file that needs editing, I'll often use Vim, a vi editor seen in Figure 3-2. Because of Emacs's bulk, it loads much more slowly than vim does. However, I prefer the way XEmacs shows me currently open files in tabs and that Emacs is not modal, as vi is.

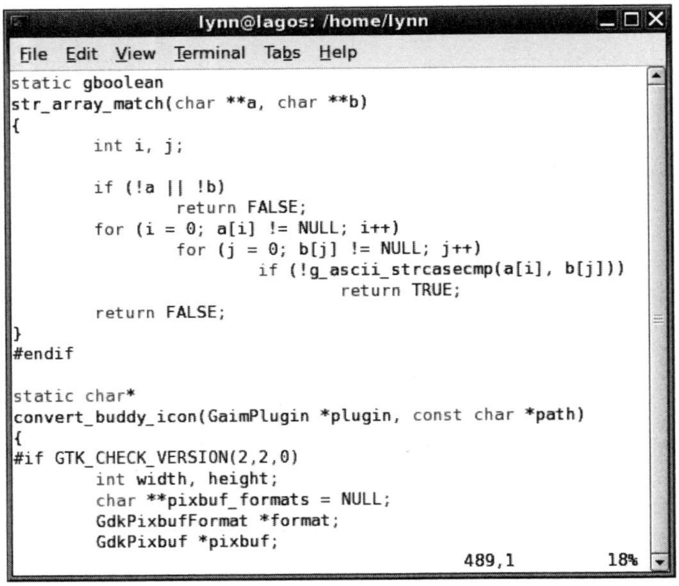

Figure 3-2. *The Vim editor*

Modes

vi is modal, meaning it has two different modes: insert and command. When in insert mode, everything you type is inserted in the current document. When in command mode, everything you type is a command. Using vi requires you to constantly move between the two modes.

vi fans say this a good thing, that they can always keep their fingers on the home keys of their keyboard without needing to move them to hit the Control or Meta key. I, personally, would prefer to move my hands occasionally to avoid the confusion of forgetting what mode I'm in, causing text I attempt to insert to issue commands. The opposite happens too, and I've written code that strangely contains vi commands.

vi starts in command mode. To enter insert mode, press the I key. It will move you to insert mode; you can tell this because the bottom line of the screen will read -- INSERT --, as seen in Figure 3-3. To return to command mode, hit the Escape key.

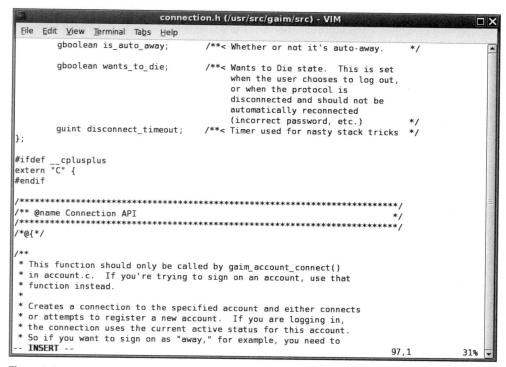

Figure 3-3. *vim in insert mode, as evidenced by the bottom line on the screen*

Commands

The variant of vi I use, Vim, is a console-based application, and like Emacs, native versions exist for most any platform you would want it for. There are also GUI versions, such as GVim (which run on X or Windows). They include menus and toolbars, but because not waiting for a GUI to load is the major advantage for me in using Vim over XEmacs, I enter all my commands with the keyboard.

vi commands do not use modifier keys such as Control or Meta as Emacs does. vi commands are entered in the command line and are usually short words or just single characters. Whereas Emacs commands that deal with file management start with C-x, the same commands in vi start with a colon. These commands are listed in Table 3-5.

Table 3-5. *vi Commands for Manipulating Files*

Command	Description
:r	Opens a file.
:w	Saves a file.
:q	Quits vi if there are no changes to save. If there are, vi will not quit and will instead warn about unsaved changes; you'll need to use one of the two following commands.
:wq	Saves and quits.
:q!	Quits without saving.

vi also allows you to navigate the file with cursor keys, but most people recommend navigating with the keys shown in first four rows of Table 3-6 so that you can keep your hands in place. Like Emacs, vi can navigate through a file more than one character at a time. Some of the commands to do this are found in Table 3-6.

Table 3-6. *vi Commands for Navigating Within a File*

Command	Description
h	Moves the cursor left one column.
j	Moves the cursor down one line.
k	Moves the cursor up one line.
l	Moves the cursor right one column
w	Moves forward one word.
b	Moves backward one word.
L	Moves to the bottom of the screen.
H	Moves to the top of the screen.
0	Moves to the beginning of the current line.
$	Moves to the end of the current line.
-	Moves to the first non-whitespace character of the current line; useful for skipping indentation.
<num>	Goes to the line specified in <num>. For instance, to move to line 44, do :44.

Also like Emacs, vi allows you to delete segments of text as well as just characters. These commands build on top of the navigation commands. To delete from the cursor to another location, type d and then the command to move the cursor to that location. To delete until the end of the current line, for instance, you would do d$. As a special case, dd deletes the entire current line. As in Emacs, deleted text is automatically "cut" to the clipboard. To insert text, use the p command.

By default, vi does not do incremental search; you must search for an entire phrase (of course, you could just search for the first few characters of your search term, but you will have to skip through nonmatches manually). Table 3-7 shows the vi commands for searching and replacing text.

Table 3-7. *vi Commands for Searching and Replacing Text*

Command	Description
/<word>	Searches for <word>. To search for "twinkies," do /twinkies.
?<word>	Searches for <word> backwards through the document.
n	Repeats the previous search.
:s/<search string>/<replacement string>/g	Replaces elements of <search string> with <replacement string>. The g means "global," and causes all instances of <search string> to be replaced. To do it only to the first instance, leave off the g.

■**Note** Many UNIX developers are so familiar with vi's search and replace syntax that they use it in e-mails, IRC, and IM. If someone IMs you s/apples/bananas/g, he means "replace 'apples' with 'bananas' in what was just said."

As you can see, Emacs and vi offer essentially the same features, but with considerably different user interfaces. An alternate user interface that may be more familiar to Windows developers is the Integrated Development Environment, or IDE, which integrates the editor with other development tools.

IDEs

Windows developers are probably familiar with Integrated Development Environments such as Microsoft Visual Studio or Microsoft Visual Basic. IDEs integrate the editor, compiler, and debugger into a single program. Due largely to tradition, these tools are rarely used on UNIX. Instead, developers use each program in the GNU build system separately.

However, various free software IDEs for C programming are available for Windows and UNIX. I'll list a few of them here.

Anjuta

Anjuta, pictured in Figure 3-4, is an IDE for UNIX's GNOME desktop environment. As such, it integrates well with the GNOME environment (see Chapter 5 for more on GNOME). In addition to a fully functional editor, Anjuta integrates with GCC (the GNU Compiler Collection) and GDB (GNU Debugger), which I'll cover later in this chapter.

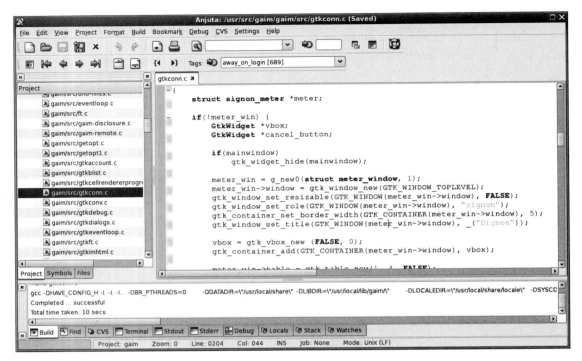

Figure 3-4. *The Anjuta IDE*

Because it's developed for GNOME, it is particularly well suited for developing GNOME applications. When you create a new project in Anjuta, it will automatically create a build environment that links to the required GNOME libraries. It will also create skeleton source code to create a window. You can then create a GUI using Glade, GNOME's WYSIWYG interface builder, and edit the code to suit your application. This certainly is less work than writing everything manually. However, Gaim and other UNIX applications typically do not use IDEs or interface builders, and prefer that everything is written manually.

You can download Anjuta from `http://anjuta.sourceforge.net/`.

KDevelop

KDevelop is to the KDE environment as Anjuta is to the GNOME environment. It offers the normal editor, compiler, and debugger integration you'd expect from any IDE, but it also offers functionality specific to developing KDE applications. You can see KDevelop in Figure 3-5.

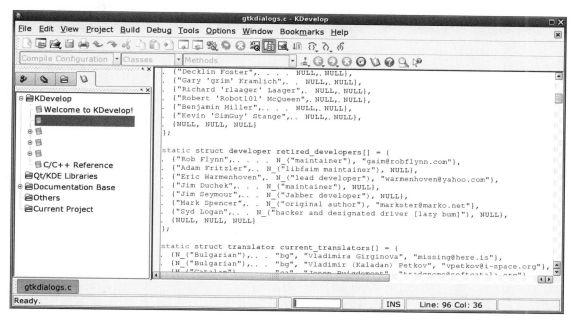

Figure 3-5. *KDevelop is an IDE specially suited for creating KDE applications.*

KDE applications use Trolltech's Qt (pronounced "cute") toolkit, whereas Gaim uses GTK+. Therefore, many of KDevelop's features are specifically tailored for Qt and not appropriate for developing Gaim or other GTK+ applications. KDevelop does, however, have some support for GNOME applications and is the most mature UNIX IDE for development in C.

You can download KDevelop from `http://www.kdevelop.org`.

Dev-C++

Dev-C++, seen in Figure 3-6, is an IDE for Windows. It uses MinGW, the Windows version of GCC capable of creating Windows-native applications, and the Windows port of GDB, the GNU debugger.

Like KDevelop and Anjuta, Dev-C++ is modeled after Microsoft Visual Studio, which makes it easy to use for Windows developers coming from those environments. Also like the others, Dev-C++ contains features specifically useful for developing for its target platform, Windows.

Dev-C++ is available under the GPL license from Bloodshed Software at `http://www.bloodshed.net`.

Using an IDE will obscure many of the details of the build and debugging process I will discuss in the next few sections. Each of the IDEs listed here are just front ends to these tools, however, so it is still important to understand what they are and the basics of how they work.

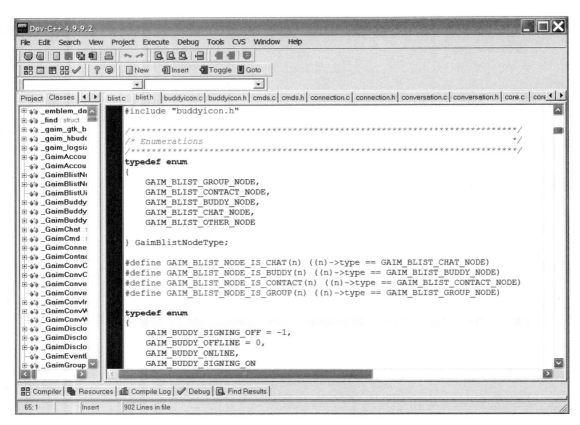

Figure 3-6. *Dev-C++, an IDE for Microsoft Windows*

GCC

GCC is the commonly used acronym for the GNU Compiler Collection (http://gcc.gnu.org/). It was originally the GNU C Compiler, but that name is no longer accurate as GCC is now capable of compiling source in C, C++, Objective-C, Fortran, Java, and Ada. It is very portable; GCC is capable of compiling source for nearly every platform imaginable, and because GCC is written in C and compiled by itself, GCC is likewise available on most platforms. It is the compiler used by Gaim, almost all free software, and other non-free software.

GCC is the crux of the GNU build system. The GNU build system, used to compile nearly all free and open-source software, consists of GCC and GNU Autotools, discussed later this chapter.

■**Note** MinGW is a Windows version of GCC; everything I say about GCC here is true of MinGW as well.

The compiler is the lowest-level tool in the development toolchain. Its task is straightforward; it reads source files and compiles them to binary executable files. Because it's so low-level, developers rarely invoke GCC directly but allow it to be invoked by other tools. However, to properly configure these tools for your project, you should know the basics of how to use GCC and how GCC works. The process of compiling source to executable happens in two main, yet distinct, phases: compilation and linking.

How a Program Is Built

Most C applications of any considerable size take up more than one file. Each of these files is first compiled individually into an object file with the same base name as the source file, but with an .o extension. Thus, when you compile account.c, it creates a file called account.o. This file contains all the executable machine code for the source code contained within account.c, as well as the location of variables and functions.

The linker takes a number of object files and compiles them to a single executable. The linker matches references to a function or variable in one object file to the correct location of that function or variable in another object file. If account.c calls the gaim_connection_new() function from connection.c, the linker will find gaim_connection_new() from connection.o and match it to the call from account.o.

It's possible to perform compilation and linking on the same command line. This is the default behavior of GCC when no arguments are given. However, that would require recompiling the entire program every time a single source file changed. Therefore, one typically compiles each source file as it's changed, a task made simple with the make tool, discussed later. make is the tool that invokes GCC with the appropriate arguments.

Invoking GCC

GCC uses command-line arguments to affect the compilation process. These options can change a wide array of behaviors, from how the language is parsed, to what language features are enabled, to how well optimized the resulting executable should be. The most basic command-line options, though, merely specify what files the compiler should compile, link, or both compile and link.

Compiling and Linking

The default behavior for GCC when passed no arguments other than source files is to compile all the provided source files and link them into an executable called a.out. To create an executable with a different name, use the -o command-line option:

```
gcc -o exampleprogram *.c
```

This command compiles all the C source files in the current directory and links them to an executable called exampleprogram. If you've already compiled the source files, you can link the object files by providing only a list of them to GCC, using the -o option if desired:

```
gcc -o exampleprogram *.o
```

This command creates the exampleprogram executable from the object files in the current directory. It will not recompile source files, even if they've changed. To do that, specify source files to compile with the -c option:

```
gcc -c *.c
```

This will create object files for each source file. Usually, though, each file is compiled on a separate invocation of GCC. The typical process in compiling multiple source files into a single binary executable would look like this:

```
gcc -c file1.c
gcc -c file2.c
gcc -c file3.c
gcc -o exampleprogram file1.o file2.o file 3.o
```

The first three commands create object files for each source and the fourth links them to an executable called exampleprogram. This process would work fine for small projects with no external dependencies, but once a project depends on some external library, GCC must be told where that library is located.

Dependencies

Your application will likely compile and link against a number of libraries, such as GTK+. Libraries your application uses are called *dependencies* and need to be located in both the compilation and linking processes. During compilation, the compiler needs to be given the location of .h header files that are #included by the project. Without them, the compilation would fail: the headers would not be located and the compiler would not know about the data types and functions provided by the library.

During linking, the compiler needs to know the location of each library on disk. These libraries are typically "dynamically linked," meaning that the code in your application isn't actually linked with the code in its libraries until right before the program runs. Nonetheless, the linker needs to know what libraries the executable will be linked against and where those libraries are located. The location of the library files and header files are unrelated to each other; they must be determined and specified to GCC separately through a series of command-line options.

To provide the compiler with a list of locations to fetch header files from, use the -I command-line option, followed by a path to the directory. You will need one -I for each directory you compile against. Gaim compiles against a large number of libraries, so each invocation of GCC has nearly 20 -I options. Fortunately, the task of maintaining these options is handled by GNU Autotools, discussed later this chapter.

The linker takes two different command-line options for specifying which libraries to link against. The first option, -l, specifies which libraries to link against. The name you specify isn't a file name, but a library name. It will correspond to a file with the specified name prefixed with lib and postfixed with .a. Thus, when the build environment gives an -lglib-2.0 option to GCC, it links against a file named libglib-2.0.a.

This file, libglib-2.0.a, is located in a directory specified by the -L command. -L works just like -I. Each directory is specified with its own argument. Often, each library will require both an -l and an -L argument, if the library file is not found in a standard location.

Other Options

Other important options to GCC include -D, which defines a preprocessor statement during compilation. This allows the programmer to selectively choose what to compile at compile-time. One common use of this is to allow additional debugging support by providing -DDEBUG to GCC. Then, within your code you could write

```
#if DEBUG
printf("%s\n", debug_msg);
#endif
```

The printf() line will be compiled in only if DEBUG is defined by the -D argument.

-W provides another useful set of compiler options. These allow you to specify how compile warnings are handled. Compile warnings are bits of code that are not illegal according to the specification, but are still most likely wrong. If your code has warnings in it, it will compile, but it may have bugs. -Wall will activate all warnings; the default is to show only the most serious ones. -Werror causes GCC to treat warnings as errors; the process exits as a failure.

Finally, to enable debugging information, provide -g GCC while linking. This will allow you to usefully run the GNU debugger, GDB, on the resulting executable. I will discuss GDB later this chapter.

All these command-line options plus the sheer number of times GCC is invoked during the process of building a project makes it quite unwieldy to perform the task by hand. The make utility is the next step in the build process; it allows you to describe the build process in a *makefile*, which make uses to provide the appropriate command options to GCC.

make

make is an extremely useful part of the build process. By creating a file called Makefile, you describe to make exactly how to build your application. make can then intelligently determine how to build your application without necessarily rebuilding the entire application.

If you build Gaim and then change a single source file, only that source file needs to be recompiled. The other object files are up-to-date. All that needs to be done is to compile that one source file and link the resulting object file with the other, older object files. By creating a proper makefile, you can specify this behavior by specifying separate *rules* for each sub-task in building your application.

Makefile Rules

A makefile is essentially a set of rules. Each rule typically describes how to create a given file. A rule contains the name of the file to create, prerequisites that the file depends on, and the process for creating the file:

```
exampleprogram : file1.o file2.o file3.o
    gcc -o exampleprogram file1.o file2.o file3.o
```

This example is the rule for creating a file called exampleprogram. The target file is located at the beginning of the first line. Following the target is a colon and then a list of prerequisites. In order to build an up-to-date exampleprogram, make must first build an up-to-date file1.o, file2.o, and file3.o. If exampleprogram does not exist, or it does exist but happens to be older than file1.o, file2.o, or file3.o, make will execute the command on the next line. If exampleprogram is newer than its prerequisites (including the prerequisites of its prerequisites), make realizes that exampleprogram is also current, and doesn't need to execute the command.

The line the command starts on begins with a tab followed by the command that will be given to the shell to execute. In this case, it tells GCC to link the object files to an executable called exampleprogram, using the syntax seen in the section on GCC. If all the .o files are up-to-date, it will issue that command and link them. However, if an .o file needs to be updated, make will figure out how to do it with its own makefile rule:

```
file1.o : file1.c
    gcc -o file1.o -c file1.c
file2.o : file2.c file2.h
    gcc -o file2.o -c file2.c
file3.o : file3.c
    gcc -o file3.o -c file2.c
```

Each object file gets its own makefile rule. The dependencies include the source file as well as any headers in the rule. Because the headers are included into the source file, the source files need to be recompiled if a header changes. Fortunately, the GNU Autotools will automatically keep track of which header files should be used as prerequisites.

Implicit Rules

Notice that the rules for the three .o targets above are essentially the same, differing only in the filenames. With a large project, like Gaim, with over 100 source files, maintaining a separate, nearly identical build target for each would be inconvenient and error-prone. Because of this problem, make allows you to create *implicit rules*. These rules don't describe how to build a specific file, but rather a rule that describes generally, for instance, how to create an .o from a .c file. Gaim's Windows makefile includes a rule like this:

```
%.o: %.c
    $(CC) $(CFLAGS) $(INCLUDE_PATHS) $(DEFINES) -c $< -o $@
```

This allows you to avoid excessively long, largely redundant, difficult-to-maintain make-files. If make is told to build an .o file, it will first look to see if that specific file has a rule in the makefile. If not, it will attempt to match it to an implicit rule. The % in %.o matches to any word; %.o matches any file ending with .o. In the prerequisite section, the % matches the same word, so if account.o were matched to %.o, it would depend on account.c.

The command looks different from the command shown earlier in this section. The $ symbol is used to start variables. Every term starting with a $ is a variable. The last two, $< and $@, are automatic variables, which are evaluated to the input file and the output file, respectively. The first few, $(CC), $(CFLAGS), $(INCLUDES), etc., are declared elsewhere in the makefile.

Variables

Because certain aspects of the build environment are very dynamic and one build environment may vary greatly from another, it needs to be easy to change certain aspects of the build process. You can accomplish this by declaring anything likely to change as variables, listed at the top of the file.

Recall the first example of a makefile rule I provided:

```
exampleprogram : file1.o file2.o file3.o
    gcc $(LIBS) -o exampleprogram file1.o file2.o file3.o
```

Notice how the list of object files is duplicated. Because adding, removing, or renaming source files is not uncommon during the development process, this list will likely change often. Every time it's changed, this makefile rule needs to be updated in two places (in both lines of this makefile rule). It might be easy to forget to update both, resulting in a broken makefile.

It would be easier, then, if we used a variable called $(OBJECTS) to represent the list of all the object files in the program. Then, the makefile rule would read

```
exampleprogram  : $(OBJECTS)
    gcc $(LIBS) -o exampleprogram $(OBJECTS)
```

The variable declaration at the top of the makefile is the only thing that would require editing:

```
OBJECTS =   file1.o \
            file2.o \
            file3.o
```

Note that backslashes are used to split the declaration among several lines to make it easier to read. Other things are useful as makefile variables as well. The implicit rule example uses $(CC), $(CFLAGS), $(INCLUDE_PATHS), $(LIBS), and $(DEFINES). These variables correspond to the compiler command (gcc), compiler flags (-g -Wall, perhaps), header file locations (-I/usr/include/gtk+-2.0 -I/usr/include/glib-2.0/, etc.), and defined preprocessor statements (-DDEBUG), respectively.

For compiling GTK+ applications, you will want to set $(CFLAGS) and $(LIBS), to point to GTK+'s header files and shared object files, respectively. A convenient way to do this is to invoke pkg-config, which I'll cover in greater detail in the Autotools section of this chapter. Typical variable definitions might look like this:

```
CFLAGS=`pkg-config --cflags gtk+-2.0`
LIBS=`pkg-config --libs gtk+-2.0`
```

Multiple Directories

Another notable point is that for projects with more than one directory, make can be used recursively. The command for a given makefile rule can run make in another directory. This is useful because most source trees contain multiple directories for different types of files: Gaim includes source code to be compiled in src/ and plugins/. The top-level makefile—the makefile in the top-level directory—just dispatches make commands to its subdirectories.

Because no files are actually created in the top-level directory, Gaim's makefile uses a phony target called all, which builds the entire project. Several of these phony targets are fairly standard as they're created by GNU Autotools, discussed later in this chapter. Other common targets include clean, which deletes all of the compiled binaries, install, which installs the resulting executables in the proper locations, and dist, which creates a release tarball. A typical all target would look like this:

```
all:
     $(MAKE) -C src/
     $(MAKE) -C plugins/
     $(MAKE) -C pixmaps/
```

This rule would merely run make in each of the subdirectories provided. The person compiling this project would then just run

```
$ make all
```

to execute this target and build the application. If all is the first target defined in the makefile (which is usually the case), you just run

```
$ make
```

Running make is easy to run; most of the time (because of the behavior of Autotools), all is the first target defined, so you just run make and it builds the all target. However, you can also build any target you want on the command line. In the context of Gaim, this is particularly useful for compiling your own plug-ins. The makefile in Gaim's plugin/ directory contains an implicit rule for creating a plug-in from a .c file. To compile myplugin.c into myplugin.so (or whichever the correct file extension is for plug-ins on your system), put it in plugins/, and from that directory run the following:

```
make myplugin.so
```

This will match the implicit rule for building .so files from .c files, and properly build your plug-in.

This is also useful when building the phony targets specified earlier. After building Gaim with just plain make, you need to build the install target. This is done just by running

```
make install
```

from the top-level directory.

Another useful command-line option to make is -f, which allows you to specify what file to use as the makefile. By default, make will look for a file called Makefile, and you don't need to specify this file manually. For a project like Gaim, however, building on Windows is vastly different from building on UNIX. Gaim, therefore, has two sets of makefiles. When building on Windows, you must specify to use the Windows makefile (called Makefile.mingw):

```
make -f Makefile.mingw
```

make is very useful, as it keeps you from manually invoking GCC hundreds of times. However, creating and maintaining a makefile, as you can tell, isn't very easy. Also, because one system varies greatly from another, a makefile would need to be edited for every new machine it was compiled on. Header file locations, for instance, can be almost everywhere.

Fortunately, the GNU Autotools exist so that users do not have to manually edit the makefile themselves. Autotools creates a shell script called configure that automatically determines what variables need to be set and generates a set of makefiles appropriately.

Autotools

When you know beforehand the exact configuration of the build environment, it is easy to create a working makefile for it. This is the case for Gaim's Windows build. In Chapter 1, I explained that in Windows each library is installed to a very specific location. Gaim's `Makefile.mingw`, used for building on Windows, is written assuming those locations. If you're developing solely on Windows, you can skip this section on Autotools.

Another time you can manually write an accurate makefile is if you're developing only on your own computer. You know the specifics about your own system. You know where each library is installed, and you can write your makefile accordingly. However, once you want to distribute your source tree to other people, you need to expect a huge variety of build configurations. GNU Autotools exists to create accurate makefiles from generic, higher-level descriptions of the build process. This allows makefiles to be built on almost any system imaginable.

Autotools consists of three utilities: Autoconf, Automake, and Libtool. These three applications work together to create a `configure` script that will generate relevant makefiles for a given system when invoked.

Autoconf creates the `configure` script. It uses a file called `configure.ac` as input. `configure.ac` specifies the variables in the build environment. Automake creates files called `Makefile.in`. These files are similar to makefiles in that they explain how the program is built. However, `Makefile.in` does it in a more general way, such that the `configure` script can process it with its own machine-specific information to create pertinent makefiles. Libtool is used to abstract the details involved in creating shared libraries. Because this book is about creating desktop applications, I will not discuss Libtool here. It's very simple to integrate into the rest of your build environment, however; if you're interested, visit http://www.gnu.org/software/libtool/libtool.html.

Figure 3-7 shows how Automake, Autoconf, and their respective input and output files interact. This may seem confusing right now, but this section will clarify things.

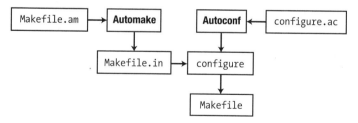

Figure 3-7. *How GNU Autotools interact with each other*

Autotools are very useful, but they're notoriously difficult to use properly for large-scale projects. This problem is escalated by the fact that different versions of the Autotools behave considerably differently. What worked fine on one version may fail miserably on another. The overview provided here remains simple enough to explain the tools' capabilities, and should work on any version of Autotools currently in use.

Automake

Automake takes a file called Makefile.am and turns it into a file called Makefile.in. This file will later be converted to Makefile when the configure script is written. Makefile.am is a very general way of describing how to build the project, and Makefile.in is essentially a makefile with some missing variables. When these missing variables are added by the configure script, it becomes the makefile for your project.

Automake can also determine which header files are included by each source file and can automatically maintain those as prerequisites as needed.

Makefile.am uses the same syntax as Makefile, and with a few exceptions, anything you include in Makefile.am will be added, verbatim, to Makefile. Because of this, you can add your own custom make targets to Makefile.am just as you would to Makefile, using the syntax discussed earlier. What makes Makefile.am different, then, are certain variables that have special meaning to Automake.

The first variable you'll want to set is bin_PROGRAMS. This is a list of all the executables to be created by your project. This will likely be only one, but you aren't limited to that. Gaim builds and installs two executables: gaim and gaim-remote, a small program that communicates with an existing Gaim session.

Variables in Makefile.am are defined just like any other variable:

```
bin_PROGRAMS = gaim gaim-remote
```

This tells Automake that it needs to build two programs: gaim and gaim-remote. Makefile.am then provides a brief description of how each of those programs is built using other variables.

The portion of a variable name in all capital letters is called a *primary*. These all have special significance to Automake. The lowercase words that prefix the primary further qualify it. bin_PROGRAMS implies a list of programs to be installed in the normal path for executables, typically /usr/local/bin. Programs normally executable only by the superuser (also called *root*) are typically installed into another directory, such as /usr/local/sbin. You could set sbin_PROGRAMS to list programs like this.

The descriptions you provide of how the programs in bin_PROGRAMS are built follow this same pattern. There are several primaries for each: most importantly, SOURCES and HEADERS. These are prefixed with the name of the program from bin_PROGRAMS:

```
gaim_SOURCES = file1.c \
               file2.c \
               file3.c
gaim_HEADERS = file2.h
```

This describes the program gaim as requiring three source files and one header file (the real Gaim is much larger). gaim-remote would be defined similarly, but the name of the program needs to be *normalized*. Because make disallows any characters other than alphanumerics and underscores in variables, you must convert any non-alphanumeric character to an underscore. For gaim-remote, this means the hyphen is converted to an underscore:

```
gaim_remote_SOURCES = gaim-remote.c \
                      prefix.c
gaim_remote_HEADERS= prefix.h
```

This is all that is required to have Automake create valid makefiles that build your application properly. Using the information determined by the configure script, the exact method of converting the provided sources and headers into binary executables will be determined. If your application requires other files, such as documentation, icon images, or sounds, Automake provides other primaries for those.

DATA is used for icons, sounds, and other data that needs to be installed without modification. SCRIPTS is similar. It is used for shell scripts. These are installed without modification also, but with different permissions. MANS is used for man pages, which are installed differently depending on the machine on which you compile the project. You can set the variable EXTRA_DIST with files that are distributed with your source, but not built or installed otherwise. This ordinarily includes your changelog and license agreement. Finally, for a project with subdirectories, set the SUBDIRS variable to contain them. Your top-level Makefile.am will probably be little more than setting SUBDIRS.

A final variable of note is AM_CPPFLAGS. This and the LDADD primary allow you to provide your own flags to the compiler and linker, respectively. This is especially useful when interacting with Autoconf. I'll discuss uses for these in the next section.

Anything else you put in Makefile.am will be copied exactly into the resulting Makefile. You can add your own targets directly to Makefile.am. Gaim does this with its doc target, allowing you to type make doc to generate documentation for Gaim's plug-in API.

Running automake from the top-level directory will read Makefile.am and process it and the Makefile.am files in each of its SUBDIRS. However, in order to do this, it first needs more configuration information as provided by configure.ac, the input to Autoconf.

Autoconf

Autoconf creates a configure script using the rules defined in configure.ac. The script it produces determines all the system-specific details of the environment the project is being built on. It determines what compiler to use, what options to pass to it, and where library dependencies are located. It also allows you to pass command-line arguments to configure that affect the way the project is built. The ultimate goal of configure is to use the Makefile.in files created by Automake and output Makefiles. However, the nature of configure.ac allows the configure script to do nearly anything.

Just as Makefile.in is essentially a makefile with a few fields that needed substitution, configure.ac is a shell script with a few fields that need replacement. However, where the fields replaced in Makefile.in are just variables, configure.ac uses macros. These macros— written in a macro language called m4—are very powerful and can be thousands of lines long. Autoconf and Automake provide a few standard macros, useful for building projects. You will rarely have to write your own macros (especially since you can write pure shell code in configure.ac).

The purpose of the configure script is to check various system properties. Autoconf makes checking for these properties simple; the hard part tends to be figuring out which properties to check for. Autoconf and Automake offer a large number of macros, only a fraction of which will be useful to you. You should be able to start small, with only a few mandatory macros, and then expand as your project becomes more complex.

The first required macro is AC_INIT, which initializes Autoconf. You provide to it your project name, the version number, and the e-mail address where users are expected to send bug reports. m4 macros have a syntax very similar to C preprocessor macros, which in turn are similar to C function calls. The main difference is that *everything* in an m4 macro is a string, so quotation marks aren't needed. However, arguments should always be quoted with square brackets such that Autoconf knows to treat it as a single argument. This is especially true when using other macros as arguments, as they may return code that contains commas. Quoting with brackets ensures that Autoconf knows that what's inside the quotes is all a single argument:

```
AC_INIT([gaim], [1.2.1], [gaim-devel@lists.sourceforge.net])
```

Next you must initialize Automake. AC_INIT has itself defined a few new macros you can use given the information provided to it. AM_INIT_AUTOMAKE, the macro that initializes Automake, also needs the package name and version number, so you can call the following:

```
AM_INIT_AUTOMAKE([AC_PACKAGE_NAME], [AC_PACKAGE_VERSION])
```

Next, you can have configure locate the command to use for the compiler. This is done with the AC_PROG_CC macro:

```
AC_PROG_CC
```

Finally, have configure create your makefiles. Unlike Automake, which uses one Makefile.am for each directory, there's only one configure script and likewise only one configure.ac. This script must create the makefile in every directory; this is done with the AC_OUTPUT macro:

```
AC_OUTPUT([Makefile
          src/Makefile
          ])
```

This command creates makefiles in the top-level directory and in src/. This very basic configure.ac, shown in its entirety in Listing 3-1, is enough to build a simple project with no dependencies. However, when you start depending on libraries, you'll need to check each of them and determine how to compile against them.

Listing 3-1. *A Very Simple Makefile*

```
AC_INIT([gaim], [1.2.1], [gaim-devel@lists.sourceforge.net])
AM_INIT_AUTOMAKE([AC_PACKAGE_NAME],[AC_PACKAGE_VERSION])
AC_PROG_CC
AC_OUTPUT([Makefile
          src/Makefile
          ])
```

Historically, every library has had its own way of properly locating itself and determining the correct flags to use when compiling or linking. The most common way was for each library to install an executable file somewhere within the user's $PATH to provide the version, compiler flags, and linker flags, depending on the arguments given. If I wanted to check if GTK+ was at least version 1.2, I would call

```
gtk-config --version
```

Then if I wanted to find out what compiler flags to use, I'd call

```
gtk-config --cflags
```

Obviously, having a separate executable for each library installed on your machine was cumbersome and resulted in a lot of duplicated efforts. Fortunately, many libraries (especially those related to GNOME, such as GTK+, GLib, and other related libraries) have moved to a common solution called pkg-config.

pkg-config does the same thing as gtk-config, but rather than require each library to provide its own binary, it has each library provide a .pc file that contains the relevant information and provides an identical interface for dealing with each library. Most importantly for this discussion of Autoconf, it also provides an Autoconf macro, called PKG_CHECK_MODULES:

```
PKG_CHECK_MODULES([GTK],[gtk+-2.0],[has_gtk=yes],[AC_MSG_ERROR([
* GTK+-2.0 is required to build Gaim])])
```

This macro call is a bit more complicated than the others seen. The purpose of this call is to determine what flags need to be sent to the compiler. The macro will return these in two variables. The first argument specifies a prefix to use for these variables; in this example, GTK_CFLAGS and GTK_LIBS will be set.

The second argument is a list of dependencies required from pkg-config. Here, it requires just the existence of one package. It can also be a list of packages ([gtk+-2.0 glib-2.0]) or a list of packages with required version dependencies ([gtkspell-2.0 >= 2.0.2]).

The third and fourth arguments are code to run when the package is found or not found, respectively. In this example, if GTK+ is found, it sets a variable called has_gtk to yes. If GTK+ is not found, another macro is executed. This macro is called AC_MSG_ERROR, and it prints an error message and exits the configure script. After your call to PKG_CHECK_MODULES, you'll want to be sure the information in GTK_CFLAGS and GTK_LIBS is included in the makefile.

Remember I said that Makefile.in is just a makefile with a bunch of variables missing. These variables are inserted to the eventual Makefile with the AC_SUBST macro:

```
AC_SUBST([GTK_CFLAGS])
AC_SUBST([GTK_LIBS])
```

These variables were set by PKG_CHECK_MODULES, and by calling AC_SUBST, they will be included in the resulting makefiles. However, you still need a way to provide these compiler options to the compiler; having them defined in a makefile doesn't do anything, otherwise.

Earlier I mentioned that AM_CPPFLAGS and the LDADD primary were important in interacting with Autoconf. I mentioned that those variables will be given as command-line options to the compiler and to the linker. In Makefile.am, you can set these to variables that will eventually be provided by the configure script:

```
AM_CPPFLAGS = $(GTK_CFLAGS)
gaim_LDADD = $(GTK_LIBS)
```

Doing this will pass the proper compiler flags along to the compiler. You can include a variable like this for each library you depend on.

Other Required Files

Automake requires that you add some additional files to your source tree other than configure.ac and Makefile.am. These files aren't actually used for anything but are included in the tarball distribution as standard documentation. These files are NEWS, AUTHORS, ChangeLog, and README.

These files have standard usage, but Automake does nothing to enforce that usage. Further, not following the recommended use of each file won't break the build, but it may confuse people accustomed to the standard. Gaim does not follow the standard. It uses ChangeLog as NEWS is supposed to be used, for instance.

ChangeLog is intended to log every change. Any time anyone changes a bit of code, it is supposed to be logged in ChangeLog. Further, the format of ChangeLog is specified. It should contain the date the change was made, the developer who made the change, the files that were affected, and the changes made in the following format:

```
Sean Egan <seanegan@gmail.com>

* gtkblist.c  Fixed an off-by-one bug
```

However, because Gaim uses CVS for development, this sort of ChangeLog isn't really necessary (I'll discuss CVS later this chapter). Our ChangeLog serves the purpose that NEWS is supposed to: it provides a brief list of important, user-visible changes. Many of the changes in a new version of Gaim are never documented in NEWS or ChangeLog.

AUTHORS provides a list of the developers who worked on the project. This can be in any format you desire. README gives a brief description of what the project is and how to get started using it. Once you have created these four files, configure.ac, and a Makefile.am for every directory, you can bootstrap your build environment.

autogen.sh

Bootstrapping is the term for invoking the Autotools and creating a configure script and makefiles. The process is straightforward, but is usually delegated to a shell script to make the process even easier.

Create a file called autogen.sh in your top-level directory in an editor. Then add the following commands to it:

```
aclocal || exit;
autoconf || exit;
automake --add-missing --copy || exit;
./configure $@
```

Save the file and give it write permissions (chmod +x autogen.sh). The || exit on each line tells the shell to exit the script if the command preceding it fails. If autoconf fails for some reason, autogen.sh will not attempt to run automake. The $@ following ./configure is a variable representing all the arguments provided to autogen.sh. This allows you to provide your configure command-line options to autogen.sh.

You know what autoconf, automake, and configure do, but you've not yet seen aclocal. Remember that Autoconf and Automake provide a ton of useful m4 macros for use in Autoconf? The aclocal command copies those macros into the project. This way, you can distribute your program to other people without them needing the same macros you have. The --add-missing and --copy arguments to automake are for similar reasons; they add automatically generated, required files to the project.

Using the Build Environment

Once you have your build environment set up, you should be able to run autogen.sh, which will bootstrap the environment, creating a configure file. When that's done it will execute configure. You should see configure performing its standard tests, which will probably look familiar to you if you've ever compiled an application before. Then, when configure is finished, you will have a Makefile in your current directory. Run

```
make
```

and the application will build. Then run

```
make install
```

as root to install it. You've created a working build environment and you now understand what makes it work and how to extend it as your project grows. Using Autotools makes your application very accessible to everyone. Autotools does the hard work of figuring out how to compile an application on a given machine.

Unfortunately, nobody will want to run your application if it's buggy. When bugs occur in your application, you will find the GNU Debugger, GDB, extremely useful in locating them.

GDB

The most notorious bug on UNIX systems is the *segmentation fault*, or *segfault*. A segfault occurs when your program attempts to access memory not allocated to it. The operating system terminates the application. Windows users know the same error as a general protection fault. Because C is very permissive in what it will allow you to do and because it makes heavy use of pointers, the segfault is one of the most common types of errors in C programming.

Fortunately, GDB makes it easy to track down segfaults. GDB has many other features as well, but I very rarely use it for anything other than tracking down segfaults. If you're interested in learning what else GDB can do, visit http://www.gnu.org/software/gdb/gdb.html.

First, before you can even start using GDB, make sure your application was compiled with debugging support. Recall that this is done by setting -g to the linker. If you're using Autotools to create your build environment, set -g in AM_CPPFLAGS. This will provide the appropriate debugging hooks within the resulting executables.

Running Your Application Within GDB

There are two ways of capturing information about a crash in GDB. The first way is to run the application within GDB. When the operating system attempts to kill the segfaulting application, GDB will notice and provide an interface to debug it. To run an application within GDB, say Gaim for example, run

```
gdb gaim
```

GDB will launch and display a copyright notice and a prompt:

```
GNU gdb 6.3-debian
Copyright 2004 Free Software Foundation, Inc.
GDB is free software, covered by the GNU General Public License, and you are
```

welcome to change it and/or distribute copies of it under certain conditions.
Type "show copying" to see the conditions.
There is absolutely no warrenty for GDB. Type "show warranty" for details.
This GDB was configured as "i386-linux"...Using host libthread_db library
"/lib/tls/i686/cmov/libthread_db.so.1 ".

(gdb)

(gdb) is the GDB prompt. To run Gaim, type run at the prompt. Running Gaim in GDB
is useful for reproducible errors; you can launch it and quickly do exactly what is required to
make it crash. When it does crash, you will be returned to the (gdb) prompt.

Analyzing Core Dumps with GDB

For non-reproducible errors, though, it's inconvenient to have the debugger constantly running.
When the application is killed it will leave a *core dump* behind. A core dump provides essentially a
snapshot of the process's memory when it crashed. Because these files are potentially very
large, many UNIX distributions disable them by default. However, if your application is crashing
sporadically with no obvious cause, it may be worthwhile to enable core dumps. You can do
this with the ulimit command:

```
ulimit -c unlimited
```

When you enable core dumps and your application crashes, it will leave behind a core
dump in the directory from which the application was launched. The name of the core dump
varies from system to system, but is almost always a combination of the word "core," the name
of the application that produced it, and the process identifier (PID) of the particular process
that caused it. When you have a core dump, you can load it into GDB by associating it with a
given application on the command line:

```
gdb gaim core.13905
```

This tells GDB to load the provided core dump that was produced by the Gaim command.
GDB will show the same copyright notice shown in the previous section and bring you to a
(gdb) prompt. Whether you've run Gaim and had it crash or you've loaded the core dump of an
already crashed Gaim, you now have access to the same debugging features.

Debugging Segfaults

The most useful of the debugging features is the backtrace. A backtrace shows the function that
Gaim crashed in, and a list of all the function calls that led to that function, starting at main().
For example, if main() calls functionA() and functionA() calls functionB(), the backtrace will
show this. You can get a backtrace from the (gdb) prompt with the bt command. In the next
chapter, I will introduce you to Gaim development with a simple example plug-in. For demon-
stration here, I've intentionally introduced a bug to it. Watch how I isolate the bug with GDB.
First, I ask for the backtrace:

```
(gdb) bt
#0  0x40559a4e in g_strdup () from /usr/lib/libglib-2.0.so.0
#1  0x4030f0b1 in gtk_window_set_title () from /usr/lib/libgtk-x11-2.0.so.0
```

```
#2  0x401b0fc1 in gtk_dialog_new () from /usr/lib/libgtk-x11-2.0.so.0
#3  0x401b1053 in gtk_dialog_new_with_buttons () from /usr/lib/libgtk-x11-2.0.so.0
#4  0x080dd199 in gaim_gtk_notify_message (type=GAIM_NOTIFY_MSG_INFO,
     title=0x1 <Address 0x1 out of bounds>, primary=0x0, secondary=0x40d3c900 "Ive
     written a plugin", cb=0, user_data=0x0) at gtknotify.c:113
#5  0x0807f3b2 in gaim_notify_message (handle=0x0, type=GAIM_NOTIFY_MSG_INFO,
     title=0x1 <Address 0x1 out of bounds>,
     primary=0x40d3c915 "Hello World!", secondary=0x0, cb=0, user_data=0x0)
     at notify.c:55
#6  0x40d3c842 in plugin_load (plugin=0x81d9418) at helloworld.c:9
#7  0x0807fed6 in gaim_plugin_load (plugin=0x81d9418) at plugin.c:340
#8  0x080e583e in plugin_load (cell=0x85f4928, pth=0x0, data=0x85f4268) at
     gtkprefs.c:1960
```

I've shown only the first eight lines of the backtrace here. The actual backtrace is 34 lines long, going all the way back to main(). Here we see that the segfault occurred in g_strdup(). g_strdup() was called by gtk_window_set_title(), which was called by gtk_dialog_new() and so on.

■Tip Sometimes it's possible to corrupt memory at one point in your code but not cause a crash until much later, typically in code entirely unrelated to the bug. This makes debugging far more difficult. Because of this, on Linux systems, you can specifically tune memory allocation functions to detect errors sooner with environment variables. Set MALLOC_CHECK_ to 2, and your program will segfault as soon as a memory error is detected. Running this way normally is not recommended, however, as it is considerably slower.

Although it's not unheard of for GTK+ itself to have a bug, it's usually quite stable. Most of the time when you see GTK+ calls (or calls to other libraries) at the top of your backtrace, it's the result of providing the library with bad data further down. Garbage in, garbage out, as they say. Here, line 4 looks particularly suspicious the way it reads title=0x1 <Address 0x1 out of bounds>. Also, I recognize it as a function within Gaim, which is generally less stable than GTK+. I decide to look at line 4 more carefully with the frame command:

```
(gdb) frame 4
#4 0x080dd199 in gaim_gtk_notify_message (type=GAIM_NOTIFY_MESSAGE_WARNING,
    title=0x1 <Address 0x1 out of bounds>, primary=0x0, secondary=0x40d3c900 "I've
    written a plugin", cb=0, user_data=0x0) at gtknotify.c:113
113    dialog = gtk_dialog_new_with_buttons(title ? title : GAIM_ALERT_TITLE,
```

The frame command shows the function that was called, gaim_gtk_notify_message(), and the arguments provided to it. It shows the exact relevant line in the source and even prints it to the screen. You can see here that the variable that came in (title=0x1) was passed on directly to gtk_dialog_new_with_buttons(). Again, Garbage In, Garbage Out. Because the 0x1 argument was passed into this function, I check the function that called it:

```
(gdb) frame 5
#5  0x0807f3b2 in gaim_notify_message (handle=0x0, type=GAIM_NOTIFY_MSG_INFO,
    title=0x1 <Address 0x1 out of bounds>,
    primary=0x40d3c915 "Hello World!", secondary=0x0, cb=0, user_data=0x0)
    at notify.c:55
55          info->ui_handle = ops->notify_message(type, title, primary,
```

Again, the bogus variable was fed as input to this function. In some instances, you may be able to design your functions to be more tolerant to invalid inputs. For example, it's very common to check for NULL, which is never a valid memory address. However, any variable may be invalid sometimes, and valid other times. It changes on a process-to-process basis, depending on what memory is allocated by the operating system. Because gaim_notify_message() is also given the invalid variable, I try on layer higher:

```
(gdb) frame 6
#6  0x40d3c842 in plugin_load (plugin=0x81d9418) at helloworld.c:9
9               gaim_notify_info(NULL, title, "Hello World!", "I've written a plugin");
```

The 0x1 variable seems to be sourced here. There is no title input, but it outputs a local variable called title. Plus, helloworld.c is my newly written plug-in that hasn't been tested yet. This seems like a likely place for the bug to be. I check out the value of the title variable with the print command.

```
(gdb) print title
$2 = 0x1 <Address 0x1 out of bounds>
```

print will print any variable that's valid in the current scope, that being the function specified by the frame command. Here it shows me that the value of title is indeed 0x1. I'll need to check the source code to see where that value comes from. I open up helloworld.c and navigate to around line 9. Reading the function, I see the following:

```
char *title = 1;
```

That's where the 0x1 has come from. I change the value of title to 0, which is a valid argument meaning "no title." I recompile the plug-in, and it loads without error.

One of the most cited advantages of the open source development process is that it allows an extraordinary number of people the ability to locate and fix bugs using tools like GDB. However, the task of getting such a large number of people to easily work simultaneously on the same code is not trivial. Fortunately, there are systems in place that attempt to make the task as painless as possible. The system Gaim uses is called CVS.

CVS

The Internet enables open source development to succeed perhaps more than any other tool. Whereas before the Internet, developers who wanted to work on the same code would need to be at the same computer, the Internet allows developers from all over the world to discover and contribute to any project run by any stranger anywhere. Over 200 people have contributed to Gaim this way. CVS is the system that enables hundreds of developers access to the same source code and manages multiple people working on it simultaneously over the Internet.

Versioning

However, the primary goal of CVS is versioning. Think of versioning as a superpowerful "undo" feature. Anytime you make a change to the code, that change gets recorded in CVS as a new revision, and CVS allows easy ways to revert the code to its state at any time prior.

Imagine you start noticing a new bug in your program, and you can't track it down with GDB alone. However, you know it's just sprung up in the past three days. You can tell CVS to isolate for you all the changes made in the past three days. When you read just those changes, you easily find the bug, fix it, and commit it back to CVS so that others can use it.

Versioning also includes *tags*, which let you mark particular moments in the code with some label. For example, every time Gaim makes a release, after we've all made final changes to the code in CVS, we tag it with the version number of the release. This way, we have a very easy way of telling CVS to give us the exact state of the code included in the 0.60 release, for instance. A related feature to tags is *branches*.

Branches

Sometimes you need to branch off of your development sources and create a separate parallel branch of your development tree. For instance, as I write this, Gaim development is happening in two branches simultaneously. One branch is used for stable, bug-fix releases, while active development on what will become Gaim 2.0.0 is happening in the main branch, called HEAD. This is the most common use of branches; you can create stable releases off of a stable branch, while doing major development on HEAD. Branches can also be used to test experimental code without affecting the rest of the code at large.

CVS is a very useful tool for allowing collaborative development. In the next few sections, I will discuss how you, as a developer, will use CVS to access a single source repository with fellow developers.

Using CVS

When you need to work on a project in CVS, you check it out of the central repository. You then have a local copy of the source on your machine. When you're satisfied with your changes, you commit them back to the central repository. Each developer maintains his own source trees, and CVS intelligently merges them together when needed. In this section, I'll walk through the typical usage for most developers using CVS, explaining how to use its commands and what they're good for.

Logging In

The first thing to do is tell CVS what server to use and where on the server your repository is located. You can do this by setting the CVSROOT environment variable, or by setting it on the command line. I prefer the second option and specify the CVSROOT on the command line.

Many projects, including Gaim, have anonymous CVS. The Gaim developers strongly discourage using builds from CVS in favor of the most recent release. However, people who wish to start contributing to development prefer to retrieve the source from CVS to make sure they're not duplicating effort or working on old code. To facilitate this, many projects will allow everyone to read from their CVS repository, but not write to it. If you're using anonymous CVS, you will be provided a specific CVSROOT username and password, which may be different from what the developers use. You should consult whoever maintains your CVS server about how to access it. To log in to Gaim's anonymous CVS, run

```
cvs -d':pserver:anonymous@cvs.sourceforge.net:/cvsroot/gaim' login
```

It will ask you your password. SourceForge.net's anonymous CVS does not have a password; just hit Enter. Once you're logged in, you can download the latest source code from the central CVS repository.

Checking Out

In your CVS repository, you can maintain several modules. These modules are normally entirely unrelated to each other; and so they're kept separate so that developers working on one module are not affected by developers working on another module. Gaim's CVS repository hosts two modules: gaim, where the Gaim source code is stored, and web, where the code for our website is stored.

You must again specify the correct CVSROOT either in the environment variable or the command line. Then, rather than login, the command is checkout <modulename>. To check out Gaim from anonymous CVS, run

```
cvs -d':pserver:anonymous@cvs.sourceforge.net:/cvsroot/gaim' checkout gaim
```

Common commands have abbreviations, so instead of checkout, I could use co:

```
cvs -d':pserver:anonymous@cvs.sourceforge.net:/cvsroot/gaim' co gaim
```

This will create a directory in your current folder with the name of the module, in this case gaim. This directory will store all the files in the repository and files used internally by CVS. Because it stores its own information, CVS will no longer require you to specify a CVSROOT when working within this directory; it saves that information itself.

After CVS creates the directory, it will begin to populate it with the files in the repository. You will see them listed, one at a time, each prepended with U. This U is used to describe what is happening to the file, and is mostly useful while updating your local tree.

Updating

Gaim has consistently been the most actively developed open source project out of nearly 100,000. With development that active, you can imagine that it won't take long for your freshly checked-out tree to become out-of-date. Fortunately, CVS can update your tree to be up-to-date with the current tree. This has two significant advantages.

Advantages of Updating

First, CVS will send you only the parts of the file that have changed. Gaim's source distributions are about 8 megabytes; the entire source tree is larger. It would be a waste to receive all 8MB. By sending only what's changed, you save time and bandwidth.

The second advantage is made possible by the first. Because CVS can keep track of the changes you've made to your local tree and is provided the changes that have been made since your last update, CVS can intelligently merge your changes along with the changes of other developers. Suppose I need to work on gtkaccount.c for a while; I would update it from CVS and make my changes. While I was working on my changes, another developer committed a few bug fixes to that file.

For instance, assume I'm working on some changes to the `gaim_conv_write()` function in `gtkconv.c`. This is a complicated change, and it takes a few days to complete. In the meantime, another developer makes a one-line bug fix to another function in `gtkconv.c`. The version of the source code I'm working on predates the fix.

Without CVS, I would have to examine the file, see the changes he made, and manually incorporate them into my tree before uploading the file. CVS can figure out when two changes are made to different parts of the file and automatically merge them in your local tree. It will warn you if there are any errors in merging, and when you're happy that there are none, you can commit your changes.

How to Update

To update your local tree to the current repository, run

```
cvs update -d
```

or, shorter,

```
cvs up -d
```

The `-d` option tells CVS to create new files in the local tree if they've been added to the repository. It's usually unnecessary, but without it you often won't discover new files have been added until make fails. Sometimes you want to completely revert to current CVS, and remove all your local changes. I usually do this when I realize I've taken the completely wrong approach to something and I want to start over. A few commands used together will result in you entirely restoring your local tree. Fortunately, these commands are very easy to remember:

```
cvs up -dCRAP
```

Updating to Past Revisions

Lastly, I've explained that CVS's primary purpose is to provide versioning. CVS makes it easy to restore your source code from some time in the past. If you're interested only in one file and you know its revision history, you can request a version of it by its revision:

```
cvs up -r 1.175 gtkaccount.c
```

This reverts `gtkaccount.c` to revision 1.175. I most typically look at revision information from a Web application called ViewCVS. I'll discuss it briefly later. More useful than updating to a specific revision is updating to a specific tag. Revision numbers and tags are treated the same way, so to update my entire tree to when it was tagged v1_1_1, I'd run

```
cvs up -r v1_1_1
```

Branches are considered just special types of tags, so if you need to sync your tree with a different branch, use the branch name as a tag name. It's also sometimes useful to revert your tree to its state at some arbitrary moment in the past. This uses the `-D` argument, which is very flexible in how it lets you specify dates. All the following are legal CVS commands:

```
cvs up -D "April 5, 2003 12:00:00"
cvs up -D "yesterday at midnight"
cvs up -D "5 weeks ago"
cvs up -D "last week"
cvs up -D "a fortnight ago"
```

You can essentially describe in plain English to CVS when you want a tree from, and it will comply.

Output from cvs update

After you issue your command to update CVS, you'll see a list of the files it's updating. Like the output from checkout, each file will be prepended by a single letter representing its status. Table 3-8 shows what these characters mean:

Table 3-8. *Output from* cvs update

Character	Meaning
U	The file was brought up-to-date with no problems. This is what you see when checking out.
P	This is effectively the same as U, but where U indicates the entire new version of a file has been transferred, P indicates that only a patch containing the relevant changes was transferred.
A	This file isn't in CVS yet, but you've told CVS to add it. It will be added the next time you commit changes.
R	This file is in CVS, but you've told CVS to remove it. Again, it will be removed from CVS next time you commit. A and R serve as reminders to commit.
M	You've made modifications to this file since your last update. CVS was able to merge your changes with any made in CVS.
C	You've made modifications to this file, but CVS was unable to reconcile your changes with changes made by other developers in CVS. (See the "Dealing with Conflicts" section that follows this table.)
?	This file is in your local tree, but CVS knows nothing about it. The file .cvsignore contains all the files whose presence CVS should ignore in a directory. This keeps the number of files marked with ? to a minimum.

Dealing with Conflicts

If you see a C in your output, it means there was a conflict in merging your changes with others. It doesn't happen often; it typically happens only when two people make changes to the same exact lines of code. You will not be able to commit your code to CVS until you resolve the conflict. CVS makes this easy.

CVS will mark up your code to show exactly where the conflict occurred. Lines will be added at a location that shows what code exists at the location in current CVS, and what you think should be there. In the example here, another developer and I decided to debug the same bit of code, but went about it slightly differently:

```
<<<<<<< gtkaccount.c
    gaim_debug_warning("account", "This doesn't look right.");
=======
    gaim_debug_warning("account", "account_name is %s\n", account_name);
>>>>>>> 1.154
```

I will explain the Gaim API in the next chapter. After reading that, you will understand what gaim_debug_warning() means; for now, know that it's a function call. This line caused a conflict because while we both added a call to gaim_debug_warning() since my last CVS update, we used a different message. My code is listed first, between the <<<<<<< and the =======. The code currently in CVS is listed second. CVS can't figure out which line is correct. I figure that the second code is more useful for debugging, I delete everything but that code, and can safely commit.

If you have made changes to your checked-out code and then updated to make sure your changes are against the most up-to-date version of the code, and you want to release your changes back to the public, you have two ways of doing it. If you have commit access to CVS, you can commit the changes yourself. If you do not, you will have to create a patch and send it to someone with commit access for consideration.

Patches

Patches are descriptions of what text has changed in a file. They are the primary way that contributors to Gaim provide their changes upstream to the core Gaim developers. Patches are plain text files that are easy for humans to read and are easily created and processed with the diff and patch tools, respectively.

Anatomy of a Patch

Gaim developers (and most other developers) prefer their patches to be in unified diff format. This format is very straightforward to read. When CVS creates a patch, it shows the files affected, what revision of the file the patch was made from and when it was made, the line numbers where the changes occur, and the changes themselves. Listing 3-2 is part of a patch submitted by Don Seiler.

Listing 3-2. *One "Hunk" of a Patch*

```
Index: src/accountopt.h
===================================================================
RCS file: /cvsroot/gaim/gaim/src/accountopt.h,v
retrieving revision 1.9
diff -u -p -r1.9 accountopt.h
--- src/accountopt.h    6 Mar 2005 06:14:26 -0000    1.9
+++ src/accountopt.h    14 Mar 2005 22:22:41 -0000
@@ -133,8 +133,8 @@ GaimAccountOption *gaim_account_option_s
 * The list passed will be owned by the account option, and the
 * strings inside will be freed automatically.
 *
- * The list is in key, value pairs. The key is the ID stored and used
- * internally, and the value is the label displayed.
+ * The list is a list of GaimKeyValuePair items. The key is the ID stored and
```

```
+ * used internally, and the value is the label displayed.
  *
  * @param text      The text of the option.
  * @param pref_name The account preference name for the option.
```

Each change in a patch file is called a *hunk*. There can be several hunks from the same file. The first line of Listing 3-2 shows the file affected. Underneath the line of equals signs can be any arbitrary text at all. If you wanted, you could edit text located here to provide a description of what your changes do. CVS automatically includes some useful information, such as when the patch was made, and off of what revision of the file.

This line is the beginning of the first hunk, as signified by the double @ sign:

```
@@ -133,8 +133,8 @@ GaimAccountOption *gaim_account_option_s
```

In this example, 133,8 describes the location of the original code; 133 is the line number where the original code started, and 8 is the number of lines in the original code. The second set of numbers is the same thing, but for the new code.

■Note Gaim developer (and this book's technical reviewer) Nathan Walp is also called a "hunk."

In this example, the two sets of numbers are equal; two lines were deleted, and two lines added. However, if I add 10 lines of code in my patch, where formerly there were only two, the two lengths would be different. Similarly, if previous hunks changed the number of lines before this, the two line numbers would be different.

The text after the second @@ can be anything; here it lists the function this hunk is within to make it easier to locate the appropriate text in an editor. This is an option provided by a command-line option to diff.

After the hunk header, the patch shows the changes made. It will show a few lines on either side of the actual change as a courtesy, to provide context. Lines that are removed are prefixed with -, lines that are added are prefixed with +. When lines are merely changes, as they are here, they're represented as lines being removed, followed by lines being added.

Following this would be a second hunk for that file, if it were changed in more than one place, or another Index: line marking the beginning of changes to a new file. If this were the only change made, Listing 3-2 would be the entire contents of the file.

Creating a Patch

Creating a patch from CVS is easy. Make the changes to your local tree, make sure it's synced to current CVS with cvs up, and run

```
cvs diff -pu
```

This uses two command-line options: -u requests a unified patch in unified format (exemplified in Listing 3-2), and -p asks diff to include the function name in the hunk header, as seen in the example.

This command will print the patch to your console. In order to send this to a developer, you'll likely want to save it to a file. This can be done with the UNIX shell's redirection functionality:

```
cvs diff -pu > gaim_account_option_list_ui.diff
```

A good filename for a patch includes the project the patch is for, a brief summary of what it changes, and a .diff extension.

You can also create a patch between any two tags or dates in the repository's history using the same context as updating to some other point in the repository's history. The main difference is that you can specify only one tag or date to see changes between that point and your local tree, or two tags or dates to see the changes between any other two points. For instance, to generate a patch of all the changes between Gaim v1.0.0 and Gaim v1.0.1, run the following:

```
cvs diff -pu -r v1_0_0 -r v1_0_1 > gaim-1.0.1-incremental_patch.diff
```

Patches like this are often useful for people who download releases, so that they needn't download a new 8MB tarball, and can instead download only new changes.

Applying a Patch

If you are a core developer with commit access to CVS, you'll probably be responsible for reviewing, applying, and committing patches that other people submit. Reviewing can be done by reading the patch file itself. The unified diff format makes it easy to see exactly what changes. Applying is also easily done with the patch utility.

patch takes a patch file from standard input, so it is usually fed via the same redirection method used to redirect the output from cvs diff to a file. patch also requires that you tell it where the files being patched are located relative to the current location. This is done with the -p option. However, CVS patches are almost always both generated and applied from the top-level directory of the project, so you don't have to understand exactly what -p is used for. You can always use -p0:

```
patch -p0 < gaim_account_option_list_ui.diff
```

This will affect the changes from gaim_account_option_list_ui.diff to your local tree. patch is very intelligent; it will be able to figure out what to change even if your local tree has changed considerably since the patch author submitted the patch. However, if your tree has changed too much, patch may skip a chunk and save the rejected hunk to a .rej file it will output on the console.

■**Tip** If you aren't sure if a patch will apply cleanly, try using the --dry-run command-line option (patch --dry-run -p0 < gaim_account_option_list_ui.diff). This will make sure each hunk applies before modifying any file.

After you commit the patch to your local tree, or after you have made your own changes and you want to share the changes with everyone else, you need to commit your changes to the CVS repository.

Committing

When you commit changes to your CVS repository, you make them publicly available as part of the official source code. From CVS, the code will be in subsequent releases, and other developers can work with it. Committing code to CVS is simple:

```
cvs commit
```

or the abbreviated form:

```
cvs ci
```

CVS will determine all the changes that need to be made, and open an editor asking you to enter a log message. CVS has its own changelog; when someone makes a commit, they write a log message about it. To be useful, this commit usually states what the patch does, who wrote it, and what potential problems it has.

Adding and Removing Files

You will need to add and remove files from the CVS repository at times. These tasks are done with the add and remove commands. To add a file to CVS, put it in your local tree and run

```
cvs add newfile.c
```

If you need to remove a file, delete it first, then run

```
cvs remove oldfile.c
```

Neither of these commands will actually take effect until you run cvs commit, providing you an opportunity to change your mind. Also, files that are removed from the repository retain all their versioning information. The file is simply moved from the main directory to the Attic, a location reserved for removed files.

Tagging and Branching

When you need to make a release, or whenever the code is at some point that you want to be able to access easily, you create a tag. Creating a tag is very straightforward. To tag for Gaim release version 1.2.1, I would call

```
cvs tag v1_2_1
```

You can also retroactively create tags at various other points in the past, using the already familiar -r and -D options:

```
cvs tag -D "November 18 at 11:18pm" OLDER_TAG
```

You can delete old tags; this is in case right after tagging for release you realize you forgot an important change. You can delete the tag, commit the change, and then retag with the same tag:

```
cvs tag -d v1_2_3
```

Branches, discussed briefly earlier, are conceptually nothing more than a special type of tag. A branch is sometimes called a *sticky* tag because when you update to a sticky tag, the tag remains with your local tree until you run cvs up with the -A argument (which is included in the cvs -dCRAP command discussed earlier). This means that when you make commits, they all affect the sticky tag.

To create a branch, call cvs tag with the -b argument:

```
cvs tag -b experimental_branch
```

This creates a new branch, called experimental_branch. When you do cvs up -dr experimental_branch, you get the code for that branch, and any code you commit goes to experimental_branch. There's no way to automatically merge changes between two branches. You must make changes to each branch individually.

Many of the commands I've demonstrated use revision numbers. It's possible to generate and view file history with the cvs command itself, but it's somewhat awkward and difficult to master. This job is made far easier with a Web application called ViewCVS.

ViewCVS

ViewCVS is a Web application installed by whomever administers your CVS server. Gaim uses ViewCVS as provided by SourceForge.net (discussed in the next section). ViewCVS provides a really simple way to view your project's versioning history. Gaim's ViewCVS is located at http://cvs.sourceforge.net/viewcvs.py/gaim/, shown in Figure 3-8.

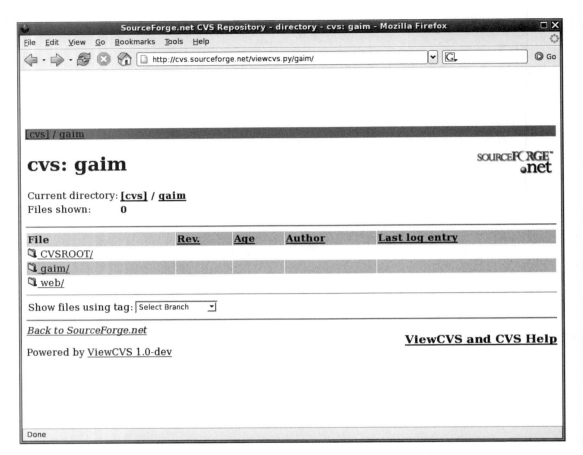

Figure 3-8. *The top-level view of Gaim's CVS repository shows the two modules contained within it.*

The top-level view in ViewCVS shows the two modules in Gaim's CVS repository. The `gaim` module is more interesting. Click its link to view the module, shown in Figure 3-9.

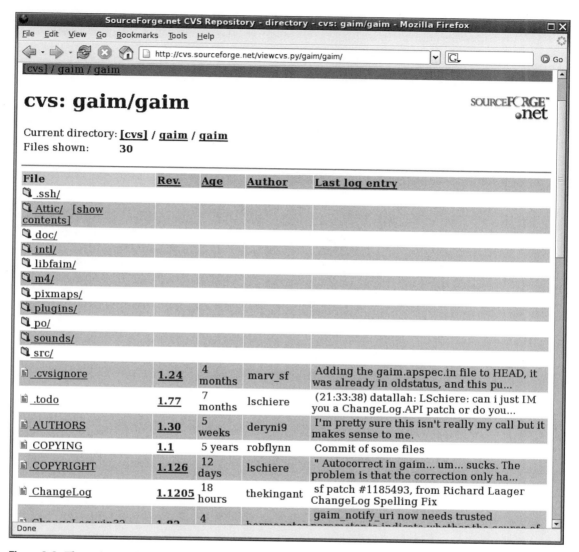

Figure 3-9. *The gaim module*

This view shows all the files and directories in this, the top-level directory of the module. Notice it also shows Attic, where old, removed files retain their versioning information.

Each file lists its current revision, how long ago that revision was made, who made it, and the changelog entry for it. Let's take a closer look at Makefile.am, a file I explained how to create earlier in this chapter. Clicking on the revision number shows the syntax-highlighted content of that revision, as seen in Figure 3-10. Clicking the filename will show the full history of the file, shown in Figure 3-11.

Figure 3-10. *The contents of a file in CVS*

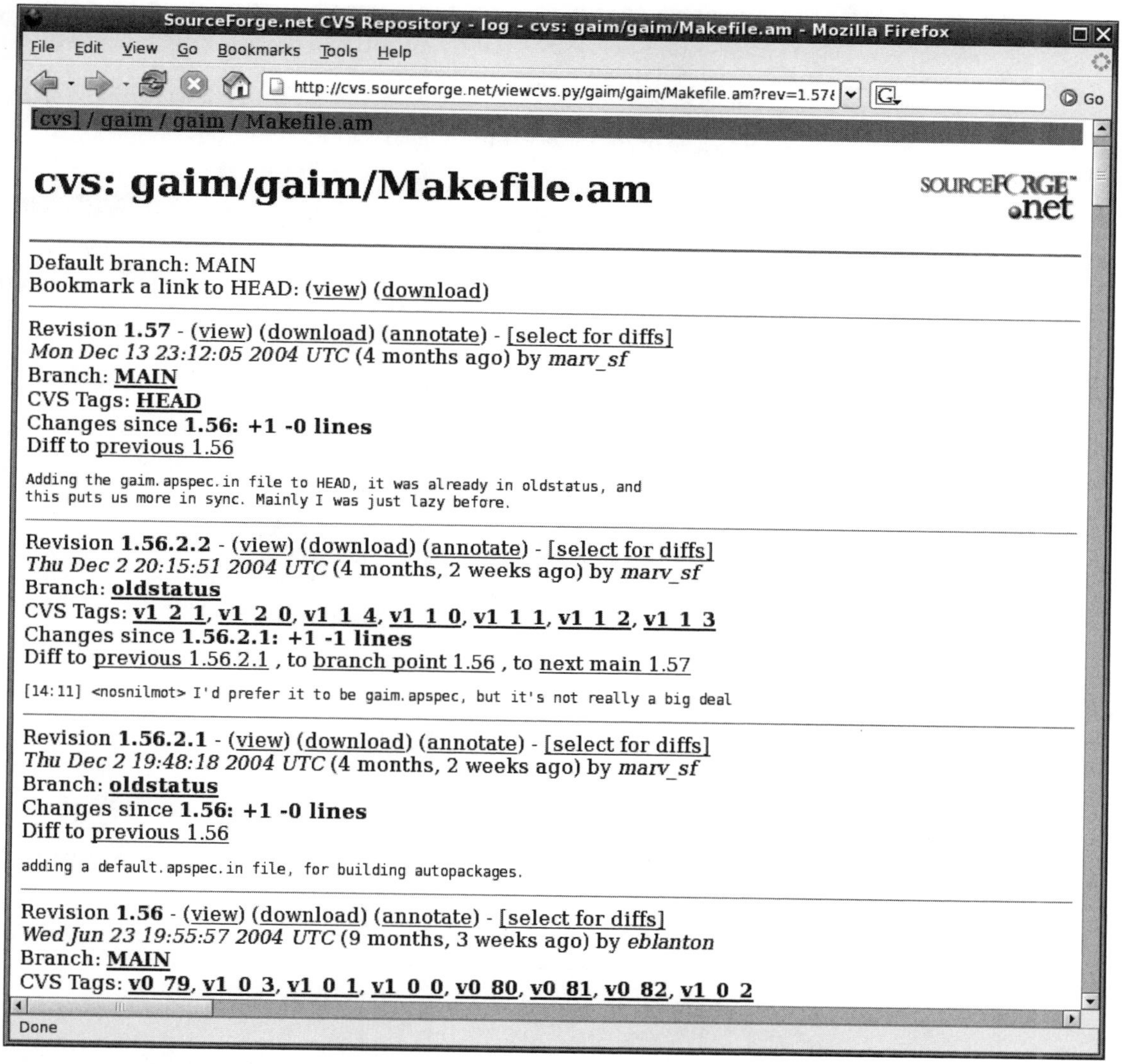

Figure 3-11. *The full history of* Makefile.am

In Figure 3-11, you see a list of each commit that affected Makefile.am. Each entry in the list contains the revision number, the date and time it was committed, who committed it, what branch the commit was to, what tags apply to it, and a link to show a patch to the previous revision. Patches in ViewCVS are slightly easier to read than they are in a typical text editor; they're color-coded to show you exactly what's been removed, added, and modified. The patch between revision 1.56 and 1.57 of Makefile.am is shown in Figure 3-12.

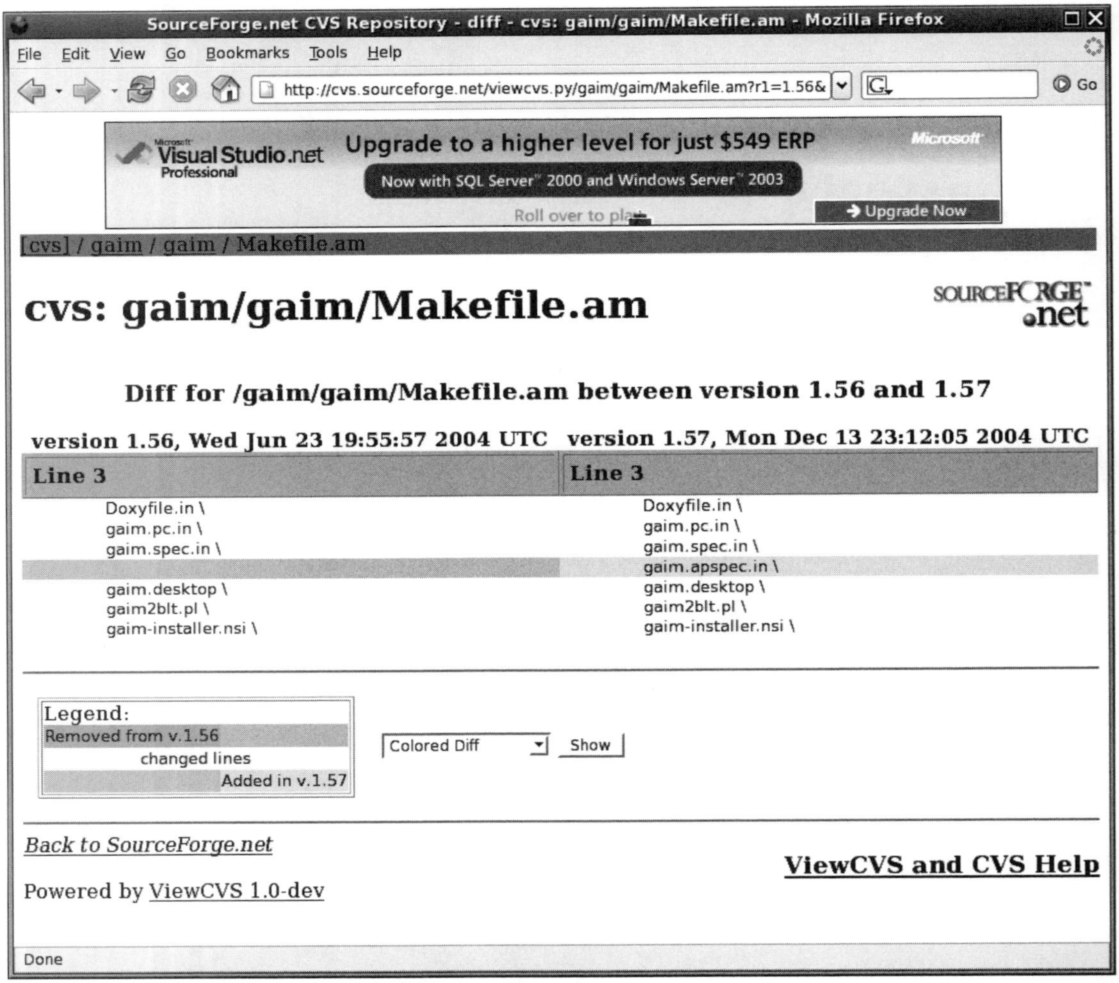

Figure 3-12. *A patch between revision 1.56 and 1.57 of* Makefile.am *as seen in ViewCVS*

ViewCVS provides a convenient interface to manage the versioning control of your project. In fact, many of the most useful tools used to manage your open source project are available on the Web. SourceForge.net is a free service that provides ViewCVS and a number of other useful means of managing your open source project.

SourceForge.net

Gaim is hosted by SourceForge.net, a site dedicated to providing open source projects with a number of free tools for managing those projects. The tools include CVS (including ViewCVS), which I've just discussed, mailing lists, project Web space, and a file-release system with a large number of mirrors around the world. The most notable unique feature to SourceForge.net is its tracker system.

■Note The concept of a tracker is not unique to SourceForge.net, but SourceForge's implementation of a tracker is. Perhaps the most popular open source tracker software is Bugzilla, from the Mozilla project, which you can read about at `http://www.bugzilla.org`.

A *tracker* is used to track issues, most prominently bug reports that lead to the alternate name "bug tracker," but anything can be considered an issue. Gaim has trackers for bugs, feature requests, submitted patches, third-party plug-ins, translations, and other items.

The best way of communicating to Gaim is to submit an item to one of our trackers. If you have found a bug, file a bug report to the bug tracker. If you wish to request a feature, file a request in our RFE (Request for Enhancement) tracker. Tracker items will remain open until they've been resolved, meaning it won't be forgotten as often happens to items submitted via e-mail or some other mechanism.

In this section, I will describe the process of working with the SourceForge.net trackers, from both the perspective of the user submitting an item, and of a developer resolving it.

Submitting a Tracker Item

A Gaim user will find a Bug Reports link in the menu along the right side of the Gaim Web page at `http://gaim.sourceforge.net`. This leads directly to the Submit New Issue page for the bug tracker, shown in Figure 3-13. Alternatively, a user can reach the page from the SourceForge.net project page (`http://sourceforge.net/projects/gaim`), which is also linked to from the Gaim Web page.

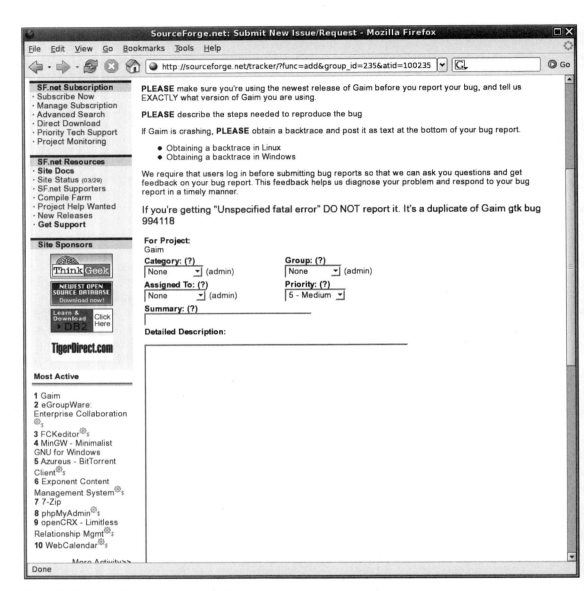

Figure 3-13. SourceForge.net's Submit New Issue page

The SourceForge.net project page, shown in Figure 3-14, has a menu along the top. This menu links to the various trackers and other services provided by SourceForge.net. Clicking Bugs brings you to the bug tracker, from which you can click Submit New, to get the same Submit New Issue page shown in Figure 3-13.

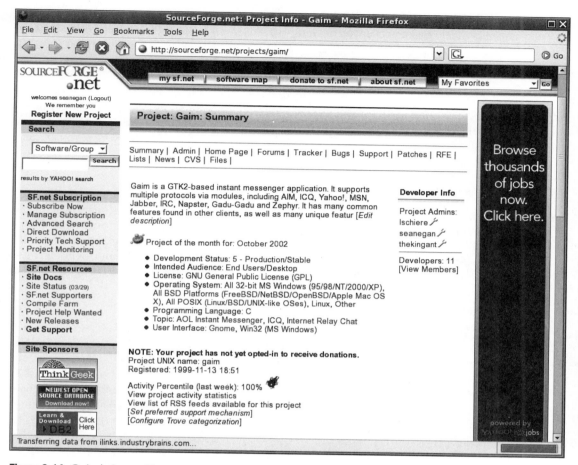

Figure 3-14. *Gaim's SourceForge.net project page*

The page shown in Figure 3-13 is specifically for the bug tracker; however, the same page is used for any tracker. Submitting a patch or a feature request uses this same interface.

The top of the page offers some instructions from the Gaim developers as to what we require from a useful bug report. As with most software projects, we need the version of the software the problem is experienced with, the process encountered to reproduce the bug, and (if the bug causes a segfault) a backtrace attained from GDB as shown earlier this chapter. Next are four drop-down boxes: Category, Group, Assigned To, and Priority.

Categorization

The four drop-down boxes allow us to more easily manage bug reports. Category describes what aspect of Gaim the bug affects. This drop-down breaks down Gaim into parts that traditionally are more bug-ridden than others. If the new bug affects one of those categories, the submitter can classify it. Otherwise, the submitter can leave it blank and let a Gaim developer set it.

Group is used to group bugs by version. This allows the Gaim developers easy access to all the bugs in any particular version of Gaim. This field must be set to the correct version because, unlike with Category, we cannot determine from context what version the submitter uses. The remaining two drop-down boxes should not be changed by the submitter.

Assigned To allows us to assign a tracker item to a particular developer, usually the one responsible for the code specified in Category. This is better done by a Gaim developer familiar with the project and each developer's specialties. Priority allows us to judge how important each bug is relative to others. A user submitting a new bug will typically be tempted to give his own bug a higher priority than appropriate. By letting a developer familiar with a large number of bugs handle priorities, they can be more accurate.

Description

Beneath the drop-down boxes are text boxes to type a brief summary and a longer description. The summary should be short but descriptive. When the developers read through a list of bugs, this is the main thing they will look at. "Gaim bug" is a poor summary; "Segfault when sending messages on ICQ" is better. The detailed description that follows should contain enough information for a developer to reproduce the bug, or at least as much information as possible about what causes the bug.

File Attachments

You may want to attach a file to your tracker item. For patches and plug-ins, the use of this is obvious; you need to attach your patch or plug-in. For feature requests, a mocked-up screenshot may be appropriate. For bugs in the GUI, a screenshot of the bug may be helpful.

The biggest mistake in attaching a file to a tracker item is failing to click the Check to Upload and Attach a File check box. A huge number of tracker items are submitted and nearly immediately the submitter updates the item to comment that he forgot to check that check box. To choose a file, click the Browse button or type the path in the provided text box. Then enter a description of the file and hit the Submit button to submit the new tracker item.

Receiving Updates

As the submitter of the item, you will be notified by e-mail when the tracker item is updated, be it assigned to a developer, resolved, or merely commented on. Often a tracker item cannot be resolved without more information. The Gaim developers will add a comment to the item requesting more information; you will receive an e-mail with a link to the tracker item. The page for updating tracker items, seen in Figure 3-15, allows you to change all the aspects you set when creating the item. The description, however, cannot be changed. Instead, you can view a list of comments left about the item, and leave your own comment.

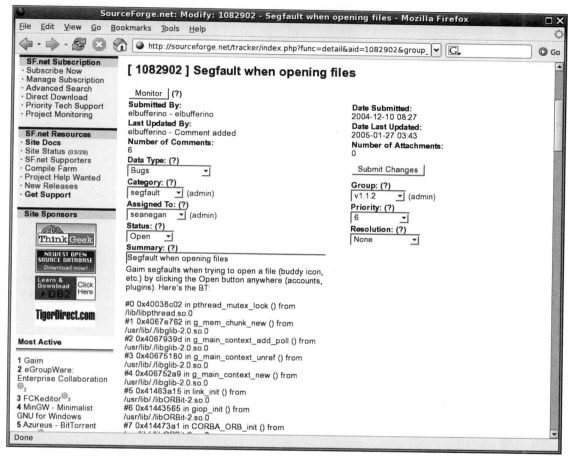

Figure 3-15. *The page SourceForge.net uses to update tracker items*

Managing Tracker Items

Managing individual tracker items is done from the page shown in Figure 3-15. One considerable difference between creating a new item and modifying an existing one is that modifying an item provides two additional drop-down boxes for Status and Resolution.

The status for all newly created tracker items is Open. Developers can than change it to Deleted, Pending, or Closed. Most commonly, an item will move from Open to Closed. Occasionally, one will change to Pending if the developer was unable to reproduce the error himself, but believes he's fixed it anyway. In this case, the submitter needs to confirm that the bug is actually fixed by changing the status from Pending to Closed. Deleted is rarely used—typically only when a bug report was filed by mistake.

When you close a bug, you provide a resolution for it. This depends on the type of tracker item. Patches are typically Accepted or ejected, bugs are typically Fixed, Duplicate (for issues that have already been reported), Won't Fix (for reports that don't describe actual bugs, but a difference in design opinion), or occasionally Works for Me (for bugs that are entirely irreproducible and, therefore, unfixable).

SourceForge.net offers a lot of other functionality to help you manage your project. The administration interface allows you to provide various levels of access to members of your project and to determine the membership of your project itself. If you are interested in learning more about how to use SourceForge.net's other features, read its documentation at `http://sourceforge.net/docman/?group_id=1`.

Summary

The growth of open source software has resulted in a large number of very high-quality, useful tools for managing software projects. This, in turn, has opened the door for more open source development. The GNU development tools and SourceForge.net provide everything a potential open source developer needs to get started.

With these tools in hand, in the next chapter you'll begin acquiring the knowledge you need to get involved in Gaim development. I will discuss some of the underlying principles behind Gaim development and some specifics to Gaim itself.

■ ■ ■

CHAPTER 4

Programming Gaim

In this chapter, I will introduce you to extending Gaim with plug-ins. Plug-ins are dynamically linked libraries with access to all the functions exposed by Gaim's application programming interface, or API. I will start by explaining the anatomy of a Gaim plug-in. Then I will present some useful programming techniques used extensively throughout Gaim. Finally, I will provide an overview of Gaim's API, highlighting important concepts, data structures, and functions.

Gaim plug-ins can be written in C, Perl, or Tcl. Because Gaim is written in C, its native API is also in C. Support for Perl and Tcl merely wrap the C API to provide the same interface with different semantics. In fact, Perl and Tcl are implemented as plug-ins themselves. Therefore, the plug-ins you will see throughout this book will be written in C. As other languages attempt to provide the same interface, the principles covered here will apply regardless of what language you choose.

Although Gaim is written in C—traditionally a procedural language—it uses mostly object-oriented techniques. Later in this chapter I will explain what makes a language "object oriented," and explain how the same techniques can be accomplished from a procedural language like C. First, however, let's examine the essential parts of a Gaim plug-in by building a simple Hello World plug-in. All you need is the build environment and the Gaim source tree you created in Chapter 1.

Compiling Your First Plug-In: `helloworld.c`

Let's start by compiling a simple example plug-in. Listing 4-1 is a simple plug-in that will display a dialog box at load. This plug-in is little more than a skeleton to demonstrate the bare minimum that every plug-in needs. I'll explain what each line does following the listing.

Listing 4-1. *The* `helloworld.c` *Program*

```
01 #include "internal.h"
02 #include "plugin.h"
03 #include "notify.h"
04
05 static gboolean
06 plugin_load(GaimPlugin *plugin)
```

```
07 {
08      gaim_notify_info(NULL, NULL, "Hello World!", "I've written a plugin");
09      return TRUE;
10 }
11
12 static GaimPluginInfo info =
13 {
14      GAIM_PLUGIN_MAGIC,
15      GAIM_MAJOR_VERSION,
16      GAIM_MINOR_VERSION,
17      NULL,
18      0,
19      NULL,
20      GAIM_PRIORITY_DEFAULT,
21      "helloworld",
22      "Hello World",
23      "1.0",
24      "Example plugin",
25      "Merely display a \"hello world\" dialog when loaded.",
26      "Sean Egan <seanegan@gmail.com>",
27      "http://apress.com",
28      plugin_load,
29      NULL,
30      NULL,
31      NULL,
32      NULL,
33      NULL
34 };
35
36 static void
37 init_plugin(GaimPlugin *plugin)
38 {
39 }
40
41 GAIM_INIT_PLUGIN(history, init_plugin, info)
```

Save this plug-in as `helloworld.c` in the plug-ins directory of your Gaim source tree and, if you're using Linux or UNIX, issue the following command:

```
make helloworld.so
```

If you're using Windows, use this command instead:

```
make helloworld.dll
```

This will create a Gaim plug-in with that name in the plug-ins directory of your Gaim source tree. To install this plug-in, drag the file from a graphical file manager into the plug-in selector in Gaim preferences, or copy it to the directory `$HOME/.gaim/plugins/`.

▐Note I will use $HOME throughout this book to refer to the home directory as used by Gaim. In Chapter 1, Windows users installed a Cygwin installation that included its own home directory. Because you compiled Gaim as a native Windows program, your Cygwin home directory is irrelevant and Gaim will use your Windows application data directory (most likely C:\Documents and Settings\Your Name\Application Data\). For users of UNIX-like operating systems, there is most likely no distinction.

You will see a new Hello World entry in your plug-in list. Click the check box to load it, and a dialog will pop up, as seen in Figure 4-1.

Figure 4-1. `helloworld.c` *creates this Hello World dialog box when loaded.*

Anatomy of a Gaim Plug-in

Often, you will find that code written in C tends to be written in a "backward" sort of way; the most important functions are at the bottom, and less useful utility functions are at the top. This is because C specifies that, unlike in other languages, functions and data structures can be used only after they are defined within the same file (or included with an #include statement, which is why such statements are always found at the top of files). Because this plug-in is no exception, I will explain how it works from the bottom up.

GAIM_INIT_PLUGIN

GAIM_INIT_PLUGIN, shown in Listing 4-2, is a preprocessor macro defined in gaim/src/plugin.h. A preprocessor macro is a statement handled by the C preprocessor, a program that alters the source code the compiler sees at compile time. For instance, #include is a preprocessor directive that includes the entire contents of another file at that point in the source code. The C compiler never sees #include statements, but rather all the function prototypes and data type declarations are included in-line.

The preprocessor is often used to allow certain features to be activated or deactivated at compile time. You can instruct the preprocessor to include only a bit of code if some certain flag is #defined. GAIM_INIT_PLUGIN is similar. It allows the user to compile plug-ins statically at compile time and is called from line 41 in the helloworld.c plug-in shown in Listing 4-1. The macro is presented in Listing 4-2, after which I'll explain more about how preprocessor statements work, and how GAIM_INIT_PLUGIN works in particular.

Listing 4-2. *GAIM_INIT_PLUGIN*

```
#if !defined(GAIM_PLUGINS) || defined(GAIM_STATIC_PRPL)
# define GAIM_INIT_PLUGIN(pluginname, initfunc, plugininfo) \
    gboolean gaim_init_##pluginname##_plugin(void) { \
        GaimPlugin *plugin = gaim_plugin_new(TRUE, NULL); \
        plugin->info = &(plugininfo); \
        initfunc((plugin)); \
        return gaim_plugin_register(plugin); \
    }
#else /* GAIM_PLUGINS  && !GAIM_STATIC_PRPL */
# define GAIM_INIT_PLUGIN(pluginname, initfunc, plugininfo) \
    G_MODULE_EXPORT gboolean gaim_init_plugin(GaimPlugin *plugin) { \
        plugin->info = &(plugininfo); \
        initfunc((plugin)); \
        return gaim_plugin_register(plugin); \
}
#endif
```

A C compiler acts on a C source file in several distinct steps. Before being compiled into machine code, C code is *lexically analyzed* (broken down into *tokens*, i.e., each parenthesis, quotation mark, variable name, or any other element is identified as such, and each bit of text is recognized as a keyword or a symbol name). After being lexically analyzed, it is parsed. The parser understands C syntax and, using the lexical tokens that the lexical analyzer provided to it, interprets the code according to the grammar of the C programming language. However, before either of these components is called upon, the C preprocessor (or CPP not to be confused with .cpp, the file extension most often used by C++ source files) preprocesses the code.

The C preprocessor identifies preprocessor directives in the source and header files, and executes them. In C, preprocessor directives are identified by the hash sign, #, being the first character of the line. You are probably already familiar with the most common CPP directive, #include, which I discussed earlier in this chapter. GAIM_INIT_PLUGIN is declared with the #define directive, which replaces any instances of the term being defined with its definition This is often used to declare constants, such as

```
#define PI 3.1415927
```

but can also be used to declare entire functions, as is the case with GAIM_INIT_PLUGIN. One thing that separates a CPP macro from a function, however, is that a macro may be #defined differently depending on certain compile-time options that the user provides.

When Gaim detects a plug-in, the first thing Gaim does is call the plug-ins gaim_init_plugin function, which it locates by its function name. However, Gaim provides the ability to have plug-ins compiled statically—that is, to include the plug-in's code in the Gaim binary itself rather than load it separately at runtime.

If more than one plug-in is compiled statically, however, each plug-in would contain its own gaim_init_plugin function, and the compiler would be unable to disambiguate between them. Because of this, the GAIM_INIT_PLUGIN macro causes the plug-in's gaim_init_plugin to be renamed according to the name of the plug-in if it is to be compiled statically. This way, each plug-in's gaim_init_plugin function can be discerned from the others.

The first line in the code presented in Listing 4-2 is an #if directive. #if directives are used to check certain parameters at compile time, and accordingly, alter the code to be compiled. For instance, if I wanted to print a message to the screen using the printf() function, to indicate whether the program was compiled for Windows, I would note that Windows recognizes _WIN32 as a true statement and write the following:

```
#if _WIN32
printf("You are using Windows");
#else
printf("You are not using Windows");
#endif
```

Likewise, GAIM_INIT_PLUGIN is defined within an #if directive that checks whether plug-ins are to be compiled statically. For each case it creates a function called either gaim_init_plugin or gaim_init_pluginname_plugin, where pluginname is the name of the plug-in. Note that the macro's line breaks are "escaped" with the backslash character.

C uses the backslash character to escape a character that otherwise would not be allowed in the context. For example, a literal string is text surrounded by quotation marks. If you wished to include a quotation mark within a literal string without ending the string, you would need to escape it with a quotation mark: "This is an example of escaping \"quotation\" marks." Similarly, because what's included within an #if directive is allowed to be only a single line, you must escape the line breaks so that the preprocessor can interpret them as a single line. The function created by GAIM_INIT_PLUGIN, which is called when Gaim discovers the plug-in, creates a new plug-in object, initializes some data provided to it by the plug-in, and registers the new plug-in to Gaim, which then presents the plug-in to the user to be loaded. You will understand more about objects after reading about object-oriented programming later this chapter.

GaimPluginInfo

GaimPluginInfo, shown in Listing 4-3, is a data structure that is instantiated in lines 12–33 of helloworld.c. It provides the Gaim core with all the information it needs to recognize and load a plug-in. When Gaim loads, it will call ask the plug-in for this data structure, get its name, version, and other data. The plug-in will then be added to the list of available plug-ins. When the plug-in is loaded, Gaim will call a function provided by GaimPluginInfo to make the plug-in start running. The GaimPluginInfo structure is declared in plugin.h.

Listing 4-3. *GaimPluginInfo*

```
struct _GaimPluginInfo
{
    unsigned int magic;
    unsigned int major_version;
    unsigned int minor_version;
    GaimPluginType type;
    char *ui_requirement;
    unsigned long flags;
    GList *dependencies;
    GaimPluginPriority priority;
```

```
    char *id;
    char *name;
    char *version;
    char *summary;
    char *description;
    char *author;
    char *homepage;

    gboolean (*load)(GaimPlugin *plugin);
    gboolean (*unload)(GaimPlugin *plugin);
    void (*destroy)(GaimPlugin *plugin);

    void *ui_info;
    void *extra_info;
    GaimPluginUiInfo *prefs_info;
    GList *(*actions)(GaimPlugin *plugin, gpointer context);
};
```

The first seven elements of GaimPluginInfo are used to identify important properties of the plug-in, needed by Gaim's plug-in handler. I'll introduce each element, reproducing the appropriate line for clarity. The first three elements are as follows:

```
unsigned int magic;
unsigned int major_version;
unsigned int minor_version;
```

It's important that Gaim attempt to load only valid plug-ins it knows will work properly. If a plug-in was built against a version of Gaim too old or too recent to work with the version of Gaim that's running, it might crash if it attempted to run. magic, major_version, and minor_version tell Gaim what version the plug-in was built against, and Gaim then decides whether the plug-in can be safely loaded.

Prior to 1.0.0, the versioning in GaimPluginInfo was limited to a single API Version field. If a new version of Gaim attempts to load one of these older plug-ins, it needs a way of detecting that it's invalid. Because old plug-ins use this API version as their first field, Gaim can demand that valid plug-ins use as their first field a value not used in old plug-ins. magic, therefore, is set greater than the last used API version, so that old plug-ins will be detected properly and rejected if they lack the proper magic number in their first field.

Since version 1.0.0, Gaim has a "major.minor.micro" versioning system. This system describes what plug-ins will work with Gaim. The "major" version number, the first digit, is incremented when plug-ins built against older versions of Gaim are no longer guaranteed to work. This happens if, say, a function or data type is removed from the API. The major version number would be incremented from 1 to 2. If Gaim sees that the plug-in's major_version is not equal to Gaim's major version, it won't load the plug-in.

The minor version number—the second digit—is incremented if it adds functions or data types to the API such that plug-ins built against this version of Gaim cannot be guaranteed to work on older versions of Gaim. If Gaim sees that the major version numbers are the same, it will check if minor_version is greater than its own minor version. If so, it won't load the plug-in.

The micro version number is incremented if the API has not changed at all. Because that doesn't affect whether a plug-in can be loaded at all, it's not included in `GaimPluginInfo`.

All three of these fields should always be set to the #defined constants `GAIM_PLUGIN_MAGIC`, `GAIM_MAJOR_VERSION`, and `GAIM_MINOR_VERSION`, which will let the compilation process fill in the correct values automatically.

`GaimPluginType type;`

`type` is what this plug-in does. Currently supported types are *protocol plug-ins*, which implement IM protocols; *loader plug-ins*, which load scripts written in scripting languages; and *standard plug-ins*, which do anything else. Most of the plug-ins in this book, including this one, will be of type `GAIM_PLUGIN_STANDARD`.

`char *ui_requirement;`

Gaim is designed to allow alternate user interfaces, a concept called *core/ui split*, which I'll discuss later this chapter. Therefore, a plug-in may be designed to work only with one specific user interface. If this is the case, one would include the name of that user interface in `ui_requirement`. Most of the plug-ins in this book will either not use a UI (leave `ui_requirement` as `NULL`), or use `"gtk"`, Gaim's default user interface.

`unsigned long flags;`

`flags` is a variable that can contain many settings, although currently it contains only one. If you wish for this plug-in to not be shown in the plug-in list, but instead to be loaded invisibly, set this to `GAIM_PLUGIN_FLAG_INVISIBLE`.

`GList *dependencies;`

If this plug-in depends on other plug-ins, it can set `dependencies` to indicate this. Gaim would then load the required plug-in additionally, and the two can communicate to each other using inter-plug-in communication functions.

`GaimPluginPriority priority;`

Gaim currently does not handle `priority`, but it is included in `plugin.h` to accommodate its use in the future. Because its value is currently ignored, all plug-ins in this book will use `GAIM_PRIORITY_DEFAULT`.

`char *id;`

Each plug-in has a unique ID describing what it does. This plug-in is called `helloworld`, and sets the `id` variable accordingly.

The next six fields provide some metadata about the plug-in, which will be made available to the user when he views the list of available plug-ins. These should be self-explanatory. They provide a way for the plug-in author to attach his name, a description, a version number, and a URL for the plug-in's website.

Following these, the next three elements are functions that will be called when certain events occur to the plug-in.

```
gboolean (*load)(GaimPlugin *plugin);
gboolean (*unload)(GaimPlugin *plugin);
void (*destroy)(GaimPlugin *plugin);
```

When Gaim starts, it probes certain file system paths for plug-in files. When it finds one, it calls the plug-in's gaim_plugin_init function, retrieves this information, and presents it in the plug-in list to be loaded. When the plug-in is loaded, it calls the load function defined in the GaimPluginInfo structure. Then, when the plug-in is unloaded it calls the unload function. This function should "undo" everything did in load. Finally, when Gaim quits, it calls destroy, which undoes everything done in gaim_plugin_init. All three of these variables are declared as function pointers.

Function pointers are declared with the following syntax: int (*example)(int parameter1, int parameter2), where the first int is the return type of the function, example is the name of the pointer variable, and parameter1 and parameter2 are parameters for this function. After declaring and setting this function pointer to an existing function that matches this prototype, you can call example(1, 2); from anywhere example has scope.

```
void *ui_info;
void *extra_info;
```

ui_info and extra_info allow the plug-in to store information to be used by various code outside of the plug-in-loading code without the plug-in-loading code needing to know what the provided data are. For instance, ui_info holds data specific to a certain user interface. For Gaim's default GTK+ interface, ui_field is set to a GTK+ user interface object. extra_info is used for special types of plug-ins, such as protocol plug-ins, and provides additional information about what the plug-in does. For a protocol plug-in, this includes data such as the protocol name and icon.

```
GaimPluginUiInfo *prefs_info;
GList *(*actions)(GaimPlugin *plugin, gpointer context);
```

Finally, prefs_info defines certain plug-in preferences and actions is a list of actions to appear in the Tools ➤ Plugin Actions menu of the buddy list.

plugin_load()

```
05 static gboolean
06 plugin_load(GaimPlugin *plugin)
07 {
08     gaim_notify_info(NULL, NULL, "Hello World!", "I've written a plugin");
09     return TRUE;
10 }
```

Lines 5–10 in helloworld.c (Listing 4-1) define the function plugin_load. This is set as the load variable in the GaimPluginInfo structure, and therefore when Gaim needs to load this plug-in, it will find plugin_load's function pointer in the GaimPluginInfo struct and call this function.

Line 5 declares the function as static, and the return type as gboolean. static means that functions outside of this source file will not be able to call this function by name. This is useful for two main reasons.

First, by essentially hiding this function from other files, you are ensuring that the function will never be called from outside the plug-in. By explicitly declaring which functions can and cannot be used throughout Gaim, you force yourself and others to follow your design. I will discuss this principle of application design more throughout this chapter.

Declaring functions static is also useful to avoid conflicts among different files. For example plugin_load is a common function name for the load function of a Gaim plug-in. Because more than one of these plug-ins contains a function with this name, code outside this file that called plugin_load would not be able to discern which function to call. Because the plugin_load function need be accessed only from this file, it is declared static to avoid this issue. Another way to avoid this issue is via *namespacing*, the act of giving each function or variable a name that represents what portion of the program it is part of. I will discuss this further later this chapter, when discussing object-oriented programming.

The return type for plugin_load is gboolean. The GLib library, a library of utility functions used extensively throughout Gaim and GTK+, includes a set of data types designed for ease of use and portability. gboolean is a type that represents a Boolean value.

gboolean represents a truth value, either TRUE or FALSE. It is included in GLib because ANSI C, unlike other languages, does not contain a Boolean type itself.

■Note The C programming language has been revised several times. The original version of C is often known as K&R, referring to its creators Brian Kernighan and Dennis Ritchie. In 1983, the American National Standards Institute (ANSI) standardized a new version of C, known as ANSI C. This is still the most prevalent implementation of C. Even though C was revised again in 1999 (known as C99), adding a Boolean type and other features, it is usually preferable for you to write your code in ANSI C to ensure your code compiles even on older C compilers.

---

plugin_load returns FALSE if, for some reason, the plug-in failed to load. Under normal circumstances, it will return TRUE (see line 9).

gaim_notify_info()

```
08       gaim_notify_info(NULL, NULL, "Hello World!", "I've written a plugin");
```

In line 8, plugin_load calls gaim_notify_info. gaim_notify_info presents a message to the user, in a manner determined by the UI. In Gaim's default GTK+ UI, this function causes a message dialog to appear. This function (actually a convenience macro #defined in notify.h, but the difference here is negligible) takes a handle and three strings. The handle parameter (the first parameter, which is NULL in this example), is used to identify the source of the message.

If this message was, for example, related to a specific conversation, you would get a handle for that conversation, and use that for the parameter. Then, when the conversation was closed and the message no longer relevant, Gaim would close the dialog window itself. Leaving this as NULL means this message has no particular source, and should remain visible until the user closes it. The other parameters, three strings, represent the title of the message, and the primary and secondary texts for this message, in that order.

The title of the message box is used as the title of the window. Gaim dialogs will often set this to NULL, which means "no title." The reason for not including a title is that the title is often redundant with the text in the dialog. As the purpose of such a dialog is to present important information to the user in the most efficient way, the title is an unnecessary encumbrance. This philosophy derives from the GNOME HIG, the UI style guide after which Gaim models its UI; it will be discussed at greater length in the next chapter. You can read the GNOME HIG at http://developer.gnome.org/projects/gup/hig/.

The primary text is the main point of the dialog. In Gaim's GTK+ interface, it is shown in large, bold text. The secondary text is ancillary information that serves to further explain the primary text. Other types of messages are able to be displayed by almost identical functions: gaim_notify_error and gaim_notify_warning. More functions available to the Gaim API are covered in the "Gaim API" section later this chapter.

#include Statements

Finally (or initially, depending on your point of view), at the top of helloworld.c are three #include directives. These include function prototypes, and data types required by this plug-in, without which the compiler will be unable to recognize data types and functions linked from Gaim proper.

The internal.h header file consists mostly of #include directives to system libraries. This results in a vast reduction in the number of #include statements required in each file. Rather than using #include on the required system headers (see "Library Dependencies" in Chapter 1 for a list of them), a plug-in needs only to #include internal.h.

The notify.h header file is required, as it contains the declaration of gaim_notify_info and its related functions. Similarly, the plugin.h header file contains the GAIM_INIT_PLUGIN macro and the GaimPluginInfo object declaration.

You should now understand how to create a Gaim plug-in skeleton that Gaim will recognize and load. The next few sections will explain how to flesh out that skeleton. You will learn how to create plug-ins that interact with Gaim through its plug-in API. First, however, you must understand some underlying concepts of Gaim's design.

Object-Oriented Programming

Gaim is written using the object-oriented programming (OOP) paradigm. Object-oriented programming makes extensive use of objects: sets of data and related functions (or methods) used to manipulate the data. Object-oriented programming puts emphasis on these objects, which represent most aspects of the program. This is opposed to the more traditional paradigm, procedural programming, which puts stronger emphasis on the actions your program performs than on the data it contains.

Suppose a programmer is given the task of writing a program to keep track of recipes. Part of this program lets the user enter a new recipe, add it to the cookbook interface, and have it save to disk. The programmer may choose to do this with procedural code or object-oriented code. In pseudocode, the procedural program's code might look something like this:

```
File f = create_new_file(recipename);
add_to_list(cookbook->recipe_list, recipename);
write_to_file(f, recipename);
write_to_file(f, ingredients);
write_to_file(f, directions);
```

Similarly, everywhere in the procedural program that this code was accessed, the code would make similar low-level calls, accessing files. The object-oriented program would create a Recipe class and a Cookbook class that took care of the low-level tasks like writing to disk. The code could then manipulate them without knowing how they actually work. This code might look something like this:

```
Recipe r = new Recipe(recipename, ingredients, directions);
cookbook.add(r);
r.save();
```

Note that the first example is a list of actions to perform, and the second example is a set of messages (such as add and save) sent to objects representing recipes and cookbooks. Despite merely looking simpler and easier to understand, object-oriented programming emphasizes several key advantages over procedural programming.

The major advantage object-oriented programming has over procedural programming is modularity and reusability, two concepts that go hand in hand. This means that each object serves as somewhat of a subprogram on its own, which operates by sending and receiving messages from other objects. How the object handles these messages is irrelevant; the objects are emphasized, not the actions.

Abstraction

Suppose the cookbook application needs to be updated. Instead of saving recipes to files, you decide it would be better to store them in a database server. The procedural program needs changes everywhere recipes are accessed, likely spread throughout many different parts of the program. The object-oriented program is much easier to update.

Because a recipe's methods are encapsulated within the recipe object, the only code that needs to be changed is in the recipe object itself. Rather than changes to low-level implementation details throughout the entire project, the object-oriented program needs only a few changes. Implementation is important only to the object itself. Those low-level disk-writing calls will still be needed, and they will still be updated to use the database server, but a programmer working on another part of the application never needs to know how this works. This is an advantage of abstraction.

Inheritance

Inheritance is a concept that allows different objects to share common functionality. It allows a programmer to say object A is a special type of object B, with a few more characteristics. B is then said to inherit from A.

If the cookbook application is updated to include different types of recipes, say diet recipes, that include nutrition information in addition to ingredients, instructions, and what we've already used in this example, an object-oriented programmer would create a DietRecipe object that inherits from a Recipe class.

By inheriting from Recipe, the DietRecipe class automatically has access to all the data and functions of a recipe, but can also include data and functions of its own. Hence, one can call methods that belong to DietRecipe (maybe showNutritionInformation() or something similar) but can also call methods that belong to Recipe, such as save(). But what if a DietRecipe object needs to save different information than a normal Recipe object?

Polymorphism

Polymorphism is a blanket term that can be applied to several different things, but in general, it refers to code that will operate as expected, regardless of the type of object given to it. If the cookbook has a bunch of recipes and calls the save() function of each one, each recipe should save all the information that object needs. To do this, the DietRecipe object will *overload* the save method by implementing its own.

How the overloaded method is called instead of Recipe's save() function varies depending on how object orientation is implemented in the programming language being used.

Object-Oriented C

Now that you understand the basic precepts of object-oriented programming, you may be thinking that OOP requires the use of an object-oriented programming language. But that's not true. The object-oriented programming paradigm can be implemented in many procedural languages, including C.

■Note GTK+ uses the GObject library to achieve more powerful object-oriented support than described here. Objects used in Gaim itself do not use GObject. You can find more about GObject at http://www.gtk.org/.

The most important element in object-oriented programming is the object. An object is a self-contained entity consisting of data and procedures to manipulate the data. In C, objects are dynamically allocated structs.

Objects

In C, a struct is a collection of different data types stored as a single data type. For instance, consider the following code from blist.h:

```
struct _GaimBlistNode {
    GaimBlistNodeType type;
    GaimBlistNode *prev;
    GaimBlistNode *next;
    GaimBlistNode *parent;
```

```
        GaimBlistNode *child;
        GHashTable *settings;
        void *ui_data;
        GaimBlistNodeFlags flags;
}
```

This code represents a buddy list node. A node can be any entry in the buddy list. It could be a group, a buddy, a contact, or a chat. struct _GaimBlistNode contains all the data common among all those types. If you've done object-oriented programming before, you're probably used to seeing object types like GaimBlistNode: one word, capitalized. When doing object-oriented programming in C, you will use typedefs to achieve that same effect. Rather than writing "struct _GaimBlistNode" everywhere you refer to this type, you can alias it to GaimBlistNode, matching the typical object-oriented syntax:

```
typedef struct _GaimBlistNode GaimBlistNode;
```

Alternately, you can usually add the typedef in the struct declaration itself. Here, however, you cannot because the struct declaration contains references to itself. You must then put the typedef before the struct declaration for the compiler to understand it. The following is an example including the typedef in the struct declaration just so that you know the syntax:

```
typedef struct foo {
    int value;
    char string[8];
} GaimFoo;
```

Note that instead of BlistNode, we've typedefed this object as GaimBlistNode. Also, the struct is called struct _GaimBlistNode, with an underscore. Because C lacks many of the features of object-oriented languages, some of these features are duplicated in naming conventions. Calling the object a GaimBlistNode rather than just a BlistNode is an example of namespacing.

A namespace ensures that two separate classes of objects can have the same type. It would be doubtful that any other code in Gaim has a buddy list node object, but other types certainly can overlap—a conversation, for instance. Gaim has its own representation of a conversation, but a library used to implement some protocol might also have its own representation of a conversation. Both objects cannot be simply Conversation, or they'd conflict. Namespaces resolve this problem. For most object-oriented languages, a pair of colons is the common syntax, so you would see Gaim::Foo and Bar::Foo.However, because C doesn't support namespaces natively, they're done semantically by prepending the namespace to the beginning of classes of that type.

The underscore is another semantic duplication of a feature. Many object-oriented languages have a private keyword, or something similar, that specifies that a data type is not to be used outside of the encapsulated object. C doesn't have this, so the effect is achieved semantically. Variables, functions, or data types prefixed with an underscore are considered private and should not be used. There's nothing in C that can actually enforce this; it's just a rule you're expected to follow.

Now that you've typedefed GaimBlistNode, to declare a GaimBlistNode object, merely do this:

```
GaimBlistNode *node;
```

This is a pointer; the object will be dynamically created. Object-oriented languages usually reserve a keyword such as new to instantiate a new object. That allocated memory is then passed to a constructor function you write that initializes the object. In C you will create your own constructors that allocate and initialize memory, such as this:

```
GaimBlistNode *gaim_blist_node_new()
{
    GaimBlistNode *node = (GaimBlistNode*)g_malloc(sizeof(GaimBlistNode));
    node->type = GAIM_BLIST_OTHER_NODE;
    node->prev = NULL;
    node->next = NULL;
    node->parent = NULL;
    node->child = NULL;
    node->settings = NULL;
    node->ui_data = NULL;
    node->flags - NULL;
    return node;
}
```

This constructor allocates memory for the new GaimBlistNode, sets most of its members to NULL, but its type to GAIM_BLIST_OTHER_NODE, indicating that it's not one of the already known node types. Note that the function is namespaced, too, with the name of the object class preceding the relevant part of the function name. Now consider what happens if you call

```
GaimBlistNode *node = gaim_blist_node_new();
```

This call will allocate enough memory to store a GaimBlistNode, and the node variable will be set to the memory location where the object is stored. The object will be initialized to a default value. We can now call methods of this object using node as an instance.

In object-oriented languages, the methods are treated as elements of the instance. You would execute something like this:

```
node->remove_setting("buddy_icon");
```

Although this is *possible* with C, it is much simpler to bind functions to objects lexically, as you did with the constructor. GaimBlisitNode's remove_setting function (which removes a setting from the node) looks like this:

```
void gaim_blist_node_remove_setting(GaimBlistNode *node, const char *key)
{
    g_return_if_fail (node != NULL);
    g_return_if_fail (node->settings != NULL);
    g_return_if_fail (key != NULL);

    g_hash_table_remove(node->settings, key));

    gaim_blist_schedule_save ();
}
```

The first three instructions check to make sure the provided arguments are valid. This is akin to the assert command in some object-oriented languages. The call to g_hash_table_remove() actually removes the setting, and then gaim_blist_schedule_save() saves the change to disk. This function is called like this:

```
gaim_blist_node_remove_setting(node, "buddy_icon");;
```

Inheritance

Another important aspect of object-oriented programming is known as *inheritance.* By inheriting from another class, an object can retain all the data and methods from its parent, and add new data and methods. An inherited class is often a special type of that class, such as a GaimGroup. A GaimGroup is an entry in the buddy list, so you can still call functions like gaim_blist_node_remove_setting() on it. However, a GaimGroup has more data stored with it than what's included in GaimBlistNode (such as its name). It also has its own methods to manipulate the additional data. You can allow this special subclass of GaimBlistNode by making a pointer to a GaimGroup also be a pointer to a GaimBlistNode simultaneously.

Because every object-oriented object in C is represented as a struct, when you create a new GaimBlistNode, the program allocates memory for a new struct. Unlike the advanced data structures discussed later this chapter, a struct is entirely flat; it is merely a block of memory in a size equal to the cumulative size of the data members within it, as illustrated by Figure 4-2. The second item in a struct resides in a memory location right next to the first item. The compiler, which knows how large each item is, can then just access the second item. No additional data about the struct need be saved.

type	prev	next	parent	child	settings	ui_data	flags

Figure 4-2. *How memory is mapped in a* GaimBlistNode *struct*

The value returned by gaim_blist_node_new() is a pointer to the beginning of this GaimBlistNode struct. To create an object that inherits from GaimBlistNode, you make the first element in the struct a GaimBlistNode:

```
typedef struct {
    GaimBlistNode node;
    char *name;
    int totalsize;
    int currentsize;
    int online;
} GaimGroup;
```

When creating a new GaimGroup, the constructor will allocate a struct in memory, like in Figure 4-3.

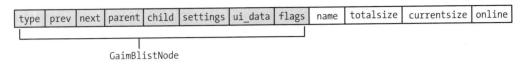

Figure 4-3. *How memory is mapped in an inherited object*

A pointer to the beginning of this object is also a pointer to the beginning of a GaimBlistNode. GaimBlistNode methods will treat the elements of GaimGroup's parent class just as it would a GaimBlistNode. To facilitate accessing node's data from an inherited class, use accessor functions.

Accessor and Mutator Functions

Object-oriented programmers are probably used to accessor and mutator functions. Rather than allowing direct access to an object's data (by referencing group->name, for example), there exists an appropriate *accessor* or *mutator* function. An accessor returns data from an object, and a mutator changes data in an object.

In an object-oriented language, an accessor would probably look like the following: node->getName(); in C, it will look like this: gaim_group_get_name(node). Likewise, to set the name data member with a mutator, do gaim_group_set_name(group, name). Disallowing access to data members of an object is part of a concept called *encapsulation*.

Encapsulation ensures that only an object can directly change the data associated with it. If another object wishes to change a member of an object, it has to utilize the interface provided it. Because each object can be thought of as a subprogram, this is an important aspect of object-oriented programming. Accessors and mutators are also necessary to maintain binary compatibility, ensuring that code written and compiled on one version of Gaim will continue to work even if the Gaim internals change.

If I write a Gaim plug-in, it should not need to be recompiled for every version of Gaim. Suppose I access a member of GaimGroup directly, such as char *l = group->name;. When I compile Gaim, the compiler sees that I access the string member of the object group. The compiler knows what a GaimGroup is composed of, and knows that the address of name is the address of group plus the size of a GaimBlistNode (assume 28 bytes). Now suppose a new release of Gaim makes a change to the GaimGroup object. I decide that it would be really useful to have the number of currently offline buddies stored within the GaimGroup object, in addition to the number of online buddies.

To facilitate storing the number of offline buddies, I add another integer type to GaimGroup. It now looks something like Figure 4-4.

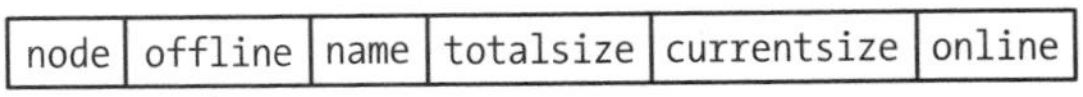

node	offline	name	totalsize	currentsize	online

Figure 4-4. *The new memory footprint of a GaimGroup object*

Without recompiling the plug-in, I attempt to use it. When the plug-in accesses group->name, it still attempts to access a string at address f+28. This no longer points to a string, though; it now points to online_count. This will result in a bug and quite likely a crash. By calling gaim_group_get_name(group), the plug-in relies on Gaim to provide the correct value. Because Gaim is recompiled with the changes to GaimGroup, it will always know the correct offset, even when a plug-in compiled for an older version may not.

Data Structures

Data structures are ways of organizing data in an efficient way. Different data types are better suited for different applications. Because they are so important, many programming languages have their own implementation of these data structures built in; C does not. Because of this, the GLib library includes implementations of many data structures. In this section, I will review a few common data types used in Gaim and, where applicable, their GLib implementations.

Linked Lists

A linked list is one of the simplest data structures. The most basic linked list is defined like this:

```
typdef struct _LinkedList LinkedList
struct _LinkedList {
    void *data;
    LinkedList *next;
};
```

The LinkedList represents a *node*, an item within the list. Each node contains whatever data you add to it and a pointer to the next node in the list. Because it contains links to other items of the same type, this is known as a *recursive* data structure.

There are several variations of a linked list, which can be more efficient in certain situations. The most common variation is the doubly linked list.

A singly linked list (see Figure 4-5) contains links in only one direction; start at the front of the list and work your way forward. In some cases, it might be more efficient to work backward through the list as well. In these cases, a doubly linked list is used.

Figure 4-5. *A singly linked list*

A doubly linked list contains two LinkedList pointers. In addition to next pointing to the next item in the list, it also contains a prev pointer, which points to the previous item. This allows you to iterate through the list in either direction.

Algorithms

To iterate a linked list, start at the first node of the list and, in a loop, keep accessing the next element until it is NULL (the end of the list). The following algorithm iterates through a linked list, searching each node for the given data.

```
gboolean linked_list_find(LinkedList *list, void *data)
{
    LinkedList *iterator = list;
    while (iterator != NULL) {
        if (iterator->data == data)
            return TRUE;
        iterator = iterator->next;
    }
    return FALSE;
}
```

The while loop iterates through all the nodes of the list; if iterator->data equals data, then the data was found, and the function returns TRUE. If data is not in the list, the while loop terminates when it reaches the end (the last item in the list will point to NULL), and the function will return FALSE. Alternately, the same algorithm can be implemented with a for loop:

```
gboolean linked_list_find(LinkedList *list, void *data)
{
    LinkedList *iterator;
     for (iterator = list; iterator != NULL; iterator = iterator->next) {
        if (list->data == data)
            return TRUE;
    }
    return FALSE;
}
```

Both are implementations of the same algorithm; the difference is entirely aesthetic. You will see both syntaxes used throughout Gaim. Because it's a very simple, primitive data type, Gaim makes extensive use of linked lists, using GLib's implementation, GList.

GList

The doubly linked list implemented in GLib is called GList. There also exists a singly linked list called GSList. The API is nearly identical for both of them.

■**Note** I will provide only a broad overview of the most common uses of GLib functions. You can find full documentation for GTK+, GLib, and other related libraries at http://www.gtk.org/api.

If you want to create a new, empty, GList, merely declare one and set it to NULL:

```
GList *list = NULL;
```

To add items to this new list, use g_list_append() (which adds new items to the end of the list) or g_list_prepend() (which adds new items to the beginning of the list). Both of these functions can change which node is the first node in the list.

Take, for instance, the empty list—a single pointer to NULL. Adding data to this list will cause a new node to be allocated. This new node will now be the first node in the list. Be sure to set your pointer to the new first node:

```
list = g_list_append(list, data);
```

or

```
list = g_list_prepend(list, data);
```

Note that you need never create new GList objects yourself. g_list_append() and g_list_prepend() take as arguments the data you are adding, and create the new GList object themselves. Likewise, g_list_remove() takes data as an argument, and will free the GList object itself:

```
list = g_list_remove(list, data);
```

Again, note that this function may change the first node in the list, so it's crucial to update your pointer accordingly. g_list_remove() will remove only the first instance of given data in a list. To remove *all* instances, use g_list_remove_all():

```
list = g_list_remove_all(list, data);
```

The main problem with linked lists is that its algorithms take too much time. linked_list_find(), for instance, has to iterate the entire list if the data is not found. For large lists, this may be unacceptable. For instances like this, you can use more-efficient data structures, such as hash tables.

Hash Tables

A hash table is a data structure in which data is *hashed* to generate a key. To hash data is to generate a new value from it which is irreversible, but reproducible, When a hash table hashes data, it creates a unique key. This key is a number that can then be indexed in the table immediately, regardless of how many items are stored in the hash table. You normally do not need to iterate through other items of a hash table to locate an item by its key. For instance, suppose you need to keep a hash table of your friends' shoe sizes.

■**Note** Computer scientists refer to the efficiency of an algorithm in "big-oh" notation. This notation represents the speed of an algorithm in proportion to the size of the input, n. Because the linked list algorithm iterates every item in the list, the algorithm completes in time exactly proportionate to the number of items in the list. This is called $O(n)$. Because the hash table operates at the same efficiency regardless of input, it is said to run in $O(1)$ time.

If you were to create a linked list, storing a name and a shoe size in each node, the code will have to iterate through all your friends, comparing the name stored at each node with the name you're looking for. With a hash table, you would create a hash of your friends' names.

The hash is generally determined by two steps. First, create a unique integer based on the name, then use the modulo operator against the size of the hash table to create an index within the necessary bounds.

■**Tip** The modulo operator in C is %. Modulo means you should divide the first operand by the second operand and return the remainder. Thus, 5 % 2 = 1 (5 / 2 = 2 with a remainder of 1). Because the remainder can never be greater than the divisor, using the modulo operator will ensure the index will not be outside the bounds.

A simple hash function is "add the ASCII values of each letter in the name." Suppose the hash table is 50 elements long. My name would hash to 83(S) + 101(e) + 97(a) + 110(n), modulo 50. The ASCII values summed equal 441. 441 % 50 = 41. Thus, my shoe size (12) would be stored at index 41 in the hash table. To look up my shoe size, calculate the hash of my name again, and retrieve the value at index 41. (See Figure 4-6.)

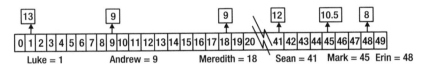

Figure 4-6. *A hash table containing the shoe sizes of me and several of my friends. Indices 21–39 are omitted for simplicity.*

However, a problem still exists if two names result in the same hash. My friend Rachel, for instance, also hashes to 41, but her feet are much smaller than mine. When two different names result in the same hash, it's known as a *collision*. There are several ways to resolve collisions.

The way collisions are resolved in GLib's implementation of a hash table is that the data themselves (shoe sizes in this example) aren't indexed, but rather linked lists, as seen in Figure 4-7. Located at each index is the first node in a linked list of names, and shoe sizes that hash to that index. This way, more than one shoe size can share the same index if their hashes collide. By searching that list with an appropriate function for the key, you can find the element representing your key.

Because collision results in a linear search with the same efficiency problem we set out to avoid, the task of choosing a hash function to result in as few collisions as possible is very important. Thankfully, GLib provides several efficient hash functions in its hash table implementation, GHashTable.

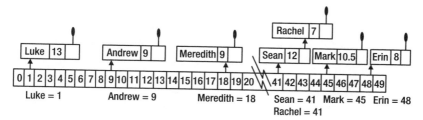

Figure 4-7. *Collision resolution using linked lists*

GHashTable

GHashTable is GLib's implementation of a hash table. It's designed to be versatile and efficient, and can be used anywhere a hash table is needed. To create a GHashTable, call

GHashTable *hash = g_hash_table_new(hash_func, key_equal_func);

hash_func is a function pointer that points to a hash function, as described earlier in this chapter. As I mentioned, GLib provides three hash functions for us to use: g_str_hash, g_int_hash, and g_direct_hash. These are used if your key is a string, an integer, or a pointer to some other object, respectively. This should suffice for the majority of applications.

key_equal_func is the function that will search the linked list for the key when a collision has occurred. Similar to hash_func, GLib provides functions for strings, integers, and pointers: g_str_equal, g_int_equal, and g_direct_equal, respectively. These functions all take two arguments of their appropriate type, and return TRUE if they are equal.

To add an item to the hash table, you needn't worry about creating the hash yourself. Call g_hash_table_insert(hash, key, value), and GLib will do the necessary work itself. Likewise, to retrieve a value from the hash table, call g_hash_table_lookup(hash, key). This will return the value you added with that key. To remove a value from the hash table, call g_hash_table_remove(hash, key). This will remove the value associated with that key from the hash table.

A hash table is extremely useful for quick access to data that can be associated with a key. Other tasks, though, lend themselves well to other data types, such as trees.

Trees

A tree is another recursive data structure; that is, each node in the tree points to other nodes. However, where a linked list links to one (or two, in the case of a doubly linked list) other list node, a tree node can link to many other tree nodes to represent a tree structure, such as the one seen in Figure 4-8.

Trees are most useful when representing hierarchical data (such as Gaim's buddy list, represented by a tree of GaimBlistNode's) and for quick searching. Gaim uses this latter kind of tree to search for smileys in a conversation. Other types of search trees include binary search trees and red-black trees; neither of these, however, is used in Gaim.

Because Gaim's trees are specific to a certain task, they don't use GLib's implementation of tree types (which you can read about at http://www.gtk.org/api). Instead, I will discuss the trees used in Gaim. The buddy list will be discussed in the next section.

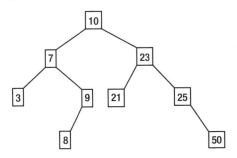

Figure 4-8. *A binary search tree*

The Gaim API

Now that you understand some important concepts of object-oriented programming in C, and a few important data structures, I will briefly explain some of the important objects used in Gaim, how they interrelate, and how to manipulate them in plug-ins. Not only will this overview introduce Gaim plug-in development, but it will also provide an example of sound object-oriented application design. For a complete reference of the Gaim API, consult the API documentation at http://gaim.sourceforge.net/api.

Core/UI Split

Gaim attempts to keep its user interface as separate from its *core* as possible. The core refers to the base functionality of Gaim: connections to IM servers, abstract notions of conversations and buddy lists, implementations of IM protocols. This way, other developers can use the Gaim core (which is available as a library called libgaim), to create their own interfaces without needing a thorough understanding of IM protocols or having to duplicate the hard work of Gaim developers. To facilitate this distinction, objects are separated between core objects and UI objects.

■**Note** Currently two projects make use of libgaim in providing alternate UIs to Gaim. The first project is Gaim for Qtopia (http://qpe-gaim.sourceforge.net), which uses Trolltech's QPE graphics toolkit library for the Sharp Zaurus handheld device. The other is a Mac OS X client called Adium (http://www.adiumx.com).

Each core object has a corresponding pointer to a UI operations object. This object contains function pointers that will be called when the UI needs to be notified of something. Figure 4-9 illustrates the relationship between these two types of objects.

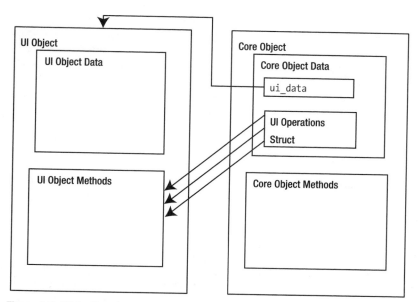

Figure 4-9. *This diagram represents the relationship between a core object and a UI object.*

Here is the UI operations object for Gaim's file transfer support:

```
typedef struct
{
    void (*new_xfer)(GaimXfer *xfer);
    void (*destroy)(GaimXfer *xfer);
    void (*add_xfer)(GaimXfer *xfer);
    void (*update_progress)(GaimXfer *xfer, double percent);
    void (*cancel_local)(GaimXfer *xfer);
    void (*cancel_remote)(GaimXfer *xfer);
} GaimXferUiOps;
```

This object is contained as a member of the GaimXfer object. The UI object for file transfer, GaimGtkXfer calls a function gaim_ft_set_ui_ops() with a pointer to this struct:

```
static GaimXferUiOps ops =
{
    gaim_gtkxfer_new_xfer,
    gaim_gtkxfer_destroy,
    gaim_gtkxfer_add_xfer,
    gaim_gtkxfer_update_progress,
    gaim_gtkxfer_cancel_local,
    gaim_gtkxfer_cancel_remote
};
```

In this `struct`, each member is a pointer to functions that match the core prototypes. When a Gaim user, for example, cancels a file transfer, the core calls the `cancel_local` member of the UI operations, corresponding to `gaim_gtkxfer_cancel_local()`. This function notifies the user that the transfer was canceled by manipulating the appropriate `GaimGtkXfer` object.

The `GaimGtkXfer` object corresponding to a `GaimXfer` is stored in `GaimXfer` in its `ui_data` data member. When the core calls its `new_xfer` UI operation, `gaim_gtkxfer_new_xfer` creates a new `GaimGtkXfer` object, and sets the `GaimGtkXfer` object as the `GaimXfer`'s `ui_data`. For subsequent UI operation calls, the UI will be able to access the `GaimGtkXfer` from here.

▪Tip Void pointers are pointers the compiler will allow to point to any data type. They are useful in situations in which different UIs will need to associate different data with a file transfer. They should not be abused, though, as strict typing will generally lead to fewer bugs.

I've used `GaimXfer` as an example here, but the same principles are used throughout Gaim. I will discuss the UI objects in the next chapter. The remainder of this chapter will focus solely on core objects.

GaimAccount (`account.h`)

Perhaps the most fundamental object in Gaim is the `GaimAccount`. This object represents an IM account. It encapsulates a user's screen name, password, the IM protocol used, and account options such as privacy settings and buddy icons. Accounts are stored in an XML file called `$HOME/accounts.xml`.

To create new account, call

```
gaim_account_new(const char *name, const char *protocol_id);
```

▪Note When you see a function that takes strings as arguments, the strings will usually be defined as `const char*`. The `const` means that the compiler won't let the value of the parameters change in any way. The strings are strictly read-only. You should declare string parameters this way to enforce encapsulation of data.

After creating the new account, you can set and get attributes related to it using the various accessor functions you'll find documented at `http://gaim.sourceforge.net/api`.

GaimConnection (`connection.h`)

`GaimConnection` represents a `GaimAccount`'s connection to an IM server, and is manipulated mostly by protocol plug-ins. A `GaimConnection` is associated with exactly one `GaimAccount`, and a `GaimAccount` can support only one `GaimConnection`, as demonstrated in Figure 4-10.

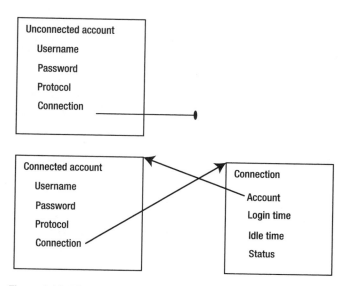

Figure 4-10. *The relationship between* GaimAccount *and* GaimConnection

When a protocol plug-in is told to connect a GaimAccount, it will create a new GaimConnection by calling

```
GaimConnection *gc = gaim_connection_new(GaimAccount *account);
```

■**Tip** When developing large applications, you'll often find that you wind up giving certain objects the same variable names repeatedly. This turns into a variable naming convention that can easily identify the type of an object from its variable name. If you see a variable called gc in Gaim, for example, it's almost always a GaimConnection.

It will then use functions such as gaim_connection_set_state() and gaim_connection_disconnect() to keep Gaim informed of the status of this connection.

The protocol plug-in contains a set of functions that Gaim will call when communication with the server is necessary (sending messages, adding buddies, sending files, etc.). These functions will all take a GaimConnection as a parameter. GaimConnection also contains a proto_data member (as a void pointer) in which the plug-in can store protocol-specific data. Protocol plug-ins will be explained in detail in Chapter 8.

GaimConversation (conversation.h)

A GaimConversation is an IM or a chat room. An IM is uniquely identified by a GaimAccount and a screen name.

To create a new conversation, call

gaim_conversation_new (GaimConversationType *type*, GaimAccount, **account*, const char
*name)

■**Note** GaimConversationType is an enum. An enum (short for enumeration) is merely a set of names
for numbers. To avoid the "magic number" problem, you can use GAIM_CONV_IM and GAIM_CONV_CHAT for
type, rather than 0 and 1.

Because Gaim conversations are tabbed, a GaimConversation will always exist inside a
GaimConvWindow. A GaimConvWindow is essentially a linked list of GaimConversations, as shown in
Figure 4-11. Because newly created conversations will automatically place themselves in a
window, creating a new one if necessary, you will rarely deal with GaimConvWindows unless
you're editing the conversation UI. UI aspects will be discussed in greater detail in the next
chapter.

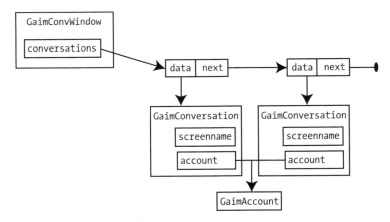

Figure 4-11. *A GaimConvWindow holding two conversations from the same account*

The most important function for GaimConversations is gaim_conversation_write (which
will probably be wrapped by gaim_conv_im_write or gaim_conv_chat_write, depending on the
conversation type). This function will print a message to the conversation, taking such factors
as the user's preferences and the type of conversation into consideration.

GaimBuddyList (blist.h)

GaimBuddyList is somewhat unique in that only one exists for all of Gaim. It contains only two
notable data members. The first is an object itself, a GaimBlistNode.

GaimBlistNode

A GaimBlistNode is a recursive data structure containing pointers to other GaimBlistNode objects as to represent a tree, as shown in Figure 4-12. The GaimBlist contains a pointer to the first node of the tree. A GaimBlistNode object can represent a group, a buddy, a chat, or a GaimContact (discussed later in this section).

As you saw earlier in this chapter, a GaimBlistNode contains very little data by itself—mostly just references to other GaimBlistNodes. Most of the data comes from derived objects, such as GaimBuddy and GaimGroup, which inherit from GaimBlistNode. In fact, nowhere in Gaim is GaimBlistNode used apart from within a derived subclass.

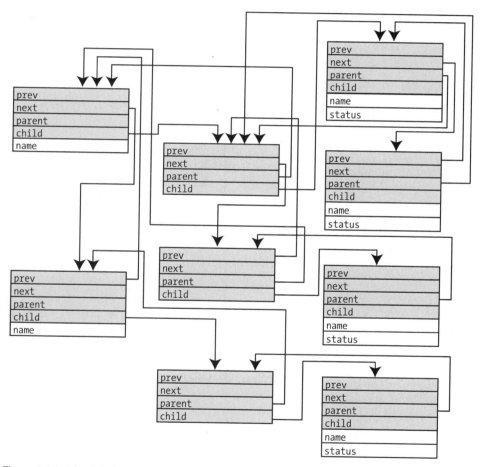

Figure 4-12. *A buddy-list tree data structure*

GaimBuddy

A GaimBuddy is uniquely identified by a GaimAccount and a screen name. The GaimBuddy object contains other data relevant to the buddy, such as buddy icons and the buddy's status.

GaimGroup

A GaimGroup stores information about how many buddies are in the group, and how many of them are logged in. This information is shown next to the group name in the buddy list. Buddies stored within the group are contained beneath it in the tree structure, i.e., node->child.

GaimContact

A contact is a mostly transparent grouping of buddies that represent the same human person. Using contacts, if your friend has an account on AIM and another on MSN, you can consolidate them to a single entry in your list.

In the buddy list tree, every GaimBuddy exists as child of a GaimContact. Because the concept of a GaimContact is mostly transparent, a user cannot distinguish in the UI between a GaimBuddy and a GaimContact with a single buddy in it.

GaimChat

By adding GaimChats to a buddy list, a Gaim user can easily join his favorite chat rooms by double-clicking their entries in the buddy list. The GaimChat object contains data that the protocol needs to identify a chat room and then join it.

The Hash Table

The other noteworthy member of GaimBlist is a hash table. The GaimBlistNode tree does an ideal job of representing the hierarchical tree structure of the buddy list. However, finding a node in the tree is an expensive operation; iterating every item in the list takes an unacceptably long time. To facilitate this, GaimBlist contains a hash table called buddies.

Each GaimBuddy in the buddy list is entered in the hash table using, as a key, a combination of its account and screen name. Then, when a GaimBuddy object needs to be accessed, it will call gaim_find_buddy(), which will search the hash table.

Summary

You should now have a working understanding of object-oriented programming, how it is implemented in C, and efficient ways of storing data. If you're a bit unsure, don't worry; some of these concepts are very complex. You will see plenty of examples of object-oriented design in the next chapter, in which I will introduce GTK+, the graphical user interface library used by Gaim and many other applications.

CHAPTER 5

■■■

GTK+ Basics

I've mentioned that GTK+ is the library Gaim uses to create its graphical user interface, or GUI. In this chapter, I'll introduce GTK+. You'll learn some of the principles behind it, such as widget packing and event listeners. Then I'll introduce some common *widgets*, the individual elements such as buttons and scrollbars that comprise a GUI. Throughout, I'll provide practical examples of the techniques I'm discussing. For the complete API documentation, visit http://www.gtk.org/api.

Overview of GTK+

GTK+ is a powerful object-oriented widget toolkit written in C, but with bindings available in many languages. The toolkit has its origins in the X Window System used by most UNIX-like operating systems, but ports are available for Windows and the Linux framebuffer.

■**Note** A language binding allows you to use a library that isn't native to the language you're programming in. GTK+ is written in C, but bindings allow you to use it in C++, Perl, Python, and other languages.

History

GTK+ was originally spawned by the GIMP, the GNU Image Manipulation Program (http://www.gimp.org). The GIMP (seen in Figure 5-1) is a powerful editor for photos and other digital images, not unlike Adobe Photoshop. When Peter Mattis and Spencer Kimball began work on the GIMP in 1995, they knew they wanted to create a completely free-as-in-freedom image editor for the UNIX platform. However, they were unable to find a suitable library with which to create their GUI.

There were plenty of choices in UI libraries for UNIX in 1995, but none were suitable for this task. Originally, Mattis and Kimball used a library called Motif, but because Motif was not free, many potential users were unable to run the GIMP as not everyone had access to the library. Mattis decided to create his own free replacement for Motif.

Although the GIMP Toolkit, or GTK, was created specifically for the GIMP, it quickly found use in other projects with similar needs. When inheritance was added to the library, making it more object-oriented, the plus sign was added to signify the difference. Today, the library is officially called GTK+, but in common conversation, the plus is often dropped.

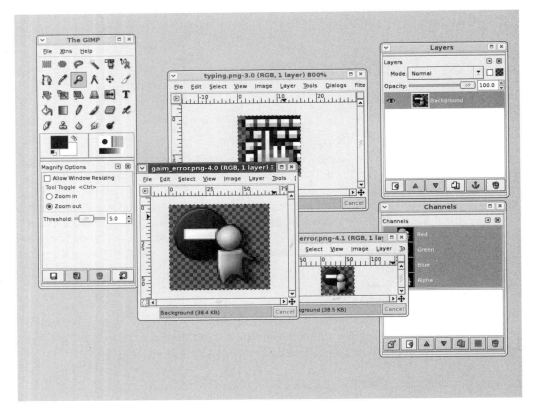

Figure 5-1. *The GIMP*

GNOME

In 1997, a student named Miguel de Icaza announced his intention to create an entirely free and open source integrated desktop environment for the UNIX environment. A desktop environment is the collection of integrated tools and applications that comprise the desktop user experience. Some operating systems, notably Windows and Mac OS, obscure the difference between the desktop environment and the operating system. Due to UNIX's more modular structure, though, a relatively wide choice is available.

At the time the most promising such desktop, KDE, was not free because it used the proprietary Qt widget toolkit, which did not offer its users the ability to modify or redistribute the toolkit.[1] Miguel de Icaza attempted to convince Trolltech, the creators of Qt, to consider a free software license. Unable to do so, he created the GNOME project. The GNOME desktop is shown in Figure 5-2.

One of the major advantages to the open source development model is that the community at large benefits from the work of others in the community. Because Peter Mattis and Spencer Kimball created a free toolkit for their needs, de Icaza was able to use it in his own free software projects. Currently, Miguel de Icaza's desktop environment, GNOME, is the most prevalent use of the GTK+ library, and development of GTK+ falls under the realm of the GNOME project.

---

1. Qt has since been relicensed under the GNU General Public License. Thus, KDE is now entirely free.

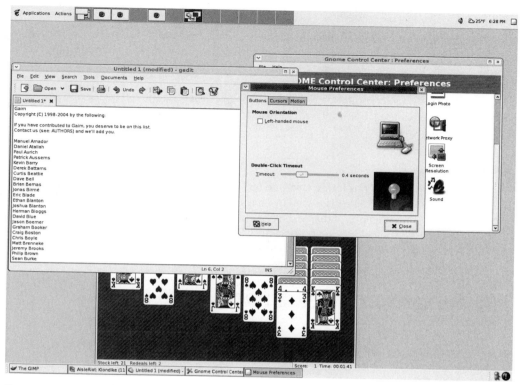

Figure 5-2. *The GNOME desktop environment*

Architecture

GTK+ is a fairly high-level library that delegates lower-level functionality such as drawing to the screen or rendering text to other support libraries that operate closer to the system being run on. These libraries are developed alongside GTK+, and although they can be used separately from GTK+, they are most useful in the context of a GTK+ application and can be thought of as part of GTK+ for most purposes.

This chapter will focus primarily on GTK+ itself. In the following few sections, I will provide only a brief introduction to what these libraries are and what they are used for. In the next chapter, I'll explore the internals of GTK+, and these libraries will be examined in greater depth.

GDK

GDK is the GTK+ Graphics Development Kit and is responsible for drawing GUI elements to the screen. It provides functions for drawing graphics to the screen; receiving input from the user from the keyboard, mouse, and other input devices; and system-independent methods of accessing interoperability features such as drag and drop and copy and paste.

To allow GTK+ to be platform-independent, GDK consists of an assortment of different back ends, each of which knows how to work with a different system. The most commonly used back ends are X, which draws to the X Window System—used by most UNIX-like computers—and Win32, which draws to Windows.

GdkPixbuf

GdkPixbuf is used to manipulate images. It can read and write image files in an assortment of common graphics formats including .jpeg, .gif, .png, .bmp, and .ico. It offers simple editing functions such as scaling, overlaying, and desaturating. It also allows direct access to the image data, allowing you to directly edit it however you please.

GdkPixbuf is most commonly used to load images for icons, but can be used wherever images need to be loaded, manipulated, or saved. In Gaim, this includes buddy icons and IM images.

Pango

Pango is a library used for rendering Unicode text in any language. It represents blocks of text in UTF-8, a text encoding to be discussed in Chapter 10. The developer can then apply various attributes to different portions of this text. These include color, size, weight (such as boldness), font family, background color, style (underlining for instance), and numerous other attributes (see Figure 5-3). Pango will then format the text according to your specification, taking into account various issues of internationalization and typesetting.

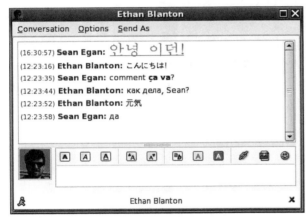

Figure 5-3. *Because of Pango, Gaim can render text in any language in a variety of different styles.*

Application developers using GTK+ rarely need to use Pango calls directly; most of its relevant functionality is wrapped within the various GTK+ widgets that use it. This includes the use of the Pango Markup Language.

Pango Markup Language is an XML-based markup language used for assigning text attributes to certain ranges within a string. These ranges are called *spans*, and the attributes are set as XML attributes of those spans.

For example,

```
<span weight="bold">This text</span> is bold.
```

would render as

```
This text is bold.
```

To allow the most common attributes to be set more easily, convenience tags are provided. These convenience tags provide a syntax very similar to HTML for most purposes. Thus, the above example can also be specified as

```
<b>This text</b> is bold.
```

A complete specification of Pango Markup Language can be found at `http://developer.gnome.org/doc/API/2.0/pango/PangoMarkupFormat.html`.

GLib

As I discussed in the previous chapter, GLib provides utility functions, common data structures, and cross-platform compatibility. The most important data structures were discussed in the previous chapter; important text manipulation functions will be discussed in Chapter 10, as will the library's compatibility functionality. GLib also provides core functionality for developing GTK+ applications.

Part of this core functionality is the *main loop* that GTK+ applications use to continually manage input from the user and update the GUI accordingly. The main loop will be discussed later this chapter.

Language Bindings

GTK+ is written in C, as are many applications that use it, Gaim included. However, the library contains bindings to many other languages, including C++, Perl, Python, and C#. Regardless of what language you choose, GTK+ most likely supports it. This book will cover only its C API, but most of the differences are minor, merely translating C's object-oriented syntaxes to those of the other language. As an example, consider the following command:

```
GtkWidget *button = gtk_button_new("Button");
```

In GTK# (the C# binding) this command translates to

```
Button button = new Button ("Button");
```

The underlying concepts about using GTK+ presented here will be the same, regardless of programming languages, although the syntax will be different.

■**Note** If you are interested in writing GTK+ applications in other languages, see `http://www.gtk.org`.

Anatomy of a GTK+ Application

A GTK+ application does not resemble most procedural C programs. Rather than a clear linear program path where you can easily trace everything that will happen from beginning to end, a GTK+ application is essentially a large group of disjoint functions. These functions are usually not explicitly called from within your application; you create user interfaces and instruct GTK+ that when certain events occur—say a button is clicked—one of your functions should be called.

GTK+ decides when to call each function and when the function returns, control is passed back to GTK+. Figure 5-4 contrasts a traditional procedural program with a GTK+ application.

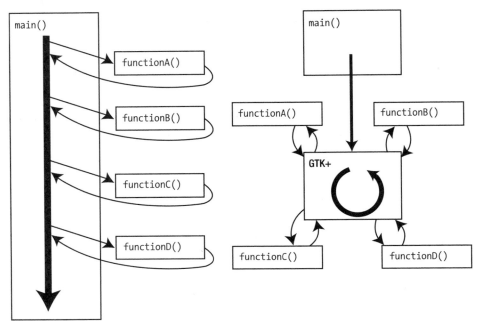

Figure 5-4. *The program flow of a GTK+ application (right) contrasted with that of a traditional procedural program (left)*

If you want a button that saves a file when clicked, you create that function and tell GTK+ to call it when the button is clicked. Likewise, if a button needs to create a new window, you create a function that creates a new window and tell GTK+ to call it when the button is clicked. Most of what your main() function does is initialize GTK+ and any other parts of your application, then hand off control to GTK+, which will call the other functions in your application as appropriate.

You should already know that main() is the first function called in any C program, and that the program terminates when the main() function returns. A program with a graphical interface stays in main() until the user quits. This is done with a main loop that constantly waits for user input and redraws the interface when necessary. With just two function calls, you can write a graphical application that will initiate itself and then cede control to GTK+.

The gtk_init() Function

Before calling any other GTK+ function in your program, you must call gtk_init(). This function initializes the library and processes the command-line options passed to it.

All GTK+ applications have certain command-line options provided to them by GTK+. These include various options for debugging and low-level system functionality of limited use to average end users. gtk_init() will process your command-line options, act only on those it understands, and remove those from the list of command-line options so that you can parse those that remain.

Command-line options are passed to your main() function in the argv parameter, and the number of options is provided in argc. The gtk_init() function takes as arguments pointers to the argv and argc parameters. By using pointers, it can modify the value of argc and argv.

Note In case you've forgotten, the main() function is typically defined as int main(int argc, char *argv[]). Command-line options are set in the argv array when your program starts, and the length of that array is set in argc.

In C, passing a pointer to a function provides that function with a *reference*, or memory address, to the data being passed. The called function can then access the data at (or *dereference*) that pointer to read the value stored at it and then change that value. If the parameter is passed by *value*, the called function cannot change it.

By passing a reference to the command-line options, GTK will remove the options it recognizes from the list. The syntax to do this uses the ampersand operator, which returns the address of the given argument:

```
gtk_init(&argc, &argv);
```

The Main Loop

Your application will be in the GTK+ main loop for the life of the process. The main loop is an infinite loop that repeatedly retrieves input from the keyboard, mouse, and possibly other devices; updates the display; and processes events such as "a button was clicked," through a system of signals and callback functions I will discuss later this chapter. From main(), simply call gtk_main(). This argument takes no parameters and will not return until gtk_main_quit() is called elsewhere in your code.

The shortest valid GTK+ application you can write consists of only these two function calls:

```
#include <gtk/gtk.h>
int main(int argc, char *argv[])
{
    gtk_init(&argc, &argv);
    gtk_main()
    return 0;
}
```

This application will not do anything; it will be stuck in gtk_main() forever. A practical main() function will create the application's initial UI between the calls to gtk_init() and gtk_main(). I will return to this example later this chapter when I demonstrate how to build a UI.

As mentioned earlier, GTK+'s main loop is actually part of GLib that provides several useful functions for interacting with it. Gaim uses these functions intensively for communicating on the network. This will be discussed in Chapter 7. Another useful function of GLib's main loop is timeouts.

Oftentimes it's useful in an application to do something after waiting a certain amount of time. GLib provides a callback mechanism to do this. Calling

```
g_timeout_add(guint interval, GSourceFunc function, void *data);
```

will call "function" after "interval" microseconds. The callback function can return TRUE to specify that the callback should recur, or FALSE if the timeout should be removed. I will discuss the concept of callbacks in more detail later in this chapter.

User Interface Principles

Traditionally, free software has had a reputation of being technically sound but having barely usable user interfaces. This is often said to be a result of developers catering their UIs to what the software is capable of rather than what the users want. However, when users' opinions are considered, this often results in a UI lacking a single clear focus, representing an amalgamation of various usage habits. Gaim is part of a growing trend in free software to focus on simple, usable UIs that do one thing, and do that one thing right.

Elegance

Because free software is traditionally used predominantly by technically savvy individuals, their UIs have generally been designed with the power user in mind. This is in contrast to many proprietary projects that tend to focus on the average computer user.

The power user is presented with a wide assortment of features and preferences, allowing for a wide range of flexibility and customization. Because this requires a certain level of knowledge, many users find themselves limited in terms of what functions they are allowed to perform. However, this is changing due to the recognition that, regardless of experience level, everyone wants the same thing from their software: they want it to do what they want, as simply as possible. As such, interfaces are getting simpler, without crippling the functionality. Google has taken over Yahoo; Firefox is making significant gains on Internet Explorer. Many free software projects have embraced this philosophy as well, and as a result, they are no longer used only by the technically savvy.

By creating an interface that is *elegant*, Gaim allows the power user to do everything he wants to do without complicating things so much that his mother can't use it. Rather than dumbing down the interface for the inexperienced, or complicating it for the computer whizzes, Gaim strives towards a happy medium that works for everyone.

Of course, Gaim is far from perfect in this regard, but strides are constantly being made to improve the UI by simplifying it. To do this, we look toward the GNOME Human Interface Guidelines (HIG), the work of the GNOME project's usability experts.

GNOME HIG

Starting with their 2.0 version, the GNOME desktop emphasized its focus on usability. This focus stressed not just simplicity, but more importantly, standardization of the look and feel of applications running on GNOME.

Consistency across all the applications on your desktop allows a user to reinforce his familiarity with your UI design by using other similarly designed interfaces. Consistent menu locations, button placement, colors, and icons all enhance the user's experience and make him feel more comfortable. Although Gaim isn't part of the GNOME project, Gaim attempts to follow the HIG as both projects use GTK+.

GNOME's Human Interface Guidelines are designed with this in mind. The HIG makes recommendations on a wide range of topics, from how many pixels to use as spacing between buttons to which colors to use in your icons. Following these guidelines will ensure your application is consistent with other applications in the GNOME environment. You may notice some aspects of Gaim's interface that are directly inspired by the HIG.

The HIG recommends that window titles, when used, show relative information that distinguishes one window from others. It also discourages the persistent "branding" seen in many commercial applications. Because of this, the term "Gaim" is rarely seen in the Gaim interface and Gaim's window titles are all brief, unique descriptions. The buddy list is "Buddy List," and a conversation with SeanEgn is "SeanEgn".

Gaim's buttons are also inspired by the HIG. The HIG recommends that action verbs be used in button captions. A typical Windows application may ask, "Do you want to remove *SomePerson* from your buddy list?" and provide OK and Cancel as options. Buttons in HIG-compliant applications specify exactly what the user is about to do. Instead of OK, the button in Gaim is Remove Buddy.

The ordering of these buttons is also sanctioned by the HIG and may feel uncomfortable to Windows users. Windows applications put the most commonly chosen option farthest to the left, the rationale being that it will be the first button seen as most people scan written text from left to right. Gaim uses the reverse ordering.

In Gaim dialogs (and dialogs of other HIG-compliant applications) the most commonly chosen function is placed farthest to the right. The authors of the HIG argue that we don't scan the contents of a dialog window the same way we scan a page in a book. When a button is the rightmost in a dialog, it is always in the lower-right corner. In a Windows-style dialog, the position of the most commonly used button depends on the other buttons. If it is the only button, it will be in the lower-right corner, but if there are five other buttons, it may be closer to the left side of the dialog. The HIG contends that a consistent location for this button is necessary, which is why Gaim's button ordering may seem out of place to you if you use Windows.

The HIG also provides a color palette that icons and other colored UI elements should use. You'll notice that all of the icons in Gaim have a consistent look because of this (and because of other guidelines specific to icon design). Even when we color the screen names in a conversation, we use colors from the HIG palette rather than pure blue or pure red.

The HIG calls for *direct manipulation*. This means that you should always allow your users to work with interface objects directly rather than forcing them to use commands. Direct manipulation is most often done through the drag-and-drop concept, which is used heavily through Gaim. To send your buddy a file, just drag the file into his conversation window or buddy list entry. To set a buddy icon for your account, drag the image to the Modify Account window.

One of the prominent concepts throughout the HIG is "simple and pretty." The interface should be kept clean; every unused interface element is a distraction to the user and interferes with her ability to efficiently use your application. You can read the GNOME HIG in its entirety at http://developer.gnome.org/projects/gup/hig.

Creating Dialogs in GTK+

A dialog is a GUI window. Each element within the dialog is called a *widget*. Widgets include buttons, text labels, check boxes, text boxes, lists, and any other GUI element. In GTK+, a widget is any object that inherits from the GtkWidget class; essentially every UI element is a widget, including the windows themselves. Creating a GUI is a matter of creating the appropriate widgets and laying them out in a window.

Though creating a GUI in GTK+ is not unlike creating GUIs in other object-oriented APIs you may be familiar with, a few significant differences are important to note—and I'll point them out here. But once you're familiar with the various widgets and some underlying principles surrounding them, you'll find it easy to create dialogs in GTK+.

Widget Packing

Perhaps the most significant difference in writing a UI in GTK+ compared to other APIs, such as Win32, is that specifying widget locations and size explicitly is discouraged in favor of GTK+'s *packing model*.

The packing model is advantageous because it automatically adapts to features such as font preferences and localization. The latter is relevant when using languages that write from right to left. GTK+'s packing model will automatically adjust the UI to the correct direction.

■**Note** Although widget packing is preferred, it is still possible to explicitly position widgets in a window in GTK+ by using the GtkFixed widget.

In the packing model, widgets are added as "children" within "parent" widgets. These parent widgets, or *containers*, are responsible for calculating the size and shape needed to hold all their children according to certain rules set by the developer. For every window, there is a root GtkWindow widget that acts as a container in which the other dialog elements are embedded. For example, a button might be packed within the window. The button, a container itself, can likewise have widgets packed into it—normally a text label and icon as shown in Figure 5-5.

Figure 5-5. *This button widget has a label widget and an icon widget packed inside it.*

Container Widgets

Any widget in which other widgets can be packed descends from GtkContainer. Because the packing paradigm is used so thoroughly, GtkContainer objects are very common throughout GTK+. Containers can generally be grouped into subcategories based on function: layout containers, and decoration and function containers.

Layout Containers

The most commonly used GtkContainer subclasses used for layout are GtkBox and GtkTable. The former is further subclassed into GtkHBox and GtkVBox. The purpose of these container widgets is to determine the size and location of widgets packed into it. If you pack two button widgets into a GtkHBox, the GtkHBox will do all the work in determining how big each button should be and where on-screen it should be drawn. The programmer doesn't concern himself with these details when multiple widgets are competing for the same space.

However, the programmer certainly is concerned about the general appearance of the UI. Having a check box take up 95% of the area of a window and forcing the rest of the contents into the remaining 5% certainly wouldn't be appropriate. Because of this, each layout container provides its own functions to use when adding widgets to it, each providing a set of tunable parameters that specify generally where to place each widget and how large it should be. I will discuss these parameters in the section for each specific widget.

Layout containers are very important because they create the entire structure of your GUI. Each window in GTK+ is composed of various layout containers packed inside one another. I will return to this notion when discussing GtkBox, the most often-used layout container.

Decoration and Function Containers

GtkContainer objects are also used for decoration and function. These are typically derived from the GtkBin subclass of GtkContainer. These containers are less concerned with size and location; in fact they hold only one child and allow it all the space it needs.

Containers in this category change the way their children appear and behave. This allows GTK+ to include only a small number of basic widgets for displaying text and images, and then pack them inside other widgets to add more-complex behaviors. The text label widget, GtkLabel, for example, is a very basic widget used prominently throughout GTK+. When GtkLabel is packed within a layout container, it merely displays a string of text. When packed inside a GtkButton, however, a frame forms around it, giving it the appearance of a button, and it becomes clickable. Complex widgets are almost always built up from smaller widgets packed together.

Because layout isn't a concern for decoration and function containers, they typically don't have special functions for packing widgets inside them. Because they all derive from GtkContainer, you can use gtk_container_add(), which I'll discuss later this chapter.

GtkWindow

GtkWindow is a container widget that represents a top-level window. Every other widget in your GTK+ application will be packed inside a GtkWindow. To create a window, call gtk_window_new, which takes one argument, a GtkWindowType.

There are only two different GtkWindowType values currently: GTK_WINDOW_TOPLEVEL and GTK_WINDOW_POPUP. You will most likely use the former exclusively. GTK_WINDOW_TOPLEVEL is a standard application window with a title bar. GTK_WINDOW_POPUP is an unmanaged window with no title bar, and is used for things such as tooltips and menus. Both types of window are shown in Figure 5-6. An empty window is the most basic UI element you can create and show in GTK+. If I take the example main() function from earlier, I can create a window by adding a line between gtk_init() and gtk_main():

```
#include <gtk/gtk.h>
int main(int argc, char *argv[])
{
    GtkWidget *window;
    gtk_init(&argc, &argv);
    window = gtk_window_new(GTK_WINDOW_TOPLEVEL);
    gtk_widget_show_all(window);
    gtk_main()
    return 0;
}
```

Calling only gtk_window_new() will create a window in memory, but do nothing else. A widget will not appear on the screen until gtk_widget_show() is called on it. However, because it's often tedious to call gtk_window_show() on every widget individually, it's common to call gtk_widget_show_all() on a container widget such as GtkWindow, which will show the container and all its children recursively.

Figure 5-6. *Gaim's About dialog is a* GTK_WINDOW_TOPLEVEL GtkWindow *and the hyperlink context menu is a* GTK_WINDOW_POPUP GtkWindow.

As with all GTK+ objects, attributes of a GtkWindow are set with mutators. Some commonly used mutator functions for GtkWindow include the following:

- gtk_window_set_title(GtkWindow *window, const char *title) sets the window title. By default, GTK+ uses the command name of your program (such as gaim.exe), but the HIG recommends useful, relevant titles.

- gtk_window_set_default_size(GtkWindow *window, gint width, gint height) sets the initial size of the window.

- gtk_window_set_icon(GtkWindow *window, GdkPixbuf *pixbuf) sets the icon for this window. GdkPixbuf is an object representing an image, which I'll discuss next chapter.

By setting some attributes and calling gtk_widget_show_all() on the window, you have a simple program that creates an empty, but titled, window:

```
#include <gtk/gtk.h>
int main(int argc, char *argv[])
{
    GtkWidget *window;
    gtk_init(&argc, &argv);
    window = gtk_window_new(GTK_WINDOW_TOPLEVEL);
    gtk_window_set_title(GTK_WINDOW(window), "Window");
    gtk_window_set_default_size(GTK_WINDOW(window), 100, 100);
    gtk_widget_show_all(window);
    gtk_main();
    return 0;
}
```

This code creates, names, and shows an empty window, shown in Figure 5-7. This application won't do anything useful; it won't even terminate when the window is closed. In order to have the application terminate, you will need to request notification when the window is closed. Upon receiving the notification, you can call gtk_main_quit(). I will return to this in the "Event Listeners" section of this chapter.

Figure 5-7. *An empty GtkWindow*

GtkWindow is an inherited subclass of GtkContainer. Thus, to add widgets to a GtkWindow, use gtk_container_add(). Because GtkWindow is a decoration and function container, it has only one child. Therefore, any window that requires more than one widget packed inside it will need to pack some layout container within it, most often a GtkVBox, which we'll look at in the next section.

To close a window, call

```
gtk_widget_destroy(window);
```

As the namespace suggests, this function will work on any `GtkWidget`, but because changing your UI while a window is visible is usually a bad idea, it is almost always called on a `GtkWindow`. The function will recursively destroy any widget within a container, so destroying a `GtkWindow` will destroy all its contents, as well.

GtkBox

`GtkBox` is the most commonly used layout widget in GTK+ applications. It comes in two varieties, seen in Figure 5-8:

- `GtkHBox` lays out its children horizontally.

- `GtkVBox` lays out its children vertically.

Figure 5-8. *Icons packed inside a GtkVBox (left), and a GtkHBox (right).*

Most UIs will be created as a combination of the two, nested within each other.

To create a `GtkBox`, call either `gtk_hbox_new()` or `gtk_vbox_new()`, depending on which type of box you require. Both these functions take two arguments that affect how widgets will be packed inside. The first argument is `homogeneous`. If set to `TRUE`, the box will allocate equal space to all the widgets packed inside. If `FALSE`, it will allocate to each child only the space required by the widget. The second parameter, `spacing`, specifies the number of pixels to place between each element.

■**Tip** The GNOME HIG suggests that `spacing` should always be a multiple of six. Closely associated items, such as an icon and its corresponding text, should have little spacing between them. Items less closely related should increase the spacing by multiples of six accordingly.

GUIs tend to be vertical in nature; that is, structured from top to bottom. Therefore, you will most likely create a `GtkVBox` first and add that to your `GtkWindow`:

```
GtkWidget *window;
GtkWidget *vbox;

window = gtk_window_new(GTK_WINDOW_TOPLEVEL);
vbox = gtk_vbox_new(FALSE, 12);

gtk_window_set_title(GTK_WINDOW(window), "Window");
gtk_container_add(GTK_CONTAINER(window), vbox);
gtk_widget_show_all(window);
```

Note the `GTK_WINDOW` and `GTK_CONTAINER` macros. Because C has no concept of inheritance, GTK+ widgets are almost always declared as `GtkWidget`, as opposed to its specific class (GtkButton or GtkWindow). This allows for easier generic programming. Therefore, macros are provided to cast a `GtkWidget` to each specific type of widget. `GTK_WINDOW(window)` is equivalent to `(GtkWindow*)(window)`.

Because `GtkBox` descends from `GtkContainer`, `gtk_container_add()` could be used to add new widgets to vbox, but `GtkBox` provides a better interface for doing that in `gtk_box_pack_start()` and `gtk_box_pack_end()`, which allow you to specify certain rules the `GtkBox` should use when packing.

`gtk_box_pack_start()` packs widgets in the "start" of the box, and `gtk_box_pack_end()` packs them at the "end." For `GtkVBox` objects, the start is the top of the box, and the end is the bottom. For `GtkHBox` objects, this depends on localization settings. For languages that write from left to write (like English), the start is the left and the end is the right. This is reversed for languages that write from right to left (often referred to as *RTL languages*). You can see the result of this in Figure 5-9. The developer need do nothing else to achieve this effect; GTK+ does everything.

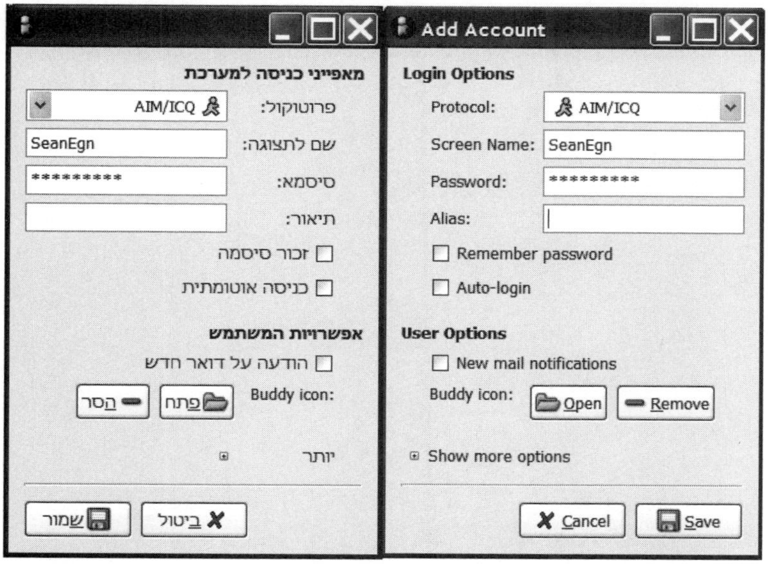

Figure 5-9. *Gaim's Add Account dialog in English and in Hebrew*

Both the `gtk_box_pack_start()` and `gtk_box_pack_end()` functions are otherwise identical. Each takes five arguments:

```
gtk_box_pack_start (GtkBox *box,
                    GtkWidget *widget,
                    gboolean expand,
                    gboolean fill,
                    guint padding);
```

- The box argument is the box in which to pack.

- The widget argument is the new widget to pack within box.

- The expand argument and the two following arguments precisely control how much space should be allocated and how it should be used. If expand is TRUE, the widget being added will evenly split any additional room in the GtkBox with any other widgets set to expand. If all widgets in the box have been packed not to expand, the remaining space in the box will be left empty. Figure 5-10 shows the effect of the expand parameter.

- The fill argument is used to determine how to use the space allocated to this widget if expand is set to TRUE. If both expand and fill are set to TRUE, additional space allocated to this child widget will be given to the child; the widget will be larger. If fill is FALSE, the widget will remain the same size, and the additional space will be left empty on either side of the widget. This empty space is referred to as *padding*, and can be explicitly set by the fifth argument.

- The padding argument is used to add additional space on either side of the newly added widget. This space is in addition to space added from the spacing argument used when creating the GtkBox. Thus, if you used a padding of 6 on a GtkBox with spacing of 12, there will be 18 pixels between this widget and its neighbors.

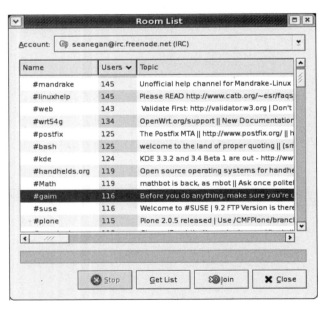

Figure 5-10. *The list of chat rooms in this widget is packed into its GtkVBox with expand set as TRUE. The drop-down menu above it and the progress bar and buttons beneath it are packed with expand set as FALSE. The other widgets take only as much room as they need, whereas the list gets allocated all the extra space available.*

You will probably never need a dialog window with all its widgets aligned in only one direction. You will need to nest GtkHBox objects inside your GtkVBox. You may then need to nest another GtkVBox in your GtkHBox. Figure 5-11 shows the nested GtkBox structure of Gaim's conversation window. A second way to lay out your widgets in two dimensions is the GtkTable widget.

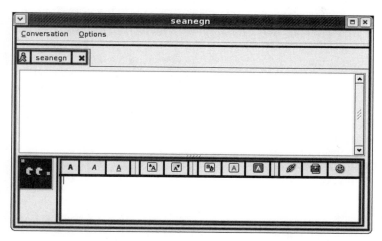

Figure 5-11. *Gaim's conversation window, like most GUIs, is composed of a series of nested containers. This screenshot shows how its widgets are packed into its structure.*

GtkButtonBox

GtkButtonBox, seen in Figure 5-12, descends from GtkBox and provides similar functionality. While GtkBox is used for generic GUI layout, GtkButtonBox is specifically tailored to laying out a set of related buttons.

Figure 5-12. *Gaim dialog boxes pack their buttons into a GtkButtonBox.*

A GtkButtonBox maintains a consistent look to the buttons contained within it with regard to size and spacing. Its children will be the same size, and appropriately spaced according to parameters you specify. Like GtkBox, GtkButtonBox is available in both horizontal and vertical varieties known as GtkVButtonBox and GtkHButtonBox. Creating one of these is straightforward:

```
GtkWidget *button_box = gtk_hbutton_box_new();
```

Because GtkButtonBox descends from GtkContainer, use gtk_container_add() to add widgets to it. You may also use gtk_box_pack_start() and gtk_box_pack_end() because it descends from GtkBox, but because the layout methods of GtkBox are overridden, there is no difference between using the GtkBox functions or the GtkButtonBox functions.

Usually, the default packing parameters will not need to be altered; rather than setting the packing parameters for each widget individually, you should set them for every button in the box with gtk_button_box_set_layout().

gtk_button_box_set_layout() takes a GtkButtonBoxStyle enum, which specifies how the buttons will be laid out within the box. Two of the possible styles are illustrated in Figure 5-13. GtkButtonBox shares the same concept of end and start as its parent class, GtkBox; end refers to a different position depending on locale. For English speakers, though, end means either the bottom or the right, depending on the orientation of the box. GtkButtonBox extends the possible layout styles. It might be helpful to make an analogy to a word-processor program:

- GTK_BUTTONBOX_END packs the widgets towards the end of the box. This is like "right-aligned," and is the most common layout setting.

- GTK_BUTTONBOX_START packs its widgets towards the start of the box. This is like "left-aligned."

- GTK_BUTTONBOX_SPREAD spaces out the buttons evenly throughout the box, leaving margins between the buttons and the edges of the box. This is like "centered."

- GTK_BUTTONBOX_EDGE is like GTK_BUTTONBOX_SPREAD but doesn't leave space between the edges of the box. This is like "justified."

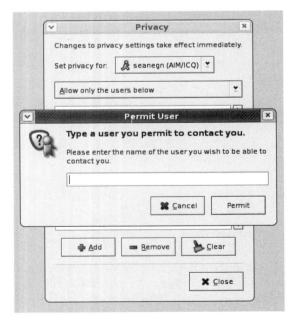

Figure 5-13. *Three GtkButtonBox objects are seen here in Gaim's Privacy dialog and its Permit User dialog. The main GtkButtonBox objects, at the bottom of each dialog, use GTK_BUTTONBOX_END. The GtkButtonBox for the permit list uses GTK_BUTTONBOX_SPREAD.*

GtkTable

When your dialog needs a level of alignment otherwise unattainable with nested vertical and horizontal boxes, a GtkTable can be used. A GtkTable allows you to add widgets in even rows and columns, as shown in Figure 5-14.

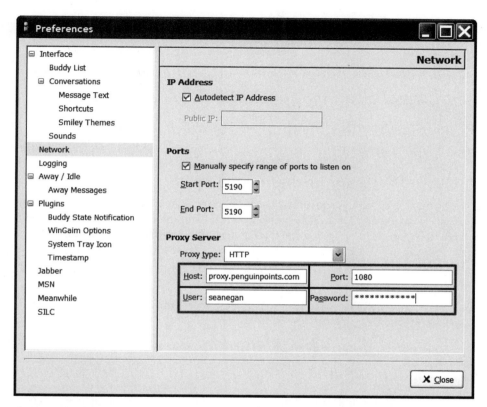

Figure 5-14. *The entry widgets for proxy details are arranged in a manner unachievable with GtkBox objects. The highlighted widgets are laid out with a GtkTable.*

When creating a GtkTable, you specify the number of rows and columns. You also specify whether you want the table to be homogeneous—that is, whether every cell should be the same size. To declare a table with two rows and four columns that takes as little space as possible, one would call

```
GtkWidget *table = gtk_table_new(2, 4, FALSE);
```

To add a widget to a table, use gtk_table_attach(), which accepts ten arguments defined as follows:

```
void gtk_table_attach (GtkTable *table,
                       GtkWidget *child,
                       guint left_attach,
                       guint right_attach,
                       guint top_attach,
                       guint bottom_attach,
                       GtkAttachOptions xoptions,
                       GtkAttachOptions yoptions,
                       guint xpadding,
                       guint ypadding);
```

- The table argument is the GtkTable affected by this operation.

- The child argument is the GtkWidget to be added to table.

- The left_attach argument specifies where in the table the left edge of widget should lie, starting at 0. To place a widget in the upper-leftmost cell in the table, one would use 0 here. The Host box in Figure 5-14 uses 0 as its left_attach.

- The right_attach argument specifies where the right edge of widget should lie within table, also starting at 0. This will normally be one greater than left_attach, but you may need to make your widget span more than one column, in which case the right side will be more than one away from the left side. If you're familiar with HTML, you can liken the difference between left_attach and right_attach to the colspan argument of a <td> element.

- The top_attach argument is like left_attach; it specifies the location of widget's top edge within table.

- The bottom_attach argument allows you to control how many rows the widget occupies. Like right_attach's relationship with left_attach, bottom_attach will usually be one greater than top_attach.

- The xoptions argument is a bitmask that allows you to fine-tune how the widget is packed, similar to the expand and fill options of gtk_box_pack_start(). The options set here affect the horizontal packing of the widget. Setting GTK_EXPAND and GTK_FILL are the GtkTable equivalent of setting expand and fill as TRUE in a GtkBox, respectively. GtkTable provides a third possibility, GTK_SHRINK, which causes the widget to shrink to the smallest possible size.

- The yoptions argument is exactly like xoptions, but it affects the widget's vertical packing.

- The xpadding argument is exactly like GtkBox's padding argument. It allows you to specify how much blank space should be left between this object and its neighbors to its left and right in pixels.

- The ypadding argument is like xpadding, but for vertical padding. ypadding specifies how many pixels should be left between the widget and its top and bottom neighbors.

■**Note** A bitmask is often used to consolidate multiple Boolean options into a single variable. Each option is designated a bit, usually by defining a constant as a power of two. These bits are then manipulated using the bitwise operators—mostly & and |. To set `GTK_EXPAND` and `GTK_FILL`, one would use "`GTK_EXPAND | GTK_FILL`". When the called function needs to check if `GTK_FILL` is checked, it will check if "`xoptions & GTK_FILL`" does not equal zero.

GtkScrolledWindow

Some widgets are too large to reasonably fit in a window without scrollbars that allow the user to choose only part of the widget to view at a time. To provide scrollbar functionality, add these widgets to a `GtkScrolledWindow`, shown in Figure 5-15.

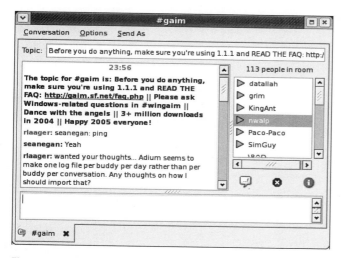

Figure 5-15. *Neither the user list nor either text area in this chat window support scrolling by themselves. All three are packed into a* `GtkScrolledWindow` *that provides that functionality.*

A `GtkScrolledWindow` is created by calling the following:

```
GtkWidget *gtk_scrolled_window_new(GtkAdjustment *hadjustment,
                                   GtkAdjustment *vadjustment);
```

The `GtkAdjustment` argument represents a value within a given range. It is mainly used internal to GTK+. As such, you can probably make both arguments to `gtk_scrolled_window_new()` NULL, which will cause the widget to create and maintain `GtkAdjustment` objects itself.

As with all container widgets, because `GtkScrolledWindow` derives from `GtkContainer`, you can add a widget to `GtkScrolledWindow` with `gtk_container_add()`. Few widgets support scrolling natively, although you'll rarely need scrollbars on other widgets. If you do wish to add scrollbars to another widget (perhaps you wish to add a `GtkBox` to a scrolled window) you can do so with `gtk_scrolled_window_add_with_viewport()`, which will add the necessary hooks. However, if this is necessary, you'd probably be better off rethinking your UI design.

GtkScrolledWindow also contains functions that affect its appearance. gtk_scrolled_window_set_shadow_type() allows you to add a bezel to its child as seen in Figure 5-15. gtk_scrolled_window_set_policy() controls when the scrollbars are visible. It's recommended you use GTK_POLICY_AUTOMATIC, which will show them when and only when they're necessary.

GtkNotebook

GtkNotebook is an interesting container in that it shows only one of its children at a time. The user can choose which child to view by selecting a tab provided by the GtkNotebook UI. Tabs are useful in limiting the amount of UI presented to the user at one time, such as in a preferences dialog, and in consolidating redundant UI to a single window, such as in Gaim's tabbed conversation windows, seen in Figure 5-16.

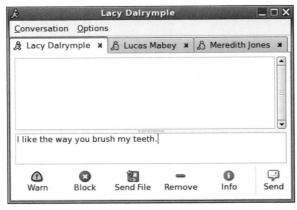

Figure 5-16. *Gaim's familiar tabbed conversation windows use* GtkNotebook *to provide those tabs.*

GtkNotebook's constructor takes no arguments. To create a GtkNotebook object, just call

GtkWidget *notebook = gtk_notebook_new();

To add children to a GtkNotebook, call gtk_notebook_append_page() to insert it after the other children, or gtk_notebook_prepend_page() to insert it before the other children.

gtk_notebook_append_page() and gtk_notebook_prepend_page() are otherwise identical and each takes three arguments:

```
gtk_notebook_append_page( GtkNotebook *notebook,
                          GtkWidget *widget,
                          GtkWidget *tab_label);
```

- The notebook argument is the GtkNotebook affected by this call.

- The widget argument is the widget to add. This can be any widget, but will almost always be a GtkBox or some other layout container.

- The third argument is a widget that will show in the tab corresponding to this child. This will probably be just a GtkLabel; the widget that shows a string. However, this can be anything—Gaim's conversation windows use a GtkBox packed with an icon and a label.

To add a container widget, vbox, to a notebook, with tablabel used as the label widget, call

```
gtk_notebook_append_page(GTK_NOTEBOOK(notebook), vbox, tablabel);
```

In addition to gtk_notebook_append_page() and gtk_notebook_prepend_page(), gtk_notebook_insert_page allows you to insert a page to a specific location within the other tabs. This location is given in a third argument and starts from 0. To make the new child the fourth tab in the notebook, call

```
gtk_notebook_append_page(GTK_NOTEBOOK(notebook), vbox, tablabel, 3);
```

GtkPaned

The containers discussed so far will size and position their children themselves, usually obeying some rules set by the developer. GtkPaned, shown in Figure 5-17, is unique in that it allows the user to resize its children.

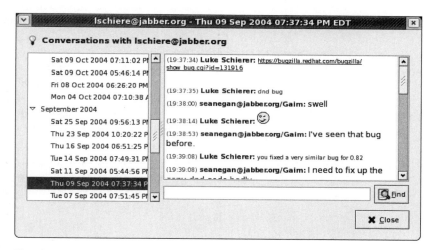

Figure 5-17. *Gaim's log viewer uses* GtkPaned, *allowing the user to choose how much of the window each UI element occupies.*

A GtkPaned container has exactly two children and comes in a horizontal and vertical variety, GtkHPaned and GtkVPaned respectively. To create a GtkHPaned object, call

```
GtkWidget *paned = gtk_hpaned_new();
```

Then adding children is as simple as calling

```
gtk_paned_add1(GTK_PANED(paned), widget1);
gtk_paned_add2(GTK_PANED(paned), widget2);
```

gtk_paned_add1() adds the child to the top of a GtkVPaned and the left (or right, in right-to-left locales) of a GtkHPaned object. gtk_paned_add2() logically adds its child to the other side.

GtkBin

A final subclass of GtkContainer is GtkBin. GtkBin is a container with only a single child. This is not used for layout purposes, but for decorative or functional purposes. Examples include

GtkFrame, which provides decoration to its child by drawing a thin line around it, and GtkButton, which provides functionality by allowing its child to be clicked.

Event Listeners

Now that you know how to present your interface to the user, how does the application respond to user interaction? The answer is in GTK+'s event system. When creating your UI, you will attach callbacks to various *signals* that represent UI events such as a button being pressed. When this event happens, the callback will be triggered.

Signals

Because your program waits within gtk_main() for the duration of the process, signals are used to give control to other functions in your code. The act of associating a function with a signal is called *connecting* to that signal. You will connect to a signal, such as "clicked", with a callback function and when that signal is sent (emitted), by the user clicking the widget, your callback is called. Signals are specific to a type of widget (or other object) and are identified by strings.

The signal system is part of GLib, so any GObject may emit signals. Also, if an object emits a signal (such as GtkButton's "clicked" signal), inherited classes (such as GtkToggleButton) will also emit that signal when applicable.

This results in a few very low-level signals implemented in GtkWidget that all widgets can then call. Many of these correspond directly to events in the X Window System and are appropriately named by suffixing them with "-event." These are typically useful only when extending GTK+ beyond its default behaviors and abilities, which will be discussed in the next chapter.

You will generally rely more on higher-level signals emitted by widgets. To connect a callback function to a signal, call g_signal_connect():

```
g_signal_connect (GObject *instance, const char *signal_name,
                  GCallback *callback, void *data);
```

The instance argument represents the object you're connecting to. You must attach to each instance of the object individually; you obviously don't want the same behavior for every button. You may, however, connect the same callback to more than one instance. The "clicked" signal of each Send button in a Gaim conversation is connected to the same function, but to a different button from the Get Info button. The signal_name argument is the string identifier for this signal that is listed in the API documentation. The callback argument is the function to be called when the signal is emitted. The data argument is a pointer passed to that callback function.

When you connect more than one instance of a button (or other widget) to the same function, the data argument determines what instance triggered the callback. When Gaim connects to the "clicked" signal of a Send button, it uses a pointer to the conversation as its data. That way, the callback knows which conversation it should send from.

Callbacks

The callback is a function pointer, the arguments and return type of which will depend on the signal. The arguments will provide any relevant information about the signal that was emitted. Callbacks rarely require a return value, but when they do (as in the low-level X Window System events that are rarely used in normal applications) they most often allow the developer to *short-circuit* the signal, that is to prevent it from propagating any further.

The first argument of the callback will always be the object the signal occurred on, and the last will be the data argument you gave to g_signal_connect() (unless you used g_signal_connect_swapped(), which swaps the two arguments). Other arguments may exist, sandwiched by these two.

Note that there is only a single void pointer for assigning data to be sent to the callback function. If you need to send more than one variable, you will need to create your own struct and pass a pointer to it. Make sure to clean up any allocated memory in the callback function if necessary. But be sure not to free any memory until you're sure the callback will never be called with that data again. This may mean not destroying it until the widget is destroyed. You can connect a callback to the "destroy" signal of a widget to receive that notification. This is also the signal to connect to in order to detect when a GtkWindow is closed.

A Sample GTK+ Application

So far this chapter, we've created an application that creates an empty window. However, because we don't have any code to run when the window is closed, the program continues to run with no visible UI. Let's create a callback function that calls gtk_main_quit() and attach it to the "destroy" signal of the window:

```
#include <gtk/gtk.h>

/* This is our new callback function. */
/* The names of callback functions are often appended with _cb */
void window_destroy_cb(GtkObject *window, void *data)
{
    /* This call causes gtk_main() to return, terminating your application */
    gtk_main_quit();
}

int main(int argc, char *argv[])
{
    GtkWidget *window, *toolbar, *tool_button;
    gtk_init(&argc, &argv);
    window = gtk_window_new(GTK_WINDOW_TOPLEVEL);
    gtk_window_set_default_size(GTK_WINDOW(window), 100, 100);
    gtk_window_set_title(GTK_WINDOW(window), "Window")
    /* Here I attach the signal. I won't need any extra data in;
     * the callback, so I use NULL as the data */
    g_signal_connect(G_OBJECT(window), "destroy", window_destroy_cb, NULL);
    gtk_widget_show_all(window);
    gtk_main();
    return 0;
}
```

This program will create an empty window and terminate when the window is closed. I will use the same signal concept throughout the rest of this chapter as I explain what signals are emitted by widgets.

Gaim Signals

Gaim itself has its own signals system used by plug-ins. Using these signals is very similar to using GTK+'s signals, but Gaim signals are better suited to what Gain plug-ins need.

While GTK+ signals communicate interface events, such as a check box being toggled, Gaim signals communicate events such as "a buddy signed on," or "a message was received." Signals like these are useful for plug-ins; most of them are specifically interested in processing incoming and outgoing messages.

Gaim plug-ins will often want to know anytime a message comes in or a buddy signs off, for instance. Unlike GTK+ signals, which are closely tied to an instance (they get triggered only when one particular button is clicked), Gaim signals are globally called when any buddy signs in or conversation receives a new message. As such, they aren't tied to a GaimBuddy, a GaimConversation, or any single object, but rather to a *handle* representing all buddies or all conversations.

Signals can come from a variety of sources, each with its own handle:

- gaim_accounts_get_handle() returns a handle for account signals such as when an account's away status or profile information changes.

- gaim_blist_get_handle() returns a handle for buddy list signals. These signals are emitted when your buddies sign on, sign off, or otherwise change status.

- gaim_connections_get_handle() returns a handle for connection signals. These are emitted when one of the user's accounts signs on or off.

- gaim_conversations_get_handle() returns a handle for conversation signals. These signals include notifications when messages are sent or received.

To connect to a Gaim signal, call gaim_signal_connect(), which is very similar to g_signal_connect().

```
gaim_signal_connect(gaim_conversations_get_handle(),
                "received-im-msg", plugin, msg_rcv_cb, NULL);
```

You should recognize that gaim_conversations_get_handle() is here used where a widget is normally used. The name of the signal is represented as a string as with GTK+ signals. msg_rcv_cb and NULL are here the callback function and the data sent to it. The only remaining argument is plugin.

When your plug-in is unloaded, its callback function is invalid and can no longer be called. This means that the callback must be disconnected. One way to accomplish this would be to require every plug-in to disconnect its own signals. This would be tedious and error-prone, though. It's better to have Gaim disconnect from the signals itself. To do this, it must know what plug-in is making each call to gaim_signal_connect(). A plug-in must then pass its GaimPlugin object to gaim_signal_connect().

This is rarely any effort, as the GaimPlugin object is passed to the plug-in's plugin_load() function, from which almost every gaim_signal_connect() call is made:

```
static gboolean plugin_load(GaimPlugin *plugin)
{
    gaim_signal_connect(gaim_conversations_get_handle(),
                        "received-im-msg",
                        plugin, msg_rcv, cb, NULL);
    return TRUE;
}
```

A complete list of all of Gaim's signals is available at http://gaim.sourceforge.net/api/pages.html.

GTK+ Widgets

Widgets can be grouped into a few distinct categories. I've already discussed layout widgets—such as GtkBox and GtkTable—and mentioned decoration widgets such as GtkFrame. What remains are the most crucial widgets, namely those that provide input and output.

GtkLabel

GtkLabel is perhaps the most straightforward widget included with GTK+. A GtkLabel simply displays text. This text can either be plain unformatted text, or it can be formatted with Pango markup. All the text seen in Figure 5-18, except the window title, are GtkLabel widgets.

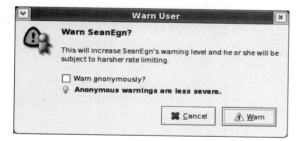

Figure 5-18. *GtkLabel displays a small bit of text, but it can still use a vast array of formatting, as seen in the Warn User dialog.*

Creating a GtkLabel is straightforward. Just call

```
GtkWidget* gtk_label_new(const char *str);
```

The str argument is the text to use for the label. If you need to change this text later, call

```
void gtk_label_set_text(GtkLabel *label, const char *str);
```

with your new text assigned to the str argument. If you want to use formatted text with Pango markup, call

```
void gtk_label_set_markup (GtkLabel *label, const gchar *str);
```

Additionally, both of these functions have variants that allow you set a *mnemonic* for this label. A mnemonic is an underlined character in a GtkLabel. Although useless by itself, when the GtkLabel is used to identify the purpose of another widget (such as packed inside a button or next to a check box), it provides the user with a keyboard shortcut to activating that widget. To add a mnemonic, call

```
void gtk_label_set_text_with_mnemonic(GtkLabel *label, const char *str)
```

or

```
void gtk_label_set_markup_with_mnemonic (GtkLabel *label, const gchar *str);
```

Be sure to add an underscore before the character you want underlined. For example, to create a label that reads "Cancel," you would set your label text to "_Cancel".

To associate the widget with this label, call

```
void gtk_label_set_mnemonic_widget (GtkLabel *label, GtkWidget *widget);
```

where widget is the widget this label will activate.

GtkImage

GtkImage is another straightforward widget that merely shows an icon to the user. This icon can come from a variety of sources, but will most commonly come from file or from *stock*. Like GtkLabel, GtkImage widgets are often used packed within other widgets wherever an image is needed. Figure 5-19 shows a GtkImage widget inside a button.

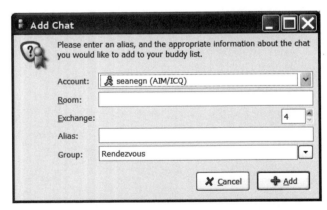

Figure 5-19. *The "question" icon and the icons on the buttons in the Add Chat dialog are all GtkImage objects.*

GTK+ provides a system of stock items. These allow you to easily create commonly used buttons, toolbars, and menus with user-themed icons and text already translated into over 50 languages. Stock items include GTK_STOCK_OPEN, GTK_STOCK_EDIT, GTK_STOCK_ERROR, and GTK_STOCK_UNDERLINE. A complete list can be found with the GTK+ documentation.

These stock icons come in a variety of sizes for different uses. They can be small for menus, medium-sized for toolbars, and large for dialogs. A set of different-sized icons for the same stock item is called a GtkIconSet. GTK+ provides APIs for retrieving images from a GtkIconSet (check the documentation on GtkIconFactory), but GtkImage provides useful convenience functions that allow you to forgo using it in creating GtkImage objects.

To create a new GtkImage object from a stock icon, call

```
GtkWidget* gtk_image_new_from_icon_name (const gchar *icon_name, GtkIconSize size);
```

where the icon_name argument is the name of your stock icon, such as GTK_STOCK_INFO, and the size argument. GTK+ #defines several sizes for you to use for various purposes:

- GTK_ICON_SIZE_MENU is used in menu items.

- GTK_ICON_SIZE_SMALL_TOOLBAR is used in small toolbars, such as the formatting toolbar in Gaim conversation windows.

- GTK_ICON_SIZE_LARGE_TOOLBAR is used in large toolbars. Gaim doesn't use any large toolbars, but one can be seen in the gedit application in Figure 5-2.

- GTK_ICON_SIZE_BUTTON is used for icons in buttons. Many buttons in Gaim have icons as well as text in them; these are sized to GTK_ICON_SIZE_BUTTON.

- GTK_ICON_SIZE_DND is used for creating an icon that represents an object being dragged with the mouse. Because most widgets implement drag-and-drop themselves, this is used mostly internal to GTK+.

- GTK_ICON_SIZE_DIALOG is used for creating the large icons seen in dialog boxes, such as the "question" icon seen in Figure 5-19.

Of course, for less commonly used images, you can create an image from file. To do this call

```
GtkWidget* gtk_image_new_from_file (const gchar filename);
```

Note that you cannot change the image when creating a GtkImage from file. If you need to make simple changes to the image, such as scaling to a certain size, you will need to create a GdkPixbuf, edit it, and then create your GtkImage with

```
GtkWidget* gtk_image_new_from_file (GdkPixbuf *pixbuf);
```

I will demonstrate creating and manipulating images with GdkPixbuf in Chapter 6.

GtkProgressBar

GtkProgressBar, shown in Figure 5-20, is a visualization that some action is currently taking place. When your application performs a task that will not complete in time that can be perceived as "instant," you should use a progress bar to indicate that it is working.

GtkProgressBar can behave in two distinct manners: If the activity being performed will take a predictable amount of time and the progress can be measured, *percentage mode* should be used. In percentage mode, the GtkProgressBar appears as a bar continually growing to fill an empty space.

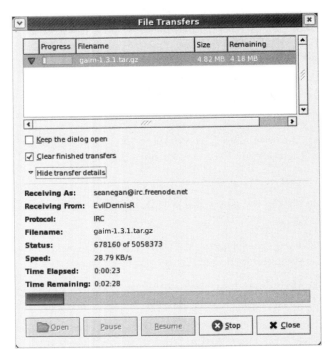

Figure 5-20. *Gaim's File Transfers dialog uses a* GtkProgressBar *object at the bottom of the window to display the progress of the selected transfer.*

If your task is less predictable, use a bar in *activity* mode. In this mode, a small bar will pulse back and forth within the empty space when activity has occurred, indicating that the application has not locked up but is busy processing.

To create a GtkProgressBar object call

```
GtkWidget* gtk_progress_bar_new (void);
```

By default this will behave in percent mode. When your activity has made progress—perhaps a byte of a file transfer was downloaded—call

```
void gtk_progress_bar_set_fraction  (GtkProgressBar *pbar, gdouble fraction);
```

where the fraction argument is the percentage of the task completed. Note that this value is from 0.0 to 1.0, not from 0 to 100.

You needn't explicitly put the GtkProgressBar object into activity mode. If you call

```
void gtk_progress_bar_pulse (GtkProgressBar *pbar);
```

on a percentage-mode progress bar, it will implicitly change to activity mode. Likewise, calling gtk_progress_bar_set_fraction() on a GtkProgressBar object in activity mode will return it to percentage mode. You will need to pulse the bar yourself on a regular basis to keep it moving.

Other functions included with GtkProgressBar allow you to customize the appearance of the bar. You can choose which direction the bar travels with gtk_progress_bar_set_orientation(). You can set text to appear on top of the bar with gtk_progress_bar_set_text(). And you can set the width of the pulsing bar used in activity mode with gtk_progress_bar_set_pulse_step().

GtkEntry

GtkEntry is a widget used to allow the user to type a short single line of text. Gaim uses it in dialogs to request data like screen names or passwords, as seen in Figure 5-21. Longer, multi-line text is typed into a GtkTextView widget, discussed later in this chapter. In addition to the user typing text himself, the text and the way it's displayed can be modified by the application programmatically.

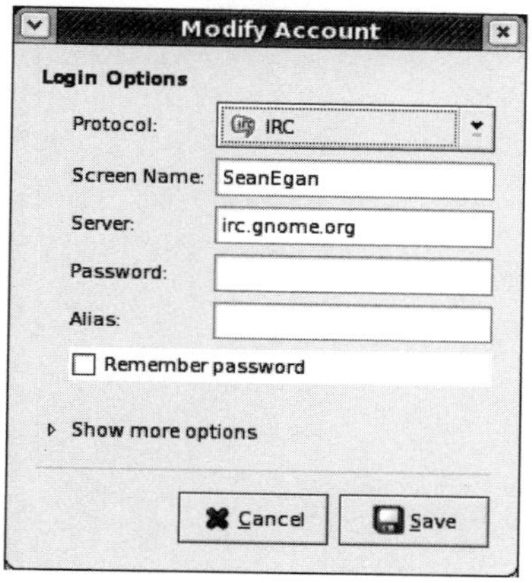

Figure 5-21. *The Modify Account dialog has four* GtkEntry *widgets to input small amounts of text.*

To create a GtkEntry, call

```
GtkWidget *gtk_entry_new();
```

This will create an empty GtkEntry widget ready to accept text. To set the text to some default, call

```
void gtk_entry_set_text(GtkEntry *entry, const gchar *text);
```

where the text argument is the text you're setting. After creating the widget, setting the default text, and presenting it to the user by adding it to a container window, you will likely want to wait for a signal to be passed (often to some other widget such as a button associated with the GtkEntry object, although GtkEntry does offer some signals you might find useful here). When you receive this signal and need to retrieve the contents of the GtkEntry object, call

```
const gchar *gtk_entry_get_text( GtkEntry *entry );
```

which returns the text in the widget. The most important signal emitted by GtkEntry—one that will be emitted by many other widgets, as well—is the "activate" signal.

A widget emits the "activate" signal when the user activates it; what that means depends mostly on the widget. In the context of GtkEntry, it usually means that the user has finished entering his text and pressed the Enter button.

A Sample GTK+ Application

Now that you've seen two widgets, how to add them to a window, and how to receive notifications from events, see if you understand how the short program in Listing 5-1 works.

Listing 5-1. *An Example Creating, Packing, and Connecting Callbacks to a GtkEntry Object*

```
01 #include <gtk/gtk.h>
02
03 static void activate_cb(GtkWidget *entry, void *data)
04 {
05     const char *text = gtk_entry_get_text(entry);
06     printf("%s\n", text);
07 }
08
09 int main(int argc, char *argv[])
10 {
11     GtkWidget *window, *hbox, *entry, *label;
12     gtk_init(&argc, &argv);
13     window = gtk_window_new(GTK_WINDOW_TOPLEVEL);
14     gtk_window_set_title(GTK_WINDOW(window), "Window");
15     hbox = gtk_hbox_new(FALSE, 6);
16     gtk_container_add(GTK_CONTAINER(window), hbox);
17     label = gtk_label_new("Text");
18     gtk_box_pack_start(GTK_BOX(hbox), label, FALSE, FALSE, 0);
19     entry = gtk_entry_new();
20     g_signal_connect(G_OBJECT(entry), "activate", activate_cb, NULL);
21     gtk_box_pack_start(GTK_BOX(hbox), entry, TRUE, TRUE, 0);
22     gtk_widget_show_all(window);
23     gtk_main();
24     return 0;
25 }
```

When compiled and run, the code in Listing 5-1 shows the window shown in Figure 5-22. When text is typed in the GtkEntry widget and the Enter key is pressed, the typed text is output to the console. Let's take a closer look at this code:

```
03 static void activate_cb(GtkWidget *entry, void *data)
04 {
05     const char *text = gtk_entry_get_text(GTK_ENTRY(entry));
06     printf("%s\n", text);
07 }
```

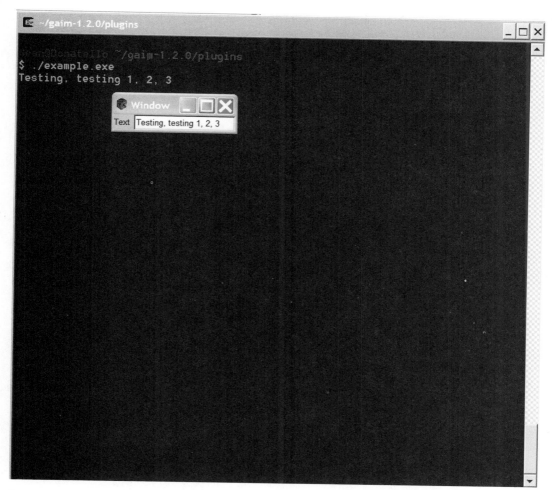

Figure 5-22. *A window with a* GtkEntry *and a callback connected to its* "activate" *signal.*

Lines 3–7 are the callback function from the GtkEntry "activate" signal. This signal provides no arguments of its own. The callback takes the two default arguments given to any callback: the object which emitted the signal, and the data given to it by g_signal_connect(). Because the instance of GtkEntry in which the user hits Enter is the instance that emits the signal, I can use the entry parameter in my call to gtk_entry_get_text(). I then printf() that result. This is a simple example of a callback function; a more complex callback might create more windows itself. When you double-click someone's name in the Gaim buddy list, a callback that creates a conversation window is called. Before that callback returns, a new window is created, the appropriate widgets are packed into it, and callbacks are attached to its signals.

In the main() function, I first initialize GTK+, and create and name a window. You should be familiar with this procedure from earlier examples this chapter. Next, I start building the UI within the window.

There are basically three things you must do for every widget you create:

- **Create the widget.** This much is obvious; you must create the widget by calling its constructor, such as gtk_entry_new().

- **Pack the widget into a container.** Unless the widget is added to a container within a window, it will always be invisible. The one exception, of course, is GtkWindow, the widget into which all other widgets are ultimately packed.

- **Show the widget.** A common mistake is to forget to call the gtk_widget_show() function on the new widget. Fortunately, calling the gtk_widget_show_all() function on the GtkWindow to which the widget is added has the effect of calling gtk_widget_show() on every widget within.

There are several different ways of doing this. Some people prefer to create all the widgets, then add each into a container, and then finally show them all. Others prefer to create, pack, and show all at once before moving on to the next widget. I prefer to create and pack at the same time, and then show later, when I've created the entire window, by calling gtk_widget_show_all(). I also call methods belonging to each widget, and connect to its signals as I create them. This way all the code relating to a specific widget is found in one place, as seen in Listing 5-1.

The order in which I create the widgets is essentially dictated by the UI's structure; I can't add a widget to a container that doesn't yet exist. Then, because within a GtkBox I can only pack new children to either end (i.e., I can't pack them in between two widgets already added), I create the widgets in the order they'll be packed. Here, I create them as they'll appear from left to right.

Because g_signal_connect() takes a GObject, it's necessary to cast entry to a GObject. The callback here is activated_cb() and takes no arguments other than the entry affected and the data attached:

```
15      hbox = gtk_hbox_new(FALSE, 6);
16      gtk_container_add(GTK_CONTAINER(window), hbox);
```

hbox is the first widget I create so that I can than pack other widgets into it. In line 16, I add the box to the window.

```
17      label = gtk_label_new("Text");
18      gtk_box_pack_start(GTK_BOX(hbox), label, FALSE, FALSE, 0);
```

In lines 17 and 18, I create and pack a GtkLabel widget.

```
19      entry = gtk_entry_new();
20      g_signal_connect(G_OBJECT(entry), "activate", activate_cb, NULL);
21      gtk_box_pack_start(GTK_BOX(hbox), label, TRUE, TRUE, 0);
```

In lines 19–21, I create the GtkEntry object, connect the callback to its "activate" signal, and pack it into the box. Finally, in line 22, I show all the widgets I've packed inside the window:

```
22      gtk_widget_show_all(window);
```

GtkSpinButton

GtkSpinButton, seen in Figure 5-23, descends from GtkEntry and is specifically suited for entering numeric values. In addition to allowing the user to type a numeric value, two buttons are displayed next to the entry, allowing the user to increase or decrease the value depending on which he presses.

Figure 5-23. *In Gaim's Auto-Away preferences, a* GtkSpinButton *object is used to input how long a user can be idle before his away status changes.*

Like GtkScrolledWindow, described in the "Container Widgets" section of this chapter, GtkSpinButton makes use of the GtkAdjustment object to control the current value and certain parameters defining how the buttons will affect it. These parameters include upper and lower bounds and the amount by which the value is incremented when a button is pressed. To create a GtkSpinButton, you must first create a GtkAdjustment or use a convenience function that will do this for you.

To create a GtkSpinButton without worrying about creating your own GtkAdjustment, call

GtkWidget *gtk_spin_button_new_with_range(gdouble min, gdouble max, gdouble step);

- The min argument is the minimum value allowed to be entered in the spin button.

- The max argument is the maximum value allowed to be entered in the spin button.

- The step argument is the how much the value will be incremented or decremented each time one of the buttons is clicked.

Because GtkSpinButton descends from GtkEntry, you can use gtk_entry_set_text() and gtk_entry_get_text() to set values, but because you are dealing solely with numeric values, you'll usually want to use gtk_spin_button_set_value() and gtk_spin_button_get_value().

You may sometimes be interested in connecting to the "value-changed" signal emitted by GtkSpinButton. It is emitted whenever the value changes; a callback is called, from which you may call gtk_spin_button_get_value() to discover what the value changed to. However, you will often not care about changes to either GtkEntry or GtkSpinButton when they happen.

In a standard dialog, several fields of information are requested and an OK button is provided to acknowledge the values entered. In GTK+, this means you'll often call gtk_spin_button_get_value() and gtk_entry_get_text() not from their own callbacks, but from a callback triggered when a GtkButton is pressed.

GtkButton

GtkButton is a container widget that draws a raised border around its child and allows it to be clicked. The Room List dialog shown in Figure 5-24 includes several buttons. Although any widget can be packed inside a GtkButton, almost always this will be a GtkLabel widget or a GtkImage widget (or more accurately, a GtkVBox object containing a GtkLabel widget and a GtkImage widget).

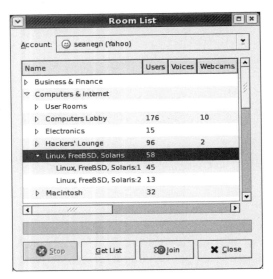

Figure 5-24. *The Room List dialog includes four GtkButton objects at the bottom.*

The gtk_button_new() function will return an empty GtkButton into which you can pack a GtkWidget. However, it's often more useful to use one of the convenience functions to create GtkButton objects with commonly used widgets already packed inside.

The first of these convenience functions is gtk_button_new_with_label(). This function takes a single argument—a string—and uses it to create a GtkLabel() within the button. It would be called as such:

```
GtkWidget *button = gtk_button_new_with_label("Button");
```

If you want to create a keyboard access key for this button, use gtk_button_new_with_mnemonic(); the syntax is exactly the same as gtk_button_new_with_label() but prepends the mnemonic character with an underscore to indicate it as such. Calling

```
GtkWidget *button = gtk_button_new_with_mnemonic("B_utton");
```

creates a button with a label that will look like "Button." This mnemonic is a cue to the user that if he hits Alt-U, the program will behave just as if he pressed it with the mouse. This keystroke is also programmatically identical to pressing the button; the "clicked" signal will be emitted. Pressing the button with the mouse and using the mnemonic keystroke are identical to your program.

The final convenience function uses stock items, already discussed for GtkImage. Calling

```
GtkWidget *button = gtk_button_new_from_stock(GTK_STOCK_CANCEL);
```

will create a stock Cancel button, containing a GtkLabel object with text translated in the current language and the standard Cancel icon as seen in Figure 5-25.

Figure 5-25. *Gaim's dialogs use stock items when available, such as the Cancel button created for the Add Group dialog with* gtk_button_new_from_stock(GTK_STOCK_CANCEL).

A GtkButton object will emit several signals as the user interacts with it. None of the callback functions have return values or parameters other than the button object itself and the data given to g_signal_connect():

- The "clicked" signal is, by far, the most important. It is emitted when the button is pressed.

- The "pressed" signal is emitted when the button is pressed, but before it is released.

- The "released" signal is emitted when the button is released.

- The "enter" signal is emitted when the mouse cursor enters the area occupied by the button and hovers over it.

- The "leave" signal is emitted when the mouse cursor hovers over the button. The "enter" and "leave" signals have little practical use in most applications.

The following program will create a window with a GtkEntry and a GtkButton. When the button is pressed, the program will print the contents of the entry to the console and quit.

```
#include <gtk/gtk.h>
#include <stdio.h>

void button_clicked_cb(GtkWidget *button, GtkWidget *entry)
{
    const char *text = gtk_entry_get_text(GTK_ENTRY(entry));
    printf("%s\n", text);

    /* gtk_main_quit causes the GTK+ main loop to terminate */
    gtk_main_quit();
}

int main(int argc, char **argv)
{
    GtkWidget *window;
    GtkWidget *vbox;
    GtkWidget *entry;
    GtkWidget *button;
    gtk_init(&argc, &argv);
```

```
    /* After initializing GTK+, but before entering the main loop,
     * we must create our intial GUI */
    window = gtk_window_new(GTK_WINDOW_TOPLEVEL);
    gtk_window_set_title(GTK_WINDOW(window), "Example");
    vbox = gtk_vbox_new(FALSE, 0);

    /* Because a GtkWindow is also a GtkContainer, add the main
     * box used for layout into it as such.  Pack the other
     * widgets into that box */
    gtk_container_add(GTK_CONTAINER(window), vbox);
    entry = gtk_entry_new();
    gtk_box_pack_start(GTK_BOX(vbox), entry, FALSE, FALSE, 0);
    button = gtk_button_new_from_stock(GTK_STOCK_OK);
    gtk_box_pack_start(GTK_BOX(vbox), button, TRUE, TRUE, 0);

    /* Here connect to the "clicked" signal, causing clicked_cb
     * to be called when the button is clicked. By attaching
     * 'entry' as the data, clicked_cb will be able to get the
     * text from it. */
    g_signal_connect(G_OBJECT(button), "clicked", button_clicked_cb, entry);

    /* Remember that all widgets are invisible until
     * gtk_widget_show() is called on them. gtk_widget_show_all()
     * recursively calls this on a container and all the children
     * within. */
    gtk_widget_show_all(window);

    /* Finally, all gtk_main(). This function will not return
     * until gtk_main_quit() is called from some callback. In
     * this example, it's called in clicked_cb(). */
    gtk_main();
    return 0;
}
```

GtkToggleButton

A GtkToggleButton is nearly identical to a GtkButton, which it descends from, with the addition of an *active* state. As shown in Figure 5-26, when the button is active, it appears depressed; an inactive button looks the same as an ordinary button.

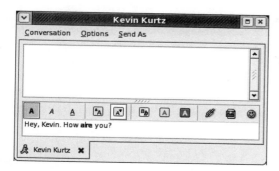

Figure 5-26. *GtkToggleButton objects are used in Gaim's formatting toolbar. Here they indicate that bold is active, while italics and underline are not.*

Creating a GtkToggleButton object is much like creating a GtkButton object. Calling gtk_toggle_button_new() creates an empty toggle button in which you can pack widgets. Just like with GtkButton, though, gtk_toggle_button_new_with_label() and gtk_toggle_button_ new_with_mnemonic() are available for the most common applications of GtkToggleButton.

Descending from GtkButton, GtkToggleButton works just like a GtkButton with a few extensions related to its active state. Two functions, gtk_toggle_button_get_active() and gtk_toggle_set_ active(), get and set the state, which is represented as a gboolean type. Also, a GtkToggleButton object emits the toggled signal whenever the state changes. Like all the signals I've discussed so far, this signal has no additional arguments, nor a return type.

GtkCheckButton

The only difference between a GtkCheckButton, shown in Figure 5-27, and its parent class, GtkToggleButton, is its appearance. A GtkToggleButton object appears just like a GtkButton object with its child inside it, state represented by whether the button appears depressed or not. A GtkCheckButton object appears as a small check box with its child to the side. The active state is represented by whether the check box is checked or not.

Using a GtkCheckButton is no different from using a GtkToggleButton. Use gtk_toggle_ button_get_active() and gtk_toggle_set_active() when appropriate by casting the GtkCheckButton object to GtkToggleButton. The only way the syntax differs is in specifying which button type to create. However, even this is merely a difference between calling gtk_ check_button_new() instead of gtk_toggle_button_new(). Even the convenience functions, gtk_check_button_new_with_label() and gtk_check_button_new_with_mnemonic() exist.

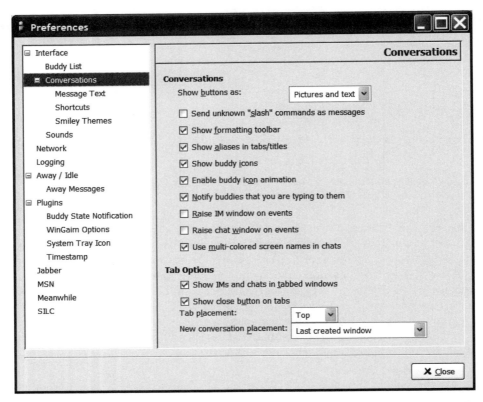

Figure 5-27. *GtkCheckButton objects are often used for Boolean preferences, as they are here in Gaim's Preferences dialog.*

GtkRadioButton

GtkRadioButton is a subclass of GtkCheckButton with the notion that several GtkRadioButton objects can be grouped together, and only one may be active at a time. GtkRadioButton is used to give a choice between several options. When one GtkRadioButton object is set as active, all the others in its group are set as inactive. GtkRadioButton is shown in Figure 5-28.

Figure 5-28. *Dragging an image file on a buddy brings up this dialog, which uses a group of GtkRadioButton objects to request what the user wants to do with this image.*

A group of GtkRadioButton objects is implemented as a GSList, GLib's singly linked list data structure. Although you can manipulate GtkRadioButton groups directly via the GSList, GTK+ provides APIs that allow you to avoid this.

gtk_radio_button_new() (and its _with_label and _with_mnemonic convenience functions) takes a GSList as an argument. To create your first GtkRadioButton object, call this function with a NULL list (GTK recognizes NULL as an empty list and will realize that this is the first radio button in this list).

For subsequent buttons in the same group, call gtk_radio_button_new_from_widget(), gtk_radio_button_new_from_widget_with_label(), or gtk_radio_button_new_from_widget_with_mnemonic(). These functions take a GtkWidget instead of a GSList. By setting that parameter to any GtkRadioButton object already in the group, it will add this GtkRadioButton object to the same group.

```
GtkWidget *radio = gtk_radio_button_new_with_label(NULL, "Option 1");
GtkWidget *radio2 = gtk_radio_button_from_widget_with_label
                             (GTK_RADIO_BUTTON(radio), "Option 2");
GtkWidget *radio3 = gtk_radio_button_from_widget_with_label
                             (GTK_RADIO_BUTTON(radio), "Option 3");
gtk_toggle_button_set_active(GTK_TOGGLE_BUTTON(radio2), TRUE);
```

Note that setting the active state of a GtkRadioButton object is no different from setting that of a GtkToggleButton object. The same is true of getting the active state. GTK+ will ensure that when one GtkRadioButton object becomes active, all the others in the group become inactive. The developer need do nothing else.

GtkTextView

GtkTextView is a rich-text, multiline text box widget. It is used to display or input large amounts of text. Because it uses Pango, GtkTextView can show text in any language with a variety of rich formatting. Figure 5-29 shows a custom subclass of GtkTextView that utilizes the features of GtkTextView.

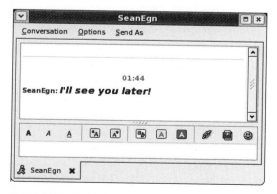

Figure 5-29. *Gaim uses a custom subclass of* GtkTextView *for inputting and showing messages.*

GtkTextView uses the Model-View-Controller (MVC) paradigm to increase its flexibility. In MVC, the tasks of the *model* (the data being shown and edited), the *view* (the user interface presenting the data), and the *controller* (the way the user can edit the data) are kept in separate objects. As you might assume, GtkTextView represents the view. It also provides the controller. The model is GtkTextBuffer.

GtkTextBuffer

GtkTextBuffer represents text with its associated formatting. This object will be displayed and edited by GtkTextView. A GtkTextBuffer represents the entire contents of the text, and GtkTextView is just a way of displaying those contents to the user and allowing her to change it.

GtkTextBuffer's constructor takes as a parameter a GtkTextTagTable. A GtkTextTagTable is used internally to store GtkTextTag objects. These GtkTextTags store formatting attributes. Leaving this parameter NULL will cause GtkTextBuffer to create its own. This is the most common use:

```
GtkTextBuffer *buffer = gtk_text_buffer_new(NULL);
```

Note If you create and use a GtkTextView without first creating a buffer, it will create an empty GtkTextBuffer for you. You can use gtk_text_view_get_buffer() to access it and edit it as described in this section.

Now that you have a buffer, you can start editing the text it represents. First, to set the text, you can call

```
gtk_text_buffer_set_text(buffer, "This is example text");
```

which will clear whatever text is currently in the buffer and replace it with the text you specify. For anything more complex than setting the entirety of the buffer's contents, you usually need to specify a range of text to affect. A range of text is specified by a pair of GtkTextIter objects.

GtkTextIter

GtkTextIter is the most commonly used object for representing a position in a GtkTextBuffer. However, if you create a GtkTextIter, it's only valid until the contents of the GtkTextBuffer object change. As soon as the contents change, the GtkTextIter is not guaranteed to represent the same position it used to. Therefore, you will almost always create it on the stack, rather than allocating heap memory for it.

Note In C, two pools of memory are allocated to your application: the stack and the heap. The stack is used for *automatic* memory allocation. When you declare a variable in a function, space is automatically allocated to it on the stack, and then invalidated when the function returns. The heap is used for dynamic allocation. When you call the malloc() function, you allocate memory from the heap. This memory is valid until you explicitly deallocate it with free().

All of the objects in GTK+ I've shown so far are allocated from the heap. That is, they are declared as pointers that are then dynamically allocated with constructor functions. This is because their lifespans are longer than the lifespan of any single function within our application. Because a GtkTextIter, however, is invalid when the content of a GtkTextBuffer object changes, it makes no sense to give it a lifespan longer than that of a function. When you allocate memory for a GtkTextIter, you do so on the stack:

```
GtkTextIter iter;
```

This is opposed to most objects in GTK+, which require a longer lifespan and are declared on the heap, leaving only a pointer to that object on the stack:

```
GtkWidget *button = gtk_button_new();
```

GtkTextBuffer offers eight functions to properly initialize GtkTextIter objects to various positions within the buffer. For most applications, the two most useful are gtk_text_buffer_get_start_iter() and gtk_text_buffer_get_end_iter(). These functions set the GtkTextIter passed to the start and the end of the text, respectively.

Once you have a valid GtkTextIter, you can insert text at it. To append text to a buffer, combine gtk_text_buffer_get_end_iter() and gtk_text_buffer_insert():

```
gtk_text_buffer_get_end_iter(buffer, &iter);
gtk_text_buffer_insert(buffer, &iter, ".  This is more text", -1);
```

Note that because GtkTextIter is declared on the stack, functions that use it always take a pointer to it such that they can change its value. In this instance, gtk_text_buffer_insert() will reset the GtkTextIter (invalidated because the contents of the GtkTextBuffer changed) to the end of the newly inserted text.

There are six ways to get a GtkTextIter other than the start or the end within a GtkTextBuffer. You can retrieve a GtkTextIter from any character offset or index, from any line. Another function allows you to get a GtkTextIter from a GtkTextMark, which I'll discuss later in this chapter.

■Note There is a difference between a character offset and a character index. The former is measured in characters, the latter is measured in bytes. In many character encodings, the two are equivalent, but you can not depend on this. Character encodings will be described in Chapter 9.

Once you have two GtkTextIter objects, you have a range of text on which you can perform a number of actions. One of the most important is deleting text. To do so call

```
GtkTextIter start_iter, end_iter;
gtk_text_buffer_get_start_iter(buffer, &start_iter);
gtk_text_buffer_get_iter_at_offset(buffer, &end_iter, 5);
gtk_text_buffer_delete(buffer, &start_iter, &end_iter);
```

This code will delete the first five characters of the GtkTextBuffer.

GtkTextTag

As stated earlier, GtkTextTag objects are associated with a GtkTextBuffer and are used to specify formatting and various other properties of text they are applied to. The best way to create a GtkTextTag is with gtk_text_buffer_create_tag(). This will cause the GtkTextBuffer to create a new GtkTextTag object and insert it into its GtkTextTagTable, thus allowing the buffer to use the tag:

```
GtkTextTag *tag = gtk_text_buffer_create_tag(buffer, "big-and-bold",
                                  "size-points", 24,
                                  "weight", PANGO_WEIGHT_BOLD,
                                  NULL);
```

Here, I create a GtkTextTag that specifies a 24-point, bold font. The first argument is the GtkTextBuffer; the second is the name of this tag.

GtkTextTag objects can be named. This allows you to easily retrieve a given tag from the GtkTextTagTable by name. Gaim, for example, stores a "link" tag that specifies blue and underlined text. Whenever we print a hyperlink, we use that tag. If you have no need for a named tag, you can leave this argument NULL. The next arguments are a NULL-terminated list of properties and their values.

Properties are defined as strings; I listed some of them in discussing Pango earlier, and a complete list can be found with the GTK+ documentation. Each of these properties expects its own type as a value. In this case, both take gint; PANGO_WEIGHT_BOLD is defined as the standard weight for bold text. Be sure to put a NULL after this list of pairs to signify the list is finished. If you don't, the code will most likely crash.

Once you have your GtkTextTag object, assign it to a range of text determined by a start and end GtkTextIter. To make all the text in the buffer "big-and-bold", you'd call the following:

```
gtk_text_buffer_apply_tag(buffer, tag, &start_iter, &end_iter);
```

Alternatively, if your tag is named, you can apply the tag by its name:

```
gtk_text_buffer_apply_tag_by_name(buffer, "big-and-bold", &start_iter, &end_iter);
```

And to save the trouble of inserting text and then applying the tag, call

```
gtk_text_buffer_insert_text_with_tags_by_name(buffer, &iter, "This example combines "
 "pretty much everything we've learned about GtkTextView so far!",
 -1, "big-and-bold", NULL);
```

Note that, like gtk_text_buffer_create_tag(), this takes a list (in this case, a list of tag names) that must be NULL-terminated. If you need to keep track of a spot in your GtkTextBuffer regardless of changes made to it, use GtkTextMark..

GtkTextMark

GtkTextMark represents a location in a GtkTextBuffer that, unlike GtkTextIter, will remain valid for the life of the GtkTextBuffer. It's sort of like a bookmark; you can rip out as many pages of the book as you want, but the bookmark may still be there. To create one, use gtk_text_buffer_create_mark():

```
GtkTextMark *mark = gtk_text_buffer_create_mark(buffer, "bookmark", iter, TRUE);
```

The second argument is the name. Like GtkTextTag, a GtkTextMark can be named to easily retrieve it from the GtkTextBuffer. In fact, GtkTextBuffer automatically already has two named GtkTextMark objects: "insert" and "selection_bound". "insert" represents the place in the text where new characters should be inserted by default (visually represented as a blinking cursor in GtkTextView). If "selection_bound" does not point to the same point in the GtkTextBuffer as "insert", it means text the text between the two GtkTextMark objects is selected. Text is most often selected by clicking and dragging over it with the mouse.

The final argument to gtk_text_buffer_create_mark() specifies how it behaves if new text is inserted at this point. If TRUE, this GtkTextMark is said to have "left gravity," and text inserted at the location of the GtkTextMark will appear after the GtkTextMark. If this is set FALSE, the text will appear before the GtkTextMark. The "insert" GtkTextMark, for instance, has right gravity. When you insert a character at that mark, the mark moves forward past it. A GtkTextMark is useful for keeping bookmarks, but not for much else. You will almost always need to convert them to GtkTextIter if you want to manipulate the GtkTextBuffer in some way. To do this, call

```
gtk_text_buffer_get_iter_at_mark(buffer, mark, &iter);
```

Or if the GtkTextMark has a name, call

```
gtk_text_buffer_get_iter_at_mark_by_name(buffer, "bookmark", &iter);
```

The same, of course, can be done for the named tags. The following code will delete everything in the GtkTextBuffer after the cursor:

```
gtk_text_buffer_get_iter_at_mark (buffer, "insert", &start_iter);
gtk_text_buffer_get_end_iter(buffer, &end_iter);
gtk_text_buffer_delete(buffer, &start_iter, &end_iter);
```

Now that you know how to programmatically change the contents of a GtkTextBuffer in your code, let's see how your user will change it in his UI, the GtkTextView widget.

GtkTextView

GtkTextView exists to allow the user to view and control the contents of a GtkTextBuffer. Because of the modularity provided by separating the model and the view, other widgets can be created to view and control a GtkTextBuffer. These widgets will usually descend from GtkTextView (as do GtkSourceView, used in code editors for syntax highlighting, and GtkIMHtml, used in Gaim to view and edit the simple HTML used in IM messages), but this is not a requirement. To create a GtkTextView, call

```
GtkWidget *text_view = gtk_text_view_new()
```

and then attach a GtkTextBuffer to it yourself, or let it create an empty one for you. If you want to attach a GtkTextBuffer to it when you create it, use

```
GtkWidget *text_view = gtk_text_view_new_with_buffer(buffer);
```

Because GtkTextView is designed to contain a large amount of text, it is one of the widgets that support scrolling natively. You will probably want to add a GtkTextView into a GtkScrolledWindow (discussed in the "Container Widgets" section of this chapter) and then pack GtkScrolledWindow where you want it.

Because the text itself is contained entirely in a GtkTextBuffer, probably the most important function in GtkTextView is gtk_text_view_get_buffer(). However, GtkTextView itself is useful in controlling how the user views the text.

For example, you can force the GtkTextView to scroll to make a certain GtkTextIter visible using gtk_text_view_scroll_to_iter(). Gaim uses this after sending or receiving a message, to make the new message visible (if the GtkTextView didn't scroll, the message would appear off the bottom). You can also control how it word-wraps with gtk_text_view_set_wrap_mode(). This can either not wrap, wrap only on word boundaries (which are detected in a language-neutral manner), or wrap on any character at the end of a line. Likewise, because GtkTextView also acts as the controller of GtkTextBuffer, you can control how the user is able to modify it.

The functions provided by GtkTextView are straightforward and well documented in the API reference. Although signals related to the contents of the GtkTextBuffer are handled by GtkTextBuffer itself, GtkTextView provides signals specific to the UI.

Signals emitted by GtkTextView include "move-cursor", which is emitted whenever the cursor moves. This signal passes information about how the cursor moved to the callback. The widget also emits signals related to clipboard functions and a signal, "populate-popup", which is called when the user accesses the right-click context menu. The spell-checking support in Gaim, provided by GtkSpell, uses this signal to add possible spelling corrections to the menu.

GtkTreeView

GtkTreeView is used to show trees and lists in GTK+. Like GtkTextView, it is separated in an MVC fashion. GtkTreeView is the view and the controller. GtkTreeModel is the model it represents. In Figure 5-30, a tree is shown along the right side of the window, and a list is shown to offer a choice of smiley themes. Both are GtkTreeView widgets.

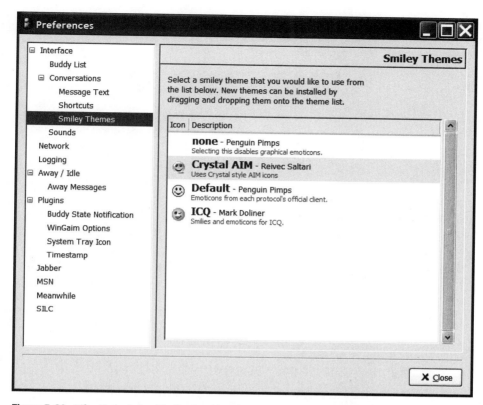

Figure 5-30. *Like Gaim's buddy list itself, this list of available smiley themes is a* GtkTreeView.

GtkTreeModel

GTK+ provides two different models compatible with GtkTreeView. These are GtkTreeStore and GtkListStore. GtkTreeStore is a nested hierarchy of items, whereas GtkListStore is a flat list. The two look identical to GtkTreeView, which is used to view and control both of them. It's also possible to create your own GtkTreeModel, but you will very rarely need to.

A GtkTreeModel, whether it's a list or a tree, is a set of rows. Each row is represented by a number of columns. When you create a GtkTreeModel (I'll use GtkListStore as an example), you specify the columns during creation. Because you need to know what columns are in your GtkListStore and what they represent, it's common to see an enum declared to keep track of this:

```
enum {
    ACTIVE_COLUMN,
    ICON_COLUMN,
    TEXT_COLUMN,
    NUM_COLUMNS
};
```

Because the columns start indexing at 0, NUM_COLUMNS will always represent the number of columns in your list. This allows you to easily change the columns in your list.

To create a GtkListStore object call

```
GtkListStore *list = gtk_list_store_new(NUM_COLUMNS,G_TYPE_BOOLEAN,
                                        G_TYPE_PIXBUF, G_TYPE_STRING);
```

The constructor takes the number of columns in the list and the types of data that will be stored in those columns, in this case a Boolean, a GdkPixbuf, and a string. The syntax for creating a GtkTreeStore is identical to the syntax for creating a GtkListStore, but called gtk_tree_store_new().

▪Note You will be able to specify which columns will appear in the GtkTreeView, which order they'll appear in, and how they'll be presented. GtkTreeModel is just a data structure. Therefore, you can add other columns to the model to store auxiliary data that won't appear in the GtkTreeView but are useful anyway. Gaim's buddy list stores pointers to the GaimBlistNode corresponding to each row in its GtkTreeStore.

GtkTreeModel emits signals when its contents change:

- "row-changed" is emitted whenever the value in a row changes in any way.

- "row-inserted" is emitted only when a row is inserted into the model.

- "row-deleted" is emitted only when a row is deleted from the model.

- "row-reordered" is emitted when a row is moved.

Like GtkTextBuffer, GtkTreeModel uses iterators to access and manipulate specific rows in the tree. These iterators are implemented by GtkTreeIter, and are used with any operation that refers to a specific row in the tree, such as adding, deleting, or modifying rows.

GtkTreeIter

A GtkTreeIter represents a row in the list or tree. Like GtkTextIter, it is invalidated when the contents of the tree change and is usually declared on the stack. To add a new row to the end of a list, call

```
GtkTreeIter iter;
gtk_list_store_append(list_store, &iter);
```

Appending a new row to a GtkTreeStore is similar:

```
GtkTreeIter iter;
gtk_tree_store_append(list_store, &iter, &parent);
```

The extra argument, parent, allows you to specify which branch of the tree to append to. If left NULL, it will be appended to the top level. Now that you have a row, you can assign values to it.

Do this using gtk_list_store_set() (or gtk_tree_store_set(); the syntaxes are identical). gtk_list_store_set() takes the GtkListStore, the GtkTreeIter pointing to your new row and, like gtk_tree_buffer_create_tag(), a NULL-terminated list of pairs. Each pair comprises the index of the row (which I've already enumerated) and its value:

```
gtk_list_store_set(list_store, &iter, ACTIVE_COLUMN, TRUE,
                                      ICON_COLUMN, pixbuf,
                                      TEXT_COLUMN, "This is text",
                                      NULL);
```

You can repeat this operation for all the data you need to enter. When you need to read this data out of the GtkListStore object, use gtk_tree_model_get(). This function takes a model, a GtkTreeIter representing a row, and a NULL-terminated list of pairs of columns to retrieve the values from and pointers to put them in:

```
gboolean active;
GdkPixbuf *pixbuf;
char *string;
gtk_tree_model_get(list_store, &iter, ACTIVE_COLUMN, &active,
                                      ICON_COLUMN, &pixbuf,
                                      TEXT_COLUMN, &string, NULL);
```

Notice the example passes pointers to the variables declared. That allows gtk_tree_model_get() to change their values.

GtkTreePath

GtkTreeIter is dependent on which type of GtkTreeModel you use. That is, a GtkTreeIter from a GtkListStore will not be compatible with a GtkTreeIter from a GtkTreeStore. Although this is fine when dealing with the models themselves, because GtkTreeView is ensured to work with any GtkTreeModel, it is often necessary to describe a position in a tree in a GtkTreeModel-neutral manner. This is done with GtkTreePath.

Whereas a GtkTreeIter is merely a collection of data that makes sense to the GtkTreeModel you're using, a GtkTreePath describes the location of a row. That is, a GtkTreePath says "go to the first top-level node and descend one level. Then choose the third child of that node, and descend one more level. Choose the first child at that level."

In fact, a GtkTreePath can be represented by a string, containing numbers separated by colons. Each number represents one level of depth; its value represents the index of the child at this step in the path. The GtkPath described in the previous paragraph would be represented as 0:2:0. You can convert a string in this format to a GtkTreePath with gtk_tree_path_new_from_string(), but it's more common to convert to and from GtkTreeIter objects.

To get a GtkTreePath from a GtkTreeIter, use

```
GtkTreePath *path = gtk_tree_model_get_path(model, &iter);
```

Then to reverse the process, use

```
gtk_tree_model_get_iter(model, &iter, path);
```

GtkTreeRowReference

GtkTreePath refers to a certain location in the tree, not necessarily a specific object. If the tree is reordered or a new row is added, the data at the position that GtkTreePath points to may change. A GtkTreeRowReference object created to point to a row will always point to that row, even if the row moves.

Create a new GtkTreeRowReference object from a GtkTreePath:

```
GtkTreeRowReference *row_ref = gtk_tree_row_reference_new(model, path);
```

This pointer will point to the node at the location the path points to as long as that node exists. When it no longer exists, gtk_tree_row_reference_valid() will return FALSE. If it returns TRUE, you can get the GtkTreePath representing its current location with gtk_tree_row_reference_get_path(), which will return NULL if the GtkTreeRowReference is invalid.

GtkTreeView

GtkTreeView displays the contents of a GtkTreeModel. It is to a GtkTreeModel as GtkTextView is to a GtkTextBuffer. To create a GtkTreeView, call gtk_tree_view_new_with_model() with your already created tree model:

```
GtkWidget *tree_view = gtk_tree_view_new_with_model(tree_model);
```

Similarly, you can call gtk_tree_view_new() and then gtk_tree_view_set_model(). Unlike GtkTextView, GtkTreeView will not create its own model (how would it know what data it would hold?); you must provide one.

Also like GtkTextView, GtkTreeView is designed to hold large amounts of data, possibly too much to fit in your UI. You will probably choose to add this to a GtkScrolledWindow.

You now have a GtkTreeView associated with a GtkTreeModel. However, the GtkTreeView still needs to be told how to present the data in that model.

GtkCellRenderer

To further increase modularity, GtkTreeView is composed of GtkCellRenderer objects that represent the data in the GtkTreeModel to the user. GTK+ comes with the GtkCellRenderer subclasses necessary for most applications, but applications can create and use their own.

The GtkCellRenderer classes included in GTK+ are as follows:

- GtkCellRendererCombo provides a drop-down list of choices from which the user can choose.

- GtkCellRendererPixbuf shows an image.

- GtkCellRendererProgress draws a progress bar.

- GtkCellRendererText shows a string of text.

- GtkCellRendererToggle provides a check box the user can click to toggle a value.

To create a GtkCellRenderer object, call its constructor function. Then, create a GtkTreeViewColumn to associate with this renderer.

GtkTreeViewColumn represents a column in the GtkTreeView. It has a title, a GtkCellRenderer, and a set of attributes. These attributes are fed from the GtkTreeModel, and used by the various

GtkCellRenderer objects. Each GtkCellRenderer uses different attributes. GtkCellRendererText, for instance, uses "text" or "markup", while GtkCellRendererProgress uses "text" and "value".

To create a GtkTreeViewColumn and set all its attributes, call

```
column = gtk_tree_view_column_new_with_attributes("Active", rend,
                                     "active", ACTIVE_COLUMN,
                                     NULL);
```

This uses another NULL-terminated list of pairs as arguments. These represent the attribute used by the renderer, and the column of the GtkTreeModel from which to get that value. After creating the column, add it to your GtkTreeView:

```
gtk_tree_view_append_column(GTK_TREE_VIEW(tree_view), column);
```

GtkTreeView and its assorted GtkCellRenderer objects emit signals related to the user's interaction with the UI. GtkTreeView emits signals when a row gets double-clicked ("row-activated"), or when a row in a tree gets expanded or collapsed, revealing or hiding its children respectively ("row-expanded" and "row-collapsed"). Signals specific to certain GtkCellRenderer objects are emitted by those objects accordingly.

GtkCellRendererToggle emits a "toggled" signal when the check box is clicked and GtkCellRendererText emits an "edited" signal when the user edits the text contained in it. The callbacks for these signals will be given the path to the affected row as a string, which you can convert to a GtkTreePath with gtk_tree_path_new_from_string().

GtkTreeSelection

The currently selected row in the GtkTreeView is represented in the GtkTreeSelection object. To get the currently selected row, call

```
GtkTreeSelection *selection = gtk_tree_view_get_selection(GTK_TREE_VIEW(tree_view));
```

Then, to get the GtkTreeIter this represents, call

```
gtk_tree_selection_get_selected(selection, &model, &iter);
```

Note that this function takes a GtkTreeModel** (a pointer to a pointer to a GtkTreeModel). This means that the function wants to edit the value of model. In this case, gtk_tree_selection_get_selected() will set model to point to the GtkTreeModel this GtkTreeSelection is part of. Assuming you already know this (or don't need to know this), you can pass this argument as NULL. Once you have a GtkTreeIter, you can read values from it as discussed earlier.

GtkTreeSelection also has one noteworthy signal, "changed", which is emitted whenever the selected row changes it. Get the GtkTreeSelection from the GtkTreeView with gtk_tree_view_get_selection() and connect to its "changed" signal. When the callback is called, you can find out which row is currently selected.

GtkComboBox

It turns out that GtkTreeModel is a useful data structure for many applications, and GtkCellRenderer is a very useful way of modularly displaying data. As such, alternate views and controllers to GtkTreeModel's model have been developed. GtkComboBox is one of them.

GtkComboBox shows a drop-down list of possible choices for the user. It uses the GtkTreeModel to represent the data shown, and employs GtkCellRender objects to draw it.

Creating a GtkTreeModel for a GtkComboBox is exactly like creating one for a GtkTreeView. Similarly, it will emit the same signals and have the same properties. Creating a GtkComboBox is much like creating a GtkTreeView.

Create a GtkComboBox with gtk_combo_box_new_with_model(), using the GtkTreeModel you've already created. GtkComboBox uses GtkCellLayout, which uses GtkCellRenderer objects to draw cells, as GtkTreeView does. Adding GtkCellRenderer objects with GtkCellLayout is very similar to adding columns to a GtkTreeView:

```
GtkCellRenderer *rend = gtk_cell_renderer_text_new();
gtk_cell_layout_pack_start(GTK_CELL_LAYOUT(combo_box), rend, TRUE);
gtk_cell_layout_set_attributes(GTK_CELL_LAYOUT(combo_box), rend,
                               "text", TEXT_COLUMN, NULL);
```

The list of attribute pairs works just like in GtkTreeView. The final gboolean argument of gtk_cell_layout_pack_start() is the "expand" argument, which works just like it does in the various layout containers. This interface works very well for complex GtkComboBox objects, but for the most common case (a combo box containing only text), GtkComboBox offers some convenience functions.

To create a GtkComboBox containing only text, call gtk_combo_box_new_text(). This function will create a GtkTreeModel with a single column of text and add it to the GtkComboBox. To add new text items to the combo box, use gtk_combo_box_append_text(), gtk_combo_box_prepend_text(), or gtk_combo_box_insert_text(), depending on where in the GtkComboBox the new item should appear.

Regardless of how you create your GtkComboBox, you'll use it in the same manner. The GtkComboBox will emit a "changed" signal when the active item in the GtkComboBox changes. You can connect to this signal and then use gtk_combo_box_get_active_iter() to find out the new value:

```
changed_cb(GtkWidget *combo_box, void *data)
{
    GtkTreeModel *model = gtk_combo_box_get_model(GTK_COMBO_BOX(combo_box));
    GtkTreeIter iter;
    char *text;
    gtk_combo_box_get_active_iter(GTK_COMBO_BOX(combo_box), &iter);

    gtk_tree_model_get(model, TEXT_COLUMN, &text, NULL);
}
```

If you created the GtkComboBox with gtk_combo_box_new_text(), you can easily get the current value with gtk_combo_box_get_active_text().

GtkToolbar

A GtkToolbar is used to present a set of buttons. In that sense, it's a lot like GtkButtonBox, discussed earlier. Although similar, toolbars and button boxes each have a very specific purpose for which each widget is best-suited.

Buttons in a GtkButtonBox are usually found at the bottom of a dialog, offering a set of choices, such as Remove or Cancel. A toolbar is a strip of buttons, usually at the top of a dialog, providing easy access to commonly used functions such as New File, Open, Save, or Paste. These buttons are usually borderless icons and are implemented in GTK+ by GtkToolButton. Like other buttons, GtkToolButton is a container widget and other widgets can be packed into it. To group toolbar buttons together, use GtkSeparatorToolItem. GtkToolButton and GtkSeparatorToolItem (and widgets that descend from them) are the only types of widgets that can be added to a toolbar, which means that any other widget must first be packed into a GtkToolButton.

To create a GtkToolbar, call

```
GtkWidget *toolbar = gtk_toolbar_new();
```

This constructor takes no arguments. This widget, like GtkButtonBox or GtkBox, is a container widget. By itself, it does nothing. But you can pack other widgets inside it. The most useful widget used in a GtkToolbar is a GtkToolButton. To create a GtkToolButton to pack inside it, call

```
GtkWidget *toolbar = gtk_tool_button_new(GtkWidget *icon_widget,
                                         const gchar *label);
```

The icon_widget argument will usually be a GtkImage, a type of widget discussed later this chapter. The label argument represents the text describing this widget. If the toolbar is set to show text and images, it will be shown. It will also be shown in tooltips for this button. For common toolbar items, you can use a stock item.

For common toolbar items, GTK+ uses the same stock item system used by GtkImage, providing commonly used toolbar items with pretranslated text labels and artwork. You can create a GtkToolButton from stock quite easily:

```
GtkWidget *tool_button = gtk_tool_button_new_from_stock(GTK_STOCK_OPEN);
```

This would, for example, create an Open button. To add this button to the toolbar, regardless of how it was created, call

```
gtk_toolbar_insert(GTK_TOOLBAR(toolbar), GTK_TOOL_ITEM(tool_button), -1);
```

The third argument to gtk_toolbar_insert() specifies the position in the toolbar. A position of 0 represents the beginning of the toolbar; 1 would make it the second item in the toolbar. A negative number (used in this example) inserts it at the end of the toolbar.

GtkToolButton provides one signal, "clicked", which is emitted when the button is clicked.

GtkToolbar is a widget and is packed into a container widget like any other. In the following example, I create a standard toolbar with New, Open, and Save, buttons created from stock:

```
#include <gtk/gtk.h>

/* Three callback functions for the toolbar button items. Here
 * I only print text to the screen. In an actual application, I
 * would do more; open_cb(), for instance might prompt
 * the user for a filename.
 */
void new_cb(GtkWidget *button, void *data)
{
    printf("New\n");
}
```

```c
void open_cb(GtkWidget *button, void *data)
{
    printf("Open\n");
}
void save_cb(GtkWidget *button, void *data)
{
    printf("Save\n");
}
/* This callback is called when the window is closed.
 * I must manually tell GTK+ to exit when this happens.
 */
void destroy_cb(GtkWidget *window, void *data)
{
    gtk_main_quit():
}
int main(int argc, char *argv[])
{
    GtkWidget *window, *toolbar, *tool_button;
    gtk_init(&argc, &argv);
    window = gtk_window_new(GTK_WINDOW_TOPLEVEL);
    gtk_window_set_title(GTK_WINDOW(window), "Window");
    g_signal_connect(G_OBJECT(window), "destroy", destroy_cb, NULL);
    toolbar = gtk_toobar_new();

    /* I create and add each toolbar one at a time */
    tool_button = gtk_tool_button_new_from_stock(GTK_STOCK_NEW);
    g_signal_connect(G_OBJECT(tool_button), "clicked", new_cb, NULL);
    gtk_toolbar_insert(GTK_TOOLBAR(toolbar), GTK_TOOL_ITEM(tool_button), -1);

    /* If you won't need to modify the tool button anymore, you can reuse its
       * variable. GTK+ manages its memory. But I can only reuse the variable
       * after making sure I no longer need this. I must, for instance, attach
       * callbacks to its signal before reusing the variable.
       */
    tool_button= gtk_tool_button_new_from_stock(GTK_STOCK_OPEN);
    g_signal_connect(G_OBJECT(tool_button), "clicked", open_cb, NULL);
    gtk_toolbar_insert(GTK_TOOLBAR(toolbar), GTK_TOOL_ITEM(tool_button), -1);

    tool_button= gtk_tool_button_new_from_stock(GTK_STOCK_SAVE);
    g_signal_connect(G_OBJECT(tool_button)," clicked", save_cb, NULL);
    gtk_toolbar_insert(GTK_TOOLBAR(toolbar),GTK_TOOL_ITEM(tool_button),-1);

    /* Now I add the toolbar to the window */
    gtk_container_add(GTK_CONTAINER(window), toolbar);

    /* And I show the window and its contents with gtk_window_show_all() */
    gtk_window_show_all(window);
```

```
    gtk_main()
    return 0;
}
```

This code results in the window seen in Figure 5-31. Clicking the buttons prints messages to the screen.

Figure 5-31. *A* GtkWindow *object packed with a* GtkToolbar *object, which itself is packed with three* GtkToolButtton *objects*

GtkMenu

GtkMenu is very much like GtkToolbar in that it offers the user a list of commands accessible with buttons. The main difference is in their appearance. Whereas a toolbar is a strip of buttons usually represented only by graphical icons, a menu is a hierarchical arrangement of text labels, sometimes with small icons to their left. Because a toolbar is always visible, it typically is used to display only the most common tasks (remember "simple and pretty"), while a menu can hold many more tasks hidden away in a hierarchy. Figure 5-32 shows a pop-up menu and a menu bar along the top of the window.

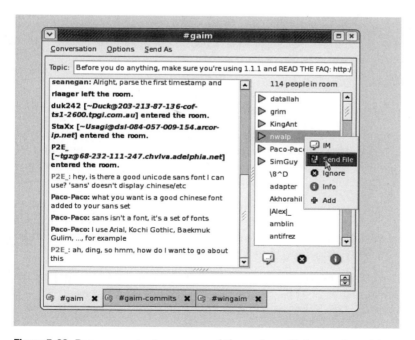

Figure 5-32. *Pop-up context menus used throughout Gaim, such as this one, are implemented with* GtkMenu.

Creating a GtkMenu is as simple as calling gtk_menu_new(), and like GtkToolbar, GtkMenu allows only objects of a specific type, GtkMenuItem. You can create a GtkMenuItem with gtk_menu_item_new() and insert your own widgets in it; a better way is to use convenience functions, which allow you to create common menu item types, avoiding the tedium of creating empty menu items and packing them manually:

- The gtk_menu_item_new_with_label() function creates a GtkLabel with the specified text.

- The gtk_menu_item_new_with_mnemonic() function also creates a GtkLabel. This function, though, uses your text as a mnemonic. This means that prepending an underscore before a character in your string will cause that character to be underlined, making it a keyboard shortcut. gtk_menu_item_new_with_mnemonic("_File"); for instance, creates a File menu, which can be accessed by hitting Alt-F.

- The gtk_image_menu_item_new_from_stock() function creates a GtkImageMenuItem, a subclass of GtkMenuItem. This type of menu item includes an icon. This function creates one using the same stock-item system used by GtkImage and GtkToolbar.

Once you have created a GtkMenuItem, insert in into your GtkMenu using gtk_menu_shell_append(). GtkMenu is a subclass of GtkMenuShell, and gtk_menu_shell_append() is straightforward:

```
gtk_menu_shell_append(GTK_MENU_SHELL(menu), menu_item);
```

After creating a menu, you'll need to display it. To do this, use the gtk_menu_popup() function, useful for pop-up context menus:

```
void gtk_menu_popup(GtkMenu *menu,
                GtkWidget *parent_menu, GtkWidget *parent_menu_item,
                GtkMenuPositionFunc func, gpointer data,
                guint button, guint32 activate_time);
```

This function's arguments are as follows:

- The menu argument represents the GtkMenu object to display.

- The parent_menu argument is used when this menu is a submenu of another menu. For instance, Gaim's buddy list menu along the top of the window contains submenus for Buddies, Tools, and Help. And the Tools menu contains submenus of its own: Buddy Pounce, and Account Actions, for instance. If the menu in the menu argument is a submenu, set its parent here.

- The parent_menu_item argument is used with the parent_menu argument to specify which item this menu is a child of. GTK+ can usually handle nested menu items itself, and you can set both parent_menu and parent_menu_item as NULL.

- The func argument allows you to set a function that will determine where to pop up the new menu. The default, specified by setting NULL, displays the menu at the current mouse pointer location. This is most suitable for almost all applications; you'll rarely need to set this yourself.

- The data argument sets data to be passed to the function specified in the func argument.

- The button argument specifies what mouse button was clicked to trigger the event. 1 is the left button, 2 is the right button, and 3 is the middle button.

- The activate_time argument specifies exactly what time the mouse button was clicked. This and the button argument are required by GTK+'s internals. If you are calling gtk_menu_popup() from a callback from the "button_press_event", you should be able to get these values from the arguments to that callback. Otherwise, use gtk_get_current_ event_time().

These bullet points are useful for pop-up context menus, but most applications feature a menu bar at the top of the window, such as the one seen on the Buddy List window in Figure 5-33. To create one of these in GTK+, call gtk_menu_bar_new(). This widget can then be added to your GUI just like any other widget. Adding other menus to it is done just like any other GtkMenuShell: use gtk_menu_shell_append() with GtkMenu objects as children. GTK+ will take care of ensuring the menus pop up when they need to.

Figure 5-33. *Gaim's buddy list provides important functions in a* GtkMenuBar.

GtkDialog

It is possible in GTK+ to create *composite widgets*. A composite widget is a GtkWidget composed of other GtkWidget objects, packed together in the ordinary ways described above. These widgets are just a set of various widgets packed into a container, but they contain their own APIs and signals affecting the composite widget as a whole. GtkDialog is one such widget.

GtkDialog, shown in Figure 5-34, descends from GtkWindow and is useful to present or request small amounts of data. A GtkDialog is a window containing a GtkVBox for content, packed in the top of the GtkDialog and an "action area" on the bottom, which is a GtkHButtonBox where buttons are placed.

When a GtkDialog object is shown (with gtk_widget_show()), the user will be presented with this dialog. When she clicks a button, the GtkDialog will emit the "response" signal. The callback will receive the GtkDialog that emitted the signal, and the response associated with the button.

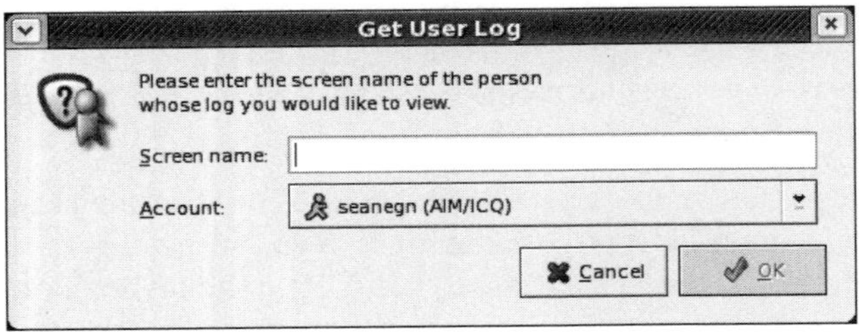

Figure 5-34. *This Get User Log dialog and many other dialog windows in Gaim are created with GtkDialog.*

Each button that you add to the GtkDialog (unless you add them directly to the GtkHButtonBox) is associated with a *response*. A response is an integer value that will be returned to your callback function. Some common responses are defined: GTK_RESPONSE_OK and GTK_RESPONSE_NO, though these responses have no inherent meaning besides how you treat them.

gtk_dialog_add_button() allows you to add a button and associate a response with it. However, the preferred way of creating a GtkDialog, gtk_dialog_new_with_buttons(), lets you add the buttons at creation time:

```
GtkDialog *dialog = gtk_dialog_new_with_buttons("Title of Window",
                    NULL, 0, GTK_STOCK_OK, GTK_RESPONSE_OK,
                          "Not OK!", 5, NULL);
```

This example creates a GtkDialog with two buttons. One is the stock OK button; the other says "Not OK!" Notice that the button text can be a stock item, or arbitrary text. Also, note the response codes are completely arbitrary. Although some have already been defined for easier readability of code, there's nothing that says you can't use your own numbers, or even use GTK_RESPONSE_CANCEL as the response for GTK_STOCK_OK.

The second argument is the parent window of this window. This can be NULL, but if you have a document-centric application and this dialog is about a specific document, you would want to use that document window as the parent. When coupled with the third argument, used for flags, you can assure the user sees an association between the two windows.

The flags argument is a bitmask of three possible options. GTK_DIALOG_MODAL causes the dialog to be modal. A modal dialog prevents users from interacting with its parent window. If the GtkDialog's parent window were NULL, it will prevent the user from interacting with any other window in the application.

Another possible flag, GTK_DIALOG_DIALOG_DESTROY_WITH_PARENT, destroys the GtkDialog if the parent window is destroyed. The final possible flag, GTK_DIALOG_NO_SEPARATOR, hides the horizontal line between the GtkVBox and the action area that is normally there by default.

After adding content to the GtkVBox, you will want to be told what button the user pressed. Attaching to the "response" signal is one way to get input back, but if you need input in the same function, you can call gtk_dialog_run(). gtk_dialog_run() creates its own event loop that won't return until the user presses a button in the GtkDialog:

```
GtkDialog = gtk_dialog_new_with_buttons("Save File?", NULL, 0,
                          GTK_STOCK_SAVE, GTK_RESPONSE_YES,
                          "Don't save", GTK_RESPONSE_NO, NULL);
GtkWidget *label = gtk_label_new("Would you like to save this file?");

int response = gtk_dialog_run(GTK_DIALOG(dialog));
switch (response) {
   case GTK_RESPONSE_YES:
        save_file();
   case GTK_RESPOSE_NO:
        dont_save();
}
gtk_widget_destroy(dialog);
```

The function pauses (or blocks) until a button is pressed. Once the button is pressed, the function resumes and gtk_dialog_run() has returned the response code of the pressed button. This means that the user will be unable to interact with any other window until responding to the GtkDialog. Because GtkDialog is such a convenient way of creating a window asking for input, GTK+ includes several subclasses of GtkDialog that make available common dialogs that will have a consistent feel among GTK+ applications. These include inputting fonts and colors, but the most common dialog is GtkFileChooserDialog.

GtkFileChooserDialog

GtkFileChooserDialog, shown in Figure 5-35, is a GtkDialog that prompts the user for the location of a file, usually for opening or saving.

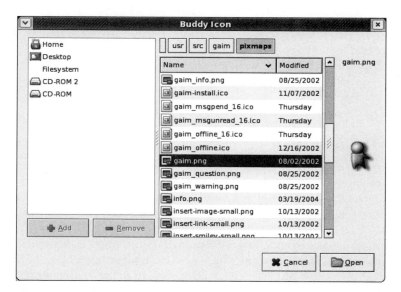

Figure 5-35. *Gaim uses GtkFileChooserDialog in many places where it's necessary to input a file path. The Buddy Icon file chooser dialog shown here is one such place.*

To create a GtkFileChooserDialog, call gtk_file_chooser_dialog_new(). This function takes similar arguments to GtkDialog: a title, a parent window, and a NULL-terminated list of pairs of buttons and their responses:

```
GtkWidget *dialog = gtk_file_chooser_dialog_new("Save File",
                    document_window, GTK_FILE_CHOOSER_ACTION_SAVE,
                    GTK_STOCK_SAVE, GTK_RESPONSE_OK,
                    GTK_STOCK_CANCEL, GTK_RESPONSE_CANCEL, NULL);
```

The first argument is the title; the second is the parent window. The third argument is the action this GtkFileChooserDialog is performing. This can be one of the following:

- GTK_FILE_CHOOSER_ACTION_OPEN requests the user choose a file for opening a document.

- GTK_FILE_CHOOSER_ACTION_SAVE requests the user choose a file for saving a document.

- GTK_FILE_ACTION_SELECT_FOLDER requests the user choose an existing folder.

- GTK_FILE_ACTION_CREATE_FOLDER requests the user choose a name for creating a new folder.

This option affects what tools and options are available to the user. The remaining arguments are pairs of buttons and their response codes, explained earlier. Before requesting input, you may want to set some parameters of the file chooser:

- The gtk_file_chooser_set_filename() function sets the chosen file. This is useful if the user has already chosen a file, but may want to change it. For instance, when choosing custom sounds in Gaim, the file chooser will show the sound file currently chosen.

- The gtk_file_chooser_set_extra_widget() function adds a preview widget. This widget should be used to preview the selected file, as seen in Figure 5-34. This can be any widget (Figure 5-34 shows a GtkImage), and it will be packed into the dialog at the location shown.

You can use either method (attaching to the "response" signal or calling gtk_dialog_run()) to receive the user's feedback. If your OK button is pressed, you'll probably want to get the chosen file with gtk_file_chooser_get_filename(). As always, complete documentation is available at http://www.gtk.org/api/.

A Gaim Plug-in Example

I have a compulsion that I must click any hyperlink I see in an IM or chat. Unfortunately, I'm often in a number of IRC channels where chat happens very rapidly and hyperlinks scroll off the screen before I ever notice them. In this section, I'll create a URL catcher, which will check every incoming IM or chat message and be capable of providing me a list of all the hyperlinks I've received in a GTK+ UI.

I will scan every incoming message by attaching callbacks to the appropriate Gaim signals. I will then check to see if the message contains a link with relatively simple string parsing. I will parse out the link, and save as many details as I can into a special data structure I will create just for this purpose. I will then hook into Gaim's Plugin Actions system to add a Show URL Catcher menu item. When it's clicked, I'll create a GUI using the techniques covered in the chapter.

I will write this section the same way I actually approach writing a plug-in. I'll provide insight as to what I'm thinking each step of the way. Hopefully, this will allow you to peer into my mind and understand the most effective way to design code with GTK+, be it a Gaim plug-in, or an entire application. The first thing I do with any Gaim plug-in is write the standard boilerplate code required by any plug-in.

Gaim Plug-in Boilerplate

```
#include "internal.h"
#include "plugin.h"
#include "notify.h"
#include "version.h"

GaimPlugin *plugin_handle = NULL;

static gboolean
plugin_load(GaimPlugin *plugin)
{
    plugin_handle = plugin;
    return TRUE;
}

static GaimPluginInfo info =
{
    GAIM_PLUGIN_MAGIC,
    GAIM_MAJOR_VERSION,
    GAIM_MINOR_VERSION,
    GAIM_PLUGIN_STANDARD,
    NULL,
    0,
    NULL,
    GAIM_PRIORITY_DEFAULT,
    "urlcatcher",
    "URL Catcher",
    "1.0",
    "Catches URLs from incoming messages",
    "Detects URLs from within incoming messages and provides an "
    "interface for viewing them.",
    "Sean Egan <seanegan@gmail.com>",
    "http://apress.com",
    plugin_load,
    NULL,
    NULL,
    NULL,
    NULL,
    NULL
};
```

```
static void
init_plugin(GaimPlugin *plugin)
{
}
```

```
GAIM_INIT_PLUGIN(urlcatcher, init_plugin, info)
```

This is the initialization code that's required of every function. I will usually copy this from some other simple plug-in, and change only the relevant fields in the `GaimPluginInfo` struct. Here, I've copied the code from the Hello World plug-in from Chapter 4.

Once I have this boilerplate, I'll compile it and make sure I haven't made any errors copying and pasting things. Once I have a working boilerplate, I'll start to flesh it out.

The Data Structures

I know I need a data structure to hold the relevant information about each incoming URL. I'll want to save the received URL, whom I received it from, when I received it, and the full message the URL was received in. The natural data structure to use for this is a `struct`.

In fact, a `struct` is the *only* data structure capable of holding items of different types provided by C. All the higher-level data structures reviewed last chapter, including object-oriented objects, are at their core `struct`s. I could attempt to use an object-oriented object for this task, but I don't think it's necessary. The `struct` has a single, specific purpose and doesn't need any additional features. I'll declare my `struct`:

```
struct url_data {
    char *url;
    char *message;
    char *sender;
    char *time;
};
```

I declare all my data structures at the very top of the file, just after the `#include` statements. This allows all the code following to use them.

I also need a data structure to keep track of all these `struct url_data` instances. In Chapter 4 I covered some data structures used to keep track of a number of objects. These included linked lists, hash tables, and trees. I'm going to use this data structure when I'm adding URLs to my UI. I'll need to loop through every received link and add them. A linked list is the most appropriate data structure for iterating through an entire collection of items. I'll use `GSList`, GLib's singly linked list:

```
GSList *urls = NULL;
```

This is a global variable, accessible by any function within the plug-in. I make the initial value of this `NULL`, which represents an empty list. After this step, I test-compile again. Compiling and testing frequently is a good idea. It makes it easy to track down errors by keeping the number of changes in each subsequent build minimal. Right now, there's no need to test the code because it doesn't do anything yet. But if you made a typo, a test compile will easily track it down. Now that I've created my data structures, I want to write code that will store the data.

Using Gaim Signals

I want to create a callback that will intercept every incoming message. Callbacks in Gaim plug-ins are usually created in the `plugin_load()` function. After checking `http://gaim.sourceforge.net/api/conversation-signals.html`, I see that there are two signals I'm interested in: `"received-im-msg"` and `"received-chat-msg"`. However, I notice that the functions they take as callbacks both use the exact same arguments and return type. Because I want to do the same exact thing regardless of whether the message came from a chat or from an IM, I can use the same callback. I'll name this callback `incoming_msg_cb()` and attach it to the two signals in `plugin_load()`:

```
static gboolean
plugin_load(GaimPlugin *plugin)
{
    void *handle = gaim_conversations_get_handle();
    plugin_handle = plugin;
    gaim_signal_connect(handle, "received-im-msg", plugin,
            GAIM_CALLBACK(incoming_msg_cb), NULL);
    gaim_signal_connect(handle, "received-chat-msg", plugin,
            GAIM_CALLBACK(incoming_msg_cb), NULL);
    return TRUE;
}
```

Scanning Messages

Next, I create the `incoming_msg_cb()` function. I'll start with creating an empty function with the correct prototype:

```
static void incoming_msg_cb(GaimAccount *account, char *sender, char *message,
                GaimConversation *conv, int flags)
{
}
```

Then I'll do another test compile, just to be safe. The main purpose of this function is to store data associated with incoming hyperlinks. The first thing I need to do, then, is to check if the incoming message (passed in the `message` argument) contains a URL. I am going to create a separate function just for this purpose.

Generally, each function should do exactly one thing. Although it's possible to check for a URL in `incoming_msg_cb()` itself, that would be poor design. Design individual functions for every task. The task of `incoming_msg_cb()` is to store data related to incoming URLs. The task of this new function will be to check a string for URLs. By keeping functions very narrowly focused like this, it allows for more-flexible code. If somewhere else you need to check a string for a URL, you can call the function devoted to it; the code isn't buried inside some function with an unrelated task. By creating a number of functions with very specific tasks, it's easy to implement higher-level tasks merely by stringing together these functions.

I'll call my new function `check_for_links()`. It needs, as input, a string to check within (in this case, the message). My first instinct is to return a gboolean that will be TRUE if the message contains a link. However, after a little bit of thought, I realize that I also need to extract the link from the input string. Because I'm already parsing the input string here, it makes sense to extract the URL, as well. If the input string doesn't contain a link, the function will return NULL. Otherwise, it will return a string containing the URL. This doesn't defy the rule about giving each function a very narrow scope. The function can still be used only to detect a URL. Returning the URL is just an added feature. Like most string-parsing functions, this function makes extensive use of pointer arithmetic, which can be difficult for novices. I've commented on the code to make it easier to understand:

```c
static char *check_for_urls(char *message)
{
    /* character pointers are often used as the
     * beginning of a string, but can also point
     * anywhere within a string. I'm trying to
     * isolate the URL from the message argument.
     * I'll use n to point to the start of the URL and
     * m to point to the end. ret is where I'll store
     * the string I'll return.
     */
    char *start, *end, *ret;

    /* I'll assume that all URLs will start with "http://"
     * strstr() sets start to the location in the string where
     * "http://" starts or, if it's not found, NULL. If it's
     * not found, the message doesn't contain a link, and so the
     * function returns NULL.
     */
    start = strstr(message, "http://");
    if (start == NULL)
        return NULL;

    /* Now that start points to the beginning of the link, I will set
     * end to that location (plus strlen("http://") and traverse the
     * string until I get to a charcter that's invalid in a URL.
     * That will be the end of the link.
     */
    end = start + strlen("http://");
    while(*end != '\0' &&
        *end != ' ' &&
        *end != ',' &&
        *end != '\n' &&
        *end != '<' &&
        *end != '>' &&
        *end != '"' &&
        *end != '\\')
        end++;
```

```
/* Now I should have pointers to the beginning and end of the URL, which
 * means the length is everything between the two. I'll allocate a string for
 * it. I need to add 1 to store the terminating NUL character.
 */
ret = g_malloc(end - start + 1);

/* And then I copy the URL into this buffer and return it. You often need to
 * manually NUL-terminate strings after using strncpy() because strncpy()
 * won't necessarily do it itself. */
strncpy(ret, start, end-start);
ret[end-start] = '\0';
return ret;
}
```

This code makes a number of assumptions that may not always be true. A more robust function would not assume that every URL begins with http://. A more robust function would also detect multiple links in a message and handle them separately. I've used these assumptions merely for simplicity.

Now, I can call this function from the incoming_msg_cb() function to check for incoming links. If the message doesn't contain a link, I'll return

```
static void incoming_msg_cb(GaimAccount *account, char *sender, char *message,
                GaimConversation *conv, int flags)
{
    char *link;
    if ((link = check_for_urls(message)) == NULL)
        return;
}
```

■Tip An assignment statement such as x = 2 has a value in C: the value that was assigned. I'm taking advantage of that here to simultaneously set the link value and detect if it's FALSE. Because assignment statements have a value, though, it's really easy to accidentally put an assignment statement in your if statement instead of a comparison statement (such as x == 2). Be careful to avoid that. Some people avoid this by writing comparison statements that are invalid if an equals sign is accidentally left off, by putting the literal value first. For example, 2 == x is perfectly valid, but 2 = x is not.

Once this check has passed, the URL is contained in link, the sender is contained in sender, the message is contained in message. The only additional data I need is the current time. I can get this by adding a single statement at the top of the function:

```
const char *timestamp = gaim_date();
```

This function is available from util.h, which I must now #include at the top of the source file. Now that I have all the data I need, I create the data structure, fill it out, and add it to the linked list. The finished function looks like this:

```
static void incoming_msg_cb(GaimAccount *account, char *sender, char *message,
                GaimConversation *conv, int flags)
{
    struct url_data *url;
    const char *timestamp = gaim_date();
    char *link;
    if ((link = check_for_urls(message)) == NULL)
        return;

    url = g_malloc(sizeof(struct url_data));
    url->url = link;
    url->message = g_strdup(message);
    url->sender = g_strdup(sender);
    url->time = g_strdup(timestamp);
    urls = g_slist_append(urls, url);
}
```

Notice I call `strdup()` on the variables passed to me. Because Gaim controls those strings, I can't rely on the fact that they will still exist when I need them. This is true even of timestamp, which is returned from `gaim_date()`. While many functions that return strings require you to free them when you're finished, `gaim_date()` returns a static buffer that may not be freed. Therefore, I have to make my own copies.

■**Note** When a variable is declared `static` within a function, its lifespan exceeds that of the function. Because most strings declared in a function are destroyed when the function exits, you can't use them as a return value, and must dynamically allocate memory for strings you'll return. `static` strings, though, may be returned, as they are not destroyed when the function exits. However, because the value of the static buffer may change the next time the function is called, it may be unsafe to keep a reference to it for an extended period of time, which is why I use `g_strdup()`in this example. You can recognize if you need to free a returned string or not by considering its return type. Allocated strings are of type `char *` while static strings like those returned by `gaim_date()` are of type `const char *`.

With this code running, the plug-in will find links within received messages and store them in the data structures I've created. Now, all that's necessary is to create the GUI and hook it into Gaim's Account Actions system.

Hooking into Account Actions

Gaim's Tools menu provides an Account Actions submenu in which plug-ins can register items. When these Account Actions are selected from the menu, a callback in the plug-in is called.

I will use this system to show the user the list of received URLs. When the callback is triggered, I'll create the window. Because Gaim's design attempts to allow multiple UIs other than just the GTK+ UI, this is done in a UI-agnostic manner. You won't create GtkMenuItem objects yourself, but rather you'll pass Gaim a list of GaimPluginAction objects, each of which contains a title and a callback. This list is created by a function that I'll call actions():

```
static GList *
actions(GaimPlugin *plugin, gpointer context)
{
    GList *l = NULL;
    GaimPluginAction *act = NULL;

    act = gaim_plugin_action_new("Show received URLs",
                                 show_dialog);
    l = g_list_append(l, act);

    return l;
}
```

Then I'll add actions() to the GaimPluginInfo struct:

```
static GaimPluginInfo info =
{
    GAIM_PLUGIN_MAGIC,
    GAIM_MAJOR_VERSION,
    GAIM_MINOR_VERSION,
    GAIM_PLUGIN_STANDARD,
    NULL,
    0,
    NULL,
    GAIM_PRIORITY_DEFAULT,
    "urlcatcher",
    "URL Catcher",
    "1.0",
    "Catches URLs from incoming messages",
    "Detects URLs from within incoming messages and provides an "
    "interface for viewing them.",
    "Sean Egan <seanegan@gmail.com>",
    "http://apress.com",
    plugin_load,
    NULL,
    NULL,
    NULL,
    NULL,
    NULL,
    actions
};
```

And then I'll create the show_dialog() function.

Creating the GUI

As a GaimPluginAction callback, show_dialog() takes one argument, the GaimPluginAction that triggered it. We won't need to use this at all, but if we had multiple Plugin Actions, all using the same callback, we could use this to discern each.

I start by creating an empty callback function:

```
static void show_dialog(GaimPluginAction *action)
{
}
```

and test-compile to make sure I haven't made any typos yet. This function will go at the very top of the file, directly underneath the data type definitions. This is because the function needs to be above other functions that call it. This must be placed above actions. I will likewise place GTK+ callbacks above this function.

■**Note** Actually, the function can be defined anywhere as long as the function's prototype appears before the first time it's used. To define a function's prototype, declare the function's name, return value, and arguments, but instead of a body, use a semicolon: static void show_dialog(GaimPluginAction *action);

I want only one link catcher window. If the user chooses Show Received URLs 50 times, I don't want 50 windows on the screen. If the window is open when the account action is triggered, I won't create the window. To do this, I need a global variable, which will be NULL if the window does not exist, and point to the window if it does. This way, I can check that variable to see if I should continue creating the dialog:

```
GtkWidget *url_window = NULL;
```

I put this declaration above the show_dialog function, and now I can check to see if it's NULL in show_dialog(). If it is not NULL, the window already exists and I should return from the function. However, if the user chose the account action, the window probably wasn't immediately visible to the user. Perhaps the window is minimized or on another workspace. I'll call gtk_window_present() on the window to ensure it becomes visible:

```
if (url_window != NULL) {
        gtk_window_present(GTK_WINDOW(url_window));
        return;
    }
```

Now that this check is out of the way, I'll start creating the window. It will be an ordinary top-level GtkWindow. I want, from top to bottom, a GtkTreeView containing a list of all the URLs received. This list will contain strings representing each URL, the time it was received, and the sender. When an item in the link is selected, the entirety of the message it was received in will appear in GtkTextView beneath it. Actually, I will use a GtkIMHtml object, which is a custom widget written specifically for displaying the subset of HTML used by AIM and other IM systems.

Lastly, beneath this, I will use a GtkButtonBox, in which I'll have two buttons: Close, and Open URL. If I were more carefully adhering to the GNOME HIG, I would probably place the Open URL button right beneath the GtkTreeView widget. A button should be placed relative to the widget it controls. The Close button affects the window, so it is placed at the bottom of the window. The Open URL button is most closely related to the list of URLs, so it should be placed near that list. For simplicity, I'll pack it at the bottom of the dialog. After following this example, you should understand GTK+ well enough to place the button wherever you like.

Because the dialog is going to be vertical in design, I'll pack a GtkVBox inside the GtkWindow to handle the window's layout. I can pack the GtkTreeView, the GtkIMHtml, and the GtkButtonBox into this, from top to bottom.

Actually, I'll need scrollbars on the GtkIMHtml and GtkTreeView. So, those will be packed inside GtkScrolledWindow objects which, in turn, will be packed into the GtkVBox. With this layout in mind, I start writing code to implement it. I declare the widgets I'll be using:

```
GtkWidget *vbox, *bbox, *sw, *tree, *imhtml, *button;
```

Notice that I don't declare a variable for the window's widget. That's because I will use the global variable I created for it. I also want to be notified when the window is closed. Unlike the previous examples in this chapter, though, I don't want to exit the application. Instead, I want to reset url_window to NULL to signify it's closed. The callback function looks like this:

```
static void
window_destroy_cb(GtkWidget *widget, gpointer data)
{
    url_window = NULL;
}
```

and the code to create, initialize, and pack a GtkWindow and GtkVBox to the window looks like this:

```
url_window = gtk_window_new(GTK_WINDOW_TOPLEVEL);
gtk_window_set_default_size(GTK_WINDOW(url_window), 300, 500);
gtk_window_set_title(GTK_WINDOW(url_window), "URL Catcher");
gtk_container_set_border_width(GTK_CONTAINER(url_window), 12);
g_signal_connect(G_OBJECT(url_window), "destroy",
                 G_CALLBACK(window_destroy_cb), NULL);

vbox = gtk_vbox_new(FALSE, 6);
gtk_container_add(GTK_CONTAINER(url_window), vbox);
```

Here, I've created a window and a vertical box, and packed the latter into the former. I've also set a default size for the window. While setting position and size explicitly is typically frowned upon in GTK+ UI design, it's acceptable here. GTK+ attempts to make its UI as compact as possible, giving each widget just as much space as required. Because the GtkTreeView and GtkIMHtml will have scrollbars, they actually need very little room to be functional. However, to really be usable they should have more room than the minimum necessary; otherwise you would be able to see only a fraction of a line at a time. The gtk_window_set_default_size() function sets a reasonable default. If the user prefers the window to be smaller, he can resize it manually.

The next item to create is the GtkTreeView.

GtkTreeView

GtkTreeView is one of the most complicated widgets in GTK+. You have to create a GtkTreeModel that represents the data you're using, then create a GtkTreeView using it. You must then add GtkTreeViewColum objects for each column, associating each with a newly created GtkCellRenderer object. Finally, you can add the data to the tree, which itself requires more than one step. The first step, though, is to create the GtkTreeModel represented by this tree.

I know I want to include the date, the sender, and the URL in the list, but the GtkTreeModel can also hold data not seen in the list. This allows you to easily associate a row in the tree with some other data. Here, it would be useful if each row were associated with the struct url_data instance. It's common to create an enum defining what each column in your GtkTreeModel is used for:

```
enum {
    TIME_COLUMN,
    SENDER_COLUMN,
    URL_COLUMN,

    MESSAGE_COLUMN,
    DATA_COLUMN,
    COLUMN_COUNT
};
```

Then I create the GtkTreeModel. Recall that GTK+ includes two types of GtkTreeModel. Because this plug-in doesn't require a hierarchical structure of URLs, I'll use GtkListStore. First, I declare it at the top of the function:

```
GtkListStore *list_store;
```

Then I create it:

```
list_store = gtk_list_store_new(COLUMN_COUNT, G_TYPE_STRING, G_TYPE_STRING,
                G_TYPE_STRING, G_TYPE_STRING, G_TYPE_POINTER);
```

■Note The version of C used in Gaim development, ANSI C, allows functions to be declared only at the beginning of function blocks, before any other statement. If you are coming from Java or C++ development, you may struggle getting used to this.

The first three columns, which will be visible in the GtkTreeView, are string types. The fourth column, the message, will not be visible in the tree, but it's useful to store it in the GtkTreeModel so that it's accessible when this list item is selected. The final column will hold pointers to the struct url_data instances and is a pointer type. This is similar to MESSAGE_COLUMN; it's included only as ancillary data rather than something that will actually be shown in the tree. With a valid model, I can now create the GtkTreeView to display it:

```
tree = gtk_tree_view_new_with_model(GTK_TREE_MODEL(list_store));
```

Then I need to add columns to the GtkTreeView. This includes creating cell renderers to draw each element in the tree and associating these renderers with the data stored in the tree model. I need to do this three times, one for each visible column in the GtkTreeView, but I will declare only one GtkCellRenderer and GtkTreeViewColumn variable and reuse them:

```
GtkTreeViewColumn *col;
GtkCellRenderer *rend;
```

Each column is associated with a renderer. These renderers have properties that are set to the values stored in the GtkTreeModel. When you create a column, you associate the renderer, and tell it where to get the values for each property it uses.

I'll be using GtkCellRendererText, which is used for displaying text data. It has a few properties that can be set, but I'll be using only its "text" property, which specifies the text it should display. Every property that you set will be associated with a column in the GtkTreeModel, so for each cell renderer I create here, I will associate its "text" property with the appropriate column number:

```
rend = gtk_cell_renderer_text_new ();
col = gtk_tree_view_column_new_with_attributes ("Time",
                                rend,
                                "text", TIME_COLUMN,
                                NULL);
gtk_tree_view_append_column (GTK_TREE_VIEW (tree), col);

rend = gtk_cell_renderer_text_new ();
col = gtk_tree_view_column_new_with_attributes ("Sender",
                                rend,
                                "text", SENDER_COLUMN,
                                NULL);
gtk_tree_view_append_column (GTK_TREE_VIEW (tree), col);

rend = gtk_cell_renderer_text_new ();
col = gtk_tree_view_column_new_with_attributes ("URL",
                                rend,
                                "text", URL_COLUMN,
                                NULL);
gtk_tree_view_append_column (GTK_TREE_VIEW (tree), col);
```

Now I have an appropriate GtkTreeModel and a GtkTreeView that is prepared to display it as I desire. The only thing remaining is to add the data to it. Because the data comes from a variable-length GSList, I will need to loop through it and add each item one by one.

To iterate through the GSList, declare a temporary variable used for iterating and set it to urls. You can then modify this variable all you want, without changing the value of urls and losing the start of the list. Also, to append new rows, I will need a GtkTreeIter, which I'll declare at the beginning of the function:

```
GSList *l;
GtkTreeIter iter;
```

Then I can start iterating. I usually iterate with a while loop, but iterating with a for loop is also possible and perhaps even more elegant:

```
l = urls;
    while (l) {
        struct url_data *data = (struct url_data*)(l->data);
        gtk_list_store_append (list_store, &iter);
        gtk_list_store_set (list_store, &iter,
                    TIME_COLUMN, data->time,
                    SENDER_COLUMN, data->sender,
                        MESSAGE_COLUMN, data->message,
                    URL_COLUMN, data->url,
                        DATA_COLUMN, data,
                    -1);
        l = l->next;
    }
```

Now I create a scrolled window, pack tree inside it, and pack the scrolled window into vbox:

```
sw = gtk_scrolled_window_new(NULL, NULL);
gtk_scrolled_window_set_shadow_type(GTK_SCROLLED_WINDOW(sw), GTK_SHADOW_IN);
gtk_scrolled_window_set_policy(GTK_SCROLLED_WINDOW(sw), GTK_POLICY_AUTOMATIC,
                                GTK_POLICY_AUTOMATIC);
gtk_container_add(GTK_CONTAINER(sw), tree);
gtk_box_pack_start(GTK_BOX(vbox), sw, TRUE, TRUE, 0);
```

At this point, the tree should properly display all the received URLs. Now is an appropriate time to test what you've written so far. Put a gtk_widget_show_all() call at the end of the function, compile, run Gaim, load the plug-in, send yourself some links, and select the Plugin Action. Compilation succeeded and I saw the dialog shown in Figure 5-36.

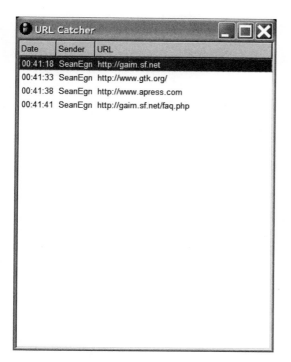

Figure 5-36. *The plug-in's GUI with only the* GtkTreeView *packed into it*

GtkIMHtml

Although GtkIMHtml is a subclass of GtkTextView, you rarely need to make GtkTextView calls on it; it's pretty self-sufficient. In this example, all I need to do is create one and add it to the UI. Of course, I must first #include its header file. I will also call a function to initialize a GtkIMHtml from gtkutils.h, so I must #include that as well:

```
#include "gtkimhtml.h"
#include "gtkutils.h"
```

Like with the GtkTreeView, I will first add it to a GtkScrolledWindow. I will also call gaim_setup_imhtml(), which sets some Gaim-specific defaults on the GtkIMHtml widget:

```
    imhtml = gtk_imhtml_new(NULL, NULL);
    gaim_setup_imhtml(imhtml);
    sw = gtk_scrolled_window_new(NULL, NULL);
    gtk_scrolled_window_set_shadow_type(GTK_SCROLLED_WINDOW(sw), GTK_SHADOW_IN);
    gtk_scrolled_window_set_policy(GTK_SCROLLED_WINDOW(sw), GTK_POLICY_AUTOMATIC,
                    GTK_POLICY_AUTOMATIC);

    gtk_container_add(GTK_CONTAINER(sw), imhtml);
    gtk_box_pack_start(GTK_BOX(vbox), sw, TRUE, TRUE, 0);
```

The text will be sent whenever a URL is selected from the list. To do this, I need a callback whenever the selection is changed. The signal this callback is connected to is emitted by GtkTreeSelection. I declare a GtkTreeSelection at the beginning of the function:

GtkTreeSelection *sel;

Then I set it from the GtkTreeView object and connect to its "changed" event:

```
sel = gtk_tree_view_get_selection (GTK_TREE_VIEW (tree));
gtk_tree_selection_set_mode (sel, GTK_SELECTION_SINGLE);
g_signal_connect (G_OBJECT (sel), "changed",
            G_CALLBACK (tree_selection_changed_cb),
            imhtml);
```

I use imhtml as the data for this callback function. This way when the callback is triggered, it will have a reference to the GtkIMHtml widget and can modify its text. The callback function gets the currently selected row as a GtkTreeIter, then extracts the values from it. I use g_strdup_printf() to create a string that will more closely resemble an incoming message by including the screen name of the sender, rather than just showing the message:

```
static void
tree_selection_changed_cb (GtkTreeSelection *selection, gpointer data)
{
        GtkWidget *imhtml = GTK_WIDGET(data);
        GtkTreeIter iter;
        GtkTreeModel *model;
        gchar *sender, *text, *message;

        if (gtk_tree_selection_get_selected (selection, &model, &iter)) {
            gtk_tree_model_get (model, &iter, MESSAGE_COLUMN, &text,
                        SENDER_COLUMN, &sender, -1);
            message = g_strdup_printf("<font color=\"#A82F2F\"><b>%s: </b></font>%s",
                        sender, text);
            gtk_imhtml_clear(GTK_IMHTML(imhtml));
            gtk_imhtml_append_text(GTK_IMHTML(imhtml), message, 0);
            g_free(message);
        }
}
```

Now all that remains is the button box.

GtkButtonBox

The button box is just a container widget that will contain two GtkButton objects. I'll create it and pack it into vbox as I've done with every other widget:

```
bbox = gtk_hbutton_box_new();
  gtk_button_box_set_layout(GTK_BUTTON_BOX(bbox), GTK_BUTTONBOX_END);
  gtk_button_box_set_spacing(GTK_BUTTON_BOX(bbox), 6);
  gtk_box_pack_start(GTK_BOX(vbox), bbox, FALSE, FALSE, 0);
```

Then I'll create buttons to pack inside the button box:

```
button = gtk_button_new_with_label("View URL");
g_signal_connect(G_OBJECT(button), "clicked", G_CALLBACK(view_url_cb), sel);
gtk_box_pack_start(GTK_BOX(bbox), button, FALSE, FALSE, 0);

button = gtk_button_new_from_stock(GTK_STOCK_CLOSE);
g_signal_connect_swapped(G_OBJECT(button), "clicked",
                G_CALLBACK(gtk_widget_destroy), url_window);
gtk_box_pack_start(GTK_BOX(bbox), button, FALSE, FALSE, 0);
```

Notice that for the Close button, I use g_signal_connect_swapped(). This function gives the user data to the callback as its first argument. This means that functions that take only one argument will be passed whatever you set as the data. Here, I connect gtk_widget_destroy(), which destroys a window, and tell it to destroy url_window when the Close button is clicked.

The View URL button has its own callback. I pass it the GtkTreeSelection object so that it can retrieve the currently selected URL just like tree_selection_changed_cb(). I call a Gaim function that opens the link in the preferred browser:

```
static void
view_url_cb(GtkWidget *widget, gpointer data)
{
    GtkTreeSelection *selection = GTK_TREE_SELECTION(data);
    GtkTreeIter iter;
    GtkTreeModel *model;
    gchar *url;

    if (gtk_tree_selection_get_selected (selection, &model, &iter)) {
        gtk_tree_model_get (model, &iter,
                    URL_COLUMN, &url, -1);
      gaim_notify_uri(plugin_handle, url);
    }
}
```

The Entire Plug-In

Finally, we generate an entire plug-in, the code seen in Listing 5-2. Compile this as you would any plug-in (make pluginname.so or make pluginname.dll), move it to a plug-in directory, start Gaim, and load it.

Listing 5-2. *The URL Catcher Plug-In*

```
#include "internal.h"
#include "plugin.h"
#include "notify.h"
#include "util.h"
#include "version.h"
#include "gtkutils.h"
#include "gtkimhtml.h"
```

```c
enum {
    TIME_COLUMN,
    SENDER_COLUMN,
    URL_COLUMN,

    MESSAGE_COLUMN,
    DATA_COLUMN,
    COLUMN_COUNT
};
struct url_data {
    char *url;
    char *message;
    char *sender;
    char *time;
};

GaimPlugin *plugin_handle = NULL;
GSList *urls = NULL;
GtkWidget *url_window = NULL;

static void
window_destroy_cb(GtkWidget *widget, gpointer data)
{
    url_window = NULL;
}

static void
view_url_cb(GtkWidget *widget, gpointer data)
{
    GtkTreeSelection *selection = GTK_TREE_SELECTION(data);
    GtkTreeIter iter;
    GtkTreeModel *model;
    gchar *url;

    if (gtk_tree_selection_get_selected (selection, &model, &iter)) {
        gtk_tree_model_get (model, &iter,
                    URL_COLUMN, &url, -1);
      gaim_notify_uri(plugin_handle, url);
    }
}
```

```
static void
tree_selection_changed_cb (GtkTreeSelection *selection, gpointer data)
{
        GtkWidget *imhtml = GTK_WIDGET(data);
        GtkTreeIter iter;
        GtkTreeModel *model;
        gchar *sender, *text, *message;

        if (gtk_tree_selection_get_selected (selection, &model, &iter)) {
           gtk_tree_model_get (model, &iter, MESSAGE_COLUMN, &text,
                        SENDER_COLUMN, &sender, -1);
          message = g_strdup_printf("<font color=\"#A82F2F\"><b>%s: </b></font>%s",
                        sender, text);
          gtk_imhtml_clear(GTK_IMHTML(imhtml));
          gtk_imhtml_append_text(GTK_IMHTML(imhtml), message, 0);
          g_free(message);
        }
}

static void show_dialog(GaimPluginAction *action)
{
  GtkWidget *vbox, *bbox, *sw, *tree, *imhtml, *button;
  GtkListStore *list_store;
  GtkTreeViewColumn *col;
  GtkCellRenderer *rend;
  GSList *l;
  GtkTreeIter iter;
  GtkTreeSelection *sel;

    if (url_window != NULL) {
      gtk_window_present(GTK_WINDOW(url_window));
        return;
    }
    url_window = gtk_window_new(GTK_WINDOW_TOPLEVEL);
    gtk_window_set_default_size(GTK_WINDOW(url_window), 400, 500);
    gtk_window_set_title(GTK_WINDOW(url_window), "URL Catcher");
    gtk_container_set_border_width(GTK_CONTAINER(url_window), 12);
    g_signal_connect(G_OBJECT(url_window), "destroy",
G_CALLBACK(window_destroy_cb), Null);
    vbox = gtk_vbox_new(FALSE, 6);
    gtk_container_add(GTK_CONTAINER(url_window), vbox);
    list_store = gtk_list_store_new(COLUMN_COUNT, G_TYPE_STRING, G_TYPE_STRING,
                        G_TYPE_STRING, G_TYPE_STRING, G_TYPE_POINTER);
    tree = gtk_tree_view_new_with_model(GTK_TREE_MODEL(list_store));
```

```
rend = gtk_cell_renderer_text_new ();
col = gtk_tree_view_column_new_with_attributes ("Time",
                              rend,
                              "text", TIME_COLUMN,
                              NULL);
gtk_tree_view_append_column (GTK_TREE_VIEW (tree), col);

rend = gtk_cell_renderer_text_new ();
col = gtk_tree_view_column_new_with_attributes ("Sender",
                              rend,
                              "text", SENDER_COLUMN,
                              NULL);
gtk_tree_view_append_column (GTK_TREE_VIEW (tree), col);

rend = gtk_cell_renderer_text_new ();
col = gtk_tree_view_column_new_with_attributes ("URL",
                              rend,
                              "text", URL_COLUMN,
                              NULL);
gtk_tree_view_append_column (GTK_TREE_VIEW (tree), col);

l = urls;
while (l) {
  struct url_data *data = (struct url_data*)(l->data);
  gtk_list_store_append (list_store, &iter);
  gtk_list_store_set (list_store, &iter,
            TIME_COLUMN, data->time,
            SENDER_COLUMN, data->sender,
            MESSAGE_COLUMN, data->message,
            URL_COLUMN, data->url,
            DATA_COLUMN, data,
            -1);
  l = l->next;
}

sw = gtk_scrolled_window_new(NULL, NULL);
gtk_scrolled_window_set_shadow_type(GTK_SCROLLED_WINDOW(sw), GTK_SHADOW_IN);
gtk_scrolled_window_set_policy(GTK_SCROLLED_WINDOW(sw), GTK_POLICY_AUTOMATIC,
                  GTK_POLICY_AUTOMATIC);

gtk_container_add(GTK_CONTAINER(sw), tree);
gtk_box_pack_start(GTK_BOX(vbox), sw, TRUE, TRUE, 0);
```

```
    imhtml = gtk_imhtml_new(NULL, NULL);
    gaim_setup_imhtml(imhtml);
    sw = gtk_scrolled_window_new(NULL, NULL);
    gtk_scrolled_window_set_shadow_type(GTK_SCROLLED_WINDOW(sw), GTK_SHADOW_IN);
    gtk_scrolled_window_set_policy(GTK_SCROLLED_WINDOW(sw), GTK_POLICY_AUTOMATIC,
                    GTK_POLICY_AUTOMATIC);

    gtk_container_add(GTK_CONTAINER(sw), imhtml);
    gtk_box_pack_start(GTK_BOX(vbox), sw, TRUE, TRUE, 0);

    sel = gtk_tree_view_get_selection (GTK_TREE_VIEW (tree));
    gtk_tree_selection_set_mode (sel, GTK_SELECTION_SINGLE);
    g_signal_connect (G_OBJECT (sel), "changed",
                G_CALLBACK (tree_selection_changed_cb),
                imhtml);

    bbox = gtk_hbutton_box_new();
    gtk_button_box_set_layout(GTK_BUTTON_BOX(bbox), GTK_BUTTONBOX_END);
    gtk_button_box_set_spacing(GTK_BUTTON_BOX(bbox), 6);
    gtk_box_pack_start(GTK_BOX(vbox), bbox, FALSE, FALSE, 0);

    button = gtk_button_new_with_label("View URL");
    g_signal_connect(G_OBJECT(button), "clicked", G_CALLBACK(view_url_cb), sel);
    gtk_box_pack_start(GTK_BOX(bbox), button, FALSE, FALSE, 0);

    button = gtk_button_new_from_stock(GTK_STOCK_CLOSE);
    g_signal_connect_swapped(G_OBJECT(button), "clicked",
                    G_CALLBACK(gtk_widget_destroy), url_window);
    gtk_box_pack_start(GTK_BOX(bbox), button, FALSE, FALSE, 0);


    gtk_widget_show_all(url_window);
}

static char *check_for_urls(char *message)
{
    /* character pointers are often used as the
     * beginning of a string, but can also point
     * anywhere within a string. I'm trying to
     * isolate the URL from the message argument.
     * I'll use n to point to the start of the URL and
     * m to point to the end. ret is where I'll store
     * the string I'll return.
     */
  char *n, *m, *ret;
```

```
    /* I'll assume that all URLs will start with "http://"
     * strstr() sets n to the location in the string where
     * "http://" starts or, if it's not found, NULL. If it's
     * not found, the message doesn't contain a link, and so the
     * function returns NULL.
     */
    n = strstr(message, "http://");
    if (n == NULL)
        return NULL;

    /* Now that n points to the beginning of the link, I will set
     * m to that location (plus strlen("http://") and traverse the
     * string until I get to a charcter that's invalid in a URL.
     * That will be the end of the link.
     */
    m = n + strlen("http://");
    while(*m != '\0' &&
        *m != ' ' &&
        *m != ',' &&
        *m != '\n' &&
        *m != '<' &&
        *m != '>' &&
        *m != '"' &&
        *m != '\\')
      m++;

    /* Now I should have pointers to the beginning and end of the URL, which
     * means the length is everything between the two. I'll allocate a string for
     * it. I need to add 1 to store the terminating NUL character.
     */
    ret = g_malloc(m - n + 1);

    /* And then I copy the URL into this buffer and return it. You often need to
     * manually NULL-terminate strings after using strncpy() because strncpy()
     * won't necessarily do it itself. */
    strncpy(ret, n, m-n);
    ret[m-n] = '\0';
    return ret;
}


static void incoming_msg_cb(GaimAccount *account, char *sender, char *message,
                 GaimConversation *conv, int flags)
{
    struct url_data *url;
    const char *timestamp = gaim_date();
    char *link;
    if ((link = check_for_urls(message)) == NULL)
        return;
```

```
        url = g_malloc(sizeof(struct url_data));
        url->url = link;
        url->message = g_strdup(message);
        url->sender = g_strdup(sender);
        url->time = g_strdup(timestamp);
        urls = g_slist_append(urls, url);
}

static gboolean
plugin_load(GaimPlugin *plugin)
{
    void *handle = gaim_conversations_get_handle();
    plugin_handle = plugin;
    gaim_signal_connect(handle, "received-im-msg", plugin,
                GAIM_CALLBACK(incoming_msg_cb), NULL);
    gaim_signal_connect(handle, "received-chat-msg", plugin,
                GAIM_CALLBACK(incoming_msg_cb), NULL);
    return TRUE;
}

static GList *
actions(GaimPlugin *plugin, gpointer context)
{
    GList *l = NULL;
    GaimPluginAction *act = NULL;

    act = gaim_plugin_action_new("Show received URLs",
                                    show_dialog);
    l = g_list_append(l, act);

    return l;
}

static GaimPluginInfo info =
{
    GAIM_PLUGIN_MAGIC,
    GAIM_MAJOR_VERSION,
    GAIM_MINOR_VERSION,
    GAIM_PLUGIN_STANDARD,
    NULL,
    0,
    NULL,
    GAIM_PRIORITY_DEFAULT,
    "urlcatcher",
    "URL Catcher",
    "1.0",
    "Catches URLs from incoming messages",
```

```
    "Detects URLs from within incoming messages and provides an "
    "interface for viewing them.",
    "Sean Egan <seanegan@gmail.com>",
    "http://apress.com",
    plugin_load,
    NULL,
    NULL,
    NULL,
    NULL,
    NULL,
    actions
};

static void
init_plugin(GaimPlugin *plugin)
{
}

GAIM_INIT_PLUGIN(urlcatcher, init_plugin, info)
```

The resulting GUI is shown in Figure 5-37.

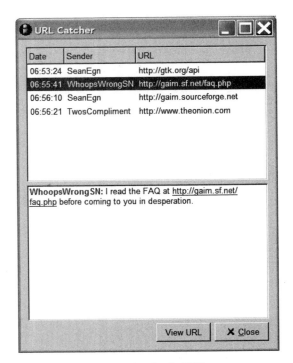

Figure 5-37. *The URL Catcher's GUI*

Potential Enhancements

If you want to play around with this plug-in to try to get a better understanding of GTK+ application design, I suggest attempting the following tasks:

- Currently, if URLs are received when the URL Catcher window is open, the list in the window will not be updated. Make the list update in real time.

- Remove some of the limitations imposed by my simplified URL detection function. Make the plug-in detect if two links were sent in the same message and handle them separately.

- Discern between URLs received from an IM and URLs received from a chat. Show which chat a URL came from, in the latter case.

- Save a few messages (sent or received) on either side of the message with the URL and show them in the GtkIMHtml widget to provide context.

- Add a protocol column to the GtkTreeView. Use a GtkCellRendererPixbuf to draw the protocol's icon. Gaim is full of examples of how to get the icon.

Summary

You should now be familiar with the most common widgets used in GTK+, and how to use them to create the vast majority of the interfaces you will need in your applications. In the next chapter, I will explain ways of extending GTK+ and taking advantage of other features it provides in order to do things not available with the default GTK+ widgets.

CHAPTER 6

■ ■ ■

Advanced GTK+

After completing Chapter 5, you should now understand how to use GTK+ to create your own applications. GTK+ offers such a rich variety of features and different widgets, but you'll likely never need to use any more than what you've already learned. However, in instances where GTK+ does not do what you require or when what you require can be done a better way, GTK+ is easily extensible.

By understanding the basic internal mechanisms that make GTK+ work, you take advantage of its modularity and create new widgets that let you do whatever you want. Gaim uses custom widgets, such as GtkIMHtml, which inputs and outputs messages in rich-text formatting. It also makes direct calls to GTK+'s support libraries to achieve effects not available in GTK itself, such as the buddy list tooltips shown in Figure 6-1, which make low-level calls to Pango and GdkPixbuf.

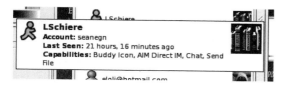

Figure 6-1. *Gaim's buddy list tooltips use Pango and GdkPixbuf directly to achieve an appearance not available through GTK+ alone.*

In this chapter, I will describe the various libraries supporting GTK+ and how GTK+ uses them. I will explain how GTK+ works internally—I'll describe the anatomy of a GTK+ widget and tell you everything you need to know to create your own.

A Sample Plug-In

To demonstrate how to extend the GTK+ library, I've written a plug-in that exemplifies the techniques discussed in this chapter. Because this plug-in is over 1,000 lines of code, I've not included it in its entirety here, but as with all the code in this book, you can download the source code to this plug-in from the Downloads page at http://apress.com.

This plug-in, called ftmakeover, changes the appearance and behavior of Gaim's File Transfer dialog as shown in Figure 6-2. It does so by implementing three custom GTK+ objects. It creates a custom cell renderer, which I use to provide a more concise view of a file transfer.

Then I create a pie-chart widget from scratch to replace the GtkProgressBar that is usually on a file transfer window. Lastly, the entire dialog is a *composite widget*, a mere aggregation of other widgets, like GtkFileChooserDialog, discussed in the previous chapter.

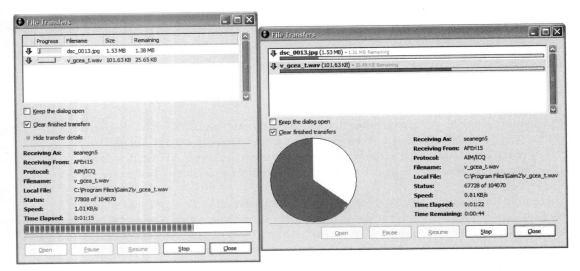

Figure 6-2. *Gaim's download manager before (left) and after (right) loading the ftmakeover plug-in*

A Gaim plug-in is not the most suitable place for immense changes like this to the GUI. However, because they're self-contained and easy to work with, they make good examples. In order to make this work as a plug-in, parts resort to unconventional programming methods you shouldn't use in actual practice. I will point these parts out to you, and tell you what you should do instead.

The first and most egregious hack is the method I used to replace the File Transfer window with a GtkWidget subclass. Gaim expects that its own File Transfer window exists and depends on its own interface to provide it. This implies that the Gaim object representing the File Transfer window must be present. Line 14 of ftmakeover.c begins the definition of GaimGtkXferDialog, the Gaim object representing a file transfer window. Later in this chapter, I will demonstrate how I integrated that into a GtkWidget, ensuring Gaim would accept the new dialog.

▪Note The three custom objects I've created for this chapter, GtkCellRendererTransfer, GtkPieChart, and GtkFileTransferDialog, I've put in the Gtk namespace. Because this namespace is reserved for GTK+ itself, this isn't good practice. If GTK+ were to create a new class called GtkPieChart, the two would conflict. Because these classes are implemented from within a plug-in, the risk is somewhat mitigated, but it's still a bad idea. GaimGtkPieChart would be more appropriate.

All three extensions to the File Transfer window have object-oriented features provided by the GObject library. Because GTK+ relies so heavily on GObject, adding features to GTK+ requires that you create a new class of GObject. The next section will demonstrate how to do this.

GObject

At the heart of GTK+ is the GObject library. GObject is a library that provides object-oriented features throughout GTK+ through the GObject class. Every object in GTK+, from GtkButton to GtkTextBuffer to GdkPixbuf, descends from GObject.

■**Note** GObject refers both to a library and to a class provided by that library. In this book, I refer to the library in normal formatting (GObject) and the class in code formatting (GObject).

Because these objects all descend from GObject, GObject's features are available in nearly everything you do in GTK+. These features add many benefits to object-oriented programming in C, as discussed in Chapter 4.

Object-Oriented Features of GObject

GObject provides features familiar to users of most object-oriented languages. In case you are not familiar with these features, I'll explain each of them and discuss how they apply to efficient GTK+ programming.

Data Typing

C provides very few data types, and as far as the language is concerned the only notable difference is how much memory each takes. A C compiler will do very little to prevent you from using the wrong type; often a compiler warning is all that occurs, and even then just casting it to the correct type will allow it to compile, even if the cast makes no sense.

Other programming languages have a strong sense of type. In these languages, you cannot call a function expecting one type with an object of another type. For an object-oriented language, the ability to know the type of an object is important, as there are infinitely more than are available in C, and consequently the chance of making a mistake is much higher.

■**Note** Static typing is done at compile time; dynamic typing is done at runtime.

Of course, GTK+ (and thus GObject) is written in C, so the previously described static typing is not possible. GObject can do only what's permissible in C. However, it offers a powerful dynamic typing system. Most functions in GTK+ that expect an object of a certain type use GObject's dynamic typing to ensure that it's been passed the correct type. If not, the function will return before attempting to use it. Importantly, GObject's typing system understands inheritance.

Classes

If you know an object-oriented programming language, you are most likely familiar with classes. In the class-based model of object-oriented programming, a "class" exists that specifies what the object is and how it behaves. Created objects must be of a certain class; these created objects are called *instances* of that class.

The GObject library is also class-based. Each object has an associated class, and just as objects inherit properties from their parents, so do their classes. When you create your own widgets, you will need to first create an object derived from GObjectClass defining certain behaviors of your widget. This allows you to set some attributes that are common to every instance of your object, such as function pointers defining how your object behaves on certain events and the various signals that objects of your class can emit.

Just as the widgets discussed in the previous chapter emit signals to indicate that some event occurred, your custom widgets will emit signals. The widget's default behavior is stored in a function pointer within the class object. This allows subclasses of a widget to override these behaviors.

Because the default behaviors are provided through function pointers, a subclass need only reassign that pointer to change the behavior. For instance, all GtkWidgets have an expose_event function pointer, called when the widget needs to draw itself. The pie-chart widget in ftmakeover reassigns this pointer to its own function, allowing it to control drawing itself.

Reference Counting

One of the trickiest aspects to programming in C for many people is memory management. In C, when you allocate new memory from the heap, it is your responsibility to explicitly free it when it is no longer of use. Other languages, such as Java and C#, have *garbage collection*, a feature wherein the program itself keeps track of when an object is no longer being used and frees memory on its own.

One way this is accomplished is through reference counting: the garbage collector keeps track of how many different references are kept to an object. When that reference count reaches zero, the object is destroyed.

GObject offers reference counting as well. Of course, as is the case with data typing, it can perform only within the bounds of what the language allows. Thus, the reference counting is not automatic. However, this still allows for objects to be heavily referenced by multiple other objects without needing to worry about freeing memory until the object is no longer needed anywhere in code.

This is why in GTK+ application development, you can create a complicated interface composed of dozens of widgets and never have to worry about freeing the memory associated with it. The GObject and GTK+ libraries handle that themselves.

Suppose you create a GtkWindow object and a GtkButton object. Each of these objects starts with a reference count of one, owned by GTK+. When you call gtk_widget_destroy() on a widget, it reduces its reference count. In this instance, the reference counts fall to zero, GTK+ notices this and frees the memory allocated to it.

Now suppose you pack the GtkButton object into the GtkWindow object. As a container widget, the window must keep track of the widgets packed inside it. This means the GtkWindow object must keep a pointer to the GtkButton object. If the memory allocated to the button were freed while the window held a reference to it, the application would crash when the window attempted to access this.

The solution is that any piece of code that keeps a reference to another object also increases and decreases the reference count of that object as necessary. In this example, the GtkWindow increases the button's reference count to two. When gtk_widget_destroy() is called on the button, its reference count decreases to one; it isn't until the window gives up its reference by decrementing the button's reference count that the memory is freed.

Signals

As discussed in the previous chapter, signals are the way in which a GObject communicates generically with the rest of the program. Communicating messages from one object to another is a crucial aspect of object-oriented programming, and various programming languages use different means of doing this. GObject uses the signal system.

Signals are a generic message-passing system between a GObject and another piece of code. You have already used signals to receive notification when buttons are pressed or text is entered; signals are the primary way the flow of your program is controlled in a GTK+ application.

As you create your own custom GTK+ widgets, they too will emit signals. Gaim's GtkIMHtml widget, for instance, emits a "url-clicked" signal, emitted when the user clicks a hyperlink. The callback is passed the URL. From the callback, Gaim launches the user's preferred Web browser. I will demonstrate how to create and emit signals later this chapter.

Properties

An object is really little more than data and functions provided to manipulate that data. While much of that data is private and used internally by the object for whatever reason, other data are public and can be accessed and changed by other parts of the program. You learned about mutators and accessors in Chapter 4; GObject offers a different way of providing encapsulation with properties.

A *property* is a bit of data associated with an instance of a class that can be changed and/or read outside of the object. GObject provides a standard way of defining, setting, and reading these values, avoiding the code duplication of countless accessors and mutators.

Last chapter you saw properties used explicitly is in the GtkCellRenderer object. Each renderer is a GObject with certain properties that affect how it draws. GtkCellRendererText, for instance, has a "text" property and a "markup" property. These properties were associated with columns in a GtkTreeModel object to display the data as required. The new cell renderer implemented by ftmakeover has numerous such properties, which affect how it draws the cell.

Because they provide a generic way of manipulating data in an object, properties are used extensively throughout GTK+. Much of the data stored within instances of an object are available as properties. Therefore, you can duplicate most of the mutator and accessor functions found within GTK+ using GObject properties. The following GTK+ function was discussed in the last chapter:

```
gtk_window_set_title(GTK_WINDOW(window), "Window");
```

It can, for instance, also be written as

```
g_object_set(G_OBJECT(window), "title", "Window", NULL);
```

You can set multiple properties with a single call such as

```
g_object_set(B_OBJECT(window), "title", "Window",
                          "default-hight", 100, NULL);
```

Arbitrary Data

Although not strictly an object-oriented feature, every instance of a GObject contains a hash table (refer to Chapter 4 for more information about this structure) associating strings to pointers. GObject offers an API for setting these pointers, and then retrieving them at a later time.

For example, suppose I created a GtkWindow (which, like all widgets, descends from GObject) for an IM conversation with someone. I can associate that someone's screen name with that GObject via a string identifier, perhaps "IM-screenname." When I receive callbacks from that GtkWindow, I can easily have it return the value stored with the key "IM-screenname."

Using GObject

In this section, I will demonstrate how to create your own GObject subclass using GtkCellRendererTransfer as an example. This cell renderer combines the capabilities of multiple cell renderers (GtkCellRendererPixbuf, GtkCellRendererText, and GtkCellRendererProgress) into a single GtkCellRenderer for a more concise appearance, specifically suited for file transfers. Because GtkCellRendererTransfer is a cell renderer, it naturally inherits from GtkCellRenderer. This, in turn, inherits from GObject. Thus, creating a GtkCellRendererText is a matter of creating a special type of GObject.

Although GObject's inheritance uses the same concept for inheritance using structs as was discussed in Chapter 4, because the GObject library makes heavy use of dynamic typing, you cannot merely create such a subclass and start using it; you must inform GObject that this new type exists and explain to it some of the object's properties. This description is referenced as a GType.

GType

A GType is ultimately just a number that serves as an identifier for the type you're creating. GObject will use the data you register with this GType as guidelines for how to create and manage objects of this new class.

Typically, your class will have a function suffixed _get_type(), which returns the value of the GType. GtkCellRendererTransfer, for instance, includes a function called gtk_cell_renderer_transfer_get_type(). It is in this function itself that the GType is registered using the *singleton pattern.*

The singleton design pattern is a mechanism for ensuring that an object is created only once. A function using this pattern creates a new object the first time the function is called, and returns a reference to that same object on subsequent calls. This is how your _get_type() function will generally operate:

```
static void
gtk_cell_renderer_transfer_class_init (GtkCellRendererTransferClass *class);
GType  gtk_cell_renderer_transfer_get_type (void)
{
    static GType cell_transfer_type = 0;

    if (!cell_transfer_type)
        {
            static const GTypeInfo cell_transfer_info =
                {
                    sizeof (GtkCellRendererTransferClass),
                    NULL,             /* base_init */
                    NULL,             /* base_finalize */
                    (GClassInitFunc) gtk_cell_renderer_transfer_class_init,
                    NULL,             /* class_finalize */
                    NULL,             /* class_data */
                    sizeof (GtkCellRendererTransfer),
                    0,                /* n_preallocs */
                    NULL              /* instance_init */
                };

            cell_transfer_type =
                g_type_register_static (GTK_TYPE_CELL_RENDERER,
                                            "GtkCellRendererTransfer",
                                            &cell_transfer_info, 0);
        }

    return cell_transfer_type;
}
```

This function uses the static modifier on the variables type and info. The static keyword in C confuses many people because it seems to play completely different roles depending on where it's used.

In this context, modifying a variable inside a function, static causes the variable to act like a global variable; it's created only once and retains its value despite subsequent calls to the function. However, unlike a global variable, only the function it's declared in can access it. The singleton pattern here uses static to ensure that once type and info are initialized, the function will be able to return type, without re-registering the type.

Registering the type is a matter of calling g_type_register_static(). This function takes four arguments:

```
GType        g_type_register_static          (GType parent_type,
                                              const gchar *type_name,
                                              const GTypeInfo *info,
                                              GTypeFlags flags);
```

- The parent_type argument is the parent this type descends from; recall that GType is aware of inheritance. If you need to create a type that does not descend from any other type (this is extraordinarily rare and of use almost solely to GObject internals), use g_type_register_fundamental() instead of this function. Because this new object is a cell renderer, the example inherits from GtkCellRenderer, specified by its type GTK_TYPE_CELL_RENDERER.

- The type_name argument is a string containing the name of the class, such as GtkWidget or GtkCellRendererTransfer.

- The info argument is a GTypeInfo struct, which defines how the GObject library will manage this class and instantiate its objects; I'll return to this point shortly.

- The flags argument is a bitmask of flags. If you are creating an abstract object, use G_TYPE_FLAG_ABSTRACT, otherwise just set this argument as 0 to indicate this new type may be instantiated.

Note *Abstract* objects are those from which instances may not be created, but serve only to provide features common to all its subclasses. GtkWidget, for instance, does nothing but provide a framework for creating GUI elements. Likewise, GObject merely provides object-oriented features to its subclasses.

GTypeInfo is a struct representing all GObject needs to properly create and maintain this class and its instances. Here, it is declared static and created with a singleton pattern, the same way as the GType itself. GTypeInfo consists mostly of function pointers and integers explaining how this object should behave:

```
typedef struct {
  /* interface types, classed types, instantiated types */
  guint16                 class_size;

  GBaseInitFunc           base_init;
  GBaseFinalizeFunc       base_finalize;

  /* interface types, classed types, instantiated types */
  GClassInitFunc          class_init;
  GClassFinalizeFunc      class_finalize;
  gconstpointer           class_data;

  /* instantiated types */
  guint16                 instance_size;
  guint16                 n_preallocs;
  GInstanceInitFunc       instance_init;

  /* value handling */
  const GTypeValueTable      *value_table;
} GTypeInfo;
```

- The class_size member tells how much memory to allocate for this class. Recall that a class is created only once, and multiple instances are created from it. The class will be declared as a struct, using inheritance just as explained in Chapter 4. I'll cover what is contained in this struct in the "Class and Instances structs" section. The size of the struct should be determined with the sizeof operator on that struct.

- The base_init member is used when creating subclasses of this class. It provides a function to allow this type's data to be initialized even when used in subclasses. It can be ignored for now and set as NULL.

- The base_finalize member is used when destroying instances of subclasses. Like base_init, this can be ignored and set to NULL for now.

- The class_init member instructs GObject how to initialize your class struct. If your class has any data to itself (most of your data will probably be unique to each instance, not within the class itself), you will need to set it to a default in class_init. More commonly, this function is where you will create the signals or properties used by this class. ftmakeover sets class_init to install its properties, which I will discuss later.

- The class_finalize member provides a suitable place to free any memory allocated in your class_init function. Note that properties and signals are removed automatically.

- The class_data member is a pointer used to send any data you want to your class_init and class_finalize functions.

- The instance_size member is the size of the struct used to represent instances of this class. Compare this to class_size, which holds the size of the struct used to represent the class itself. This will similarly be determined by sizeof.

- The n_preallocs member allows you to specify the number of instances for which GObject should initiate memory in advance. Because allocating memory in little bits over time can result in fragmented memory that can reduce performance, GTK+ and its associated libraries attempt to allocate memory in larger chunks and use it as needed. If you have an idea of how many instances this class will generate, you can set some sort of number here to cause memory for them to be more efficiently allocated in advance.

- The instance_init member is the function that initializes an instance of this class. This function will initialize the data associated with an instance to default values and do anything else it needs to create a new object.

- The value_table member provides the functions needed to implement this type as a GValue, discussed briefly next section. Because the GObject library already provides a GValue for objects, this is rarely needed and can be set to NULL.

Once you have written a _get_type() function, you may use that type. You can create objects of a specific type by using g_object_new() as shown in the following example. You may also set properties at initialization. I will discuss properties later in this chapter:

```
gpointer    g_object_new                    (GType object_type,
                                             const gchar *first_property_name,
                                             ...);
```

To make it easier to create a GtkCellRendererTransfer object, though, I include a constructor that makes the call to g_object_new() itself. It is customary and expected to include a function like this:

```
GtkCellRenderer *gtk_cell_renderer_transfer_new(void)
{
    return g_object_new(GTK_TYPE_CELL_RENDERER_TRANSFER, NULL);
}
```

A final note about GType: it's customary to define several macros when creating a new GObject. In Chapter 4, you saw one of these extensively: the macro that casts one object to another (e.g., GTK_WIDGET(widget)). These macros are not required at all, but are useful to developers working with your objects, yourself included. By providing a convention in the name of these macros, you make it easier for other developers to work with your extensions.

GtkCellRendererTransfer defines GTK_CELL_RENDERER_TRANSFER and several other standard macros:

```
#define GTK_TYPE_CELL_RENDERER_TRANSFER (gtk_cell_renderer_transfer_get_type())
#define GTK_CELL_RENDERER_TRANSFER(obj) (G_TYPE_CHECK_INSTANCE_CAST((obj), \
                GTK_TYPE_CELL_RENDERER_TRANSFER, GtkCellRendererTransfer))
#define GTK_CELL_RENDERER_TRANSFER_CLASS(klass) (G_TYPE_CHECK_CLASS_CAST ((klass),\
                GTK_TYPE_CELL_RENDERER_TRANSFER, GtkCellTransferClass))
#define GTK_IS_CELL_RENDERER_TRANSFER(obj) (G_TYPE_CHECK_INSTANCE_TYPE ((obj), \
                GTK_TYPE_GTK_CELL_RENDERER_TRANSFER))
#define GTK_IS_CELL_RENDERER_TRANSFER_CLASS(klass) (G_TYPE_CHECK_CLASS_TYPE \
                ((klass), GTK_TYPE_GTK_CELL_RENDERER_TRANSFER))
#define GTK_CELL_RENDERER_TRANSFER_GET_CLASS(obj)  (G_TYPE_INSTANCE_GET_CLASS \
                ((obj), GTK_TYPE_CELL_RENDERER_TRANSFER,
                GtkCellRendererTransferClass))
```

GValue

GType provides a way to identify a type. A GValue is essentially a GType and an associated value of that type. Using GValue allows data of any type to be handled generically. GValue is useful as a *polymorphic data type.*

Polymorphism is the concept that the same code can be applied to any data, regardless of type. A function that can take any type of value, such as GObject properties that are demonstrated later, can use a GValue. One function can be used to accept any type of value. In some cases, you will know in advance the type of GValue to expect, but GValue can attempt to convert a value from one type to another. This functionality ranges from the simple—casting a value of type char to type int—to the more complex—converting a gboolean to a string reading "True" or "False," for example.

If you know the type of GValue to expect, you can use existing standard functions to retrieve the value from within. These functions include g_value_get_char(), g_value_get_string(), g_value_get_int(), etc. These functions all take a GValue as their argument and return the corresponding C fundamental type. These functions also all have corresponding mutators, such as g_value_set_char(), g_value_set_string(), etc. available for setting a GValue.

The Class and Instance `structs`

When GObject must create an object of the class you've just created, it will first check if the class exists. If not, it will allocate the memory needed for the class struct (as you specified in class_size), then hand it off to the class_init functions of every class in its inheritance hierarchy, ending with your class_init function. Once a properly initialized class struct exists, it will allocate memory for your new instance, and call each instance_init function in the same manner. What belongs in these structs and initialization functions?

Your structs should use the inheritance technique for structs discussed in Chapter 4. That is, the first item in your class struct must be the class struct you're inheriting from. The first (and only) element in GtkCellRendererTransferClass is GtkCellRendererClass:

```
struct _GtkCellRendererTransferClass {
    GtkCellRendererClass parent_class;
};
```

It is possible that this is all you need; however, some classes require variables for data common to all instances of your class (Java and C++ developers would call these static variables, not to be confused with the two meanings of the static keyword in C) and function pointers to store the default handlers for each signal you will create.

Including overridable functions is very useful for subclasses. By creating default handlers, a derived subclass can access this function pointer and override the default behavior of its parent class. This technique can be used with other functions you wish to allow derived subclasses to override. This overriding will be done in the _class_init() function of the subclass.

GtkCellRenderer, for instance, provides a render function that subclasses may override to define how it draws a cell. GtkCellRendererTransfer overrides this in gtk_cell_renderer_transfer_class_init() called before a single GtkCellRendererTransfer is created:

```
GObjectClass *object_class = G_OBJECT_CLASS(class);
GtkCellRendererClass *cell_class = GTK_CELL_RENDERER_CLASS(class);

object_class->get_property = gtk_cell_renderer_transfer_get_property;
object_class->set_property = gtk_cell_renderer_transfer_set_property;

cell_class->get_size = gtk_cell_renderer_transfer_get_size;
cell_class->render    = gtk_cell_renderer_transfer_render;
```

Because the class struct inherits from other class structs, overriding the function pointers in other classes involves a simple cast. Notice here that GtkCellRendererTransfer also overrides functions in GObjectClass. This is to allow GObject to set and retrieve properties your class introduces in the manner discussed in the "Properties" section.

The instance struct usually contains more data than the class struct, as it contains all the data specific to each instance. Each GtkCellRendererTransfer keeps track of various properties of the file transfer it renders, including the filename, the size, the transfer status, and the current progress. All of this data is included in the GtkCellRendererTransfer struct:

```
struct _GtkCellRendererTransfer {
    GtkCellRenderer parent;

    GdkPixbuf *icon;
    gdouble progress;
    gchar *name;
    gchar *size;
    gchar *remaining;
};
```

In many cases, you would want to provide an instance_init function in GTypeInfo to initialize these data to defaults. In the case of GtkCellRendererTransfer, leaving them uninitialized is fine. In many cases, you would want to provide accessor and mutator functions for these variables. However, because GtkTreeView requires a uniform way to set data for all renderers, GtkCellRendererTransfer uses properties.

Properties

In addition to initializing any class-wide data you may have, the class_init function is where you create properties and signals.

A property is simply data that can be changed by other classes. There is little difference between using properties and merely containing in your instances a variable and an accessor and mutator function for it. However, properties provide GObjects with a cleaner, more generic API that can then be used to access data from an instance regardless of what type the instance is. When used by cell renderers, a GtkTreeView object can set values from its associated model without knowing the specifics of how each renderer works.

Creating New Properties

Just as you created a GTypeInfo before you could register a new GType, you must describe the properties you create before registering them. The GParamSpec object provides metadata about the property, most importantly its type.

Most often, you will create a GParamSpec by using a function specific to the type of property you're creating. A GParamSpec object describing a Boolean property, for instance, would use g_param_spec_boolean(). GtkCellRendererTransfer includes a few string properties created with g_param_spec_string():

```
g_param_spec_string ("name",
                     "Name",
                     "File name",
                      NULL,
                      G_PARAM_READWRITE);
```

Other property types may have slightly different arguments. g_param_spec_double(), also used by GtkCellRendererTransfer, for instance, requires that you specify a maximum and minimum value, 1 and 0 in this case. However, each GParamSpec constructor requires at least the information required by g_param_spec_string():

```
GParamSpec* g_param_spec_string          (const gchar *name,
                                          const gchar *nick,
                                          const gchar *blurb,
                                          const gchar *default_value,
                                          GParamFlags flags);
```

- The name argument is the name used internally by your code to refer to this property. It must start with a letter and can be any combination of letters, numbers, and hyphens. Underscores are also permissible in most places, but the hyphen is much preferred. Hyphens and underscores cannot be mixed in the same property name.

- The nick argument is a human-readable nickname for the property.

- The blurb argument is human-readable description of the property.

- The default_value argument is the default value for this property before it is altered by code elsewhere. Its type depends on the function called. This function requires a string.

- The flags argument is a bitmask allowing you to set certain aspects of this property. The most common of these flags are G_PARAM_READABLE and G_PARAM_WRITABLE, which specify how the developer can access and modify this property, respectively.

After describing a property, you may install it to a class with g_object_class_install_property(). Most often, g_param_spec_string() and its companion functions will be invoked within the call to g_object_class_install_property() itself. Thus, one of GtkCellRendererTransfer's calls to g_object_class_install_property() looks like this:

```
g_object_class_install_property (object_class,
                    PROP_NAME,
                    g_param_spec_string ("name",
                                         "Name",
                                         "File name",
                                         NULL,
                                         G_PARAM_READWRITE));
```

The first argument is the new class's GObjectClass, referenced by casting GtkCellRendererTransferClass; the second is a numerical identifier for this property, often declared in an enum. The property enum used by GtkCellRendererTransfer follows:

```
enum {
    PROP_0,
    PROP_ICON,
    PROP_NAME,
    PROP_PROGRESS,
    PROP_SIZE,
    PROP_REMAINING
};
```

■**Note** Because 0 is an invalid property identifier, these enums often start with PROP_0, which is never used. An alternative way to avoid an error is to start with PROP_ICON = 1, which would then start enumerating from 1.

At this point, your properties are registered and GObject has a generic interface it uses to access them. However, your object provides a way for GObject to do this. GObject knows only to call the set_property and get_property function pointers in GObjectClass; it is up to your class to specify how to internally set and get these properties. If you're using custom properties, you must provide code in the set_property and get_property functions that retrieve and set values appropriately. Because these functions are pointers in GObjectClass, they can be overridden in gtk_cell_renderer_transfer_class_init().

```
object_class->get_property = gtk_cell_renderer_transfer_get_property;
object_class->set_property = gtk_cell_renderer_transfer_set_property;
```

The prototypes for these functions are as follows:

```
void g_object_set_property (GObject *object, guint prop_id,
                                  const GValue *val, GParamSpec *pspec);
void g_object_get_property (GObject *object, guint prop_id,
                                  GValue *val, GParamSpec *pspec);
```

These functions take a similar list of arguments:

- The object argument is the object that owns this property. GObject calls the set_property function when the program must change the value within the object argument and the get_property function when it must read the value from within the object argument.

- The prop_id argument is the numerical identifier specified (likely from an enum) in the GParamSpec when first registering the property.

- The val argument is the GValue that must be assigned from the object argument in case of get_property, and assigned to the object argument in the case of set_property.

- The pspec argument is the GParamSpec created when registering this property.

Because the GObject library passes the numerical identifier specified in the property enum to both of these functions, it's common for these functions to be nothing more than a switch block. gtk_cell_renderer_transfer_get_property() is one such example:

```
static void gtk_cell_renderer_transfer_get_property (GObject     *object,
                                                     guint       param_id,
                                                     GValue      *value,
                                                     GParamSpec *psec)
{
    GtkCellRendererTransfer *cellrenderer = GTK_CELL_RENDERER_TRANSFER(object);

    switch (param_id)
```

```
    {
    case PROP_ICON:
        g_value_set_object(value, cellrenderer->icon);
        break;
    case PROP_PROGRESS:
        g_value_set_double(value, cellrenderer->progress);
        break;
    case PROP_NAME:
        g_value_set_string(value, cellrenderer->name);
        break;
    case PROP_SIZE:
        g_value_set_string(value, cellrenderer->size);
        break;
    case PROP_REMAINING:
        g_value_set_string(value, cellrenderer->remaining);
        break;
    default:
        G_OBJECT_WARN_INVALID_PROPERTY_ID (object, param_id, psec);
        break;
    }
}
```

gtk_cell_renderer_transfer_set_property() is nearly identical. Notice, though, that it frees the old string values before reassigning the variables. It is implementation details like this that make overriding set_property() and get_property() necessary to a generic property system:

```
static void gtk_cell_renderer_transfer_set_property (GObject      *object,
                                                     guint        param_id,
                                                     const GValue *value,
                                                     GParamSpec   *pspec)
{
    GtkCellRendererTransfer *cellrenderer = GTK_CELL_RENDERER_TRANSFER (object);

    switch (param_id)
        {
        case PROP_ICON:
            if (cellrenderer->icon)
                g_object_unref(cellrenderer->icon);
            cellrenderer->icon = g_value_get_object(value);
            g_object_ref(cellrenderer->icon);
            break;
        case PROP_PROGRESS:
            cellrenderer->progress = g_value_get_double(value);
        case PROP_NAME:
            if (cellrenderer->name)
                g_free(cellrenderer->name);
            cellrenderer->name = g_strdup(g_value_get_string(value));
            break;
```

```
      case PROP_SIZE:
          if (cellrenderer->size)
              g_free(cellrenderer->size);
          cellrenderer->size = g_strdup(g_value_get_string(value));
          break;
      case PROP_REMAINING:
          if (cellrenderer->remaining)
              g_free(cellrenderer->remaining);
          cellrenderer->remaining = g_strdup(g_value_get_string(value));
          break;
      default:
          G_OBJECT_WARN_INVALID_PROPERTY_ID(object, param_id, pspec);
          break;
      }
}
```

Using Properties

Now that you've created properties and provided a way to store and retrieve them, any application using this object can call g_property_set() or g_property_get(). Both functions can work with multiple properties at a time. For example, when I instruct GtkTreeView to associate certain properties of GtkCellRendererTransfer to columns in its GtkTreeModel object, it will eventually call something to this effect:

```
g_object_set(renderer, "pixbuf", pixbuf,
                       "name", "ftmakeover.c",
                       "progress", 0.74,
                       "size", "46 Kb",
                       "remaining", "12 Kb", NULL);
```

This call sets properties for renderer. The function's syntax uses a NULL-terminated list of pairs of property names and values, which you saw in the previous chapter. g_object_get() uses an identical syntax using pointers to variables instead of values:

```
char *name, *size, *remaining;
double progress;
GdkPixbuf *pixbuf;
g_object_get(renderer, "pibuf", &pixbuf,
                       "name", &code,
                       "progress", &progress,
                       "size", &size,
                       "remaining", &remaining, NULL);
```

Of course, these functions aren't limited to GtkTreeView; you can use them on any object anywhere appropriate.

Creating Signals

The other important thing to do in your class_init function is to create the signals that will be emitted by objects of your new class. An integer identifies a signal, like a GType. In order to emit these signals, you will need to use this identifier, so it makes sense to keep track of them in an array with an enum to give recognizable names to each signal. Because cell renderers rarely need to emit signals, GtkCellRendererTransfer does not create a signal. GtkFileTransferDialog, another GObject implemented by ftmakeover, implements one signal, emitted when the user indicates the transfer should be stopped. The enum and array this object uses follow:

```
enum {
    STOPPED,
    LAST_SIGNAL
};
static guint signals [LAST_SIGNAL] = { 0 };
```

Notice that because enums start counting at 0 (STOPPED is 0, LAST_SIGNAL is 1), that LAST_SIGNAL, while not representing a signal itself, will be the number of signals defined (one, in this case) and can be used to declare the array.

The class struct should also have a function pointer to serve as the default event handler for this signal. By putting a function pointer in the class struct, you provide a generic way for GObject to call the handler and a way for subclasses to override it. The callback to GtkFileTransferDialog's STOPPED signal takes one argument, a GaimXfer struct. Therefore, GtkFileTransferDialogClass includes a function pointer matching that prototype:

```
struct _GtkFileTransferDialogClass {
    GtkDialogClass parent;
    void (*stopped)(GtkFileTransferDialog *, GaimXfer *);
};
```

With an array declared to store the signals and function pointers to store the default handlers, call g_signal_new() and store the return value in your array. gtk_file_transfer_dialog_class_init() follows in its entirety:

```
static void
gtk_file_transfer_dialog_class_init (GtkFileTransferDialogClass *ft_class)
{
    GObjectClass *gobject_class = (GObjectClass*)ft_class;
    signals[STOPPED] = g_signal_new("stopped",
                    G_TYPE_FROM_CLASS(gobject_class),
                    G_SIGNAL_RUN_FIRST,
                    G_STRUCT_OFFSET(GtkFileTransferDialogClass, stopped),
                    NULL,
                    0,
                    g_cclosure_marshal_VOID__POINTER,
                    G_TYPE_NONE, 1,
                    G_TYPE_POINTER);
}
```

The g_signal_new() function takes a variable number of arguments. Nine arguments are always required, and each argument this signal's callback requires adds an additional argument to g_signal_new():

```
guint       g_signal_new                    (const gchar *signal_name,
                                             GType itype,
                                             GSignalFlags signal_flags,
                                             guint class_offset,
                                             GSignalAccumulator accumulator,
                                             gpointer accu_data,
                                             GSignalCMarshaller c_marshaller,
                                             GType return_type,
                                             guint n_params,
                            ...);
```

- The signal_name argument is the name of the signal. This name follows the same rules as property names: it must start with a letter and can consist only of letters, numbers, hyphens, and underscores.

- The itype argument is the GType of the class that will emit this signal. G_TYPE_FROM_CLASS is a macro called on your class to return its type. You could also call the gtk_file_transfer_dialog_get_type() function or the GTK_TYPE_FILE_TRANSFER_DIALOG macro that wraps it.

- The signal_flags argument is a bitmask of flags pertaining to this signal. The most commonly used ones tell GTK+ when during signal emission the object's default signal handler should be called. Except for very special purposes, G_SIGNAL_RUN_FIRST is appropriate here.

- The class_offset argument tells GObject where to find the default signal handler for this signal. G_STRUCT_OFFSET is a macro that returns the location within the struct of the default handler for this signal. It provides a convenient way of telling GObject where it can find the default handler, while still allowing the default handler to be overridden.

- The accumulator argument is a function that can be used when a signal's callback returns a value. The accumulator will be called after each callback with that callback's return value. The accumulator uses the return values of each callback function to determine whether the signal should continue to be passed to other callback functions. This feature—stopping the signal emission—is the most useful feature of the accumulator. In fact, GObject provides a preexisting accumulator g_accumulator_true_handled(). This accumulator, when set in g_signal_new(), will allow callbacks to return gboolean types and stop signal emission when they return TRUE. This is known as *short-circuiting*.

- The accu_data argument allows you to send a pointer to the accumulator that may then affect how it works.

- The c_marshaller argument is a special type of function called a *marshaller*. Because GObject deals with the polymorphic GValue internally, a function is needed to convert each GValue from g_signal_emit() into its appropriate primitive C type in order to pass the callback function the types it expects. The same function needs to convert the callback's return value to a GValue. GTK+ provides most common marshallers, so you rarely need to create your own (if you do there is a utility program named genmarshal distributed with GTK+ to help you). Marshaller function names start with g_cclosure_marshal_ and then the return value type of the callback function, *two* underscores, then a list of parameter types separated by underscores. GtkFileTransferDialog uses g_cclosure_marshal_VOID__POINTER for its STOPPED signal. This marshaller matches the prototype of this signal's callback.

- The return_type argument is the type of the callback function's return value: G_TYPE_NONE here.

- The n_params argument is the number of arguments the signal's callback takes. This signal's callback has one argument.

- The remaining arguments are a list of types of each parameter. Note that because the number of parameters is explicitly stated, this list need not be NULL-terminated unlike other variable length parameter lists covered. This signal's callback takes a G_TYPE_POINTER type.

Your object can emit the new signal when appropriate with g_signal_emit(). GtkFileTransferDialog emits the STOPPED signal when the Stop button is pressed:

```
g_signal_emit(dialog, signals[STOPPED], 0, dialog->dialog.selected_xfer);
```

Here, dialog is the instance of the class emitting the signal, and signals[STOPPED] looks into the array where you stored your signal IDs, returning the appropriate one. The third argument is used for a signal "detail," a rarely used function of signals. You can usually set this to 0. The remaining argument is the pointer to send as the argument to attached callbacks. If the callback took more than one argument, they would be included in subsequent arguments to g_signal_emit(). If the callback has a return value, the final argument is a pointer to a variable in which to store it.

Elsewhere, code attaches to the "stopped" signal:

```
g_signal_connect(G_OBJECT(dialog), "stopped", G_CALLBACK(stopped_cb), NULL);
```

When the signal is emitted, the stopped_cb callback is called:

```
static void
stopped_cb (GtkWidget *widget, GaimXfer *xfer)
{
    gaim_notify_info(NULL, NULL, "You stopped this transfer", NULL);
}
```

This results in the alert message seen in Figure 6-3 popping up when the Stop button is pressed.

Figure 6-3. *An alert dialog triggered by* GtkFileTransferDialog*'s "stopped" signal*

Other Features of GObject

The other features of GObject outlined earlier are straightforward to use. Setting and retrieving arbitrary data is simple as can be. To set data, call the following:

```
g_object_set_data(object, "key", data);
```

The key argument is the key for this data. If data is already stored with this key, it will be overwritten. Data is defined as a void pointer. If you need to store a nonpointer value, you can use GINT_TO_POINTER(data) and GPOINTER_TO_INT(data), which are two macros that will ensure the int is properly stored within the pointer.

Retrieving data is simple:

```
data = g_object_get_data(object, "key");
```

This will return the associated data, or NULL if no data is set.

Reference counting is slightly more complex, but it's rare that you will need to use it often, as it happens mostly internally. You can increase the reference count with g_object_ref() and decrease it with g_object_unref(). When manipulating the refcount of a GObject is necessary, that object's documentation will usually specify so.

Summary of GObject

Now that you understand what is involved in creating GtkCellRendererTransfer, review what you need to do to create a new GObject.

- **Create structs for your instance and your class.** You must have a struct for both your class and your instance. These must inherit from the direct parent. In the case of GtkCellRendererTransfer, its structs inherit from GtkCellRenderer.

- **Register a type from a _get_type() function.** Create a GTypeInfo struct and register this with g_type_register_static(). Do this with a singleton pattern to avoid registering the type more than once. Your GTypeInfo will contain the size of the structs created and, optionally, pointers to functions that initialize and deinitialize data.

- **Create functions to initialize or deinitialize your class and instances.** If you need to set default values for your instances' data fields, create an instance_init function and set it in your GTypeInfo struct. The class_init function is the appropriate place to install properties and signals and also to override the parent class's default behaviors.

- **Override the parent class's default behaviors.** This is the best way to introduce new behaviors into your new widget while building on old ones.

GObject is the base object class of every other object in GTK+, including every GtkWidget. Now that you understand how to create a new GObject descending from GtkCellRenderer, you'll find there are few differences in creating a GObject descending from any GtkWidget. Typically, the simplest such GtkWidgets are called *composite widgets*.

Creating a Composite Widget

As mentioned in the previous chapter, a composite widget is merely a widget composed of other widgets amalgamated into a single entity. This kind of widget can be created entirely with ordinary GTK+ API calls, but making it a widget of its own adds a level of encapsulation, which benefits the developer. The collection of widgets becomes a single, reusable object.

A composite widget is a container that comes prepacked with other widgets created and handled by the composite widget. This widget can emit signals of its own and do anything else any other GTK+ widget can do. Examples of composite widgets in GTK+ itself include GtkDialog (which descends from GtkWindow, a container widget) and GtkFileChooserWidget (which descends from GtkVBox).

For the ftmakeover plug-in, I've turned the file transfer dialog into a composite widget called GtkFileTransferDialog. To create a file transfer dialog with GtkFileTransferDialog, you can call gtk_file_transfer_dialog_new() and be returned a widget, properly packed with GtkTreeView, GtkTable, and GtkButton objects, among others. While this is possible without creating a composite widget (as evidenced by the fact that Gaim doesn't use one for the File Transfer window), creating the composite widget allows the dialog to emit its own signals and keep its own properties.

Naturally, the class a new composite widget will descend from is the container class that contains the widgets. The formatting toolbar in Gaim, shown in Figure 6-4, is a composite widget. The elements within it are arranged in a GtkHBox, so the widget descends from GtkHBox. Any function that can be called on a GtkHBox can be called on the formatting toolbar; plug-ins can add their own buttons with gtk_box_pack_start().().

Figure 6-4. *Gaim's formatting toolbar descends from GtkHBox, and can be treated as a single entity.*

Similarly, because the elements of the file transfer dialog are packed into a GtkDialog, GtkFileTransferDialog descends from GtkDialog. As explained in the previous section, declaring a new class in GObject is simply a matter of declaring a pair of structs, registering a new type and providing some basic information about the class, including the parent class, the class_init function and the instance_init function.

First, you must declare your two structs: one for the class and one for the instance. Again, both must inherit from the parent class, so GtkFileTransferDialog and GtkFileTransferDialogClass descend from GtkDialog and GtkDialogClass, respectively.

Your class struct contains class-wide variables and function pointers for default behaviors as it did in the preceding example. GtkFileTransferDialog has just one signal, discussed in the previous section.

```
struct _GtkFileTransferDialogClass {
    GtkDialogClass parent;
    void (*stopped)(GtkFileTransferDialog *, GaimXfer *);
};
```

The instance struct contains all the instance-wide variables. Often you still want to be able to access other widgets from within an encompassing composite widget, so it is often useful to contain the child widgets in the instance struct. Gaim already has a struct it uses to store all the data associated with a File Transfer window: GaimGtkXferDialog. Because this represents everything I need in a File Transfer dialog widget, and because Gaim already expects to deal with this struct when interfacing with the File Transfer window (not something I can change with a plug-in), the instance struct for GtkFileTransferDialog contains only a GaimGtkXferDialog. When I create one of these widgets, I address the GaimGtkXferDialog within it and tell Gaim to use it as the File Transfer dialog.

```
struct _GtkFileTransferDialog {
    GtkDialog parent;
    GaimGtkXferDialog dialog;
};
```

Like in most GObjects, in a composite widget the class_init function doesn't do much other than declare the signals and properties the composite widget will have. The instance_init function, however, is responsible for creating and initializing all the component widgets within.

In the examples you've seen so far, the instance_init function has not been used; there was no initialization needed on each instance. In a composite widget, however, each instance must be initialized; other widgets must be created and packed into it. This is done the same way I demonstrated in Chapter 4, but whereas creating the container widget is usually the first step, when the instance_init function is called, the composite widget is already a valid container.

When g_object_new() is called, it allocates the appropriate amount of memory and passes it to each instance_init function of the inheritance hierarchy, starting at the least-derived class. For any GtkFileTransferDialog, for instance, GObject will be the first class to initialize the memory; it will be handed essentially blank memory. It initializes the GObject-specific parts of the object. Then GtkObject does the same thing. Then GtkContainer, GtkWindow, GtkDialog, and finally GtkFileTransferDialog. When the instance reaches your instance_init function, it can be thought of as a valid yet empty, container of whatever type you inherit from. It's the responsibility of your instance_init function to fill that container, just as any other GTK+ code would.

For gtk_file_transfer_dialog_init(), for example, I took the code straight out of Gaim's gtkft.c file and, with only very minor modifications, got it to work fine. By using the same code from gtkft.c, I further ensured that the rest of Gaim will recognize this new widget as a valid File Transfer dialog.

Your composite widget class can (and most likely will) attach to signals that the component widgets emit. Again, this is done just like any other GTK+ code, with g_signal_connect(). From the callbacks you attach to component widgets, you'll process them and emit signals of your own when appropriate. The composite widget will emit these signals; other code using this widget won't access each component widget individually but treat them all as a single entity with its own properties and signals. Take a look at how GtkFileTransferDialog is able to emit the "stopped" signal itself when the Stop button is pressed. First, look at how the Stop button is created in gtk_file_transfer_dialog_init():

```
/* Stop button */
button = gtk_button_new_from_stock(GTK_STOCK_STOP);
gtk_box_pack_start(GTK_BOX(bbox), button, FALSE, FALSE, 0);
gtk_widget_show(button);
dialog->stop_button = button;
g_signal_connect(G_OBJECT(button), "clicked",
                 G_CALLBACK(stop_button_cb), ft_dialog);
```

Despite being part of a widget implementation, this code is undistinguishable from any other GTK+ code. It creates the button, adds it to a container (which is part of the GtkDialog), shows it, and connects a callback to it. It uses ft_dialog as the data to the callback, which is the widget itself. The callback, stop_button_cb(), then emits a signal, originating from the widget:

```
static void
stop_button_cb(GtkButton *button, GtkFileTransferDialog *dialog)
{
    g_signal_emit(dialog, signals[STOPPED], 0, dialog->dialog.selected_xfer);
}
```

Really, all a composite widget needs is a class_init function to create signals, and an instance_init function to create child widgets, attach to their signals, and add them to the container. More-advanced applications of a GtkWidget will require you to override functions from inherited classes. You will often want to change the appearance of your widget. To do this, you need to know how various graphical elements are represented in GTK+.

GdkPixbuf

A GdkPixbuf object represents a graphical image stored in memory. Any graphic you see in a GTK+ application was most likely originally represented as a GdkPixbuf object. At its core, a GdkPixbuf is just an array of pixels. Although you can access this array yourself, GdkPixbuf is a full-fledged GObject with a rich set of functions provided for creating and manipulating the image data.

Note Like GObject, GdkPixbuf is both a library and a data type. I will use GdkPixbuf to refer to the library and GdkPixbuf to refer to the data type.

Working with Image Files

A GdkPixbuf object represents an image as a two-dimensional array of bytes, but numerous other means to represent images exist. Most image formats introduce some element of compression, allowing for smaller file sizes. Other formats are used for very specific tasks and are designed specifically with those tasks in mind. Because you will often need to work with images in an assortment of formats, GdkPixbuf provides powerful functions to automatically recognize and convert to and from these formats.

Common formats supported by GdkPixbuf include JPEG, GIF, PNG, BMP, ICO, and SVG. GdkPixbuf will recognize the file type on its own; you needn't know it in advance. To create a GdkPixbuf from a file, call

```
GdkPixbuf *pb = gdk_pixbuf_new_from_file(const char *filename, GError  **error);
```

The filename argument represents the image file you're loading. The error argument is a pointer to a GError object. GError is a data type used by GLib for reporting runtime errors. It can be likened to the *exceptions* system found in Java and C++, for example. For gdk_pixbuf_new_from_file(), possible errors include the file not existing or not being a valid image file. In either of these cases, the function will set GError to describe the error, but if you're interested only in *if* a function using GError failed rather than *why*, you can simply check the return value.

Assuming no error occurs, gdk_pixbuf_new_from_file() will return a new GdkPixbuf object. GdkPixbuf is one of those few areas in GTK+ development in which you need to worry about manual reference counting. The new GdkPixbuf object will be created with a reference count of one. Make sure to g_object_unref() it when you're through with it. Other parts of GTK+ that use it, such as GtkImage, will do the same and the GdkPixbuf object will be destroyed only when it is no longer needed anywhere.

Saving a GdkPixbuf object to a file is similarly straightforward:

```
gdk_pixbuf_save(GdkPixbuf *pixbuf, const char *filename,
                const char *type, GError **error, ...);
```

The pixbuf, filename, and error arguments should be self-explanatory. The type argument is the format to save in: either "jpeg", "png", or "ico" with a default GdkPixbuf installation. Other formats can be added modularly. The last options are yet another NULL-terminated list of pairs of image properties and their values.

Each format provides its own parameters for saving files. For example, "jpeg" being a *lossy* format (that means the file size can be reduced by reducing the quality of the image) includes a "quality" property, using an integer from 0 to 100. For most common applications, these settings won't often be used and a simple NULL will suffice, causing the GdkPixbuf library to use the default properties.

GdkPixbufLoader

Sometimes you'll need to create a GdkPixbuf object from a source other than a file. Gaim does this with IM images, which are images that can be embedded within certain IMs. Because these images come directly from the network, it's inefficient to save the data to disk and then have gdk_pixbuf_new_from_file() read it back to memory. Other times, you may need to display the image as it loads; this can be the case if you're downloading it from the network (think of how images load in your Web browser), or if it's a particularly large file that takes a while to read from disk. In these cases, you should use GdkPixbufLoader.

GdkPixbufLoader is an object that progressively loads an image as you feed data to it. Like gdk_pixbuf_new_from_file(), it will automatically create a GdkPixbuf object from the same variety of automatically detected formats. gdk_pixbuf_new_from_file is merely a wrapper function around GdkPixbufLoader for convenience.

To create a GdkPixbufLoader, call gdk_pixbuf_loader_new(). This function takes no arguments. As you receive data to feed to it, call the following:

```
gdk_pixbuf_loader_write(GdkPixbufLoader *loader, const guchar *buf,
                                gsize count, GError *error);
```

buf points to the new data to add, and count is the number of new bytes in buf. As soon as GdkPixbufLoader has received enough data about the image to know its format and dimensions, it will create an empty GdkPixbuf with those specifications. As it receives more data about the image, it will begin to fill in the pixels of that GdkPixbuf. You can access this GdkPixbuf with gdk_pixbuf_loader_get_pixbuf(). Even though the data may not have loaded, you can still have a perfectly valid GdkPixbuf. Some of it, however, will be empty (again, think of how a Web browser loads an image). If you are presenting this GdkPixbuf to the user as it loads, you will want to connect to a few signals emitted by the GdkPixbufLoader.

The first signal you should connect to is "area-prepared". This signal is emitted when the GdkPixbuf object has been created with the appropriate size. When creation of the GdkPixbuf object invokes your callback, you can call gdk_pixbuf_loader_get_pixbuf() and present the empty GdkPixbuf object to the user. The next important signal is "area-updated". This signal is emitted when more data has been added to the GdkPixbuf. You should connect to this when you need to redraw the image presented by a GdkPixbuf. The final signal you may want to connect to is "closed". "closed" is emitted when the GdkPixbufLoader has been closed and no more data will be written to the GdkPixbuf. This signal will be emitted only after you manually call gdk_pixbuf_close(), as the GdkPixbufLoader has no other way to know when there is no more data.

Animations

GdkPixbuf also provides a way to work with animations. These animations, usually coming from a GIF file, consist of a series of frames. GdkPixbuf obscures most of the implementation; all it requires is that you ask it to return the GdkPixbuf that should represent the animation when the frame changes.

To create a new animation from a GIF file (or any other file that supports animation), call

```
GdkPixbufAnimation *anim = gdk_pixbuf_animation_from_file_new(const char *filename,
                                GError **error);
```

It should be noted that GdkPixbufAnimation will treat a nonanimated image as an animation with only one frame. If you don't know in advance whether the image is animated or not, GdkPixbufAnimation can be used identically, regardless.

When you want to start showing the image, you'll need to get a GdkPixbufAnimationIter object representing the current frame of an animation. To get this, call

```
GdkPixbufAnimationIter *iter = gdk_pixbuf_animation_get_iter(GdkPixbuf *pixbuf,
                                const GTimeVal *start_time);
```

The start_time argument is the time the animation begins, represented as a GTimeVal struct. Because this time is most likely "now," you can set this as NULL, which GdkPixbufAnimation will consider "now."

Immediately after creating an iterator, the animation begins. To get the first frame of animation, call gdk_pixbuf_animation_iter_get_pixbuf() on it. Then call gdk_pixbuf_animation_iter_get_delay_time() which returns the amount of time this frame should be shown for. Use g_timeout_add() (see last chapter) to attach a callback triggered after this amount of time. When the timeout is triggered, call gdk_pixbuf_animation_iter_get_pixbuf() and gdk_pixbuf_animation_iter_get_delay() repeatedly for as long as you need to animate.

Similar to the problem of how to represent images on the screen, solved by GdkPixbuf, is the problem of how to represent text on the screen. Pango solves this problem.

Pango

Pango is a system for the generic layout and rendering of internationalized text. It's generic in that it's not tied to any particular application. Its use within GTK+ is its most prominent application, but it can be used anywhere text need be drawn by computers, be it on-screen or in print.

Laying out text may not seem inherently difficult, but Pango needs to take into account many factors, such as font selection and word-wrapping, that will drastically affect the output. The real challenge, though, is in ensuring that text in any language will be rendered correctly. Some of these issues will be addressed in more detail in Chapter 9 but other languages have very complex rules that Pango must comprehend and utilize.

To achieve this, Pango has a modular structure in which each language is implemented modularly. This provides the same advantages that GdkPixbuf receives by modularizing its support for various image formats. Each language can be developed separately and new languages can be easily added.

PangoLayout

Just as a GdkPixbuf object represents the visual appearance of an image, a PangoLayout object represents the visual appearance of a paragraph of text. It represents a paragraph, as that's the smallest unit of text that can be laid out independently. Think of it as a set of instructions for rendering a bit of text.

A PangoLayout object contains a string of text, a set of *attributes* defining how the text should appear (these include what font to use, what size to render it, what color, etc.—I'll discuss attributes shortly), and it includes various properties affecting how the paragraph as a whole should be rendered (such as line spacing, indentation, alignment, and the width to word-wrap to). The best way to create a PangoLayout object is with gtk_widget_create_pango_layout():

```
PangoLayout* gtk_widget_create_pango_layout (GtkWidget *widget,
                                             const gchar *text);
```

The widget argument is the widget this text will appear as part of. It is used to determine the correct colors to match the GTK+ theme. The text argument is what text the PangoLayout should represent. You can change this at any time with pango_layout_set_text():

```
pango_layout_set_text(layout, "This is text", -1);
```

The -1 in this call is the length argument. Usually this will be -1, indicating that the provided string is NULL-terminated—the standard representation of strings in C. I will discuss in depth how text is represented in computers in Chapter 9. That chapter will also address some of the concerns you may have about representing foreign text with Pango.

You can also now set the various parameters that affect the appearance of the paragraph described earlier. Each of these is accessible with accessor and mutator functions. To set attributes that affect only a range of text within the paragraph (such as a single bolded word), you will need to apply PangoAttributes to this PangoLayout.

PangoAttribute

A PangoAttribute is composed only of two indices indicating the range of characters the attribute affects. Through inheritance, many sorts of attributes have been created that all subclass from PangoAttribute.

Each of these subclasses has its own constructor function, which takes the value of the attribute. Bold text, for example, requires a new weight attribute. To create such an attribute, specifying bold text, call

```
PangoAttribute *attr = pango_attr_weight_new(PANGO_WEIGHT_BOLD);
```

You will then need to manually specify the range of characters in a PangoLayout this attribute affects. This range is in bytes, which is not the same as the number of characters for most non-English languages. I'll discuss the distinction further in Chapter 9.

Presume the first four bytes of text need to be bold. Directly modify the start_index and end_index fields of the PangoAttribute:

```
attr->start_index = 0;
attr->end_index = 4;
```

This causes the PangoAttribute to affect the first four bytes of the text it is applied to. How is it applied to text? With a PangoAttrList, a list of attributes applied to a PangoLayout.

To create a PangoAttrList, call pango_attr_list_new(), and then make calls to pango_attr_list_insert() for each attribute you've created:

```
PangoAttrList *list = pango_attr_list_new();
pango_list_attr_insert(list, attr);
```

The PangoAttrList stores attributes in a structure convenient to Pango, sorted by each attribute's start_index. Having added all these PangoAttributes to the PangoAttrList, associate the list with your PangoLayout:

```
pango_layout_set_attributes(layout, list);
```

Dealing with each PangoAttribute, explicitly setting its range, and worrying about PangoAttrList can be difficult and error-prone. Thankfully, it is rarely necessary. As mentioned in the previous chapter, Pango offers a markup language that lets you specify attributes in XML applied to a range of text.

Pango Markup Language was discussed in Chapter 5; you should see the parallels to manually creating PangoAttributes. Each span element in the XML file represents the range of a Pango attribute. The XML attributes of a span correspond to the type of PangoAttribute. The preceding example, which sets a PangoLayout object's text to "This is text," and then sets the first four bytes bold can be represented as Pango markup: `<span weight='bold'>This</span> is text.`

Pango markup also provides shortcuts for commonly altered attributes. These attributes resemble HTML. Therefore, `<span weight='bold'>This</span> is text` can also be represented as: `<b>This</b> is text.`

To set a string of Pango markup to a PangoLayout call:

```
pango_layout_set_markup(layout, markup);
```

Note that this has the effect of calling both pango_layout_set_text() and pango_layout_set_attributes() in one call. Any attributes or text you've already set will be replaced.

You should now see how straightforward it is to create a new PangoLayout to represent how a paragraph of text should be drawn. However, it is not Pango's responsibility actually to draw the text. Neither is it GdkPixbuf's responsibility to draw images. Both exist solely as representations of drawn data. Although any code that draws images can use a PangoLayout or GdkPixbuf, for the purposes of GTK+ applications, both are done by GDK, the GTK+ Graphics Development Kit.

GDK

GDK is an abstraction layer. It provides an interface for interacting with a user through graphical output to the screen and input from the keyboard, mouse, and other input devices. It is an abstraction because it hides the details of the implementation to the developer using it. This allows the developer to draw to the screen without understanding how the drawing is actually happening. It also means that the implementation can be changed entirely without requiring any changes to programs using GDK. This is what allows Gaim and other GTK+ applications to run on Windows and X, despite the two having radically different back-end interfaces.

The X Window System

Although GDK is platform-neutral and will run on Windows and the Linux frame buffer, the X Window System—or just X—is the platform it was originally created for. Thus, many of the concepts in GDK come directly from X and it helps to understand a little about how X works.

Server-Client Model

Probably the most unique aspect of X is that it uses a server-client model. An application that runs on X is called a *client*. When it wants to show a window, it connects to the X server. The server is the software that runs where the user is; it shows the GUI and processes user input. The client and server then communicate back and forth with each other; the client sends commands about how to draw windows, and the server sends the input from the user.

What makes this interesting is that, although the client and the server are usually running on the same machine, they don't have to be. This connection between the server and the client can occur over the Internet. I can run Gaim (the X client) on a computer across the world and have it act just like any other program connected to my X server.

An X server provides one or more *displays*. A display represents the monitors, keyboard, and mouse that the user will be using. Many functions in X programming take a display as an argument to accommodate this. Likewise, GDK provides the concept of a display.

Window Management

X aims to be as modular as possible. The core X implementation does little more than allow clients to draw onto windows and receive input notification. X relies on other code, built on top of X, to provide any higher-level function. This is the very reason GTK+ exists. Unlike other systems, like Windows, which themselves provide mechanisms to create widgets, X delegates this task elsewhere. One area where this design philosophy is particularly evident is in window management.

Window management refers to the positioning and sizing of windows. Operating systems such as Windows handle this task themselves, usually offering the application the possibility to do whatever it wants. In X, this task is delegated to a separate application called a *window manager*. Applications running on X can request their own size and location, but they inevitably have to deal with whatever the window manager gives them. The window manager has the final say.

Because of this, a vast array of different window managers exists. Some of these would be instantly usable to someone with a Windows background (such as Metacity, GNOME's default window manager, shown in Figure 6-5); others are quite different (such as Ion, which arranges windows in tiled frames with tabs as shown in Figure 6-6).

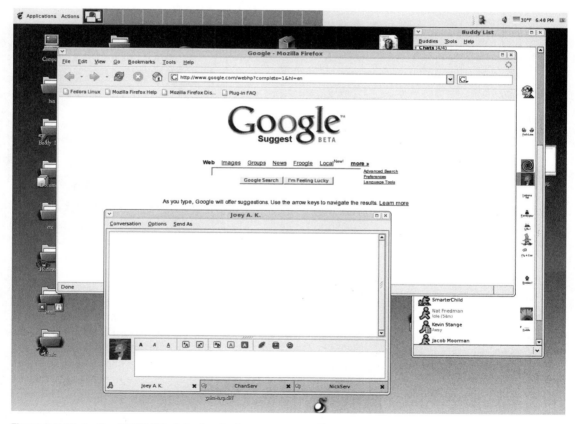

Figure 6-5. *Metacity, GNOME's default window manager, offers an interface very familiar to users coming from other operating systems.*

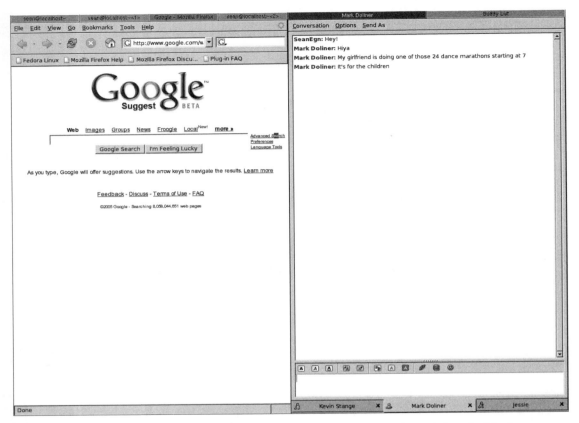

Figure 6-6. *Ion has a unique approach to window management. Windows are tiled and tabbed.*

GDK encapsulates client communication to the window manager as well as the X server.

GdkDrawable

As mentioned, X provides practically no functionality when it comes to drawing GUIs, other than providing a decent way of saying "draw a line from this point to this point." Likewise, GDK does little more than wrap this behavior. GTK+, which provides the higher-level GUI function-ality, draws these widgets by telling GDK where to draw the appropriate lines, rectangles, and other drawing primitives. These graphical elements are drawn to a class called GdkDrawable.

A GdkDrawable object corresponds to an X Drawable object, which represents something that can be drawn to. There are two types of drawables in X: windows and pixmaps. These correspond directly to GdkWindow and GdkPixmap.

In X, both exist on the X server and act nearly identically. The only significant difference is that a window is drawn on-screen and a pixmap exists only as memory off-screen. The latter is often used to "double buffer." You can create a complex image in a pixmap, and then copy it to a window all at once, rather than making numerous changes directly to the window, which could result in flicker.

For the purposes of simplification, I'll deal solely with GdkWindow objects, but be aware that all the functions for drawing on a GdkWindow object will work exactly the same with any GdkDrawable.

Drawing Functions

When drawing to a GdkDrawable object, it's often necessary to specify colors, fonts, line widths, and all sorts of stylistic variables. Rather than demanding you specify all these in each API call, resulting in extraordinarily long lists of arguments, GDK uses a struct called GdkGC for *graphics context* that will specify any parameters needed by a drawing function.

It is possible to create and initialize a GdkGC for each drawing call every time you need one, but fortunately this is rarely necessary in a GTK+ application. Because GTK+ is themeable, there is usually a predefined consistent style for elements within each widget. In fact, there are many different predefined styles for each widget, depending on the widget's state. A widget with focus can look entirely different from a widget without focus. All this information is contained within a GtkStyle.

GtkStyle

As is obvious from the namespace, GtkStyle is not part of GDK. However, if you want your widget to fit in with the rest of your application, you will use the GtkStyle associated with your widget every time you need to draw to a GdkDrawable object. The GtkStyle will tell you the appropriate colors, fonts, etc. to use.

A GtkStyle object contains arrays of GdkGC structs and GdkColor structs (which represent a color). Each array represents a certain element of the UI. If you needed the color in which to draw text, you would use the text array. If you needed a background color, you would use the bg array.

Each of these arrays holds five objects, corresponding to the five distinct visual states the widget can have. These states are defined in a GtkStateType enum.

- GTK_STATE_NORMAL is the ordinary default state.

- GTK_STATE_ACTIVE is the state the widget appears in when activated, such as an active toggle button.

- GTK_STATE_PRELIGHT allows widgets to change their appearance when the mouse cursor hovers over them.

- GTK_STATE_SELECTED is used when a GUI element is selected from a list or menu.

- GTK_STATE_INSENSITIVE is what widgets should appear in when they are inactive and unresponsive to interaction.

GtkCellRendererTransfer uses three of these GdkGC arrays to properly determine what colors to draw its progress bar:

```
gdk_gc_set_rgb_fg_color(gc, &widget->style->fg[GTK_STATE_NORMAL]);
gdk_draw_rectangle (window, gc, TRUE,
            cell_area->x + cell->xpad + icon_width + 2,
            cell_area->y + cell->ypad + string_height + 2,
            width - icon_width - 2, 7);

gdk_gc_set_rgb_fg_color(gc, &widget->style->bg[GTK_STATE_NORMAL]);
gdk_draw_rectangle (window, gc, TRUE,
            cell_area->x + cell->xpad + icon_width + 3,
            cell_area->y + cell->ypad + string_height + 3,
            width - icon_width - 4, 5);

gdk_gc_set_rgb_fg_color(gc, &widget->style->bg[GTK_STATE_SELECTED]);
gdk_draw_rectangle (window, gc, TRUE,
            cell_area->x + cell->xpad + icon_width + 3,
            cell_area->y + cell->ypad + string_height + 3,
            (width - icon_width - 4) * celltransfer->progress,
            5);
```

First, it draws a rectangle using the widget->style->fg[GTK_STATE_NORMAL] color. This is the normal color for foreground elements. Because foreground elements must stand out from their surroundings, this makes an effective border.

GtkCellRendererTransfer then draws a rectangle with widget->style->bg[GTK_STATE_NORMAL], which provides a suitable background for the progress bar.

Finally, GtkCellRendererTransfer draws the progress bar with widget->style->bg[GTK_STATE_SELECTED]. Because it's important to know when an item is selected, this color contrasts well with the background color for GTK_STATE_NORMAL.

As you can tell, in practice the colors defined by a GtkStyle are not used the way they were intended. When writing new windows, you must sometimes be creative with the colors you use. When writing custom widgets, though, always use colors from the widget's GtkStyle. Otherwise, your widget will not be themeable with the rest of GTK+ and will stand out negatively because of it.

Drawing Functions

Drawing functions in GDK include simple geometric shapes such as lines, points, and arcs. Images and text, represented by GdkPixbuf and PangoLayout as already discussed, can be drawn to a GdkDrawable object through the use of those libraries.

Each geometric primitive in GDK is represented by a series of straightforward numbers: a point is an x-coordinate and a y-coordinate; a polygon is a set of points. Each primitive has a corresponding function in GDK to draw it.

Each function takes a GdkDrawable object (recall that means GdkWindow or GdkPixmap), a GdkGC (discussed earlier), and enough data to represent the primitive. Consult the GDK documentation at http://gtk.org/api for specifics.

GtkCellRendererTransfer draws three types of primitives. It draws rectangles for the progress bar, PangoLayout objects for the text, and GdkPixbuf objects for the icons:

```
static void gtk_cell_renderer_transfer_render (GtkCellRenderer *cell,
                             GdkWindow      *window,
                             GtkWidget      *widget,
                             GdkRectangle   *background_area,
                             GdkRectangle   *cell_area,
                             GdkRectangle   *expose_area,
                             guint           flags)
{
    GtkCellRendererTransfer *celltransfer = (GtkCellRendererTransfer *) cell;
    GdkGC *gc = gdk_gc_new(window);
    PangoLayout *layout = gtk_widget_create_pango_layout(widget, NULL);;
    GtkStyle *style = widget->style;
    gchar *markup;
    gint width, height, icon_width, string_height;

    width = cell_area->width;
    height = cell_area->height;

    /* Icon */
    icon_width = gdk_pixbuf_get_width (celltransfer->icon) + 2;
    gdk_pixbuf_render_to_drawable(celltransfer->icon, GDK_DRAWABLE(window), NULL,
                    0, 0,
            cell_area->x + cell->xpad,
            cell_area->y + cell->ypad,
            -1, -1, GDK_RGB_DITHER_NONE, 0, 0);

    /* Text */
    markup = g_strdup_printf("<b>%s</b> (%s) - <span size=\"smaller\" col-
or=\"gray\">%s Remaining</span>",
                                celltransfer->name, celltransfer->size, celltrans-
fer->remaining);
    pango_layout_set_markup(layout, markup, strlen(markup));
    pango_layout_get_pixel_size (layout, NULL, &string_height);
    gtk_paint_layout (style, window, GTK_STATE_NORMAL, FALSE,
            NULL, widget, NULL, cell_area->x + cell->xpad + icon_width + 2,
                                cell_area->y + cell->ypad, layout);
    g_free(markup);

    gdk_gc_set_rgb_fg_color(gc, &widget->style->fg[GTK_STATE_NORMAL]);
    gdk_draw_rectangle (window, gc, TRUE,
            cell_area->x + cell->xpad + icon_width + 2,
            cell_area->y + cell->ypad + string_height + 2,
            width - icon_width - 2, 7);
```

```
gdk_gc_set_rgb_fg_color(gc, &widget->style->bg[GTK_STATE_NORMAL]);
gdk_draw_rectangle (window, gc, TRUE,
            cell_area->x + cell->xpad + icon_width + 3,
            cell_area->y + cell->ypad + string_height + 3,
            width - icon_width - 4, 5);

gdk_gc_set_rgb_fg_color(gc, &widget->style->bg[GTK_STATE_SELECTED]);
gdk_draw_rectangle (window, gc, TRUE,
            cell_area->x + cell->xpad + icon_width + 3,
            cell_area->y + cell->ypad + string_height + 3,
            (width - icon_width - 4) * celltransfer->progress,
            5);
}
```

The cell renderer first draws the icon from a GdkPixbuf object using gdk_pixbuf_render_to_drawable(), which takes 12 arguments:

```
void        gdk_pixbuf_render_to_drawable    (GdkPixbuf *pixbuf,
                                              GdkDrawable *drawable,
                                              GdkGC *gc,
                                              int src_x,
                                              int src_y,
                                              int dest_x,
                                              int dest_y,
                                              int width,
                                              int height,
                                              GdkRgbDither dither,
                                              int x_dither,
                                              int y_dither);
```

- The pixbuf argument is the image to draw. In GtkCellRendererTransfer, this is the icon indicating status.

- The drawable argument is the GdkDrawable on which to draw. This is provided to the render function by GtkCellRenderer.

- The gc argument allows you to specify a graphics context to use. For this application of GdkPixbuf, a GdkGC is unneeded and can be passed NULL.

- The src_x and src_y arguments allow you to draw only part of a GdkPixbuf. As the cell renderer wants to draw the entire icon, these are both set as 0.

- The dest_x and dest_y arguments specify the destination within drawable to draw this. GtkCellRenderer provides the coordinates and dimensions of the layout, and GtkCellRendererTransfer takes padding between cells into account.

- The width and height arguments specify the size of the GdkPixbuf to draw. Setting these as -1 causes the function to draw the full dimensions, which is desired for showing the entire icon.

The rest of the arguments are for dithering, which is a technique for dealing with low-color displays. This widget has no need for it.

The widget then creates a string with g_strdup_printf(), and creates a PangoLayout for it. It then draws the PangoLayout object with gtk_paint_layout():

```
void          gtk_paint_layout                    (GtkStyle *style,
                                                   GdkWindow *window,
                                                   GtkStateType state_type,
                                                   gboolean use_text,
                                                   GdkRectangle *area,
                                                   GtkWidget *widget,
                                                   const gchar *detail,
                                                   gint x,
                                                   gint y,
                                                   PangoLayout *layout);
```

- The style argument is the GtkStyle to draw this text with. For a GtkWidget, this should be widget->style.

- The window argument is the GdkWindow to draw to. It is provided as an argument to gtk_cell_renderer_transfer_render().

- The state_type argument includes the states enumerated in the previous section.

- The use_text argument specifies whether you want to use the style intended for text (TRUE) or for foreground elements (FALSE).

- The area argument specifies a bounding rectangle outside of which text will not be drawn.

- The widget argument is the widget doing the drawing, in this case the GtkTreeView instance.

- The detail argument allows you to further qualify to the GTK+ theme how this text should be drawn. I use NULL, but if I used a string literal such as "transfer-renderer", GTK+ themes could be developed to treat this string differently.

- The x and y arguments are the coordinates provided by GtkCellRenderer.

- The layout argument is the PangoLayout object to draw.

Lastly, the cell renderer draws a progress bar out of rectangles using a drawing function similar to those shown in the "GDK" section:

```
void          gdk_draw_rectangle                  (GdkDrawable *drawable,
                                                   GdkGC *gc,
                                                   gboolean filled,
                                                   gint x,
                                                   gint y,
                                                   gint width,
                                                   gint height);
```

- The `drawable` argument is the GdkDrawable object to draw on.

- The `gc` argument is the graphics context to use. `GtkFileTransferDialog` sets this argument's colors before each call to the function, resulting in three different colored rectangles.

- The `filled` argument, if `TRUE`, results in a filled rectangle, or otherwise just a rectangular border.

- The `x`, `y`, `width`, and `height` arguments specify the location and dimensions to draw the rectangle.

Other drawing functions work very similarly to these three. They specify where to draw, what to draw, and how to draw. You can discover more drawing functions in the GTK+ documentation and use them to alter how existing widgets appear through subclassing.

Overriding `GtkWidget`

If you understand how `GtkWidget` works, your inherited subclasses can have incredible control over how they look and behave. By overriding the event handlers in the `GtkWidget` class, you affect the widget's behavior at the lowest possible level.

The `ftmakeover` plug-in implements a widget called `GtkPieChart` that displays file-transfer progress in a pie chart. Because they serve the same purpose, this widget inherits from `GtkProgressBar`. Both widgets display progress, and because the new widget inherits from `GtkProgressBar`, this subclass causes no code changes to cope with the new widget. You can use it just as you would a `GtkProgressBar`. The only difference is in its appearance.

`GtkPieChart` is a simple widget. It inherits from `GtkProgressBar`, and adds no data, signals, or properties to it. All it does is override two of the functions provided by `GtkWidget`. Of course, to effectively override the functionality of a `GtkWidget`, you must understand how a `GtkWidget` works.

Data Fields of `GtkWidget`

A `GtkWidget` instance contains only a few data fields. The `GtkStyle` struct in its `style` member, which has already been discussed, consists of the parameters governing the way this widget should be drawn. It contains `requisition`, a `GtkRequisition` struct that contains a height and a width. This is the size requested by the widget, but not necessarily the size it will receive.

Each widget requests a certain size, but must accommodate any size. Often, the widget will receive a larger size than it requested, due to container packing. Generally, a widget will always request the smallest area it needs to work properly, and GTK+ will make sure it gets that area. The amount of area it actually gives to a widget is available in the `allocation` field of `GtkWidget`.

The allocation is the size and position provided to the widget. The position is relative to its parent's window, which is the window the widget will draw in. The widget is held responsible for drawing only within the allocation provided, although that represents only a subset of the entire area in the window.

Finally, `GtkWidget` keeps a reference to the window it draws in. This can be a window unique to this widget, but usually is the window of the container the window is packed in.

The important things in drawing for a new widget are to use `widget->style` in your calls to the `GtkStyle` API, make those calls draw to `widget->window`, and paint only within the bounds specified by `widget->allocation`.

Overriding Functions

Remember that a `GObject` subclass can override its parent class's functions in its own `class_init` function by merely casting its own class to that of its parent class and changing function pointers within. This is how much of GTK+'s inheritance gets its power. `GtkWidget` contains important functions that control creating new widgets, sizing widgets, and drawing widgets that need to be overridden in any widget that draws to the screen.

In the case of `GtkPieChart`, only two functions are overridden: `size_request`, which requests the size GTK+'s layout engine will give it, and `expose`, which draws the widget to the screen:

```
static void gtk_pie_chart_class_init (GtkPieChartClass *class) {
    GtkWidgetClass *widget_class = GTK_WIDGET_CLASS(class);

    widget_class->size_request = gtk_pie_chart_size_request;
    widget_class->expose_event = gtk_pie_chart_expose;
}
```

Overriding these two functions alone gives you complete control over how your application appears.

size_request

The `size_request` function is used to determine the appropriate size to allocate to this widget. The widget should calculate the smallest amount of space it needs, and set the value of the provided `GtkRequisition` accordingly.

Obviously, the method used to determine the minimum size depends entirely on the widget itself. Container widgets will call `gtk_widget_size_request()` on its children, and add in the needed space for spacing and padding. A text label widget will create a `PangoLayout` and request the size of that.

`GtkPieChart` arbitrarily chooses 20 pixels in height and 20 pixels in weight. I figure this is the smallest the widget can reasonably be without being completely unreadable:

```
static void
gtk_pie_chart_size_request (GtkWidget *widget, GtkRequisition *requisition)
{
    requisition->height = 20;
    requisition->width = 20;
}
```

Now, when GTK+ lays out a dialog, it will make sure that a `GtkPieChart` gets at least a 20 × 20 square. In all likelihood, it will get more due to the packing model. `ftmakeover` adds this to a `GtkAspectFrame` object, a container widget whose goal is to ensure a constant aspect ratio. By using this, I ensure my `GtkPieChart` is always a circle.

expose

Next, override expose which draws the widget to a GdkDrawable. The rules for drawing are the same as earlier:

- Use the GTK+ style API

- Draw on widget->window

- Draw only within the bounds of widget->allocation.

You are free to draw whatever you want given the techniques discussed earlier. GtkPieChart gets the percentage to display from the properties system and makes three calls to gdk_draw_arc(), which it uses to draw ellipses and arcs:

```
static gint
gtk_pie_chart_expose (GtkWidget *widget, GdkEventExpose *event)
{
    double progress;
    GdkGC *gc = gdk_gc_new(widget->window);

    gdk_gc_set_rgb_fg_color(gc, &widget->style->base[GTK_STATE_NORMAL]);
    gdk_draw_arc(widget->window, gc, TRUE,
    0, 0, widget->allocation.width, widget->allocation.height,
            0, 64*360);

    g_object_get(widget, "fraction", &progress, NULL);
    gdk_gc_set_rgb_fg_color(gc, &widget->style->bg[GTK_STATE_SELECTED]);
    gdk_draw_arc(widget->window, gc, TRUE,
    0, 0, widget->allocation.width, widget->allocation.height,
            64*90, (64*360)*progress);


    gdk_gc_set_rgb_fg_color(gc, &widget->style->fg[GTK_STATE_NORMAL]);
    gdk_draw_arc(widget->window, gc, FALSE,
    0, 0, widget->allocation.width, widget->allocation.height,
            0, 64*360);
    return FALSE;
}
```

If your custom widget can't neatly inherit from an existing widget, you may need to inherit from GtkWidget directly. You would then to manage its own data, and create its own GdkWindow objects if necessary. You would also need to receive notification on user input by overriding the widget's event handlers.

Receiving Events

There are other GtkWidget default handlers you may want to override for other events. Recall that an *event* is a signal generated by X (or by another GDK back end emulating X events). GtkWidget contains overridable function pointers for all these events.

Handling an event is just like overriding any other default signal handler. In your `class_init` function, cast your class to a `GtkWidgetClass`, and set the appropriate function pointers to your function. After doing this, your function will be called whenever your window receives an event. You can use these events however you need to, sometimes processing them, altering the widget's state, and emitting signals of your own.

Summary

In this chapter, you've seen how `GObject` is used to create powerful object-oriented classes in C, and how subclasses of `GtkWidget` can be used with various degrees of complexity to merely add features to an existing widget, or to create a new widget entirely from scratch. Combining this with knowledge of the external GTK+ API, you should be able to create any interface you could possibly need.

In the next chapter, I'll explore how to interface your GUI with the Internet, allowing your application to communicate on the network. I'll explain how networking code works in general, and explore how you can easily integrate this with GTK+'s main loop.

■■■

CHAPTER 7

Sockets

Internet-based applications, such as instant messaging clients, Web browsers, and e-mail clients are now an essential part of most computer users' lives. New applications for the Internet emerge constantly, from peer-to-peer file sharing to voice-over IP telephony. Even programs that don't obviously deal with networking enrich themselves with Internet accessibility, be it downloading up-to-the-minute help files or checking if an upgrade is available.

It's apparent this trend will increase, constantly allowing for greater collaboration and interaction. Understanding the programmatic interface for connecting to the Internet is therefore crucial to much software development now and in the future.

This chapter will review this interface, known as *sockets*. I will then explain how to tie networking with sockets into GLib's main loop, allowing your GTK+ interfaces to work seamlessly with the Internet. First, however, I'll offer a background of networking, explaining some key concepts of networking, which will help you better understand how to work with it.

Networking

To understand the design decisions of the sockets API, you need to be somewhat familiar with networking. The overview here is very brief, but is enough to understand what sockets are used for.

Networking is simply transferring binary data, 1s and 0s, from one computer to another. That alone is useless; but when protocols are added to give some meaning to these 1s and 0s, many wonderful things can happen.

These protocols are used for various tasks, including instant messaging. In the next chapter, I will examine a couple of IM protocols: how 1s and 0s get translated to and from instant messages and presence updates. This, however, is only the top layer of a seven-layer system called the Open Systems Interconnection (OSI) seven-layer model.

The OSI was an initiative in the early eighties to end the trend that saw numerous incompatible proprietary networks. The OSI approach called for seven protocol layers, each providing a different service. Under this scheme, networking is essentially modularized; each layer builds on another, and any combination of these protocols could be used and still interoperate. Figure 7-1 illustrates the seven layers in the OSI design.

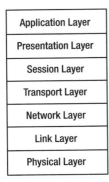

Figure 7-1. *The seven-layer OSI model*

Ultimately, two protocols in particular, Internet Protocol (IP) and Transmission Control Protocol (TCP) proved to be superior to other protocols for most tasks, and today most applications use TCP and IP. However, although the OSI vision of many interchangeable protocols has not been fully realized, the OSI design remains an important aspect of understanding networking.

The OSI Seven-Layer Model

In the OSI model, a *packet* is bit of data that is transmitted over the network as one single entity. Depending on the protocol, a packet usually contains a header, describing the purpose and other metadata about the packet (such as how long it is). Following the header is the packet data—this is the information actually being sent. In the OSI-model, the data of a low-level packet is an entire packet of the next level. You can see this nested behavior on every packet, such as the one shown in Figure 7-2; it seems to start with a bunch of headers for different protocols until it reaches the application layer, which is highlighted.

An IM protocol exists in layer 7, the application layer. An IM packet exists as the data of a packet of a lower-level protocol, such as TCP, which is the data of a lower-level protocol, IP. Each layer adds new functionality to those provided at layers beneath it.

In real-world implementations of the OSI model, rarely are all seven layers implemented. For this discussion, I will omit layers 5 and 6, which many applications, including Gaim, don't implement.

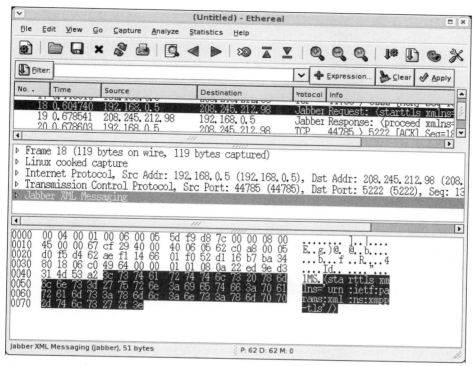

Figure 7-2. *Ethereal is a program for intercepting and comprehending Internet traffic. Here, you can see the nested nature of an Internet packet. A Jabber packet is the data of a TCP packet, which is, in turn, the data of an IP packet, which is the data of an Ethernet packet. I'll discuss Ethereal in the next chapter.*

The Physical Layer

The lowest layer, the physical layer, describes how to transmit data physically over the connection. For wired connections, this includes what voltages to use and over what type of wire to use them. Wireless connections specify their own parameters. The physical layer also defines how to represent 1s and 0s which, in networking, is rarely as simple as "on" and "off."

Because network transmissions often have troubles with long strings of the same bit, i.e., lots of 1s in a row or lots of 0s in a row, the physical layer will often introduce some encoding scheme to ensure greater reliability. This often includes using extra bits, such as using seven bits to encode every five bits. These two extra bits are used to prevent long sequences of the same value, which can cause the computer to get confused with regard to timing (it's hard to tell the difference between 50 1s in a row and 51 1s in a row when transmitting at the high speeds used in modern networks).

Obviously, there are many different implementations of the physical layer. Home Internet users are probably familiar with 10Base-T, used by most broadband ISP services. Wireless networks, specified by the 802.11 set of protocols, are growing in popularity. You may have heard of different variations of 802.11, such as 802.11b, and 802.11a. These differ only in the physical layer.

The physical layer specifies the physical methods to send and receive 1s and 0s from a single computer. Networking, of course, involves numerous computers. How a computer interacts with its network is specified in the link layer.

The Link Layer

The link layer introduces the concept of a network, as opposed to the physical layer, which merely provides the concept of a way to send and receive data. To establish the concept of multiple computers, an addressing system is required.

Every computer on a network has a network address. At the link level, this address is known as the MAC (Media Access Control) address. This address is hardwired into each network device at the factory, and guaranteed to be unique. The link layer provides a protocol to send data targeted to a given machine by its address.

The link layer also provides mechanisms for identifying where a machine is located on the network and routing messages accordingly. However, this is usually done by flooding the entire network, i.e., sending packets to every machine. Clearly, this is not something that would work well on the Internet; each machine would need to remember the location of millions of other machines, and find out where they are by flooding the entire network looking for them.

As with the physical layer, there are numerous implementations of the link layer; the best known is Ethernet, which has surpassed most other implementations in popularity. However, other implementations, such as 802.11 wireless, are still in use. The creators of the Internet faced the challenge of inventing a way for various types of networks to talk to each other. This challenge is met with the internet protocol (IP) in the network layer.

The Network Layer

Before the Internet, there existed a number of relatively small networks, each speaking its own link-layer protocol and using its own addressing scheme. Eventually people invented devices known as switches that would translate from one link-layer protocol to another. One might allow an Ethernet network to work with a token-ring (another link-layer protocol) network. However, given the vast majority of different link-layer protocols, it would be difficult to create switches to translate between every combination of network there is; too many issues exist, such as packet size and, most importantly, addressing.

Each link layer implementation has its own addressing scheme, and a switch needs to be able to convert addresses from one scheme to another. The larger the networks are, the more challenging this becomes. Further, MAC addresses are created by the manufacturer, leaving no way to find the correct route to other hosts on the network without flooding. A scalable solution was needed.

IP exists as a *lingua franca*, a common protocol used by all networks, regardless of their link layer implementation. By using IP, a switch needn't know how to translate to and from an assortment of different link-layer implementations. A switch need just understand IP and, regardless of where the packet comes from, the Internet will understand it. IP packets have even been transmitted by carrier pigeons (http://www.blug.linux.no/rfc1149/).

IP is one implementation of the network layer, but not the only one. A successor to IPv4 (which is the version of IP currently used by the Internet as a whole), called IPv6, is slowly being deployed. This new version offers a few important advantages over IPv4, most notably a much larger address space. Because IPv4 addresses are only 32 bits, only about 4.3 billion addresses are possible. Because of the way addresses are assigned, many addresses go unused, resulting in a shortage of usable IP addresses. IPv6 increases the address space to 128 bits, supporting about 340 undecillion (34 followed by 37 zeroes) addresses. This solves the problem, but is a very *destructive* technology, meaning every machine on the entire Internet must be updated to support it. Because cheaper, nondestructive technologies are being developed to solve the address-shortage problem, many doubt IPv6 will ever be completely adopted.

IP has its own aggregatable addressing scheme. This allows route information to be conveyed within the IP address. Routers, points on the Internet that join several networks together, are configured to know where to direct packets based on their IP addresses. This combination of scalability and implementation-independence are what make the Internet possible, although they don't make the Internet reliable. Many points on such a large network could be a source of failure. The transport layer adds additional services on top of IP that make it more usable.

The Transport Layer

The data of an IP packet is a packet of a transport protocol, most commonly TCP or User Datagram Protocol (UDP). UDP doesn't provide many additional services over IP and is used mostly in areas where reliability must be sacrificed for speed, such as video conferencing. It's important that you get each frame as quickly as possible, even if it means a few frames are lost on the way. TCP, however, ensures that each packet arrives, unmodified and in the correct order. It also provides other services to ensure reliability and functionality.

IP only allows a packet to be directed at a computer, but most computers run many Internet-based applications simultaneously. How does the computer know which packets should go to a Web browser and which should go to an IM client? TCP *multiplexes* IP with *ports*.

A port is a numerical identifier that the operating system uses to route TCP packets to the correct application. As you will see in the next section, creating a TCP connection involves specifying which port to send data to. The port must be known beforehand, so the assignment of these values has been largely standardized. The AIM protocol, called OSCAR, uses port 5190. The MSN Messenger protocol uses port 1863.

TCP provides reliability, ensuring that the data received is exactly the same as the data sent. To the programmer, it makes the data on the network appear as a stream of never-ending bits, whereas it's really a set of individual packets. This stream abstraction causes, from a programmer's perspective, a TCP connection to have many of the same characteristics of a file, which are also read from and written to as a stream of endless bits. This similarity is the crux of the sockets API, which I will discuss in the next section.

The Application Layer

Finally, packets in the application layer are the data of a TCP (or UDP) packet. This can be anything, depending on the application. Gaim implements nine IM protocols in its regular distribution, plus additional protocols, such as SOCKS and HTTP that are required for other assorted features.

I will explain some basics about how IM protocols are designed, using real life examples, in the next chapter. I will also explain how these protocols are commonly implemented in code.

Domain Name Service

IP addresses make it very convenient for one computer to locate another on the Internet. However, requiring a human to remember the IP addresses of every computer she wanted to reach would be impossible. For this reason, the Domain Name Service (DNS) exists.

DNS is a hierarchical system of servers that accepts requests to return the IP address for a given domain name. Because of DNS, a device need only know the IP address of the DNS server (which is usually provided by your ISP at the same time an IP address is assigned to your computer), and that server will provide the IP addresses.

When you try to connect to `login.oscar.aol.com`, the server used by AIM and ICQ, the application asks the operating system to return the IP address of `login.oscar.aol.com`. The operating system contacts its DNS server by its IP address and the DNS server responds with the IP address.

DNS is implemented at the application layer. It uses UDP as its transport protocol.

Sockets

The sockets API, first implemented in the Berkeley Software Distribution (BSD) variety of UNIX, was developed at the University of California at Berkeley. For this reason, the API is also called Berkeley sockets or BSD sockets. Despite this origin, the sockets API is the standard C API for accessing the Internet on most any operating system, including Linux and Windows.

Sockets are based on the idea that a network connection is very much similar to a file. Reading and writing to a file on disk correspond neatly with receiving and sending data over the network. Once the connection is established, a socket appears, to your application, identical to a file. The major difference is in establishing the connection.

■**Note** *man* is the standard documentation system in UNIX and a *man page* is the documentation for a specific program, function, file type, or other entity. To read the documentation for any of the functions in the sockets API, run `man functionname` from the console. The `man` program is also available in Cygwin.

Connecting to a Server

Because the sockets API is designed to be network-agnostic, allowing any implementation of the OSI model, connecting to a server is somewhat complicated. Even though TCP/IP is the most commonly used type of connection, at nearly every stage in using the sockets API you must explicitly state that you're using these protocols.

■**Tip** Because TCP/IP connections are so frequently used within Gaim, it offers a convenient function that creates one with a single call. The function, `gaim_proxy_connect()`, takes a hostname, a port, and a callback function called when the connection is established (or when it has failed).

The steps you must take to connect to a server are

- **Resolve the hostname.** You can't connect to a server without knowing its IP address. You discover the IP address from a hostname by querying the DNS system.

- **Create a socket.** Creating a socket reserves a file descriptor to use with this connection.

- **Create a** `struct sockaddr`. A *socket address* describes a network address by specifying the type of network, the address, and the port. Most of this data comes from the `struct hostent` returned from `gethostbyname()`, described later.

- **Connect.** Finally, connect the socket to the `sockaddr`. You can then use the socket as you would any other file descriptor.

■**Note** A "connection" is not part of IP. The appearance of a connection that is established and then disestablished by disconnecting is one of the services provided by TCP. Subsequently, a UDP socket need not connect. It must, though, create a socket.

Domain Name Resolution

Before connecting to another computer on the Internet, you will need to resolve its hostname into an IP address. An IPv4 address, although often represented in writing as four numbers separated by periods, is just a 32-bit integer. However, because the sockets API attempts to work regardless of the network protocol, and because a domain name may resolve to more than a single IP address, the sockets API uses a structure called `hostent` to represent the result of a DNS resolution.

■**Note** So far, we've used `structs` as objects in object-oriented programming. The sockets API is a set of system calls and is not object-oriented. Be sure to not confuse the two.

`struct hostent`

A `hostent` structure is defined as such:

```
struct hostent {
    char *h_name;          /* official name of host */
    char **h_aliases;      /* alias list */
    int h_addrtype;        /* host address type */
    int h_length;          /* length of address */
    char **h_addr_list;    /* list of addresses */
};
```

- The h_name field is the official name of the host, probably the hostname you specify when you perform the search, but not necessarily. gaim.sourceforge.net and gaim.sf.net, for instance, both resolve to the same host. Only the former is in h_name.

- Alternate names are stored in the h_aliases field, a NULL-terminated array of alternate names for this host. gaim.sf.net would appear in this array.

- The h_addrtype field gives the network-layer implementation of this host. It will probably be AF_INET, which is IPv4, although it could possibly be AF_INET6, which corresponds to IPv6.

- The h_length field is the length of an address. IPv4 addresses are 4 bytes long, so this will likely be 4.

- Lastly, the addresses themselves are stored in the h_addr_list array. Because you'll probably need only one address for a host, h_addr_list[0] is most likely what you want. For convenience, h_addr is #defined as h_addr_list[0], so anywhere you would want to use hostent->h_addr_list[0], you can use hostent->h_addr.

gethostbyname()

To get a hostent structure, use gethostbyname(). This function, simply enough, takes a domain name and returns a pointer to a struct hostent:

```
struct hostent *hostent = gethostbyname("gaim.sourceforge.net");
```

Following this call, the hostent pointer will point to a valid hostent for this host or NULL if for any reason the host was not found.

Tip gethostbyname() is a blocking function; i.e., it won't return until the operation has completed. Because the time this takes depends on the network, it may cause irresponsiveness in the UI. For this reason, you may consider finding some way of performing it asynchronously. On UNIX, Gaim spawns a helper process that feeds the IP address back in a pipe. You may also consider alternate methods, such as threads.

---

socket()

A socket is created with the socket() function. The function takes three parameters:

```
int fd = socket(int domain, int type, int protocol);
```

- The domain parameter specifies the protocol-layer implementation being used. You will most likely be using PF_INET for the domain. This specifies that the socket is intended for IPv4. Other networking protocols, including IPv6, are available, and local UNIX sockets, used for communicating between two programs on the same computer, can also be specified in the domain. However, for connecting to the Internet, PF_INET is most likely what you need.

- The type parameter refers to the type of connection this will be. In this case, you will choose between TCP (SOCK_STREAM) or UDP (SOCK_DGRAM). Think of domain as specifying the network layer and type as specifying the transport layer.

- The protocol parameter is only used when there is more than one protocol used for this combination of domain and type, which is rare. For sockets in the PF_INET domain, this should be left 0, which specifies the default.

The return value for socket() is an integer that serves as a file descriptor. In UNIX every open file is identified by an integer. System calls that write or read to this file pass the file descriptor to the operating system, which uses it to look up its own representation of a file in some data structure. Because this is a convenient method of doing input and output, UNIX makes these same semantics available to other appropriate areas.

For example, UNIX specifies that for text-based programs, 0 is the file descriptor for what the user types (STDIN), 1 is the text terminal display the user sees (STDOUT), and 2 is used for printing error messages (STDERR). Thus the same call to write a string to a file could be modified to write to the screen just by changing the file descriptor to 1. A socket, the value returned by socket(), is also nothing more than a file descriptor. However, for a TCP connection, the operating system cannot write to or read from it until it is connected to another host with the connect() function. Before connecting, though, you must specify the network address and port to connect to.

sockaddr

Because the API allows for such a diverse range of sockets, specifying an address needs to be done in a very general way. connect() uses a struct called sockaddr to accomplish this.

One specific type of sockaddr, sockaddr_in, is designed for use on the Internet. It contains all the fields necessary to specify an address and port number on the Internet. It is defined as follows:

```
struct sockaddr_in {
    short sin_family;
    unsigned short sin_port;
    struct   in_addr sin_addr;
    char sin_zero[8];
};
```

- The sin_family member is the same family name you used when creating the socket, and is also returned in the hostent structure from gethostbyname() in its h_addrtype member.

- The port, specified in the sin_port member of struct hostent is set here. Make sure it is in network byte order when setting it.

■Note *Byte ordering* is the way in which values of more than one byte are represented by a computer. An Intel x86 machine, for instance, is little-endian. It stores the least significant byte first. A Macintosh running PowerPC, on the other hand, is big-endian. It stores the most significant byte first.

The way we write numbers of more than one digit, for example, is big-endian. We write one hundred twenty-three as 123. The most significant digit comes first. If we were little-endian, like the x86 processor, we might write the same number as 321. Obviously, when networking computers of various types, a standardized way of interpreting numbers is needed. This way is called network byte order, and is big-endian.

To convert a value of type short int, such as the port number, on the local machine from its native byte ordering to network byte ordering, use htons() (Host TO Network Short). To convert it back, use ntohs(). The htonl(), and ntohl() functions do the same for values of type int. To set the port to 80, do

```
hostent.sin_port = htons(80);
```

Tip Even if you're developing on a big-endian platform, don't neglect to use htons(). It won't change the value when compiled on your machine, but it will make the code portable to run on a little-endian machine.

- The sin_addr member is the IP address, which is also contained in struct hostent. It is a structure of type in_addr, which is really just a convenient way for you to set its value in a variety of different formats. If you want to copy the value from a hostent struct, you should use memset to copy the memory from your hostent to your sockaddr.

```
struct sockaddr sockaddr;
memcpy(sockaddr.sin_addr.s_addr, hostent.h_addr, hostent->h_length);
```

- The remaining field, sin_zero, is an empty array used to make a sockaddr_in struct fit the profile of a sockaddr struct. You should fill it with zeroes by using memset:

```
memset(&(sockaddr.sin_zero), 0, sizeof(sockaddr.sin_zero));
```

connect()

Once you have a struct sockaddr, representing a network address and a port, you can finally connect to it with the connect() function.

connect() takes the file descriptor created with socket() and the sockaddr struct just presented, and connects it. It also takes the size of the sockaddr struct, determined by sizeof():

```
connect(fd, &sockaddr, sizeof(sockaddr));
```

This call will block until either the socket connects or the connection fails. On success, connect() will return 0. If it fails, it will return -1.

A Sample TCP/IP Client

One additional step is required for Windows applications that use networking. They must first initialize Winsock, the Windows implementation of sockets. An application need only do this one time, so it's recommended to put it in some Windows-specific initialization file. Gaim calls the code in the wgaim_init() found in win32/win32dep.c. The example in Listing 7-1 puts the initialization routine behind an #ifdef.

Listing 7-1. *A Sample TCP Client*

```
#ifdef _WIN32
#include <winsock2.h>
#else
#include <netdb.h>
#include <sys/types.h>
#include <sys/socket.h>
#endif

int main (int argc, char **argv)
{
    struct hostent *hostent;
    int fd;
    struct sockaddr_in sockaddr;

#ifdef _WIN32
    WORD wVersionRequested;
    WSADATA wsaData;
    int err;

    wVersionRequested = MAKEWORD( 2, 2 );
    err = WSAStartup( wVersionRequested, &wsaData );
    if ( err != 0 ) {
        return -1;
    }

    /* Check the version */
    if ( LOBYTE( wsaData.wVersion ) != 2 ||
         HIBYTE( wsaData.wVersion ) != 2 ) {
        WSACleanup( );
        return -1;
    }
#endif /* _WIN32 */

    if (argc != 3)
        return;

    hostent = gethostbyname(argv[1]);
    fd = socket(PF_INET, SOCK_STREAM, 0);
    if (hostent == NULL)
        return;

    memcpy(&sockaddr.sin_addr.s_addr, hostent->h_addr, hostent->h_length);
```

```
sockaddr.sin_port = htons(1118);
sockaddr.sin_family = hostent->h_addrtype;
memset(&(sockaddr.sin_zero), 0, sizeof(sockaddr.sin_zero));

if (connect(fd, (struct sockaddr*)&sockaddr, sizeof(sockaddr)) == -1)
    return -1;
send(fd, argv[2], strlen(argv[2])+1, 0);
close(fd);

return 0;
}
```

Following the Winsock initialization, notice that actually creating a connection is rather straightforward despite the complexity. The code in Listing 7-1 fetches a hostname and a string from the command line, and sends that string to the host on port 1118. When the corresponding server application (shown in Listing 7-2) is running, the two will interoperate.

Accepting Connections from Clients

You may also need to accept incoming connections in your application. Most IM protocols, for example, behave this way when doing file transfer. Rather than route large files through the IM server, using its resources, the clients arrange to connect to each other directly. One client, then, must accept incoming connections. This is also done with a socket, but instead of *connecting* to an address, the socket is *bound* to an address (in this case your own address) and is then told to *listen* for incoming connections on it.

sockaddr

Binding a socket to an address is very similar to connecting to one. The main difference is that the address used by connect() is on a remote machine, but the address used by bind() is on your own. First, fill out a sockaddr_in appropriately. In this case, you will fill out a sockaddr_in struct to your own computer. sin_family will still be AF_INET, and you can set the port to listen on (this will be the port others connect to on your machine) with a combination of sin_port and htons(). sin_addr.s_addr should be set to INADDR_ANY, which means "this computer."

```
struct sockaddr_in sockaddr;
sockaddr.sin_family = AF_INET;
sockaddr.sin_addr.s_addr = INADDR_ANY;
sockaddr.sin_port = htons(5050);
```

bind()

Binding a socket to an address is just like connecting to one. The bind() call takes the socket, created with socket(), the sockaddr, filled out in the previous example and the size of the sockaddr:

```
bind(fd, &sockaddr, sizeof(sockaddr));
```

Once the socket has been associated with a sockaddr, you can listen on it, causing the operating system to inform your program when data has been sent to the port you've bound to.

listen()

The listen() function takes two arguments: the socket to listen to and the number of simultaneous connections to allow. For an application like a Web server, you will want a relatively high number of simultaneous connections; many people may want to get content from the server at the same time. For the example of an IM client doing a file transfer, only one connection is needed:

```
listen(fd, 1);
```

listen() will block until someone connects, or returns -1 immediately if the call to listen was invalid for some reason. Otherwise, it will return 0, indicating that some other host has attempted to connect to this socket. You will need to use accept() to accept the connection.

accept()

accept()has a similar syntax to connect() and bind(). This time, however, the operating system passes sockaddr to you, describing the network address of the computer connected to you. socklen, similarly, is passed to you as the length of the sockaddr:

```
int connection_fd = accept(listening_fd, &sockaddr, &socklen);
```

accept() returns a new socket that represents the connection. To communicate with the connected machine, use this socket. The other socket, listening_fd in this example, will continue to listen for new connections. You can maintain multiple connections to your listening socket—as many as specified in listen()—so the return value from accept() will be required to discern among the various connections.

Once you have a socket returned from connect(), you can read and write to it just as a socket connected to another host, or any other file descriptor by using standard I/O system calls.

A Sample TCP/IP Server

Listing 7-2 presents the complement to the client in Listing 7-1. This program listens on port 1118 and then prints to the screen anything it receives.

■**Note** On UNIX machines, binding to port numbers less than 1024 typically requires root access. If users need to bind to a port on a protocol you're designing, keep this in mind.

Listing 7-2. *A Sample TCP Server*

```
#ifdef _WIN32
#include <winsock2.h>
#else
#include <netdb.h>
#include <sys/types.h>
#include <sys/socket.h>
#endif
```

```c
int main (int argc, char **argv)
{
    int fd;
    struct sockaddr_in sockaddr;

#ifdef _WIN32
    WORD wVersionRequested;
    WSADATA wsaData;
    int err;

    wVersionRequested = MAKEWORD( 2, 2 );
    err = WSAStartup( wVersionRequested, &wsaData );
    if ( err != 0 ) {
        return -1;
    }

    /* Check the version */
    if ( LOBYTE( wsaData.wVersion ) != 2 ||
        HIBYTE( wsaData.wVersion ) != 2 ) {
        WSACleanup( );
        return -1;
    }
#endif /* _WIN32 */

    fd = socket(PF_INET, SOCK_STREAM, 0);
    sockaddr.sin_family = AF_INET;
    sockaddr.sin_addr.s_addr = INADDR_ANY;
    sockaddr.sin_port = htons(1118);

    bind(fd, (struct sockaddr*)&sockaddr, sizeof(sockaddr));
    listen(fd, 1);

    while (1) {
        int connection_fd;
        int i, socklen = sizeof(sockaddr);
        char buffer[256];
        connection_fd = accept(fd, (struct sockaddr*)&sockaddr, &socklen);
        i = recv(connection_fd, buffer, sizeof(buffer), 0);
        if (i <= 0)
            return -1;
        printf("Received: %s\n", buffer);
        close(connection_fd);
    }


    return 0;
}
```

Like Listing 7-1, Listing 7-2 contains some Winsock initialization code wrapped in a `#ifdef` `_WIN32` statement. The major difference here is that the socket is bound to an incoming port and then an infinite loop is entered. Within the loop, the program repeatedly listens for incoming connections, which each get their own socket.

When this server is running, the client from Listing 7-1 can be run to send messages to the server. The result of this action is seen in Figure 7-3.

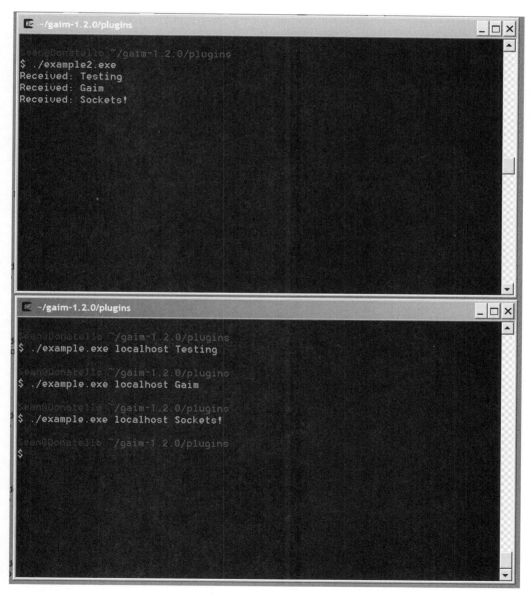

Figure 7-3. *The sample client communicating with the sample server*

Reading and Writing Data to a Socket

Reading and writing to a socket can be done just like reading and writing to any other file, by using read() and write(). You could even use functions such as fprintf() if you so desired. However, because they offer functionality specific to socket communication, recv() and send() are usually preferred.

The important thing to remember about I/O streams is that a read or a write call won't necessarily read or write all the data you want it to. Because of this, you will almost always see these calls within a loop.

recv() and send() return the number of bytes received or sent respectively, or -1 if an error occurred. Using this return value and a counter, we can loop until the number of bytes equals what we're expecting. To receive 1024 bytes from a socket, enter the following:

```
int i = 0, msg_len = 1024;
char buf[1024];
while (msg_len > 0 && (i = recv(fd, buf + (msg_len - 1024), msg_len, 0)) > 0)
    msg_len -= i;
```

recv()

Here, the first argument to recv() is the socket, fd. The second argument is a pointer to a buffer to which you'll save the received data. Notice I declared buf as an array with a size of the total amount of data to be received. Then when passing it to recv() I added (msg_len - 1024) to it.

Because recv() will be called numerous times, passing the same buffer to it each time would overwrite the data written to that buffer by previous calls. The solution is to keep track of how much data has already been received and offset the buffer by that amount. Here, the value stored in msg_len is counting down to zero, so (msg_len - 1024) accurately represents the size of the data already received.

Likewise, the third argument, the amount of data to read, must be updated regularly. Here, the counting-down nature of the msg_len counter achieves this. Finally, the fourth argument—the one that separates this call from read()—is the flags.

The flags argument is a bitmask of options affecting this call. It allows you to specify certain, mostly esoteric, options about the call. For most calls to recv(), you can leave the flags as 0, effectively making the call identical to read().

send()

Like recv(), the only difference between send() and its nonsocket cousin, write(), is the that send() provides a flag bitmask. Like write(), send() takes arguments for the file descriptor, a pointer to the data to send, and the number of bytes to send:

```
send(int s, const void *buf, size_t len, int flags);
```

Also like recv(), the flags you can set are largely useless for most applications and will most often be set to 0. The send() function returns the number of bytes written to the network. Like with the recv() example above, be sure to loop until you receive all the data you need.

close()

When you are finished with the socket, it is necessary to indicate so by closing it. The close() function takes a single argument: the socket. Closing a socket terminates the connection and invalidates the file descriptor. Remember that incoming connections can involve many sockets and it is necessary to close them all, especially the listening socket, as no other socket can bind to that port until the listening socket is closed.

Socket functions such as send(), recv(), connect(), and listen() all block; i.e., they don't return until they've completed. For some applications, this may be fine. However, GTK+ depends on control being passed back to the main loop to keep the GUI redrawn and receive events. To keep your GUI application responsive, it may be necessary to use non-blocking sockets.

Non-blocking I/O

Because a socket is a file descriptor, any function that acts on a file selector can take a socket. One notable such function is fcntl(), which offers a wide range of modifications to a file descriptor. To set a socket as non-blocking, call:

```
fcntl(fd, F_SETFL, O_NONBLOCK);
```

When a socket is non-blocking, any call made to it that the function would otherwise block returns immediately. However, because it's still impossible to send data over an unconnected socket, for example, it's still necessary to wait. The responsibility to wait for a socket to be connected or for a connection to be made or for data to be available to receive is transferred from within the operating system to the program itself.

After a non-blocking call, the program must regularly check the status of the socket to see if it is ready for the next function call to be made on it. This check is done by a function called select().

select()

The select() function waits for a file selector to change status. This could mean changing from "unconnected" to "connected," or "no data available to read" to "data available to read." When select() is called frequently enough, it can appear that the sockets are operating with no delay, and control can still be passed to other parts of the application such that it doesn't appear to lock up and freeze. The select() function takes a number of arguments that specify which file descriptors to listen to and how long to listen for:

```
int select(int n fd_set *readfs, fd_set *writefds, fd_set *exceptfds, struct time-
val *timeout);
```

The select() function can check the status of multiple file selectors at once. This is useful for an application like Gaim, which maintains multiple connections to various IM protocols simultaneously, but a more traditional use is to check the 0 file selector: STDIN. This allows a text-based application to connect to the Internet while still responding to user input. The sets of file descriptors to listen on are specified in arguments of type fd_set.

fd_set

The select() function takes three different sets of file descriptors to check for three different types of state changes in a file descriptor. select() will check the file descriptors in the readfds argument to see if their state has changed such that it can now be read from; in other words, data has been received on the socket. select() will check writefds for file descriptors that can now be written to, i.e., sockets that have finishing connecting. File descriptors in exceptfds will be watched for errors. These three arguments are of type fd_set.

Tip Because they're usually both unique to a given connection, I often tend to confuse file descriptors and port numbers when dealing with select(), causing a ton of wasted time figuring out why my sockets seem never to connect. It's probably just a quirk of mine, but be sure not to make the same mistake. Socket file descriptors have no relation to the port number they're connected to.

An fd_set is a small struct wrapping around an array of file descriptors. The sockets API provides some convenient macros for manipulating fd_set structs.

To clear an fd_set, call FD_ZERO on it. You should always do this to initialize an fd_set before using it:

```
fd_set readfds;
FD_ZERO(&readfds);
```

Then, set file descriptors to it with FD_SET:

```
FD_SET(0, &readfds);
FD_SET(fd, &readfds);
```

This example adds STDIN—the user's input to the console—and some file descriptor stored in fd, perhaps a socket, to readfds. When select is called, it will check all the file descriptors in the readfds that have been set. If the status has changed appropriately, it will clear the file descriptor from the readfds. You will then use the FD_ISSET() macro on the file descriptors you've set to check if their status has changed.

select() also specifies how long to wait for the status to change. It will block until the status of one of its file descriptors changes or until the timeout expires. For a GTK+ application, where application response is determined by how frequently program control is returned to the main loop, the timeout would benefit from being small; otherwise the application would not redraw the screen often enough. Suppose an application with a single network connection and a text interface. This program has nothing to do until input is available from either. In this case, the timeout can be infinite.

timeval

The timeout is specified in a struct called timeval. struct timeval contains two members: seconds and microseconds:

```
struct timeval {
    long tv_sec;   /* seconds */
    long tv_usesc; /* microseconds */
};
```

Filling this `struct` should be straightforward. Keep in mind that 0 seconds and 0 microseconds is a valid timeout to keep `select()` from blocking at all:

```
struct timeval timeout;
timeout.tv_sec = 0;
timeout.tv_usec = 0;
```

Non-Blocking Sockets with `select()`

After filling out your three `fd_set` structs and timeout `timeval`, you're ready to call `select()`. The only additional required information is the highest numbered file descriptor set in an `fd_set`. `select()` will use this to minimize the number of file descriptors it checks. This value, plus one, is passed as the first argument to `select()`. In my example, two file selectors are set. Because `fd` is certainly greater than 0, I would use `fd + 1` as my first argument.

If dealing with more than one variable file descriptor, you can use the `MAX()` macro to find the greater of two. For larger numbers of file descriptors, you probably want to keep track of the highest value as the sockets are created.

Once you've determined the highest value of all your file descriptors, plus one, call `select()` with it, the three `fd_set` structs, and the timeout:

```
int ret = select(1, &readfds, &writefds, &exceptfds, &timeout);
```

The return value of `select()` is the number of set file descriptors whose status has changed. If none changed before the timeout, it can be zero. To check which have changed, you must manually check each previously set file descriptor in an `fd_set` struct to see if it's still set:

```
if (!FD_ISSET(0, &readfs))
    handle_stdin();
if (!FD_ISSET(fd, &readfs))
    handle_socket();
```

You could then repeat this in a loop, continually waiting for and then processing new input. Make sure that you reset the sockets you watch, as `select()` unset them. Do this just as you did originally, with `FD_SET()`.

`select()` provides a useful way of keeping both your network connections and your GUI constantly refreshed. Because it's so useful for GUI applications, GTK+ provides convenient wrappers that mesh this constant polling of file descriptors in with its own main loop and provides a useful callback system to receive notification of these events.

Integrating into GLib's Main Loop

`GIOChannel` is provided by GLib as a portable wrapper around a file descriptor. Its goals are platform independence and tight integration with GLib's main loop. While the former goal has not yet been achieved, forcing developers who intend their applications to run on Windows to use lower-level APIs, the integration with the main loop is incredibly useful for networked GTK+ applications.

When using select() and non-blocking sockets, it's necessary to repeatedly poll the file descriptors. Ultimately, you're creating a main loop of your own, repeating the same function call over and over. GLib brings this select() call into its main loop, and instead of manually checking the status of each socket after calling select(), GLib lets you attach a callback to a socket, which gets called when its status changes. Your application can essentially treat "I received data on this socket" as an event just like "the user clicked this button."

GIOChannel

The first step to enjoying the benefits of this system is to create a GIOChannel. If your GIOChannel represents a file (remember, sockets are just special files), you can use g_io_channel_new_file(), but for a socket, call g_io_channel_new_unix().

g_io_channel_new_unix() takes a file descriptor as its sole argument and returns a GIOChannel. GIOChannel offers no mechanisms building on the sockets API, so you will still need to connect, bind, listen, and accept as described above.

You can, though, replace recv() and send() with functions provided by GIOChannel, such as the ability to send Unicode text. However, as you will see next chapter, data sent over the network will often be far more complex than Unicode text, and these functions are more useful for files than sockets.

g_io_add_watch()

After creating the GIOChannel, attaching a callback for status changes is very similar to attaching to signals on a GObject. The function g_io_add_watch() takes as arguments the GIOChannel, the event to attach to, the callback function, and data to send to the callback. This is just like attaching to a signal.

Due to the highly limited number of possible events, the event is specified as an enum rather than a string. The values that correspond to the three fd_set structs are G_IO_IN for readfds, G_IO_OUT for writefds, and G_IO_ERR for exceptfds. The callback is passed a value of this enum as its second argument; its first argument is the GIOChannel and the third argument is the user data. The callback also returns a gboolean: TRUE if GLib should continue watching this socket or FALSE otherwise:

```
gboolean socket_cb (GIOChannel *ioc, GIOCondition condition, gpointer data)
{
    printf("Data received.\n");
    return TRUE;
}
...
...
g_io_add_watch(ioc, G_IO_IN, socket_cb, NULL);
```

> **Note** The ellipsis in the preceding code indicate that I have omitted part of the code.

The return value of `g_io_add_watch()` is an integer representing an event source. This is the same type returned by `g_signal_connect()` and `g_timeout_add()`. Just like event listeners for those, the result of `g_io_add_watch()` can be disabled with `g_source_remove()`.

A Sample Gaim Plug-in

I am always online. Only on very rare occasion do I ever sign off. I do, however, leave the computer once in a while. When I do, I sometimes want to see the messages I've received since I left. In this section, I'll walk you through writing a plug-in designed to allow me to read my messages from any other computer with Internet access.

In order to be able to read my messages from another computer over the Internet, I'll need to employ the client-server model presented earlier in this chapter. Obviously, Gaim will be the server; the other computers I use will connect to mine and my computer will respond with the messages it's received. However, because I often don't have the permission to install my own software on other computers I use, it would be ideal if I could use software that already exists on every computer. For this task, I'll use a Web browser.

Essentially every computer I use with Internet access has a Web browser; therefore this is an ideal client to use for this task. Because the server and the client need to understand the same protocol, I will need to design my Gaim plug-in to speak HTTP, the protocol used by the World Wide Web.

HTTP is a fairly simple protocol. The client connects to the server and sends a request; the server then responds with a set of headers and then the content that was requested. A client can make numerous types of requests: GET is the most common, but PUT, POST, and DELETE are also used. For simplicity, this plug-in will respond to all requests the same way, with the contents of currently open conversations.

The Boilerplate

As always, I start with a simple boilerplate template, modified for this plug-in:

```
#include "internal.h"
#include "plugin.h"
#include "notify.h"
#include "version.h"

#include "gtkconv.h"
#include "gtkimhtml.h"

GaimPlugin *plugin_handle = NULL;
```

```
static gboolean
plugin_load(GaimPlugin *plugin)
{
}
static GaimPluginInfo info =
{
    GAIM_PLUGIN_MAGIC,
    GAIM_MAJOR_VERSION,
    GAIM_MINOR_VERSION,
    GAIM_PLUGIN_STANDARD,
    NULL,
    0,
    NULL,
    GAIM_PRIORITY_DEFAULT,
    "webserver",
    "Remote Web Access",
    "1.0",
    "Sends pending messages over the web when requested",
    "Implements a basic web server which listens on the network "
    "for incoming connections, and processes requests by sending "
    "the complete text within each open IM conversation",
    "Sean Egan <seanegan@gmail.com>",
    "http://apress.com",
    plugin_load,
    NULL,
    NULL,
    NULL,
    NULL,
    NULL
};

static void
init_plugin(GaimPlugin *plugin)
{
}
```

```
GAIM_INIT_PLUGIN(webserver, init_plugin, info)
```

In addition to changing the `plugin_info` struct accordingly, I also add two #include statements for header files I will need later. `plugin_load()` starts empty, but, as usual, it will be the first place I write code.

plugin_load()

Typically the `plugin_load()` function initializes data structures and connects to Gaim plug-in signals. In this plug-in, I also need to create the socket that will listen for incoming connections. I will then attach this signal to the GLib main loop with a callback:

```
static gboolean
plugin_load(GaimPlugin *plugin)
{
    struct sockaddr_in sockaddr;
    int fd;

    plugin_handle = plugin;
    fd = socket(PF_INET, SOCK_STREAM, 0);
    if (fd < 0)
        return FALSE;
    sockaddr.sin_family = AF_INET;
    sockaddr.sin_addr.s_addr = INADDR_ANY;
    sockaddr.sin_port = htons(1118);

    if ((bind(fd, (struct sockaddr*)&sockaddr, sizeof(sockaddr))) < 0)
        return FALSE;
    listen(fd, 1);
    g_io_add_watch(g_io_channel_unix_new(fd), G_IO_IN, incoming_cb, NULL);
    return TRUE;
}
```

Because this will be running as a Gaim plug-in, we can assume that Winsock has already been initialized on Windows. With that code out of the way, you can see how simple creating a socket actually is. Here, I create a socket and bind it to port 1118. Then I listen on it and add it to the main loop with g_io_add_watch(). Because I set G_IO_IN, the callback, incoming_cb, will be called when there is data to be read on the socket. Because this socket listens, "data to be read," means that a client has connected.

The callback, incoming_cb(), will need to handle incoming connections and send to them the contents of the conversations.

incoming_cb()

Typically, when receiving an incoming connection, you would read from it, then act differently. The set of rules dictating the communication between the client and server is called a protocol. I will discuss protocols in the next chapter. In this chapter, I will ignore the client request and respond to any request the same way.

The socket file descriptor is retrieved from the GIOChannel with g_io_channel_unix_get_fd(). I then treat the socket just as any other bound and listening socket. I call accept() on it to get a socket representing the new connection.

Under most connections, I'd probably use GIOChannel again on this socket to maintain the connection. For this plug-in, though, the connection is transient; I'll close it as soon as I send the messages. I can handle the entire connection in this one function.

```
static gboolean incoming_cb(GIOChannel *source,
                    GIOCondition condition,
                    gpointer data)
{
    int cfd;
    struct sockaddr_in sockaddr;
    int socklen = sizeof(sockaddr);
    char buf[256];
    char *resp=create_response();
    int fd = g_io_channel_unix_get_fd(source);
    if (condition != G_IO_IN)
        return TRUE;


    if ((cfd = accept(fd, (struct sockaddr*)&sockaddr, &socklen)) < 0)
        return TRUE;
    recv(cfd, buf, sizeof(buf), 0);
    /* Send response here */
    send(cfd, resp, strlen(resp), 0);
    close(cfd);
    return TRUE;
}
```

I read the command into the buf character buffer but ignore it. Because I'm handling all requests the same, I don't bother to check the contents of the buffer after reading into it. I just send to the connected client a string of text returned from create_response().

create_response()

The create_response() function creates the HTTP response that will be sent to the client. This code uses GString to easily work with appending data to a string without worrying about manually reallocating memory for it. The function loops through all the currently open conversations and calls gtk_imhtml_get_markup(), which returns HTML markup representing the contents of the conversation. This is perfectly suitable to return to a Web browser.

```
static char *create_response()
{
    GList *convs = gaim_get_conversations();
    GString *str = g_string_new("HTTP/1.1 200 OK\r\n"
                            "Content-Type: text/html\r\n"
                            "\r\n"
                            "<html><head><title>"
                            "Gaim Conversations</title></head><body>");
    while (convs) {
        GaimConversation *conv = convs->data;
        GaimGtkConversation *gtkconv = GAIM_GTK_CONVERSATION(conv);
        if (gaim_conversation_get_type(conv) != GAIM_CONV_IM) {
            convs = convs->next;
            continue;
        }
```

```
            char *html = gtk_imhtml_get_markup(GTK_IMHTML(gtkconv->imhtml));
            str = g_string_append(str, "<h1>");
            str = g_string_append(str, gaim_conversation_get_name(conv));
            str = g_string_append(str, "</h1>");
            str = g_string_append(str, html);
            g_free(html);
            convs = convs->next;
        }
        str = g_string_append(str, "</body></html>");
        return g_string_free(str, FALSE);
}
```

The first few lines are the HTTP header specify that the issued command (whichever it was) succeeded and that it is returning HTML text. The rest of the code is the HTML from each currently open conversation.

The Final Plug-In

Listing 7-3 shows the final plug-in. Save this to a file and compile the way you typically compile plug-ins.

Listing 7-3. *The Webserver Plug-in that Returns the Contents of Currently Open Conversations*

```
#include "internal.h"
#include "plugin.h"
#include "notify.h"
#include "version.h"

#include "gtkconv.h"
#include "gtkimhtml.h"

GaimPlugin *plugin_handle = NULL;

static char *create_response()
{
    GList *convs = gaim_get_conversations();
    GString *str = g_string_new("HTTP/1.1 200 OK\r\n"
                                "Content-Type: text/html\r\n"
                                "\r\n"
                                "<html><head><title>"
                                "Gaim Conversations</title></head><body>");
    while (convs) {
        GaimConversation *conv = convs->data;
        GaimGtkConversation *gtkconv = GAIM_GTK_CONVERSATION(conv);
        if (gaim_conversation_get_type(conv) != GAIM_CONV_IM) {
            convs = convs->next;
            continue;
        }
```

```
            char *html = gtk_imhtml_get_markup(GTK_IMHTML(gtkconv->imhtml));
            str = g_string_append(str, "<h1>");
            str = g_string_append(str, gaim_conversation_get_name(conv));
            str = g_string_append(str, "</h1>");
            str = g_string_append(str, html);
            g_free(html);
            convs = convs->next;
        }
        str = g_string_append(str, "</body></html>");
        return g_string_free(str, FALSE);
}


static gboolean incoming_cb(GIOChannel *source,
                    GIOCondition condition,
                    gpointer data)
{
        int cfd;
        struct sockaddr_in sockaddr;
        int socklen = sizeof(sockaddr);
        char buf[256];
        char *resp=create_response();
        int fd = g_io_channel_unix_get_fd(source);
        if (condition != G_IO_IN)
                return TRUE;


        if ((cfd = accept(fd, (struct sockaddr*)&sockaddr, &socklen)) < 0)
                return TRUE;
        recv(cfd, buf, sizeof(buf), 0);
        /* Send response here */
        send(cfd, resp, strlen(resp), 0);
        close(cfd);
        return TRUE;
}

static gboolean
plugin_load(GaimPlugin *plugin)
{
        struct sockaddr_in sockaddr;
        int fd;

        plugin_handle = plugin;
        fd = socket(PF_INET, SOCK_STREAM, 0);
        if (fd < 0)
                return FALSE;
```

```
        sockaddr.sin_family = AF_INET;
        sockaddr.sin_addr.s_addr = INADDR_ANY;
        sockaddr.sin_port = htons(1118);

        if ((bind(fd, (struct sockaddr*)&sockaddr, sizeof(sockaddr))) < 0)
                return FALSE;
        listen(fd, 1);
        g_io_add_watch(g_io_channel_unix_new(fd), G_IO_IN, incoming_cb, NULL);
        return TRUE;
}

static GaimPluginInfo info =
{
        GAIM_PLUGIN_MAGIC,
        GAIM_MAJOR_VERSION,
        GAIM_MINOR_VERSION,
        GAIM_PLUGIN_STANDARD,
        NULL,
        0,
        NULL,
        GAIM_PRIORITY_DEFAULT,
        "webserver",
        "Remote Web Access",
        "1.0",
        "Sends pending messages over the web when requested",
        "Implements a basic web server which listens on the network "
        "for incoming connections, and processes requests by sending "
        "the complete text within each open IM conversation",
        "Sean Egan <seanegan@gmail.com>",
        "http://apress.com",
        plugin_load,
        NULL,
        NULL,
        NULL,
        NULL,
        NULL
};

 static void
 init_plugin(GaimPlugin *plugin)
 {
 }


GAIM_INIT_PLUGIN(webserver, init_plugin, info)
```

After compiling and running this plug-in, you can connect to your computer with any Web browser by specifying to connect to port 1118. To make your browser connect on a port other than 80, specify it after the hostname with a colon. For instance, if your IP address is 127.12.51.111, you would enter the URL http://127.12.51.111:1118. Figure 7-4 shows three open conversations in Gaim, and a Web browser connected to http://localhost:1118 displaying those conversations.

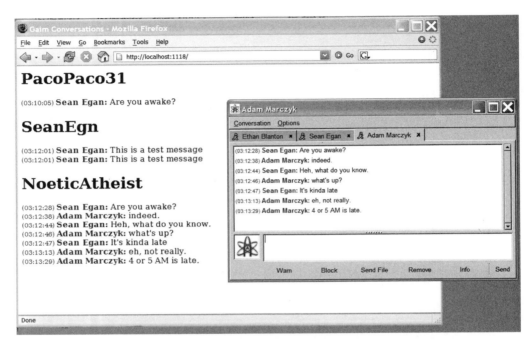

Figure 7-4. *The Gaim webserver plug-in*

Possible Extensions

This plug-in has a ton of potential extensions in case you're interested in doing some additional experimentation. Here is a short list:

- **Process HTTP requests.** This is the most obvious extension. Rather than handling any connection as a request to get the contents of the conversations, only handle valid HTTP requests.

- **Return different information.** Once you're parsing requests, you can handle them differently. For instance, allow someone to request only one active conversation by screen name. You can allow the Web browser to view past conversations, buddy icons, the current status of the buddy list, etc.

- **Make the output prettier**. The current output is quite simple and not very pretty. If you know HTML or CSS, you could make it much prettier. If you allow the Web server to request buddy icons, you can make it look even prettier.

- **Handle HTTP authentication**. It's not a good idea to let just anyone on the Internet read your messages. It would be beneficial only to let you access it. HTTP includes an authentication scheme you can support to accomplish this.

Summary

You should now have an understanding about how networking works and how the sockets API was designed around it. You should be able to use the sockets API to connect to other computers on the Internet and send and receive data from them. I've explained the troubles of trying to use sockets and maintain responsiveness in the GUI at the same time, as well as how to use select() to avoid these troubles. But more importantly, you've learned how GLib provides an API for you, allowing it to keep the GUI and your network connections running smoothly.

In the next chapter, I'll expand on how to use networking, explaining exactly what kind of data gets sent and received to implement instant messaging. Although I will use IM-specific examples, the design principles of the protocols I'll discuss apply to any network protocol, even ones you may need to design yourself.

■ ■ ■

Protocol Plug-Ins

A protocol is a predefined method for communication between two or more programs. In instant messaging, and many other network applications, protocols specify the rules as to how two computers should communicate. In the previous chapter I described the roles of some protocols such as IP and TCP that serve to make networking scalable and reliable. I also explained the OSI model and that these protocols are at a low level. In this chapter, I'll discuss protocols that occur at the application layer.

The application layer is especially interesting because it's the layer that actually does what people want. Minimizing network congestion and determining the fastest route from one computer to another aren't problems most people are interested in. Sending e-mail, sharing photos, and instant messaging are practical applications that affect people's lives very directly.

In this chapter, I will discuss application-level protocols. While I will place special emphasis on IM protocols, most of what I will write applies to all protocols in general. After reading this chapter, you should understand the general form of most networking protocols, be able to design your own protocol for a given purpose, decipher existing protocols, and implement these protocols in C based on the sockets API discussed in the previous chapter.

Protocol Design

A protocol is designed for a specific task. While the task dictates certain implementation specifics, most protocols nonetheless have a lot in common. For instance, the IM protocols discussed here all share a common task—instant messaging—so they'll obviously have a lot in common, but they also have similarities to unrelated protocols such as HTTP (Hypertext Transfer Protocol). One notable similarity between many protocols is the concept of packets.

Packet Framing

Although TCP streams are useful in their ability to provide an identical interface to file I/O, most protocols will need to break this stream into discrete packets. Figure 8-1 shows a screenshot of Ethereal demonstrating that an HTTP stream is actually a series of discrete IP packets. Most protocols work on a packet basis, where each packet represents one or more commands or messages. Therefore, one of the most important features of most protocols is determining where a packet begins and ends. There are three possible ways of doing this.

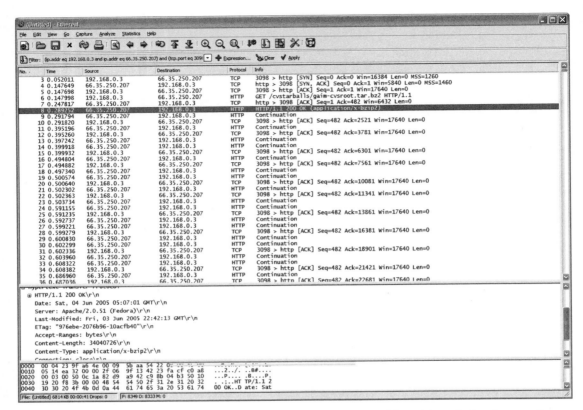

Figure 8-1. *Although the sockets API presents TCP as a steady stream of data, it's really implemented as multiple discrete IP packets.*

Note Streaming is a feature of TCP. If a protocol uses UDP, there is no need for additional framing. Most protocols, however, prefer the benefit TCP's reliability over the cost of framing packets from it.

Fixed-Length Packets

The first possibility is to require all packets to be the same length. This way, an implementation knows that every *n* bytes it receives is an entire packet. Of course, the limitations to this are obvious. The protocol is limited to an arbitrarily decided limit on packet length, i.e. messages cannot be longer than a set limit. Also, ordinarily short messages will need to fill the entire packet. This is usually done by padding it with garbage data, which is a needless waste. If your protocol is for an application for which these consequences aren't limiting—where each packet will be the same length anyway for whatever reason—this may be a good solution. However, because IM messages range from "hi" to huge paragraphs, this is typically unsuitable for IM.

Sentinel Markers

A second solution is to mark the end of packets with a special sequence of bytes, known as a *sentinel*. This is similar to marking the end of sentences with a period. However, this method prohibits us from using that sequence within the packet. Also, it requires the implementation to individually check every byte of every incoming packet to find the sequence, which is less efficient than the other methods described here.

This solution is better for IM than the first and is used by many protocols, including MSN Messenger and IRC. An oft-used sequence for marking a packet border is 0x0d0a, alternatively represented as \r\n, which represents a new line in ASCII (ASCII is a way computers represent text, explained in depth in Chapter 9). Protocols that use this delimiter, such as IRC, are commonly called *line-based protocols*.

Specified Length

The third solution is to include the length of each packet in a header at the start of each packet. This method, like the first, does put an upper limit on the size of a packet, because the length field of the header has a maximum value. However, this limit can be very large—to the point that it's negligible—without requiring all packets to be that length. Using this method, an implementation just reads the length of a header from the TCP stream, determines the length of the packet from that, and reads the rest of the packet from the network.

For instance, suppose the header of a packet contains only the length. This length is stored in an unsigned int type of four bytes. Accordingly, the maximum packet length is in the order of gigabytes: more than enough for any application. To frame a packet, you would do something like this:

```
unsigned int length;
char *buffer;
read(fd, &length, 4);
length = ntohl(length);
buffer = (char*)malloc(length);
read(fd, buffer, length);
```

After this, the data of the packet will be in the buffer variable. Note here that read(), while usually told to write to an array of chars, can write to any pointer. Here, I have it write its value to an unsigned int variable. I then must convert it to host byte order to ensure the correct value. Once I have the length, I allocate a buffer and read the rest of the packet into it. As explained in the previous chapter, read() doesn't guarantee to read the number of bytes specified. I omitted the loop here for simplicity. Of course, in most instances, a packet header will contain a lot more data about the packet than just its length.

Packet Headers

Packet headers frame and identify individual packets from a TCP stream. They will usually contain the length of the packet, and other data that identifies the protocol used and the purpose of this packet within that protocol.

The protocols used by AIM and ICQ, for example, use a header AOL calls FLAP. This header contains fields, each of which serves a different purpose. One identifies the header as a FLAP header (as opposed to some random Internet anomaly). Another identifies the packet's purpose within the protocol, and another gives the length of the data contained within it.

■Note America Online operates both AIM and ICQ, which both use the same protocol, known as OSCAR. AOL also provides a protocol called TOC, intended for third-party developers, but their support for this protocol has not been maintained and OSCAR is much better for that reason. Gaim implements the OSCAR protocol for its support of AIM and ICQ, but because it's an easier protocol to understand, TOC will be used as my example in this chapter. Both protocols, however, use FLAP headers.

Most network protocols make their packets identifiable with a "magic number" at some predefined location in the packet. For protocols that prefix each packet with a header, the header often houses the identifying string of bytes. This magic number is often the first element of the header and is a constant value the implementation can check to ensure it has a valid packet header. The FLAP header starts with a magic number: a single byte with the value 0x2A, or alternatively, '*'. If an implementation checks the first byte of a FLAP header and finds it's not '*' then there's been some error, and the connection should be dropped. Other protocols do more to detect the protocol. Yahoo! Messenger, for example, uses the string "YMSG" as its magic number and follows it with a binary version number.

The next element in AIM's FLAP header identifies the packet's role within the protocol. This is another one-byte identifier for which several values are predefined. These values include 1, for packets which negotiate logging in, 2 for standard data packets, 3 for error packets, and so on. It is common for the protocol implementation to check a value like this in a switch() statement, passing control to various functions according to the packet type.

The third element in a FLAP header is a sequence number. Sequence numbers are used to ensure that every packet is received in order. If a host receives packet 4 before receiving packet 3, clearly an error has occurred and the connection should be dropped. This sort of reliability, however, is already ensured by TCP, which AIM and ICQ are built on top of, so having a sequence number is redundant. I would speculate that the sequence number was included to ease the ability to migrate to UDP instead of TCP if that decision were deemed appropriate at some time. The sequence number is 2 bytes.

Finally, the last two bytes of the FLAP header are the length of the data following it. Note that the length of the data does not include the length of the packet, but that may vary from protocol to protocol. Also, these values are all network byte order; be sure to convert numbers any time you're dealing with network data.

An implementation of a protocol that behaves like this will likely perform this series of actions:

1. Read the number of bytes in a header to a buffer.

2. Determine the values of each header element from what you've read, knowing which bytes apply to what.

3. Check that the magic number matches what it should. Give up if it doesn't.

4. Using the length specified in the header, read the rest of the packet into memory.

5. Determine the purpose of this packet, and demultiplex accordingly, passing the data of the packet to a function designed to handle it.

Headers are used to frame packets. Although they provide data *about* the packet, they generally provide little information about what it's actually trying to *do*. The FLAP header, for example, doesn't bother explaining who the recipient of a message is. Further, line-based protocols such as IRC or MSN don't have headers at all. In most cases, the function being performed by a given packet is not found in the header, but in the packet data.

Packet Data

Once you've isolated and demultiplexed the packet data, it's necessary to interpret it. The packet data can be broadly grouped into two categories: binary and text-based. Further, because protocols tend to use one or another, and not both, the same terms apply to the protocols that use packets of that type.

The two types of protocols, however, are really quite similar. The major difference is that binary protocols are easier for computers to read and text protocols are easier for humans to read. Because this book is intended to be read by humans, I'm focusing on using text-based IM protocols: namely AOL's TOC and Microsoft's MSN protocols. However, the general principles of protocol design are the same; only the specifics differ.

Protocol packets can usually be thought of as commands or replies. Each command can have a number of arguments, and a reply can have multiple parts. For example, a packet sent in order to send an instant message will typically contain an identifier for the command and various arguments: whom to send it to and the message itself, at least. The only differences are how the commands and arguments are represented.

Binary Protocols

Binary protocols are generally preferred for their speed. Because they're highly machine-readable, it requires little computation to decipher them. The FLAP header example above, for instance, is a binary protocol. While the rest of the TOC protocol involves relatively complicated string parsing, its FLAP header involves reading a few bytes and passing it to ntohs(). I'll discuss more specifically how to implement a binary protocol in C later this chapter.

The FLAP header is a good example of a binary protocol in form. It identifies itself using predetermined numerical values. Sending 3 as the type of the packet, for instance, identifies it as an error. Binary protocols do the same with their packet data.

The first thing needed to identify the packet data is to identify what type of command the packet contains. As is done in the FLAP header, the type of command is a predetermined numerical identifier. It may, in fact, be preferable to use more than one identifier. This helps break the command into categories. For instance, assume "buddy list commands" are handled by command type 5. If you receive a packet and the command type is 5, you can then pass the packet to your buddy list handling code. Breaking down commands into groups like this doesn't add much to the usefulness of the protocol, but aids in writing modular code to implement it.

After determining the command, the arguments are left to be deciphered. This is a problem very similar to framing packets: determining where one begins and another ends. Another similarity is that an argument may want to identify itself, as certain protocols identify each packet type in the header.

Consequently, the three methods used for framing packets can be used to frame arguments. Likewise, the same shortcomings that prevent fixed-length packets from being an effective method of framing IM packets keeps it from effectively framing arguments in a packet: usually a "message" argument will be considerably longer than a "screen name" argument. Therefore, the two most commonly used techniques are headers and delineating arguments with special sequences of bytes.

An argument in a packet can have a header. The OSCAR protocol uses this technique extensively. A header for an OSCAR packet is known as a TLV, for "type, length, value," the three fields contained therein. The type identifies the argument, similar to how the FLAP packet type field identifies the type of argument. The type field marks this argument as a screen name, or as a message. The length field provides the length of the data. The data itself, the value, follows. The next TLV is found immediately after.

Yahoo!, on the other hand, breaks arguments with a special sequence of bytes. An argument in Yahoo! starts by identifying the argument, like the type in a TLV, then places the delineating byte sequence, followed by the data: the value in a TLV. The whole argument ends with the delineating byte sequence.

Although the type of argument is given in both OSCAR and Yahoo! packets, it's not strictly necessary. The argument type can be determined simply by where within the packet the argument lies. Perhaps the protocol specifies the first argument is the screen name and the second is the message. However, protocols will usually try to explicitly identify their arguments to allow for easier extensions to the protocol. It's poor design to be dependent on a particular ordering of arguments. Argument ordering is, however, the most common method in text-based IM protocols.

Text-Based Protocols

The major benefit to binary protocols is speed. It's really easy for a computer to decode and act on a message received. It's similarly very fast for it to construct and send packets. However, for a network protocol such as instant messaging, the time required to decode each packet is not the limiting factor. It takes far longer for the packet to travel from the server to the client than it does to parse it. Therefore, text protocols are often used for network protocols, including instant messaging. I will be discussing two text-based protocols here: AIM's TOC protocol, and the MSN protocol.

Text-based protocols have the advantage of being highly human-readable. Therefore, it's much easier to read and understand a text protocol than a binary protocol. However, the same concept of commands and arguments applies. Instead of being represented by binary numbers, though, commands in a text-based protocol are represented by words.

To send me an instant message with TOC, for example, send the following to the TOC server:

```
toc_send_im seanegn "Hello"
```

It's human-readable and straightforward. Let's examine the design considerations discussed for binary protocols and see how they compare to this TOC packet.

The command is a string. There is no breakdown into subcategories, but there could be. Commands are guaranteed not to contain spaces, so the first space encountered marks the end of the command and the beginning of the arguments.

Arguments are separated with a special sequence of characters: in this case, a space. As mentioned, one of the negatives of this is that it prevents that sequence from being used within the data it delineates. TOC avoids that by additionally framing each argument around quotation marks (screen names are an exception because they are not allowed to have spaces). This, however prevents you from using quotation marks within arguments. TOC avoids this with a method familiar to any C programmer: backslash escaping. Hence, to send quotation marks in an IM, they would appear as \" in the string:

```
toc_send_im seanegn "Then she said, \"conifer? I barely know her!\""
```

Unlike OSCAR and Yahoo!, which identify arguments with numerical identifiers, TOC identifies them by order alone. For toc_send_im(), the first argument must be the screen name, and the second must be the message. This is less flexible than OSCAR and Yahoo!'s method, but is common in text-based protocols. MSN uses it, as well.

MSN is a line-based protocol. Whereas TOC uses a binary header for framing and only the packet data is text-based, MSN generally frames its packets with newline characters, although it actually uses a combination of various techniques reviewed so far.

To send an instant message in MSN, you send the following to the server:

```
MSG 21 A 68
MIME-Version: 1.0
Content-Type: text/plain; charset=UTF-8

Hello!
```

Each line is separated with the newline characters \r\n.

As you can see, MSN is slightly more obtuse than TOC. Although it is still more readable than a string of hexadecimal, it's not self-explanatory. Let's see how MSN handles the issues we've been discussing.

The command name is the first thing appearing in the packet. Elements in MSN are separated by spaces, and MSN has the added restriction that command names are limited to three characters. Either fact can be used to isolate the command. The next element is called the transaction ID, abbreviated TrID. The TrID serves a similar purpose to the sequence number found in FLAP headers, but rather than solely attempting to detect errors, it serves as an identifier for the packet. I'll explain how the protocol uses the TrID later this chapter.

The three-letter command name and TrID are common to every MSN command. What for a MSG command are the arguments, which vary depending on the command. In this case, there are three arguments: an "acknowledgement type," a length, and the message itself.

■**Note** Every MSN conversation happens in a separate connection with a different socket. There is no screen-name argument because any message to this connection goes to other people in the conversation represented by this connection.

In MSN, there are three acknowledgment types. These are represented by single letters: U for Unacknowledged, A for Acknowledged, and N for Negative Acknowledged. Respectively, these request that the server tell me nothing about whether the message was received, confirm that the message was received, and only tell me when the message was not received.

The next argument is the length of the message that follows. The length breaks the normal line-based nature of the protocol and replaces it with a "length in header" model. The MSG command makes an exception and any character is allowed within the bounds set by the length argument.

In fact, the message starts after a blank line itself. The message starts with a MIME header, which itself is delineated by newlines and spaces. MIME headers are commonly used throughout networking protocols to describe content. They are used in e-mail and on the World Wide Web, for instance. Here they provide the type of message this is—plain text—and the encoding (encodings will be explained in-depth in Chapter 9).

The message starts after two newlines in a row, the sequence that marks the end of a MIME header. It ends after the number of bytes specified by the length parameter, after which the server implementation should expect a new three-letter command. The server, likewise, will send its own commands to the client. In IM protocols, these commands most frequently include updates to presence information and instant messages. These commands are just one type of packet IM servers will send to clients. Another notable type is responses to client-initiated commands.

Responses

So far I've discussed *commands*. A command can be sent in either direction. I've been using "send an IM" as an example of a command from the client to the server, but the same ideas are relevant for communication in the opposite direction. If a user on the buddy list signs on, the server sends a packet to the client. This packet can be thought of as a command: "show that this user has signed on." As such, it has the same form: a command name and arguments. A packet from the server may look different, but the same ideas permeate. For example, a TOC packet from the server informing that a buddy has signed on might look like this:

```
UPDATE_BUDDY:SeanEgn:T:0:110998697:0: 0
```

This packet looks very different from the toc_send_im() packet looked at earlier, but it uses the same principles. It starts with a command name and is followed with a series of arguments. The arguments are separated by colons. Here they reveal, in order, the screen name of the buddy in question; whether that buddy is online or not (T for True or F for False); the buddy's "warning level"; the time the buddy signed on in UNIX epoch time; the number of minutes the buddy has been idle; and the "user class," describing whether the user is away, using the AOL service (as opposed to regular AIM), and whether the user is an administrator or some other special class of user. I will discuss the various ways to figure out what fields like this mean later this chapter.

■Note One way that computers represent time is via the number of seconds since the "UNIX epoch," midnight, UTC, on January 1, 1970. That's how TOC provides the time the buddy logged in—the very large number in the preceding example.

Not every message from the server is a command like this, though. Protocols often require a method to respond to commands. There are three basic methods. One is to wait for a response after issuing a command, not sending any other packets until you get the response from the current one. This is typically how login requests are handled. The client can't do anything until it hears back from the server.

Another method has the server sending replies back at any time. The client may not know exactly which packet caused the response, but the response usually contains enough information that it can act on it. OSCAR uses this method. If you tell OSCAR to send a message to someone not signed on, it will provide a response saying essentially, "Unable to send a message to user." The client doesn't know *which* message wasn't sent, but it can relay the error to the user. Most likely, the error came quickly enough that it makes sense.

The third way is to offer responses that refer to the packet explicitly. This is what MSN uses the TrID for. A response to a specific packet will reference that packet by its TrID. Suppose, for instance, our sample MSN packet failed due to an internal server error.

The TrID of the packet was 21. So the error packet refers to this error:

```
500 21
```

500 is the "internal error" command (error packets in MSN start with three-digit numbers instead of three-letter words). 21 is the TrID that caused it. MSN implementations, therefore, need to keep track of packets they send with their TrID if they intend to keep track of what error packets refer to. However, it is also relatively safe to ignore this and handle these packets the same way OSCAR packets are handled, with little regard to which specific packet caused the error.

As demonstrated, binary and text protocols are not terribly dissimilar in their design. They each provide a way to issue a command and arguments modifying the command. Where they do differ significantly is merely in syntax. I've mentioned that binary protocols are easier for machines to understand than text protocols. In the next section, I will explain why this is. I will describe how protocols are commonly implemented in code.

Protocol Implementation in C

Binary protocols and text protocols differ in many aspects, and subsequently different techniques must be used for each. The generalities of protocol implementation, however, remain the same.

Every protocol implementation has the same basic flow of events: they all loop continuously, receiving, decoding, and acting on incoming packets, as well as forming and sending packets when called for. Thankfully, due to the integration of sockets in GLib, and GTK+'s signal callbacks, a GTK+ application already has an easy way to receive notification when there's a new packet on the wire or the user interface requires some packet to be sent. I've also shown how to frame a packet from within a TCP stream. The only remaining trick is how to decode and encode packets.

Binary Protocols

Because it's easier for computers to understand a binary protocol, its implementation is easier. However, because a binary protocol is based so heavily on knowing how many bytes each data element takes, it's first necessary to understand how the different types in C work.

Unfortunately, this isn't as straightforward as you might hope. C was designed to be as platform-independent as possible, so it remains very vague as to implementation details. A compiler for any given platform is given significant liberty to make implementing C as efficient as possible. While this generally makes C more portable, there are certain portability issues you must keep in mind to use it properly. I will address many of these issues in Chapter 10.

One important issue is that integral types (e.g., char, int, long int, etc.) do not have clearly defined sizes. The only rule defined by the C specification is that a short int has fewer than or just as many bytes as an int and an int has fewer than or as many bytes as a long int. Everything else is left to the compiler.

However, it is typically safe to make a few assumptions because few platforms are so dissimilar that they require entirely different types. For instance, a char will essentially always be 1 byte. A short will be 2 bytes, and an int will be 4 bytes. This is the best solution for 32-bit platforms, which most computers currently are. 64-bit computers are growing in number, but because so many programmers have always safely assumed the numbers stated here, 64-bit computers also keep 4-byte int types.

However, the best way to be safe about having the correct size is to use types that are guaranteed to be a certain size. GLib provides these by using some compiler-specific techniques. The relevant types are gint8, gint16, gint32 and their unsigned cousins guint8, guint16, and guint32. These types are guaranteed to be 1 byte, 2 bytes, and 4 bytes, respectively.

Now, remember how a struct is laid out in memory: each element is placed immediately after each other and the compiler keeps track of each element's offset. This is exactly how binary protocols work! Each element is placed right after each other and the implementation is left to calculate where each element is.

Therefore, it makes a lot of sense to use a struct to represent binary packet data. Here's the FLAP header struct used by Gaim's TOC implementation:

```
struct sflap_hdr {
    unsigned char ast;
    unsigned char type;
    unsigned short seqno;
    unsigned short len;
};
```

Just as specified by the protocol, it's a 1-byte magic number (ast is for asterisk), followed by 1 byte representing the type, a 2-byte sequence number, and a 2-byte length.

Warning Compilers that generate 32-bit code will often pad structs for performance reasons. This means that they add extra, unused space within the struct so that the resulting code can access elements within the struct more quickly. When defining a header like this, you need to ensure it won't be padded. With GCC, you can do this by putting __attribute__ ((packed)) after the struct declaration or by providing --fpack-struct as a command-line option at compile time.

Remember from earlier that, although a char array is most often used as the destination for a read() call, any location can be used. I used an int earlier, but you can also use a pointer to a struct. Therefore a TOC implementation could read each packet header into a struct:

```
struct sflap_hdr header;
read(fd, &header, sizeof(header));
```

However, the values in this `struct` are now in network byte order, so you convert them:

```
header.seqno = ntohs(header.seqno);
header.len = ntohs(header.len);
```

An implementation should then have a valid header in the header `struct`. A TOC implementation would then likely check the magic number to ensure no error has occurred and then read the rest of the packet into a `char` array:

```
if (header.ast != '*')
    return;
read(fd, buffer, header.len);
```

Again, remember that `read()` doesn't guarantee to read all the data requested and that I'm omitting the loop for simplicity.

Once the data is in a `char` array, the implementation varies again. For a binary protocol, these same techniques can be applied to the packet itself. For TOC, a text protocol, different techniques are used.

Text Protocols

Parsing a text protocol is technically more involved than it is for a binary protocol. However, because most developers are already familiar with manipulating text and there are numerous functions both in the standard C library and other helper libraries (such as GLib), many feel more comfortable dealing with text protocols than with binary. Indeed, working with a text-based protocol is essentially the same as working with any other strings.

As you should probably know, a string in C is most typically represented as an array of `chars`, terminated with the `NUL` character, `'\0'`. The two main ways of dealing with these strings are to manually iterate the strings, or to use library functions that manipulate them. Most code will use a combination of both.

Manual String Manipulation

Manipulating strings manually involves a lot of pointer arithmetic, which really worries some people who aren't confident with it. Working with pointers is a bit tricky if you're unfamiliar with it, and pointer arithmetic is especially intimidating because it's very common for a mistake to result in a program crash or, worse, a security vulnerability.

However, these same problems can occur any time you're dealing with strings. Passing incorrect parameters to string manipulation functions can similarly cause security vulnerabilities. Hence, it's critical to understand how strings and pointers work even if you never use pointer arithmetic.

A pointer is essentially an integer containing a memory address. A pointer has a type, the type of data stored at the memory location pointed to. Therefore a `char*` is a number holding the memory address of a `char`. If this is a standard C string, there are probably more `chars` after this in an array. However, because C is not strictly typed, there's no way of telling if this actually is a valid C string or how long the array is. The prime reason C strings are so buggy is that there's no good way to tell how many `chars` are in the array.

The standard way of marking a string's length is to end it with a NUL char. Therefore, the two most important things to keep your application from crashing are never to read and never to write past the NUL character (unless you know for a fact that there is allocated memory past it, by design).

Typically, when parsing a string, I use a few different char* variables to iterate the string. Remember that a pointer is just a number holding a memory address. If I set the value of one char* to another, there remains only one string in memory but two different pointers point to its address. So, normally setting an iterator variable to the start of the string is the first thing to do:

```
char *i = str;
```

Next, you probably want to parse over the string, checking it character for character. Because chars in C will take one byte (for practical considerations), the address of the second character in the string will be one greater than the address of the first, or i + 1. You want to do this through the entire string, until the value that i points to is '\0'. A for loop is appropriate for this:

```
for (i = str; *i != '\0'; i++)
```

Keep in mind that the asterisk in *i != '\0' is very important. The asterisk dereferences the pointer and returns the value stored at that address. If the asterisk weren't there, it would be checking the value of the memory address itself and the program would crash.

What you do in the loop depends on the protocol. For MSN, suppose you received a packet and want to identify the command by finding the end of the command and determining what it is. You'll know when you've reached the end of the command by reaching the first space:

```
for (i = str; *i != '\0'; i++) {
    if (*i == ' ') /* End of command */
```

The command is now contained between the start of the string and i. At this time, you'd likely use a combination of calls to strncmp() or some similar function to determine what the command is:

```
for (i = str; *i != '\0\'; i++) {
    if (*i == ' ') { /* End of command */
        if (!strncmp(str, "MSG", i - str))
            handle_msg(i);
        else if (!strncmp(str, "RNG", i - str))
            handle_rng(i);
```

The strncmp() function compares at most the first *n* characters of two strings to see if they're the same. The function returns a value corresponding to how the string arguments are sorted in alphabetical order. If the first argument is sorted closer to 'A' than the second, strncmp() returns a negative number. If the first argument is sorted closer to 'Z', then the second, strncmp() returns a positive number. If the two strings are identical, strncmp() returns zero. It's that last behavior I depend on here.

Here I specify the length as i - str, which is the address of the space minus the address of the beginning of the string. If strncmp() determines the strings are the same, it passes the rest of the string (i is currently pointing to the space, which implies the string starting at the space character) to different functions designed to handle specific types of packets.

These other functions will probably use similar techniques to further break down the packet. They may use loops to iterate through the string and then manipulate strings within it with various string functions.

String Functions

Because working with strings in C manually is so difficult, the C library and GLib both provide a useful set of string-manipulation functions. The GLib set of functions is largely a superset of the C library functions, providing wrapper functions guaranteed to work identically on all systems[1]. In this section I will provide a brief overview of several useful functions.

g_strdup_printf()

My personal favorite GLib string function is g_strdup_printf(). It will create a string much in the same fashion that sprintf() does, using a printf() formatting string. However, it will also determine exactly how much memory the string needs and allocate it. It's a convenient way to create a string while ensuring you don't exceed any boundaries, resulting in a bug.

To create an MSN packet to send a message using g_strdup_printf(), call

```
char *packet = g_strdup_printf("MSG %d A %d\r\n"
                               "%s\r\n",
                               trid++, strlen(msg), msg);
```

This assumes the MIME headers are already part of msg. It also increments the transaction automatically so that the next packet can use it.

g_strecsape()

Remember that in TOC, arguments are enclosed in quotation marks, forcing quotation marks within an argument to be escaped, by putting a backslash before it. g_strescape() makes this easy.

The first argument to g_strescape() is the text to be escaped. By default it will escape '\b', '\f', '\n', '\r', '\t', '\', '"', and all non-ASCII characters. In order to make it escape only '"' and '\', the second argument is a string of exceptions. Make a string of all the characters you prefer to leave unchanged as the second argument:

```
char *toc_command_escaped = g_strescape(toc_command, "\b\f\n\r\t");
```

g_strsplit()

On the receiving side of the protocol, g_strsplit() is a convenient way to break down a packet into its elements. Elements of incoming TOC packets, for instance, are separated by colons. g_strsplit() provides an easy way to break this string into its component elements:

```
char **tokens = g_strsplit(packet, ":", -1);
```

---

1. Take a look at http://developer.gnome.org/doc/API/2.0/glib/glib-String-Utility-Functions.html for complete documentation.

The `-1` tells `g_strsplit()` to split the string completely. It defines the maximum number of tokens to split the string into. A negative value specifies no limit.

After this call, `tokens` will be a valid array of strings. `tokens[0]` will hold the command, and the indices 1 and greater in the array will point to the command's arguments. The array is terminated with `NULL`, indicating no more strings exist after that. This array could then be passed to other functions, depending on the value of `tokens[0]`. When done with the array, free it using `g_strfreev()`.

Each function would expect its arguments in a certain order. The arguments expected and the order they appear in are specific to each type of packet. How does the developer learn what they are? There are two ways: protocol specification and reverse engineering.

Learning Protocols

The easier way (by far) to learn how a protocol works is via a protocol specification. A protocol specification (or *spec*) is a document that completely explains how the protocol works and how to implement it. Protocol specs are available when the designer of the protocol wants either to make it an Internet standard freely implemented by anyone (such as Jabber's XMPP) or when the designer wishes to allow third-party developers access to the systems (such as TOC).

Most public IM systems currently in use, however, do not provide specifications. These systems are called *closed*, because they don't provide a way for third parties to connect. If you want to understand these protocols, you must reverse engineer them. I'll discuss reverse engineering in the next section.

Currently the only truly open public IM protocols are Jabber and TOC. Jabber is designed to be an open standard for IM—like e-mail or the World Wide Web, both of which require a fully specified protocol to allow developers access to the systems. TOC was created by AOL in 1998 to allow third-party developers access to AIM servers. Since then, however, new features have not been added to TOC and features that used to work have disappeared. Although it still works, TOC is no longer a viable solution for full-featured instant messaging.

Similarly, Microsoft's MSN Messenger protocol was based on a published specification. However, the specification has not been updated since, despite changes to the protocol. A client that uses the specification as originally published would not be able to connect to MSN Messenger today.

Other protocols supported by Gaim, notably IRC and Zephyr, do have published specifications, but are not generally considered public IM protocols.

A protocol spec typically starts with a list of definitions and other information required to understand the rest of the document. It then provides an overview of the protocol, explaining what packets look like—i.e., how they're formed. It then includes a list of valid commands, their syntax, and use. Then, using the techniques described earlier, it should be fairly simple to translate that into code. It is far more difficult to implement a protocol when its designers don't provide any documentation for it. In fact, some protocol designers do the opposite: purposely making the protocol difficult to understand. In these cases, it's necessary to reverse engineer the protocol.

Reverse Engineering

Reverse engineering is determining how a protocol works just by observing. Because public IM systems are interested in keeping their networks closed to the outside world, reverse engineering is a necessity for a third party to access many of these networks. AIM and ICQ's OSCAR protocols, Yahoo! Messenger's protocol, and extensions to MSN Messenger's originally public protocol are all reverse engineered.

Reverse engineering can never provide as accurate an implementation of a protocol as a protocol spec can. This is because reverse engineering can be based only on what you observe. If parts of the protocol are entirely unused during your observations, you have no way of implementing those parts through reverse engineering.

IM services, notably AIM, have used this, attempting to block competitors from their network by detecting incomplete implementation. However, when new protocol features start being used, they can generally be reverse engineered fairly rapidly, resulting in a more complete protocol implementation. AOL's most recent attempts at blocking Gaim's OSCAR code also blocked certain older versions of AOL's own client. We can infer, then, that Gaim imitates AOL's own AIM clients well enough that they are indistinguishable.

If evading AOL's attempts to block Gaim and attempting to decipher AOL's secret protocols against its will seems a bit shady to you, you're right. Reverse engineering currently lies in a legal gray area.

Legal Ramifications of Reverse Engineering

There has not been a definitive court case in the United States that has determined whether reverse engineering a network protocol is legal or not. Courts have, however, found repeatedly that reverse engineering is important to innovation and fair competition. Courts have also found that mechanical reverse engineering, discovering how a mechanical device works by disassembling it, is legal.

Reverse engineering software, however, is still a hazy area. Because Gaim remains the only way for many computer users to connect to certain IM protocols, some would point out that reverse engineering these protocols allows for interoperability—a cause that courts generally look favorably upon.

To date, however, no IM provider has been willing to test whether reverse engineering its software is permissible by the law, and instead providers resort to other means of keeping their systems closed. One method is changing through technical measures that keep unwanted implementations out temporarily until the measures are reverse engineered (usually within a week, from my experience). Another method is to disallow reverse engineering in the software's license.

There's a lot of legal uncertainty about shrink-wrap and click-through licenses in general, and clauses restricting reverse engineering are no exception to the controversy. However, courts have decided that such clauses may be preempted by federal copyright law in certain applicable cases.

■**Note** For more information about the legalities of reverse engineering, see `http://www.chillingeffects.org/rerverse/faq.cgi`.

Personally, I'm not very interested in legal matters. Nobody has attempted to challenge Gaim in court, and if they do, Gaim has the backing of hundreds of thousands of users and several large corporations who could fund a legal defense. However, there are certain aspects of reverse engineering specific to free and open source software that I do keep in mind.

Legal Aspects of the GPL

The GPL, the license that applies to Gaim and many other free software projects, is built on top of copyright law. It takes advantage of the fact that only the author of a copyrighted work has permission to do anything with it. If a piece of software is not licensed, nobody other than its author has permission to alter it.

Software licenses, therefore, grant the user certain rights: most often the right to use the software under a certain set of restrictions. The GPL offers additional rights to study, distribute, and modify, but the work remains copyrighted by the original author. Because nobody apart from the author has the right to do anything not explicitly granted, only the author can license his code. I cannot take someone else's code and declare it open source.

Therefore, to include code in Gaim, I have to ensure that the author of that code gave permission to license the code under the GPL. Most of the time, the person who wrote the code is the person who submits it, and there's no problem. However, with reverse engineering, it's often possible that someone may submit code he has no claim over. When this is the case, I have to reject the patch.

White Box vs. Black Box Reverse Engineering

Reverse engineering can be broken down to two distinct types. White box reverse engineering involves breaking down the target, looking at its internals, and determining how it works from the inside. Black box reverse engineering involves figuring out how it works by observing how it interacts with the outside world.

Gaim uses black box techniques I'll cover later in this chapter. By viewing the official IM client, the reference implementation, as a black box whose internals are completely hidden, everything learned about the protocol is learned through observation. Any code written to implement the protocol, then, is an original work, not based at all on the copyrighted code of the reference implementation. This new code, therefore, is copyrightable. We claim copyright over this code and release it under the GPL.

White box techniques are less certain. For software, white box techniques include *disassembly* and *decompilation*. These techniques turn compiled machine-readable binary code back to human-readable source code. Of course, the code is barely readable, as function names, variable names, and comments are almost always missing, but with some work it's possible to tell what functions do what. Relevant parts can be extracted and incorporated into Gaim.

Disassembly is not a creative act. It does not create new source code, but rather translates compiled binary code back into source code. Therefore, someone who decompiles or disassembles code has no claim to copyright over that code. Rather, the original author who wrote the decompiled code retains copyright over it. Therefore, the person who decompiled the code has no right to relicense that code under the GPL, and I cannot accept it into Gaim.

The vast majority of reverse engineering by Gaim developers is black box. On occasion, white box techniques are used. We never disassemble or decompile code, but rather we watch how it operates within a debugger, studying the internals of the program without outright stealing its code. This is most often done for authentication procedures, which are intentionally made difficult to decipher for security reasons. Fortunately, in most cases, the rest of the protocol is straightforward enough that black box techniques may be used exclusively.

Packet Sniffing

The most important tool in black box reverse engineering network protocols is a *packet sniffer*. A packet sniffer is a program that intercepts and logs network traffic. By running a packet sniffer and using IM at the same time, you can watch the network traffic between your IM client and the IM server, which you then can use to decipher how the protocol works. The packet sniffer that Gaim developers prefer is Ethereal (see Figure 8-2).

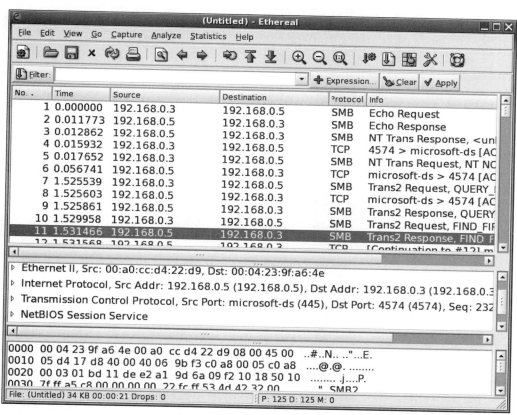

Figure 8-2. *Ethereal allows you to watch network traffic to your computer, a fundamental task in black box reverse engineering.*

Ethereal is available from `http://www.ethereal.com`, and runs on most platforms, including UNIX-like operating systems and Microsoft Windows. It is licensed under the terms of the GPL and uses GTK+ for its user interface.

Ethereal offers a rich assortment of features that make it very appropriate for reverse engineering. It has the ability to recognize and interpret 658 different protocols, including all the major IM protocols. Therefore, if you're working on reverse engineering a new feature in Yahoo!

Messenger, it already understands how the protocol works. It will separate commands and its arguments for you, as shown in Figure 8-3.

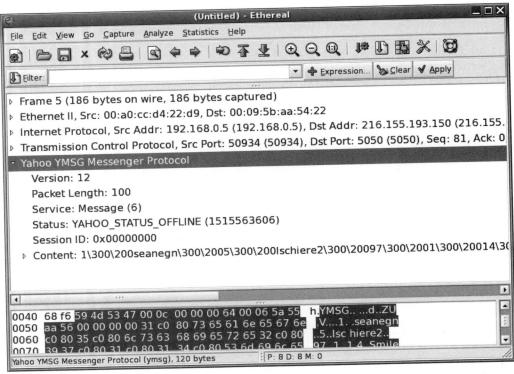

Figure 8-3. *Ethereal understands Yahoo! Messenger's protocol. In the lower pane it breaks down the contents of a Yahoo! packet to its component parts.*

Installing Ethereal should be straightforward. An installer program exists on Windows, and Linux distributions will provide standard binary packages. Install Ethereal in your operating system's preferred way. Note that because it requires the permission to read every packet on the network, UNIX users will need to run Ethereal as root.

To start collecting data, choose Start from the Capture menu on the menu bar (or press Ctrl-K). You will be presented with a window prompting for certain Capture Options (see Figure 8-4). The top frame, labeled Capture, allows you to specify what network device to use (the default should be fine if you have only one), and whether to capture in *promiscuous mode*. Promiscuous mode captures all packets on the network, as opposed to packets to and from the computer it's running on. For purposes of reverse engineering, you'll rarely (if ever) need to use promiscuous mode.

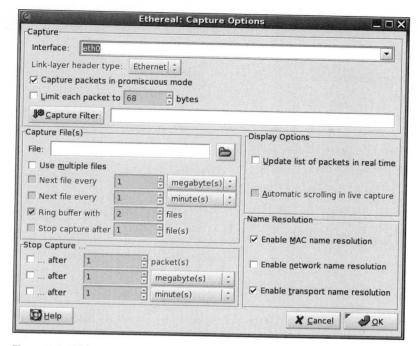

Figure 8-4. *Ethereal's Capture Options dialog*

The Capture File(s) frame allows you to automatically save packet dumps to disk. Because you can save the capture from Ethereal after the fact, there's little need to use this feature here, though it may be useful for long-term network analysis. Similarly, the Stop Capture... frame is useful for long-term packet dumping, allowing you to specify when to cease the capture. However, when reverse engineering IM protocols, you will usually stop the capture manually, when you know the packet you want to decipher has been sent or received.

Display Options specifies how you'll be presented with incoming packets, and Name Resolution allows you to see the DNS name of the systems you're communicating with, rather than only its IP address. This will result in slightly slower responses from Ethereal, as it needs to contact the DNS server for every IP address you communicate with. Once you have chosen appropriate options, click OK to start the capture.

While the packets are being captured, Ethereal shows a small window providing capture statistics and the ability to stop the capture (see Figure 8-5). While it's capturing, it will show the total number of packets received, and a breakdown of what types of packets are traveling through your machine. This breakdown is done by transport-layer type. The progress bars indicate the percentage of total packets represented by the type.

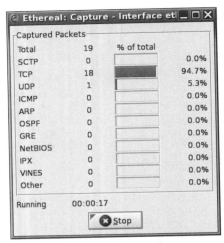

Figure 8-5. *Ethereal shows how many and what types of packets are traveling through your machine as it happens*

To stop the capture, click the Stop button. You will be returned to the main Ethereal screen. The main Ethereal screen has three panes. The top pane is a list of packets. By default, they're sorted chronologically, but that can be changed by clicking the column headers.

The middle pane breaks down the packet into its parts. Ethereal works at a low level, so TCP, IP, Ethernet, and other types of headers will all be included. You can see them in the middle pane. Further, Ethereal breaks down each header into its own parts, as well as much packet data. If Ethereal recognizes the protocol being used, it will break it down in the middle pane. Clicking parts of the protocol listed in the middle pane will highlight them in the bottom pane, the packet display.

The packet display shows the actual data in the packet in hexadecimal and ASCII formats. The hexadecimal display shows each byte in hex on the left and shows each ASCII character to the right. It should be obvious that the hex output is useful for binary protocols and the ASCII output for text protocols. However, even in binary protocols, there are numerous text aspects, such as the contents of your IMs themselves. Both views are very useful for reverse engineering techniques.

Reverse Engineering Techniques

Once you have a packet dump, you can use your newfound knowledge of protocol design to break apart a protocol into its parts and learn how it works. It's difficult to teach this. It comes with experience and even then, it's largely trial and error.

The first job is to determine whether you're dealing with a text protocol or a binary protocol. This is easy. Simply look at the ASCII readout of packets. If it's all comprehensible text, it's probably text based. Check for newlines (0A 0D) in the hexadecimal display to see if it's line-based. If not, determine what separates packets, looking for signs of the three methods discussed earlier.

Remember that IM packets are generally packets built on a TCP stream built on top of IP packets. There is no guarantee that your IM packets will match the IP packets exactly. An IP packet may contain multiple application-level packets, or just fractions of them. This is left to the operating system. The operating system looks to make networking as efficient as possible.

If your application sends ten application-level packets immediately after each other, the OS will typically consolidate them into a single IP packet. However, because IM packets are sent relatively infrequently, the OS will usually send them one at a time; if it waited for more, there would be a considerable delay. For this reason, you'll often see one application-level packet per each IP address. In other words, most of the time, each packet captured by Ethereal will correspond to exactly one application-level packet.

If you're working with a text protocol, the job is considerably easier. There are fewer variations. Commands will typically have sensible English names; arguments will typically be clearly delineated with some character (probably a space). This is what makes text protocols easier to work with for humans.

If you're working with a binary protocol, you'll have a slightly harder time. You'll need to figure out where one element of the protocol ends and where another begins. You'll have to determine what each command number does through trial and error. In general, binary protocols are much more difficult to reverse engineer than text-based protocols. However, once you've discovered how packets are framed and how their arguments are specified, you'll have the same problem with each: determining what each packet actually does.

Tip If the packet dumps you capture contain no text whatsoever, not even in IM packets, you're probably looking at an encrypted stream. Most common forms of stream encryption are vulnerable to "man in the middle" attacks, where an intruder between the two ends of the encrypted stream can break the encryption. You can exploit that by routing traffic through an encryption-breaking proxy. Look at Mozilla NSS's ssltap program as an example.

You need to collect enough packets to determine what changes from packet to packet. Some things will never change. You may notice that the "buddy signed on" command always has the same exact string of bytes at the end of its packet. If this never changes, you'll likely never know what exactly those bytes indicate. However, your implementation will include them, which will mimic the behavior of the official client.

Gaim does this all over the place. There are numerous places in various protocols where we observe that the official clients always do the same thing. We have no clue what that thing is, but we make sure to do it as well. Conforming to the official clients is important, as anything that distinguishes us from the official client can be used to selectively block us.

Likewise, parts of the protocol that never change can be used to selectively block us. If the official client is supposed to handle a certain command differently depending on its arguments and its reverse engineers never see different arguments, it will be unprepared when the service starts changing them. This technique has been used to block Gaim in the past.

So, assuming you figure out what parts of the protocol change by looking at a large number of packets from a large number of IM sessions, your next task is to figure out what the parts that do change do.

Some things will be obvious. Even in binary protocols, text will (most typically) still be readable. You'll always be able read screen names and messages, for instance. This is the part of reverse engineering that cannot easily be taught. Here, however, are some useful hints to keep in mind:

Use the official implementation as many different ways as you can. You'll often find that some things suddenly gain an obvious meaning when some highly obscure setting is changed.

Learn a bunch of open protocols with published specifications. You can be sure that the person who designed the target of your reverse engineering skills had prior experience with network protocols and was inspired by them when creating this new one. If you're familiar with the same protocols, you may recognize some aspects of it and understand it more easily.

Armed with enough knowledge about how protocols work and how to decipher that when needed, you should be able to integrate a network protocol into your GTK+ application. You know how to use GLib to have callbacks called when either the user or the IM server needs a response from you, and you know how to manipulate the UI accordingly. Gaim, however, chooses a modular approach to protocols. This approach allows Gaim to minimize duplicated code and make the UI protocol-agnostic by providing an identical interface to every protocol implemented therein.

Interfacing with Gaim

Gaim uses *protocol plug-ins*, abbreviated "prpl" (pronounced "purple"), to modularly support and unlimited number of IM protocols. These protocol plug-ins are largely identical to other plug-ins. The main difference is that they are loaded automatically when Gaim detects them; they are not available to be loaded or unloaded by the user.

Protocol plug-ins work by registering a protocol. This is done with an enormous struct containing everything Gaim will ever need to know about a protocol. After the protocol is registered, Gaim will include it as an available protocol. Accounts assigned to use it will be available, and new accounts can be created for it. Whenever Gaim needs to interact with an account, it determines the prpl it uses and passes control to that plug-in.

The plug-in on the opposite end sends and receives packets over the network. When it receives packets, it passes control to the Gaim core, which can then act on the incoming message. The functions for this communication between the Gaim core and its protocol plug-ins are implemented in server.c.

server.c

The functions documented in server.h are largely convenience wrappers to the prpls and to the rest of Gaim. For instance, when a prpl receives notification that a buddy is typing a message, it will call serv_got_typing(). serv_got_typing() then change the conversation windows accordingly and send the notification to other plug-ins with the signal system. These are public functions that the prpl could call itself, but by containing them all to a single function, Gaim employs greater code reuse (each prpl tells the core its received messages in one line) and provides a convenient place to change the behavior for every protocol.

■**Note** server.c is some of the oldest code in Gaim. As such, it doesn't follow many of the ideals I've been talking about, such as object orientation. Working on a project like Gaim is interesting in that regard; you see how code written five years ago is made to work with code written five minutes ago.

Likewise, when the core needs to send a command to a protocol, it uses functions in `server.c`. `server.c` takes care of certain things each protocol needn't worry about individually (such as when to set the account as idle or when to emit signals to plug-ins), and then looks up the appropriate function in the appropriate prpls `GaimPluginProtocolInfo` struct.

GaimPluginProtocolInfo

`GaimPluginProtocolInfo` is the enormous `struct` that a prpl provides to the Gaim core. It contains everything Gaim needs to know about how to use a prpl. Because it has to abstract a vast set of features from a potentially infinite number of protocols, it remains very vague and allows protocols to implement as much or as little as they need to.

`GaimPluginProtocolInfo` is mostly function pointers. The Gaim core calls these functions both when it needs the prpl to perform some action (such as "disconnect this account") and when it needs information ("What icon should I show for this buddy?"). Other fields in `GaimPluginProtocolInfo` are solely descriptive about the protocol itself and how it should be used. I will explain all the fields in this `struct` in the next several sections.

GaimProtocolOptions options;

The `options` field is a bitmask of features this protocol has. These options are a result of not all protocols acting as identically as Gaim would like them to. Because certain protocols do some things differently, Gaim provides a way to specify certain behaviors a protocol has in this `struct`. These options include `OPT_PROTO_NO_PASSWORD`, used by protocols that don't require a password to log in, `OPT_PROTO_IM_IMAGE`, for protocols that allow images embedded in IMs, and very Jabber-specific `OPT_PROTO_UNIQUE_CHATNAME`, which specifies that usernames in chat rooms do not necessarily correspond to their names in IMs or on the buddy list.

These options generally are added when a slightly different behavior is required for one specific protocol. This is how `OPT_PROTO_IM_IMAGE` and `OPT_PROTO_UNIQUE_CHATNAME` get included. They exist as a way to allow protocol-specific hacks within a protocol-independent architecture.

GList *user_splits

With AIM, Yahoo!, MSN, and most pubic IM protocols, every screen name is unique. There can be only one SeanEgn on AIM. However, for protocols such as IRC or Jabber, with multiple mutually exclusive networks, one can have accounts on multiple networks, all with the same username. I'm SeanEgn on both `irc.freenode.net` and `irc.gnome.org`. The old system of identifying an account by screen name and protocol is invalid.

A `GaimAccountUserSplit` is a data structure that specifies specific elements of the username that will be prompted for separately, but tacked on to the end of the screen name when necessary.

For example, Jabber sets two `GaimAccountUserSplits` in this `GList`. The first is

```
gaim_account_user_split_new(_("Server"), "jabber.org", '@');
```

This specifies that in addition to the screen name (the full name of this account), when shown in places it needs be distinguished from other Jabber accounts, a "server" should be prompted for; the default should be jabber.org and it should be appended to the screen name separated by a @ character. The second split is Jabber-specific, a "resource":

```
gaim_account_user_split_new(_("Resource"), "Gaim",'/');
```

Both these splits are appended to the user_splits linked list with g_list_append(). The result of this split is seen in Figure 8-6.

Figure 8-6. *The Modify Account dialog prompts for each split element separately, but the Accounts dialog shows it as a single entity to distingusih it from other accounts.*

GList *protocol_options

This is another list that provides information the UI should prompt the user for. These options appear under the Show More Options expander in the Modify Account dialog, as shown in Figure 8-7.

Creating an account option and appending it to this list is essentially the same as creating a user split. There are several functions for various types of account options in accountopt.h. These include gaim_account_option_bool_new(), gaim_account_option_int_new(), and gaim_account_option_string_new(). These functions all take a name the user will see, such as Chat Room List Url, a name the prpl can identify the preference with ("room_list"), and a default value. Other functions may require more data as necessary.

The core and UI will take this data about an option and handle presenting it to the user, storing it, and saving it on its own. Whenever the prpl requires the value of the option, it can call gaim_account_get_string(), gaim_account_get_bool(), or gaim_account_get_int() on the account to return the current value.

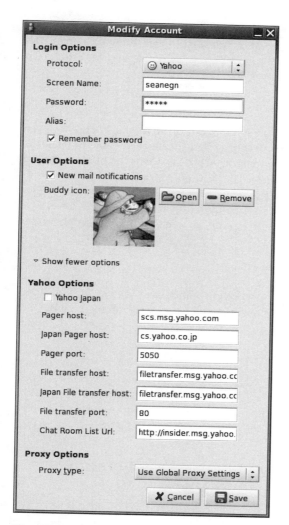

Figure 8-7. *Each protocol can specify certain protocol-specific options that appear under Show More Options in the Modify Account dialog.*

GaimBuddyIconSpec icon_spec;

Many protocols use buddy icons, though some call them by different names, such as avatars or display pictures. Each protocol has different requirements from a buddy icon. AIM, for instance, can not display PNG files, whereas MSN can display *only* PNG files. AIM icons are small, typically 50×50 pixels, whereas Yahoo! icons are about four times as large. Rather than have the user keep track of what formats and sizes are needed for each protocol, Gaim automatically scales and converts icons using the parameters defined in GaimBuddyIconSpec.

GaimBuddyIconSpec contains a minimum size, a maximum size, scaling rules (should I scale incoming buddy icons, outgoing buddy icons, or both?), and accepted file formats. Gaim's GTK+ UI, then, uses GdkPixbuf to manipulate whatever image the user selects to fit these criteria.

const char *(*list_icon)

The remaining elements of GaimPluginProtocolInfo are function pointers. list_icon() was originally used simply to provide an icon name for a given buddy on an account. Now, however, it is used as a way to uniquely identify the protocol with a string. Because OSCAR, for instance, handles both AIM and ICQ, the protocol name is given as AIM/ICQ. However, because they're separate services, we often want to make a distinction. By passing an account to the list_icon() function, we can retrieve the name of the specific service being used.

Also, because an AIM user can have an ICQ user on his buddy list, list_icon() takes a GaimBuddy parameter. If set, list_icon() will return the service that buddy is using rather than just the account.

const char *(*list_emblems)

list_emblems() is used to return a graphical representation of this user's status. The buddy list will overlay as many as four "emblems" over the user's status icon (as seen in Figure 8-8).

Figure 8-8. *SmarterChild is an AOL user and an ActiveBuddy bot, according to the emblems set by* list_emblems()*.*

list_emblems() is passed four char**s, one for each corner of the status icon. In those variables, it provides the names of status icons to use (such as "away"), or NULL to leave it blank. Most prpls start at the lower-right (which is the only emblem visible if the single-line-of-text-per-buddy "small list" is being used), then work their way clockwise.

char *(*status_text) and char *(*tooltip_text)

status_text() and tooltip_text() are similar. They both take a GaimBuddy as their sole arguments and return text to return as the second line of the buddy list node and in the tooltip for the buddy, respectively.

status_text() is necessarily short, whereas tooltip_text() is expected to be longer, formatted with Pango markup language, in the typical tooltip style (several lines of "Header: Value\n").

GList *(*away_states)

This is a list of the various status types that the prpl allows. These include "online" and "offline" states, as well as more specific states such as "on the phone." The status API uses these to determine what statuses the user can employ.

GList *(*blist_node_menu)

Like account options, this function provides a list of options the prpl should provide to the user. These options are specific to a buddy and are placed in the buddy's right-click context menu, seen in Figure 8-9.

Figure 8-9. blist_node_menu() takes a GaimBlistNode and returns a list of choices to show in the menu.

Common menu items, such as IM, Alias, and Remove, are added to every menu by Gaim itself. This function is only for protocol-specific options, such as Direct IM.

The list this function will return is specific to a GaimBlistNode. It consists of elements created with gaim_blist_node_action_new(). This function takes a name, a callback, and data to send to the callback.

Alternatively, if the menu is a submenu, it set a GList called children, which contains other GaimBlistNodeActions. Yahoo! includes Initiate Conference in its buddy menus:

```
gaim_blist_node_action_new(_("Initiate Conference"), yahoo_initiate_conference,
NULL, NULL);
```

GList *(*chat_info) and GHashTable *(*chat_info_defaults)

Each protocol requires slightly different information to join a chat. IRC requires a channel name, and occasionally a password. AIM requires a room name and an "exchange." Jabber requires a room name, a server, a handle, and a password. chat_info() and chat_info_defaults() provide a mechanism for the prpl to specify these parameters to Gaim.

chat_info works very much like account_options. It creates various options, specifying a type for them, and appends it to the GList. chat_info_default takes a chat name and provides a hash table with default values for each of the options and with an appropriate default for that chat room.

gboolean (*can_receive_file)

This function returns a Boolean argument, specifying if the intended recipient can receive a file on this connection. If this function returns TRUE for a user, the Send File option will appear in the conversation and buddy list when appropriate.

Command Functions

The previous functions are used by the core to retrieve information about a protocol. The rest of the functions are used by the core to instruct a prpl to perform some action. I will list and briefly explain them all in Table 8-1.

Table 8-1. *Functions from* server.h *That the Core Uses to Communicate to Protocol Plug-Ins*

Function Name	Description
void *(login)	Connects an account.
void *(close)	Disconnects an account.
int (*send_im)	Sends an IM. It takes the GaimConnection to send from, a screen name to send to, a message to send, and a bitmask of options pertaining to this message. It returns a code indicating whether the message was sent successfully.
void (*set_info)	Sets the profile of a GaimConnection.
int (*send_typing)	Sends a typing notification to another user. The kind of typing notification is specified: "started typing," "stopped typing," or "paused typing."
void (*get_info)	Called when the user requests someone's profile. It is up to the prpl to display the info however appropriate.
void (*set_status)	Sets an account's status to that provided.
void (*set_idle)	Sets how long an account has been idle.
void (*change_password)	Tells the prpl to change the user's password.
void (*add_buddy)	Adds a buddy to the buddy list.

Table 8-1. *Functions from* `server.h` *That the Core Uses to Communicate to Protocol Plug-Ins (Continued)*

Function Name	Description
`void (*add_buddies)`	Used when more than one buddy needs to be added at a time. Used when the prpl can add them all in a single packet, rather than bombard the server with individual packets for each buddy.
`void (*remove_buddy)`	Removes a buddy from the buddy list.
`void (*remove_buddies)`	Removes multiple buddies from the buddy list, with the same justification as `add_buddies()`.
`void (*add_permit)`	Adds a user to the Permit list, a white list of people who can IM you.
`void (*add_deny)`	Adds a user to the Deny list, a black list of people who are blocked.
`void (*rem_permit)`	Removes a user from the Permit list.
`void (*rem_deny)`	Removes a user from the Deny list.
`void (*set_permit_deny)`	Sets the privacy mode. In conjunction with the Permit and Deny lists, this determines who is blocked from IMing you.
`void (*warn)`	Warns a user. This is a very AIM-centric feature.
`void (*join_chat)`	Joins a chat room, given the parameters specified by the `chat_info()` function.
`void (*reject_chat)`	Rejects an invitation from another user to a chat room. Used when doing so should return a message to the user who invited you.
`char *(*get_chat_name)`	Given the parameters from the `chat_info()` function, returns how the chat should be named in the UI.
`void (*chat_invite)`	Invites another user to a chat.
`void (*chat_leave)`	Leaves a chat room.
`void (*chat_whisper)`	"Whispers" a message to another user in a chat. The message will appear in the other user's chat room window, but not in the windows of others in a chat. No protocols currently use this, as IMing the user you wish to whisper to is a better option.
`int (*chat_send)`	Sends a message in a chat room. It returns a code specifying if the message was successfully sent.
`void (*keepalive)`	This function is called every 60 seconds. It's generally used just to check in on the IM server and let it know the connection is still active. This is typically done with a single mostly empty packet. AIM does it with an empty *keep alive* packet (a FLAP header with a type of 5 and a length of 0). The TOC prpl sets `keepalive` to its function, which sends this packet. However, this function can be used whenever regular polling needs to be done. IRC has no buddy-list mechanism, so uses this function instead to check every 60 seconds which of its buddies are online.

Table 8-1. *Functions from* server.h *That the Core Uses to Communicate to Protocol Plug-Ins (Continued)*

Function Name	Description
void (*register_account)	Creates a new account on the IM server with the provided information.
void (*get_cb_info)	Gets the user info of a user in a chat room, as opposed to get_info(), which gets the info of a buddy on the buddy list or in an IM.
void (*get_cb_away)	Gets the status message of a user in a chat room.
void (*alias_buddy)	Sets the alias of a buddy on the server.
void *(group_buddy)	Moves a buddy on the buddy list from one group to another.
void (*buddy_free)	Frees any data allocated by the prpl for a buddy when that buddy itself if removed.
void (*convo_closed)	Called when a conversation with a user is closed. This may involve action on the part of the prpl, closing open connections if necessary.
char *(*normalize)	Returns the "normalized" name for given screen name. This is the "proper" way to represent a name such that it's entirely unique.
void (*set_buddy_icon)	Sets the buddy icon for an account.
void (*remove_group)	Removes a group from the buddy list.
char *(*get_cb_real_name)	Returns the real name of a user in a chat room.
void *(*set_chat_topic)	Sets the topic in a chat room.
GaimChat *(*find_blist_chat)	Because chats can be added to the buddy list, this function returns the appropriate buddy list node for a chat, given its name.
GaimRoomList *(*roomlist_get_list)	Requests a list of chat rooms on a connection.
void (*roomlist_cancel)	Cancels the retrieval of the room list.
void (*roomlist_expand_category)	Rooms in a list can be grouped. When a group is expanded, this returns the chats within that group.
void (*send_file)	Starts sending a file to another user.

The majority of these functions take as their first argument a GaimConnection, the object that represents a connection on a given protocol. Consequently, most of the functions in server.c also take a GaimConnection as the first argument. If server.c were made object-oriented, the functions within would fit best as methods of the GaimConnection object.

Program Flow of a prpl

It is the responsibility of the prpl to create a GaimConnection object. It does this by calling gaim_account_get_connection(), which creates a GaimConnection if one does not exist. This will typically happen in the login() function specified in GaimPluginProtocolInfo.

After the prpl creates a GaimConnection, it will create a socket for it. This socket is contained in the fd field of GaimConnection. It will typically then retrieve the server's hostname and port with gaim_account_get_string() and gaim_account_get_int(), respectively. Next, it will connect the new socket to the server.

The login() function will then set an input listener on the socket, providing a function as a callback, and the GaimConnection as its data. The login() function can then exit. Incoming packets will go to the callback function, and interface actions will go to the appropriate functions specified in GaimPluginProtocolInfo.

The callback function will receive the packets and decode them. It has the GaimConnection as its data, so it knows which connection the packets are for. As it decodes the packets, it makes calls to functions in server.h as appropriate, providing its GaimConnection so that Gaim's core knows what connection this represents. If the callback (and helper functions of the callback) realize that a message has been received, it will get the sender's name and the message from the packet, and call serv_got_im() with the GaimConnection, the sender's name, and the message.

When command functions from GaimPluginProtocolInfo are called, they receive a GaimConnection object, as well. GaimConnection has a prpl_data member which is used to store information specific to a protocol. The prpl will use this data to form a packet and send it to the socket stored at the fd member of GaimConnection.

Using server.c, the Gaim core sends and receives messages from the prpl in an abstracted, protocol-independent manner. The prpl uses the GaimConnection's fd and prpl_info elements to communicate the abstract notions from Gaim's core to and from specific protocol packets.

Summary

You now understand how network protocols typically work, and how to implement them in C using Gaim's protocol plug-in system. I've offered hints and tips about how to monitor data sent by an unknown protocol, and decipher what it all means. One such hint is that, even in binary protocols, screen names, messages, and other textual elements will always be sent in plain text. However, what is plain text? How does a computer, which understands only 1s and 0s, represent letters and words?

In the next chapter, I'll review the many ways computers can do this. This is a crucial element to working with IM protocols, for if you represent text incorrectly, your friends will not be able to read it. Whereas historical reasons make this less problematic for English speakers, for foreign users this is often problematic. I'll address localizing your application so that it's usable by as many people as possible, regardless of where they live. In addition to text encoding, I'll be discussing translation. I'll explain how the gettext system is used to provide simple translations for all the text in your application.

CHAPTER 9

∎∎∎

Internationalization

Free software licenses were created to enable the entire world to use software with as few restrictions as possible. However, unless you develop your application with foreign languages in mind, you're keeping your software from being used by most of the world's population.

Internationalization (abbreviated i18n, meaning i, followed by 18 letters, followed by n) and localization (l10n) are important steps to allowing free use of your software by everyone, regardless of language or culture.

There are two important but different subtasks in i18n. First, you must make sure your software works with the languages your users want to use. For IM clients, this means making sure messages sent in any language will reach their recipient properly and vice versa. This is taken for granted by most English speakers, but foreign users constantly have problems sending and receiving non-English text properly. I'll explain what text encodings are and how to work with them.

Gaim prides itself on its strong i18n support. We use the tools and knowledge I'll outline in this chapter to provide an entirely comfortable native-language experience. Because we use GTK+, we're able to display text in any language. We can even show characters from different languages in the same block of text (as seen in Figure 9-1), which other GUI toolkits are not capable of. I'll explain why this is difficult and how GTK+ is able to overcome this.

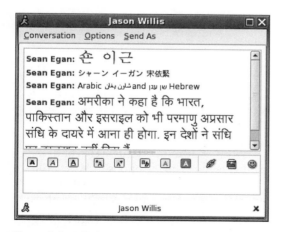

Figure 9-1. *A Gaim conversation showing multiple languages in the same message*

Gaim also fully implements the internationalization regulations provided by each protocol. Each protocol has a very specific defined system for communicating in various languages, and if the clients at each end don't both follow the regulations, it's impossible for the two to talk. The most common internationalization-related complaint from Gaim users is actually the result of other clients not following the proper procedure. Gaim is even more compliant than some of the official IM clients.

The second task I'll discuss in this chapter is how to present an interface to your users in their own language. Gaim uses a system called gettext to provide automatic translations based on the users' system settings. I'll explain how to use gettext within your application and how to create translations for it.

Gaim has a large team of translators who have translated Gaim into 42 languages from Amharic to Vietnamese. Gaim's very rapid development cycle devotes nearly a whole week to translating each new version. The Hindi translator's work is seen in Figure 9-2. I will explain how to easily add new translations to Gaim and how to set up your own projects to allow for translation.

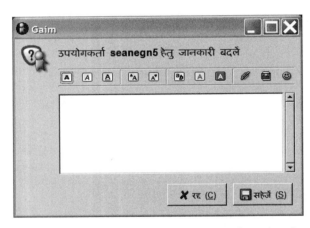

Figure 9-2. *Gaim's New Away Message window, translated into Hindi*

Internationalization Defined

Perfect internationalization is not an easy goal to accomplish. Language is one aspect of it, but even if you get this right, there is a huge number of other cultural differences to be mindful of. Some of them include:

- **Decimal format.** In the United States, we use the period as our decimal sign and commas to break up long strings of digits; other cultures do the opposite. When Americans read 3.142, they read "three and 142 thousandths." A British user would read the same numerals as "three thousand one hundred forty-two." How can you avoid confusion?

- **Date and time format.** In the United States, we express dates in Month/Day/Year order and time in 12-hour AM/PM format. Much of the rest of the world uses Year/Month/Day and 24-hour format. This is especially confusing for potentially ambiguous dates such as 4/5. Is that April 5th or May 4th? How can your code safely accommodate both date formats?

- **Alphabetical order**. Sorting text in alphabetical order, formally called "collation," is a huge problem. Different languages have different concepts of alphabetical order even when they use the same alphabet. For some languages, it's difficult even to decide what constitutes a letter. In German, is "ß" to be treated the same as "ss," or differently? How do Asian languages order ideographs?

- **Currency**. In the United States, we use U.S. dollars, but this unit won't have as much meaning to someone from another country. How can you convert currency values so that other people can understand them?

- **Paper**. Even paper can be a problem. If your application needs to print things, how do you cope with the fact that different countries use different paper sizes? Americans use 8.5 inch-by-11 inch "Letter" paper and Europeans use 210mm by 297mm A4 paper.

- **Measurements**. The U.S. is one of the only countries that still doesn't use the metric system. Can your application handle dealing with users who don't have a firm grasp of other measurement systems?

- **Names**. In the West, we commonly put the given name first, followed by the family name. Eastern cultures put the family name first. How can your program accommodate?

- **Addresses and telephone numbers**. One common mistake is to ask for contact information in a very U.S.-centric form, requesting a state and ZIP code and allowing limited flexibility as to what input you allow. Different countries use different formats for addresses and telephone numbers.

Obviously, some of these are more important than others. And, fortunately, many of them are handled for you automatically by the various system calls you use. Most operating systems have built-in support for internationalization that will handle decimal, date, and time formats automatically, for instance. Really, the most important thing to get right is language.

If you fail to get language right, nothing else matters. A user can forgive seeing a dollar sign instead of a euro sign, but if she can't interact with your application at all, it won't matter. And while your operating system probably does have support for correctly dealing with internationalized text, that support is useless unless you have a basic understanding of the principles of internationalization.

In the next section, I will explain how text is represented by computers: the fundamentals of internationalization.

Text Encoding

Computers, as you know, understand only numbers. The only way a computer can properly represent text is as a series of numbers, where each number has a predefined meaning. The method of assigning numbers to letters is known as text encoding.

There are many different encodings used today, and unless you know exactly what encoding a string uses, that string is useless to you. The Internet, and IM in particular, allows strings of text to travel around the globe. Most American developers don't understand text encoding enough to make this work correctly.

Most developers assume (usually without even realizing it) that every string they get is in an encoding called *ASCII*. They usually refer to this as "plain text." However, most of these developers don't truly understand what ASCII is.

ASCII

ASCII is the oldest text encoding still in widespread use. It assigns English letters, numbers, punctuation, and terminal control codes (things like "backspace," "newline," "terminal bell," etc.) in numbers 0 to 127, the range allowed by 7 bits.

The standard way of representing strings in C is a character array of ASCII values, terminated by the ASCII NUL character, 0. The standard C library and most other traditional string-manipulation libraries assume this is the format of all strings passed to it. However, not all text encodings represent text with the char data type. Also, not all text encodings use the NUL character to mark the end of a string. Therefore, these functions aren't guaranteed to work properly with non-English text.

ASCII is a 7-bit system. Most systems use 8 bits for their char data type. This means that there exists an extra bit in every char, unused by ASCII. This eighth bit can be used for anything, depending on the application. Historically, some programs flagged certain characters. However, its most widespread use has always been to double the number of characters used. Using an 8-bit character encoding opens up a new range of possible characters, from 128 to 255.

■Note The ASCII codes for lowercase letters are all exactly one bit different from their uppercase equivalents (e.g. 'a' 01100001 vs 'A' 01000001). Likewise, ASCII codes for numbers are all exactly one bit different from the punctuation characters they share a key with (e.g. '1' 00110001 vs '!' 00100001). This historically made keyboards easy to create. The Shift key merely toggled one particular bit.

These new characters were used for all sorts of things—again, depending on the application. One use of these characters was for "line art," boxes and lines used to create text-based GUIs. But, the most common use of these extended characters is for foreign characters.

Foreign Encodings

Foreign encodings that add extra characters to the top 128 codes are supersets of ASCII. These encodings differ from ASCII only in the one bit that ASCII ignores, and therefore the encodings are mostly compatible with ASCII. I say "mostly" because applications are allowed to do whatever they want with the eighth bit of an ASCII character. However, few if any modern applications use the eighth bit for anything other than foreign characters.

The major advantage to this compatibility is that libraries expecting NUL-terminated ASCII text (such as the standard C libraries) will work perfectly with the superset. This is because each character takes exactly one byte and the NUL character appears only at the end of a string.

Numerous encodings fit in this category. For English speakers, the most relevant encoding is ISO-8859-1, also known as Latin-1. Latin-1 is identical to ASCII from 0 to 127. From 128 to 255, it encodes the characters that make up Western European languages, such as diacritics (accents, tildes, umlauts, etc.), punctuation, currency symbols, etc.

Other encodings are used for other languages, such as KOI8-R for Cyrillic scripts, and ISO 8859-8 for Hebrew. Strings in all of these one-byte encodings share the advantage that they may be passed to any function that expects ASCII without causing an error. However, they have a limitation: they cannot display more than 256 different characters. If an Israeli computer user is using ISO 8859-8 to display Hebrew, he'll never be able to work with Russian text. 256 characters are too few for many uses. This is especially evident with East Asian languages.

For example, because languages such as Chinese, Japanese, and Korean have so many characters, they can't be encoded in a single byte. They all use Chinese characters, which number about 80,000. Just to achieve basic literacy, a Chinese reader must know 3000 characters. An educated person will be familiar with 5000 characters. ASCII contains only 128 characters. Using an eighth bit allows 256. East Asian languages, therefore, simply cannot fit in one byte and are commonly encoded in two bytes, potentially allowing 65,536 characters.

These encodings, such as Shift-JIS (Japanese), GB (Simplified Chinese, used in mainland China), and Big5 (Traditional Chinese, used in Taiwan and Hong Kong), are typically designed to attempt to be compatible with the standard C libraries. This means the encoding uses a char array and uses the NUL character only at the end of a string. Also, because ASCII is so widespread, it's useful if a valid ASCII string is also a valid string in a foreign encoding. Encodings like ISO 8859-1 accomplish this simply by their nature. Multibyte encodings require a less straightforward way to approach this.

One approach is to allow each character to take either one or two bytes. ASCII characters use one byte, and foreign characters use two bytes. The program that decodes this string would then check the first bit of each byte. If that bit is 0, the program knows the character falls within the ASCII range and goes on to the next. If the bit is 1, the program knows that this character and the next represent a non-ASCII character. This type of encoding is useful, as it allows full equivalence with ASCII.

In the past, it was enough that a computer understand one encoding. A French computer, for instance, might use ISO-8859-1, and all the applications on the computer would save their documents in that encoding. Each application could encode its documents however it wanted, and they would always work on that computer. Those documents would rarely find their way on to another computer, anyway.

However, the Internet changed that. Now an enormous number of documents are available to an enormous number of computers. Without knowing the encoding of those documents, they're useless. Therefore, Web browsers (and any other application that can view or create downloaded content) must understand an impossible number of different encodings to work properly. This problem is gradually being solved by a system called Unicode, an attempt to encode every character in every language in the world into a single system used by everyone. However, until Unicode is used universally, it remains necessary to convert documents from their own encoding to the native encoding of the system. The iconv project allows applications to do this.

iconv

iconv is a system for converting strings from one encoding to another. It includes an API for doing this from within your own application. The availability of iconv, however, varies from machine to machine. Some systems include it as part of the standard C library; others require a separate library, libiconv, for the functionality. Because these implementations are of variable availability and not all implementations are identical in functionality, GLib provides a set of wrapper functions to iconv, ensuring that a GTK+ developer has access to an iconv implementation that works the same, regardless of platform.

The most straightforward way to convert a string from one encoding to another in GLib is the g_convert function. When provided with an input string, its encoding, the desired encoding of the result string, and a few other data, g_convert returns the same string encoded in whatever encoding you requested:

```
gchar *g_convert (const gchar *str,
                  gsize len,
                  const gchar *to_codeset,
                  const gchar *from_codeset,
                  gsize *bytes_read,
                  gsize *bytes_written,
                  GError **error);
```

- The str argument is the string to convert, and len is its length. You will often be able to use strlen(str) for this argument, but remember that the standard C string libraries don't necessarily work for all encodings. AIM, for instance, uses an encoding called UCS2-BE, for which strlen() would return 0 for any English sentence. Be sure you know the correct length of a string. For an IM client, the length is often provided to you by the framing of the packet, as discussed in the previous chapter.

- The to_codeset argument is the encoding to which str should be encoded. The version of iconv on my personal computer understands 961 different encodings, many of which are just alternate names for the same encoding (such as ISO8859-1, ISO8859-1, Latin-1, and LATIN1).

- The from_codeset argument is the encoding that str is already in. Like to_codeset, it can be one of almost a thousand different encoding names.

- The bytes_read and bytes_written arguments are pointers to integers that will return the number of bytes read and written. bytes_written is the length of the resulting string, not including the terminating NUL. The actual number of bytes written is one greater than this. bytes_read will usually be equal to len, but will be less if some of the characters were not able to be encoded. For instance, if you attempt encoding Chinese text from Big5 into ASCII, only the very small number of characters that are in both will be converted; bytes_read will not include the unconverted characters.

- Finally, the error argument is provided in case the conversion fails. Errors can be caused by iconv not understanding either encoding specified, or str not being a valid string in from_codeset, for example. I explained how to use GError in Chapter 6. Remember that if catching specific errors is not required—if you need to know only if the function failed or succeeded—you can pass NULL as your error argument. The return value will indicate whether the function succeeded.

g_convert() will return a newly allocated string in the desired encoding, or NULL if the conversion fails. bytes_written will contain the new string length, which may or may not equal the strlen() of the result, depending on the encoding.

Gaim most commonly converts strings within its protocol plug-ins. All strings within GTK+ use an encoding called UTF-8. Therefore, before sending a string out over the network,

Gaim needs to be sure the string is in an encoding the reader will understand. This involves a lot of converting between UTF-8 and other encodings.

IRC, for instance, has no standard for i18n whatsoever. Every IRC server uses its own encoding, and it's not atypical for individual channels to use their own encoding. Gaim has no choice but to depend on the user to properly set what encoding to use in his account settings. When the user sends or receives a message, Gaim attempts to decode it from the user-specified encoding:

```
msg = g_convert(string, strlen(string), "UTF-8", charset, NULL, NULL, NULL);
```

Here, `msg` is the string the IRC plug-in passes back to Gaim and `string` is the string received from the network. `charset` is the user specified character encoding.

If you set the incorrect encoding for the IRC server, you won't be able to communicate. Figure 9-3 shows the results of attempting to use ISO 8859-1 on a Korean IRC channel. Fortunately, more modern communications systems have stronger methods than mere guesses to correctly negotiate which encodings to use.

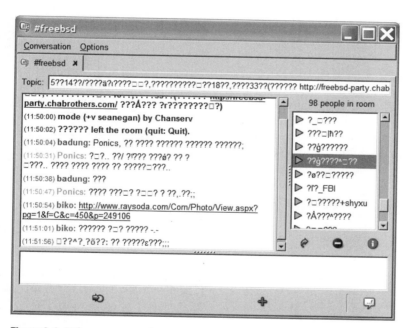

Figure 9-3. *When two people aren't using the same encoding, they cannot communicate.*

Knowing What Encodings to Use

To convert strings from one encoding to another, you must determine which encodings to use. There are two main ways to do so. A third, used by Web browsers that need to deal with Web pages not designed with internationalization in mind, is to guess based on character distribution. That method, though, is based on heuristics and prone to failure. An IM client, such as Gaim, needs to know exactly what encodings are used.

The first, most direct way, is to make a text encoding part of the protocol or API. This is generally useful only with Unicode encodings, discussed later, as only they can represent text in any language. GTK+, for instance, encodes all strings in a Unicode encoding called UTF-8.

Any code that passes to GTK+ (or GLib, or any other related library) a string that isn't valid UTF-8 is a bug and will probably make the application crash. Likewise, every string that GTK+ gives the applications (e.g., the result of gtk_entry_get_text()) is in UTF-8, and must be converted from that to whatever encoding is needed.

The second way is to specify the encoding along with the text. This is the method used by the MSN Messenger protocol, which includes an encoding name in the message's MIME header. This method is used by many protocols, as it allows the client to work regardless of what encodings it understands. Most of the character-encoding conversions in Gaim, therefore, are converting from encodings specified in a message to UTF-8, the encoding used by GTK+ and consequently, throughout Gaim's internals. For outgoing messages, Gaim simply specifies the encoding as UTF-8 for protocols that support that, or converts it to another encoding, such as UCS2-BE, used by AIM.

As you can tell, specifying various encodings and converting strings between them for every message is fairly messy. Fortunately, a system called Unicode was developed with the goal of being able to encode text in any language.

Unicode

Unicode is a character set that assigns every character in every written language to a unique number called a *code point*. Therefore, Unicode can be used regardless of language, allowing the possibility for a single encoding for all languages, and characters from different languages can be used in the same document. None of the encodings discussed so far allow Chinese characters to appear beside Arabic characters, for instance. With Unicode, a document or an IM message can contain text from multiple languages side-by-side.

■**Note** You can read more about Unicode at the Unicode Consortium's Web page http://www.unicode.org/.

Some people think that Unicode is merely a two-byte encoding capable of displaying any character in any language. This isn't true. Unicode doesn't specify at all how characters are represented in memory. Instead, it provides an abstract concept called a "code point."

Code Points

A code point is a number that represents a character. It is written like this: U+0041, where the "U+" identifies it as a Unicode code point, and the number is the hexadecimal value of the number. U+0041 is a capital A; U+C200 is a Hangul (the Korean writing system) "syon" character: 숀.

Each character is given one of these numbers, and the Unicode Consortium, which is in charge of Unicode, has done a lot of work in determining what exactly a character is. For instance, in Arabic, characters at the end of a word have a different appearance than characters appearing within a word. Unicode says that, despite the different appearance, it's the same character. GTK+ applications have very strong support for Unicode strings due to the Pango support library, which uses Unicode exclusively and follows the Unicode Consortium's recommendations in laying out and rendering Unicode text.

■**Tip** In GTK+ applications, you can insert any Unicode character by holding down Ctrl and Shift, and entering the Unicode code point. For instance, Ctrl-Shift-203D inserts an interrobang, one of the Gaim developers' favorite punctuation marks.

A string in plain Unicode, represented as a series of code points, is nothing more than a bunch of numbers with no information about how to represent it in memory. Representing these code points in memory is the job of a Unicode encoding.

Encodings

An encoding specifies how to represent a Unicode code point in memory. It's a concrete representation of the intangible code point. The first encoding was the most obvious. Because originally all the code points could fit in two bytes (this is no longer the case), the first encoding developed was UCS-2, which simply represents each code point in two bytes.

Using UCS-2, the string "Gaim" would be represented as

```
0x00 0x47 0x00 0x61 0x00 0x69 0x00 0x6D
```

Alternatively, because some systems are little-endian, it can be represented as

```
0x47 0x00 0x61 0x00 0x69 0x00 0x6D 0x00
```

These encodings are referred to as UCS2-BE and UCS2-LE, respectively. UCS2 is the Unicode encoding used throughout Windows. AIM also uses it. Instead of using an array of characters to represent strings, use an array of wchars, which are two bytes long, like a short int.

The standard C text functions won't work on UCS-2-encoded strings, because each character takes more than one byte and, for English text, every other byte has the value of the NUL character. Windows provides two versions of any function that takes a string argument to allow for either one-byte characters or two-byte characters. It's clearly undesirable to duplicate large numbers of functions, and because English text uses twice as much memory as needed, a new encoding was invented in 1992, called UTF-8.

UTF-8

UTF-8 is an alternate Unicode encoding that attempts to reduce the number of bytes needed to represent a string. Using UTF-8, every ASCII character takes exactly one byte, and foreign characters take more. This works in a way similar to how I described Asian multibyte encodings earlier.

For code points from 0 to 127, UTF-8 takes exactly one byte, leaving the first bit zero. If the first bit is a 1, that's a sign that the character takes more than one byte—the number of 1s at the start of the byte tells you how many more. Two 1s means the character takes two bytes, three 1s means it takes three bytes, and four 1s indicates four bytes. These 1s are then followed by a 0.

You may have noticed that a single 1 at the start of a byte, followed by a 0, is not used at the beginning of a character. Instead, that combination is reserved for the beginning of subsequent bytes. For instance, a character that takes three bytes will be encoded like so, where the bits of the code point are placed where the *x*s are:

1110xxxx 10xxxxxx 10xxxxxx

Why do subsequent bytes start with 10 when those bits could be used to encode character data? UTF-8 was designed specifically to be able to identify characters out of any point of a stream.

Suppose you have a device plugged in to your computer that sends it a constant stream of UTF-8 text, eight bits at a time. When you turn your computer on, you start receiving the stream at some arbitrary point. You can't assume the first byte you receive is the first byte of a character. If it isn't, your entire stream will be interpreted as garbage. Some way is needed to identify the starting byte of a character so that the program reading that stream can tell where to start. UTF-8 does this by marking every byte that *isn't* the first byte in a character with 10 as the first two bits. If you see a byte whose first two bits are 10, you know it's not the first byte of a character.

This also has the advantage that the string cannot contain a NUL character within it. A byte with the value zero is the NUL character itself, and any other byte contains at least one 1. Because the characters are represented in memory as one to four char types, and no NUL characters are used within a string, the standard C libraries can be used on UTF-8 text. You just need to keep in mind that you're dealing with bytes instead of characters, and that the two may not be equivalent. For instance, if you use the strlen() function on a UTF-8 string, it will return the number of bytes, not necessarily the number of characters. GLib provides a set of functions specifically for dealing with UTF-8. They are documented at http://developer.gnome.org/doc/API/2.0/glib/glib-Unicode-Manipulation.html.

The other thing that makes UTF-8 workable with functions that expect ASCII is that Unicode gives the first 128 code points to the characters in ASCII. And because the first 128 characters are represented in one byte with 0 as the first bit, an ASCII string is identical to its UTF-8 equivalent; an ASCII string is also a UTF-8 string. This means that English speakers don't even need to realize anything's different. Only foreign characters are encoded differently.

Because it's 100% compatible with ASCII, the most prevalent text encoding, and is able to represent all of Unicode with great efficiency, UTF-8 is gaining popularity. GTK+ uses it to represent text internally; it's also commonly used to represent text in Yahoo! Messenger, MSN Messenger, and Jabber. It's a very good way to represent text in any language. However, for your program to be used throughout the world, merely representing foreign text isn't enough.

People should be able to use your application regardless of what language they speak. To do this, your user interface must be translated into other languages. The most popular way to do this in free software is gettext.

Translations with gettext

gettext is a library for translating strings. This library is pervasive throughout the free-software world and is used by Gaim for its translations. For the developer the job is simple, and for the translator the job is straightforward. The user will automatically see text in whatever language is set in his locale settings. The gettext library does all the hard work.

An Overview of gettext

The crux of gettext is the gettext() function. gettext() takes a single argument, a string, then looks for the appropriate translation within a separate file specific to the language being used.

The files containing the translations are Machine Object, or MO files. GNU gettext gives these files a .gmo extension. These are binary files generated from .po files, Portable Objects. A .po file is a text file in a specific format that can be compiled into a .gmo file with a program called msgfmt.

Each .po file (and consequently each .gmo file) represents a single translation. To create a .po file, a .pot file (Portable Object Template) is created. This is a file in the .po format that contains no translations, allowing the translator to fill it out in his own language. This template is created by a program called xgettext, which parses the source code of your program and puts all the strings marked for translation into the .pot file. A new translator renames the file with the ISO code for his language—fr.po for French, for example—and adds that language's translations to it. These translations are in a human-readable format, containing the English strings and their translations. I'll explain this format more thoroughly later, but here I present an example translation of one string in Gaim in French.

```
#: src/gtkdialogs.c:238
msgid ""
"Gaim is a modular messaging client capable of using AIM, MSN, Yahoo!, "
"Jabber, ICQ, IRC, SILC, Novell GroupWise, Napster, Zephyr, and Gadu-Gadu all "
"at once.  It is written using Gtk+ and is licensed under the GPL.<BR><BR>"
msgstr ""
"Gaim est un client de messagerie instantanée compatible avec AIM, MSN, "
"Yahoo!, Jabber, ICQ, IRC, SILC, Novell GroupWise, Napster, Zephyr et Gadu-"
"Gadu. Il est écrit en Gtk+ et est distribué sous licence GPL.<BR><BR>"
```

When the translation needs to be updated, because the text in the program has changed, another gettext program called msgmerge merges the existing .po file with the newly generated .pot file. This leaves only new strings blank, which the translator fills in. The user, then, just runs the application and finds it in her own native language, as specified by the system locale setting.

Note Windows has a locale setting, too, but most applications ignore it and users don't even realize it exists. Gaim used to use the Windows locale setting to determine what translation to use, but because that setting is so infrequently used, users couldn't understand why Gaim was employing a different language than any other application on their machine. Now Gaim's Windows installer asks for a default translation and allows you to override that by setting the GAIMLANG environment variable.

The act of translating is straightforward for both the developer and the translator. The hardest part—as with most of the GNU development tools—is setting up gettext to work properly regardless of what version of it you use.

Setting Up gettext

Setting up gettext is so difficult, Gaim's source code includes a script called setup-gettext solely to set up various versions of gettext. As a general rule, however, the procedure is the same for every version of gettext. The differences lie in small details regarding command-line options and the like.

Complete documentation on gettext is available in the gettext manual, found on the Web at http://www.gnu.org/software/gettext/manual/.

gettextize

The first step to setting up gettext is to run gettextize, a program that creates certain directories and files necessary for any project that uses gettext. Most important of those is the po/ directory, which will originally hold only a Makefile.in.in file, which provides instructions about how to compile the .po files. As you add new translations, you will add them to the po/ directory and edit some files to indicate the new translation. gettextize will also edit your Makefile.am file, instructing Automake to process the newly created directories.

Note A .in file extension in Autotools indicates the file will be used as input to create the given output file. Makefile.in is input to the configure script to generate a makefile; Makefile.in.in is input to generate a Makefile.in.

---

gettextize has a few command-line arguments. --force is a good option to use. It will overwrite the files created from the last time gettextize was run. This is especially useful in case gettextize was upgraded or downgraded, as different versions of gettextize use the various files differently.

Another very useful command-line option is --intl. This option creates a directory called intl/ into which it installs files needed by gettext. This allows internationalization on systems that don't have GNU gettext. Also --no-changelog is an option that keeps gettext from logging changes it makes to the source code in a file called ChangeLog.

gettextize will usually be the first command invoked from your autogen.sh script, which bootstraps the entire build environment. Recall the autogen.sh script created in Chapter 3. Just add gettextize to the top of that script. Gaim's autogen.sh first checks that the user has all the tools needed to bootstrap Gaim (Autotools), and then invokes gettextize indirectly through a helper script designed to work with as many gettext versions as possible.

Configuring the Build Environment

After bootstrapping the gettext environment with gettextize, there are a few files you need to create and edit to properly configure gettext to work with your project. These configurations tell gettext what translations are available and what files are to be translated, and they tell Autoconf and Automake how to work with gettext.

po/POTFILES.in

POTFILES.in, located in the po/ directory, tells gettext which files need to be translated. The format is simple: each line is a filename relative to the top-level source directory (i.e., you specify src/conversation.c). You can also include comments, by starting the line with a hash (#), or you can add whitespace, which is ignored.

   Gaim's POTFILES.in file is simply a list of files with no comments or extraneous whitespace, in alphabetical order for easier management. Each file is listed with its path relative to the top-level source directory, such as

```
src/account.c
src/blist.c
src/conversation.c
src/ft.c
```

   When source files are added or removed, they must also be added or removed here.

po/LINGUAS

The LINGUAS file is a list of languages for which .po files are available. gettext will set the contents of this file to a LINGUAS environment variable that you can edit from within configure.ac. Gaim does not include a LINGUAS file and, instead, the LINGUAS environment variable is set within configure.ac itself:

```
ALL_LINGUAS="am bg ca cs da de en_AU en_CA en_GB es fi fr he hi hu it ja ko lt mk
my_MM nl no pl pt_BR pt ro ru sk sl sq sr sr@Latn sv tr uk vi zh_CN zh_TW"
```

   This list must be updated whenever a new translation is added. Its contents are a whitespace-separated list of ISO language codes such as fr, de, or he. The .po files also use these ISO language codes with a .po extension as their filename. The translators will usually know their own ISO code and send you a correctly named file.

configure.ac

Your configure.ac file needs to be updated to initialize gettext. This can be done with a single line. After declaring the package name and version as described in Chapter 4, add the following line, which calls an m4 macro responsible for configuring gettext to work on your project:

```
AM_GNU_GETTEXT
```

   Next, at the end of configure.ac, your AC_OUTPUT call must be modified to output makefiles in the po/ and intl/ directories created by gettextize. The files that need to be generated are intl/Makefile and po/Makefile.in. Simply add those two files to the list of files in your AC_OUTPUT call, and the configure script will create them.

config.guess and config.sub

If you called gettextize with the --intl command line, creating the intl/ directory, you need to add config.guess and config.sub to your source tree. Because the files in intl/ are platform-dependent, these files help the Autotools system determine what platform compilation is happening on.

These files are distributed with Automake and Libtool and can be copied into the top-level directory of your source tree.

aclocal.m4

The `aclocal.m4` file contains a set of macros used by Autoconf that aren't part of the standard Autoconf distribution. The macros required by gettext fall under this description.

The files containing macros that gettext needs are `codeset.m4`, `gettext.m4`, `glibc21.m4`, `iconv.m4`, `isc-posix.m4`, `lcmessage.m4`, `lib-ld.m4`, `lib-link.m4`, `lib-prefix.m4`, and `progtest.m4`. These files can all be found in the `m4/` directory of the gettext distribution. These files can be concatenated together along with any other macros that your project needs into an `aclocal.m4` file and included in the top-level source directory.

You should now have a build environment that will properly use gettext. When `./autogen.sh`, `./configure`, `make`, and `make install` are run, the gettext system will search the files specified in `POTFILES.in` for strings marked for translation, create a `.pot` file with them, merge that with the existing `.po` files from `LINGUAS`, and compile the `.po` files into `.gmo` files. It will link your application against gettext, which will then look to the appropriate `.gmo` file whenever a translated string is needed. With the files marked and translations specified, the only remaining step for the developer is to specify which strings in the source code must be translated.

Coding with gettext

With most libraries, one of the first things needed is to initialize it somewhere in `main()`; gettext is no different. gettext and Autoconf will already have done most of the work in determining the correct initialization variables and will provide them to you in a set of `#defined` constants. To initialize gettext, placing the following in your `main()` function should suffice:

```
setlocale (LC_ALL, "");
bindtextdomain (PACKAGE, LOCALEDIR);
textdomain (PACKAGE);
```

`LC_ALL`, `PACKAGE`, and `LOCALEDIR` are `#defined` by Autoconf. Once you have called these functions, you can start marking strings to be translated.

The most important element to gettext is the `gettext()` function, which takes a string argument and returns the correct translation for it. Wherever you used to enter something like

```
printf("Hello, world!");
```

you can now enter

```
printf(gettext("Hello, world!"));
```

The `gettext()` function checks the appropriate `.gmo` file for a translation for "Hello, world!" and returns it. If no translation is found, it returns the original string. That's all the developer must do to translate strings.

However, because the `gettext()` function is used so often and should be as transparent as possible in your code, it's standard practice to define a couple of macros to make things easier. Do this in a header that every source file includes:

```
#include <libintl.h>
#define __(String) gettext (String)
#define gettext_noop(String) String
#define N_(String) gettext_noop(String)
```

This defines _() to be equivalent to gettext(). Now, wherever you would normally call gettext(), you just call _():

```
printf(_("Hello, world!"));
```

The call is nearly transparent, but tells xgettext that "Hello, world!" is a string that needs to be translated and calls the gettext() function that will actually do the translation.

Another macro was defined in the example code: N_(). N_(String) is defined, through gettext_noop, as String. So when the preprocessor sees N_("Hello, world!"), it will replace it with "Hello, world!". How is this useful?

The gettext() function is normally used on string literals. However, there are places a string literal can be used where a function call is not allowed, namely array initialization. Suppose you want to translate the contents of this array, for instance:

```
char *choices[] = {"Yes", "No", "Maybe So."};
```

If you were to add _() around those strings, it would result in an error. The preprocessor would add gettext() calls within the array initializer where function calls are not allowed.

The solution is simple. Don't translate the strings within the array initialization, but rather when they're actually used:

```
printf("The choice is %s\n", _(choices[1]));
```

This will call gettext() on "No," return the translation, and then pass it as an argument to printf(). However, as choices[1] isn't a string literal, how will xgettext know the strings in that array need to be translated, anyway? That's what N_() is used for.

When you wrap a string with N_(), it merely marks a string for translation. The macro does absolutely nothing to the source code other than leave the string there. Then, when the string is to be used, translate it with the normal _() call. Another variation of gettext() is ngettext().

English has one plural form. However, other languages have more. Slovene has a special case for two of something in addition to singular and "more than two," for instance. While it's common for English programmers to add a simple if/else statement (or alternatively, use the ternary operator), how do you handle this for translations which may require the exact number? ngettext() does this.

Note The ternary operator is like a miniature if statement and is one of the most obscure constructs in C. It takes three operands: a logic statement to evaluate for truth, and values to return depending on whether the statement is true or false. Thus, an internationalization-naïve statement might use n == 1 ? "goose" : "geese" as a string argument. Multiple ternary operators may even be chained together for more complex logic statements: n == 1 ? "one" : n == 2 ? "two" : "a lot".

The ngettext() function takes three arguments: the singular version of the string, the plural version of the string, and the number:

```
printf(ngettext("%d red balloon goes by", "%d red balloons go by", number));
```

Given the singular and plural forms of the string, the number passed to it, and the information in the .gmo files, ngettext() returns the appropriate string. If the preceding example is run in English, it will print "1 red balloon goes by" if number is 1, and "99 red balloons go by" if number is 99. It will also correctly translate to any language, provided the translation is correct.

Now your build environment is properly configured to automatically handle translations, and your source code is marked up to translate appropriate strings. All you need now are translations.

Translating with gettext

Gaim's source distribution contains a gaim.pot file, which is an empty translation template that serves as the base for new translations. A translator takes that file, renames it to represent his own language, say de.po for German, and edits it accordingly.

The beginning of a .po file is metadata providing information about the translation: who translated it, when it was last translated, and of course, what character encoding it uses; as you know, all text is worthless unless you are certain what encoding it uses.

This header is a bunch of strings surrounded by quotation marks. Here is the actual header from Gaim's de.po:

```
"Project-Id-Version: Gaim\n"
"Reports-Msgid-Bugs-To: \n"
"POT_Creation-Date: 2004-12-02 18:38-0500\n"
"PO-Revision-Date: 2004-08-24 21:40+0200\n"
"Last-Translator: Björn Voigt bjoern@cs.tu-berlin.de\n"
"Language-Team: de de@li.org\n"
"MIME-Version: 1.0\n"
"Content-Type: text/plain; charset=UTF-8\n"
"Content-Transfer-Encoding: 8bit\n"
"Plural-Forms: nplurals=2; plural=n != 1;\n"
```

This is a MIME header as represented in a C string. All the fields of the header, and some of the values, will be generated by xgettext. The translators fill in the other fields as appropriate.

Following the header in the file is the list of all the strings in the program and their translations. Here is an example entry from gaim.pot:

```
#: plugins/statenotify.c:42
#, c-format
msgid "%s has become idle."
msgstr ""
```

This is a single entry. The first line is a comment providing the programmer with the location where this string appears in the source. This is useful if the string has a potentially ambiguous meaning and the translator needs more context to correctly translate it.

The second line is a comment informing the translator that this string is a C formatting string, the type that gets passed to `printf()`. The translator should understand what `%s`, `%d`, and the like mean (string argument and integer argument, respectively) and be able to handle them in his translation.

In some cases, the translator will need to change the order of the formatting arguments in a C-format string. C formatting strings provide a way of explicitly specifying which argument to use. If a translator needed to reverse the order of two arguments to a formatting string, he could translate something to the following, which is a formatting string that puts the second provided argument before the first:

```
"%2$s %1$s"
```

The two fields that matter in the translation of a string are `msgid` and `msgstr`. `msgid` is the English string and is provided by `xgettext`. Every string in your application is identified by its English value. A `.po` file is essentially a list of English phrases and their translations. Translating a `.po` file is largely a matter of reading each `msgid` and filling out each `msgstr` accordingly. Gaim's German translation, `de.po`, translates the earlier example:

```
#: plugins/statenotify.c:42
#, c-format
msgid "%s has become idle."
msgstr "%s ist inaktiv."
```

The translator translates all the `msgid`s and sends the `.po` upstream to the developers. Many projects give the developers Concurrent Versions Systems (CVS) rights and allow translators to commit their translations directly. Gaim has a special SourceForge tracker for `.po` files to be uploaded.

The developer then adds the `.po` file to CVS and edits LINGUAS appropriately, to represent the new translation. This `.po` file, along with all the others, will automatically update to reflect new strings as they're added to the source. Translators can then update their translations by checking the automatically updated translations and filling in the empty `msgstr`s. The translator then sends it back upstream and a developer updates it.

When the program is recompiled and run, and the string `"%s has become idle"` is used, the `gettext()` function searches for the German translation and uses it as seen in Figure 9-4.

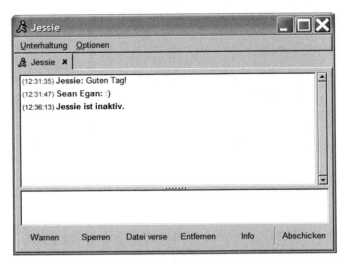

Figure 9-4. *A message translated to German*

Using Translations

Using translations is simple. Provided your system is properly configured, an application using gettext should show you an interface in your native language. It decides what language to use based on the LANG environment variable (or GAIMLANG for the Windows port, as LANG conflicted with other applications), which should be properly set. If you wish to use a language other than your system default, just set the LANG environment variable before running the program. Setting LANG (or GAIMLANG for Windows users) to something like the following will run Gaim with Canadian French as the default language:

```
$ LANG=fr_CA gaim
```

gettext will figure the appropriate .gmo file to use and will show you a French interface.

gettext Summarized

gettext is really easy to use once you get it set up in your build environment. With very slight changes, it's simple to keep your application's translations up-to-date. Just remember a pair of programming guidelines:

- When adding new user-visible strings, surround them with _() or N_() when appropriate.

- When adding new files or removing old files from the source tree, update po/POTFILES.in accordingly.

That's all the programmer *needs* to do. But the programmer *should* do a bit more to make the translators' jobs easier. This generally means including enough context in each string to make the meaning clear. This way translators will understand exactly what needs to be translated. For translators, the job is similarly straightforward:

- If a translation for your language, suppose Finnish, already exists, you'll just want to update it. Translation files are kept in the po/ directory, named with the two-letter ISO language code: fi.po in this case.

- If no translation exists, copy the empty translation template gaim.pot to fi.po. Add fi to the list of languages in the LINGUAS variable.

- Go through the file, providing the translation for each untranslated string.

Next time the project is compiled and installed, your translations will be available.

Summary

For your application to enjoy widespread use around the world, it's important that it work regardless of what language your users speak. It's vital that their language is supported—that is, that your program knows how to represent text in the appropriate language. You now have a firm understanding of character encodings and Unicode, which will allow you to ensure proper language support. It's also important that users see an interface in their own language. You now know how to use the gettext system, allowing you to translate your application into an infinite number of languages.

In the next chapter, I'll address another important issue in ensuring your potential audience is as large as possible. I will discuss portability, which is the art of ensuring your program will work regardless of what hardware or software is used. Plenty of tools exist to aid the developer in writing portable code. I will overview them and point out some of the potential pitfalls to look out for.

CHAPTER 10

■ ■ ■

Portability

If you want to maximize your software's potential audience, it's important that it run on as many machines as possible. The ability of code to run anywhere is called *portability* and is fairly easy to achieve with a suite of tools designed specifically for this task.

Gaim's portability allows it to run on any UNIX system—including Mac OS X—Microsoft Windows, and even obscure hobby operating systems like SkyOS (http://www.skyos.org). This portability comes from several layers, which I'll discuss in this chapter.

Portability and abstraction go hand in hand. In large part, portability boils down to providing the programmer with functions and techniques that are guaranteed to work without revealing the specifics of how they work. Drawing an image to screen is entirely different in UNIX than it is in Windows, but GDK abstracts the implementation away, providing a single, portable way guaranteed to work on any machine. Therefore, the tools that aid in portability can often be thought of merely as abstraction layers. Each layer builds on top of those below it, as shown in Figure 10-1.

GD
GLib
MinGW
POSIX
Libc
C

Figure 10-1. *Portability is provided in layers, each building on top of those beneath it.*

The highest-level portability layer is GDK, discussed in Chapter 8. It abstracts the implementation of interacting with the user via a GUI. GDK itself is built on a number of different portability layers beneath it, the lowest of which is the language it's written in, C.

The C Programming Language

C has been called a "portable assembly language," which is a fairly accurate description. Of all the programming languages currently in widespread use, C is probably the closest to the hardware.

Concepts like memory addresses, which are abstracted away by many other languages, are an essential part of C and must be thoroughly understood.

However, despite being so low-level, C is probably the most portable language in existence. Because it's such a simple language, it's relatively easy to port it to various architectures. C is very close to the hardware, but not to any *particular* hardware; it can be ported to nearly any hardware.

However, despite C's portability, the programmer must still be aware of certain issues in writing portable code. Because C's specification is so liberal in what it lets compilers do, it's easy to become accustomed to tricks that work on your particular compiler but are not portable to other environments. This section will help you avoid bad habits. I'll provide some common assumptions programmers make that may keep their code from being portable. However, to fully appreciate the decisions that went to making C portable, a historical perspective is useful. Much of the following is summarized from "The Development of the C Language," online at http://cm.bell-labs.com/cm/cs/who/dmr/chist.html.

History

C was developed in the early 1970s as a language with which the original UNIX kernel could be written for the DEC PDP-7 machine. The PDP-7 was greatly limited in resources, even for the time, and so the original UNIX kernel was written in assembler, as a high-level language compiler was considered too large a program to create and run for the PDP-7.

Eventually, however, the original UNIX developers, notably Ken Thompson and Dennis Ritchie, came to miss the conveniences of writing in higher-level languages; they were used to writing programs in a language called BCPL on other systems. Due to the hardware constraints, the language was forced to be as bare-bones as possible. Because it was inspired by BCPL (Basic Combined Programming Language), but stripped down in size it was simply called B.

The main feature of BCPL that was lost in B was *typing*. Typing (or datatyping) is the means by which a language attaches a semantic meaning on a variable. Because everything in a computer is merely a number, a type associated with it tells the compiler how that number should be treated. In turn, the compiler can disallow the code to perform invalid operations, such as adding an integer to a string.

B was an untyped language. Neither the language nor the compiler did anything to enforce what a variable should be used for; that was left entirely to the programmer. This did a lot to reduce the size of the compiler, was still better than assembly language, and programs written with the untyped B language were still able to run fairly efficiently given the hardware limitations. When the UNIX developers were given a better machine to work on, the PDP-11, the deficiencies of B became apparent.

The PDP-11 handled some things differently than its predecessor. In particular, the PDP-7 was word-addressed, meaning that memory addresses were assigned to groups of 18 bits. This fit nicely with B's lack of typing, as every value in B was just an 18-bit number called a cell. To deal with characters, B code was written that would access an 18-bit word and extract two 8-bit characters from it. This was the only way to handle characters in an untyped language (aside from using 18-bit characters, which was impossible due to the machine's limited memory), and is what the machine code needed to do anyway.

The PDP-11 gave every byte an address. With this system, each character could be addressed individually and B's method of storing two characters in a cell became obsolete. A character type was needed to determine whether the value was an 8-bit character or a 16-bit word.

Also, the PDP-11 would eventually receive support for floating-point arithmetic, but the normal 16-bit words of the PDP-11 weren't large enough to store floating-point numbers. A way would be needed to determine if a value was a floating-point number. Lastly, the new addressing scheme of the PDP-11 allowed the possibility for pointers to be more efficient than merely a cell representing an index in an array of words. The only way to solve these three problems was to introduce typing.

And so C was developed, introducing pointers to B and allowing it to run more efficiently on the PDP-11. This began the legacy of portability in the UNIX tradition. By creating a typed language and allowing the compiler to use those types in the manner most efficient for the system it runs on, code written in C could run with the same efficiency on any machine with a C compiler.

At the time, however, the C developers weren't interested in portability as much as simply getting C to work on the PDP-11. Over time, however, others would embrace C and write compilers for their own systems. As C progressed, it became possible to rewrite UNIX itself in C. Because UNIX was now written in a portable assembly language, it made sense to begin porting UNIX to other platforms. As new platforms were targeted, new issues would arise as they did with the PDP-11. These issues—mostly addressing type safety—were integrated into C, which became truly portable as a result.

As a portable programming language for systems programming, C's popularity increased, and C began to move outside of its UNIX origins. Because of this popularity and because the language was not formally standardized, conflicting implementations of C were created. In 1983, the standardization process began and the first C standard (known as ANSI C) was accepted in 1989.

K&R, ANSI, and C99

Standardization is an important process in portability; it specifies precisely what an implementation of the standard must and must not do. Because C is standardized, code written for one standards-compliant compiler is guaranteed to work with any other standards-compliant compiler.

Standard compliance is important not only in programming languages but in many aspects of computing. You've already seen in Chapter 8 that if a protocol is standardized, like Jabber or IRC for instance, it's easy to create an implementation guaranteed to work. Later this chapter, in the "POSIX" section, I'll explain how operating-system standards greatly aid in portability.

K&R

The first standard for C was the publication of the first edition of *The C Programming Language* (better known as K&R after the initials of its authors, Brian Kernighan and Dennis Ritchie, also the language's authors). The book was written while the language was still in active development, and although it contained a complete language specification, that specification became inaccurate as the language evolved.

Today, the first edition of K&R is no longer an accurate description of C, although a subsequent edition has been published, bringing the text up to date. Although obsolete, the first edition of K&R has lasting effects on the C language, as many people learned C from reading it. In particular, the most popular common coding style (where to put braces, indents, newlines, etc. in your code) comes from K&R and is commonly called K&R style.

■Tip The indent utility found on many UNIX machines will parse C code and automatically change the coding style however you specify. Using the -kr option will reformat the code in K&R style.

As the language evolved and K&R became inaccurate for describing the language, Kernighan and Ritchie decided to have the language more formally standardized by ISO (the International Organization for Standardization) and ANSI (the American National Standards Institute).

ANSI C

The result of the first standardization process was accepted in 1989 and is commonly known as ANSI C. ANSI C is the flavor of C that Gaim is written in, as well as most other projects using C. This is because ANSI C is the flavor implemented by most compilers.

The various versions of C aren't necessarily compatible with each other. Code written in K&R C isn't guaranteed to compile with an ANSI C compiler, nor is code written in the more recent C standard, C99. Because few, if any, compilers have complete implementations of C99, but every compiler in common usage supports ANSI C, it's recommended that ANSI C be used for all your development. Later this section, I'll present some important issues in making sure your code is ANSI C–compliant.

C99

In 1999 an update to the C standard was formalized. This update, commonly called C99, made numerous significant changes to C. The single most common mistake in writing portable C code is writing code valid in C99 but that fails to compile in a non-C99 compiler.

Recent versions of GCC have almost complete support for C99 enabled by default. Many of the changes from ANSI C come from other languages inspired by C, such as C++ or Java. Therefore, it's common for, say, a Java developer to write some C99 code that isn't ANSI C–compatible, for instance using // to mark comments.

This code will work fine on recent versions of GCC, but when released, people with other compilers may be unable to compile. Because most other compilers are not C99-compatible, this represents a significant portability issue.

Ensuring Your Code is ANSI C–Compliant

As I mentioned, most mistakes in writing non-ANSI-compliant C are matters of using a syntax from another language that was added to C99. These mistakes (often called C99isms) are easy to make if you commonly work with more than one language.

The best way to ensure your code is ANSI C–compliant is to use the -ansi command-line option to GCC. This option disables C99 features and will cause GCC to generate errors just as any other ANSI C compiler would. Here are the most common mistakes to look out for in writing ANSI C:

- **Variable declarations may appear only at the beginning of a block.** In C++, Java, and C99 you may declare a variable anywhere in your code. ANSI C restricts variable declarations to the beginning of a code block, that being at the beginning of a function, if statement, for loop, or anywhere else enclosed with curly braces.

- **Variables may not be declared within** for **loops.** This is implied by the first point, but it's still a mistake common enough to mention. In Java, C++, and C99, it's common to declare a variable within a for loop such as for (int i = 0; i < 10; i++). It's convenient, but not valid ANSI C. In this example, i must be declared outside of the for loop.

- **Text starting with** // **is not comments.** Java, C++, and C99 specify that any text following // on a line is a comment. These are called C++-style comments and are not valid in ANSI C. Only text surrounded by /* and */ are comments in ANSI C.

- **Array lengths must be specified at compile time.** It's common for developers to create an array using a variable, doing something like this:

```
void example_code(int array_length) {
    char *array[length];
        ...
```

This is not valid in ANSI C. You may only declare an array with a constant length at compile time. If you require an array with variable length, create one dynamically with calloc(). In this example, char *array = calloc(array_length, sizeof(char));.

C99 introduced many other changes, but because they don't appear in other languages, it's not common to use them mistakenly when ANSI C is desired. These other features are obscure extensions of C itself, and if writing C99 is not your intention (and I strongly recommend writing only in ANSI C), you don't need to know about them.

By writing valid ANSI C code, you ensure that your code will compile on as many compilers as possible. The C language, however, provides no built-in functions for such things as file input and output or managing memory. This functionality is introduced by the next layer of portability, the standard C library.

libc

While many languages offer functions like file I/O within the language, the purpose of B, C's predecessor, was to be as minimalist as possible. Therefore, B (and subsequently C) delegated such tasks to a library. As C was ported to different languages, so were these libraries, first as the portable I/O package, then C standard I/O routines, and finally the C standard library, or libc. This library presents a common interface of interacting with the operating system and hardware, regardless of what operating system and hardware it's running on.

GCC uses its own version of libc, called glibc (not to be confused with GTK+'s support library GLib, which is unrelated). glibc extends the C standard library as specified but as GCC and glibc are so pervasive, these extensions are used almost everywhere your code will be compiled. However, for truly portable code, you should avoid using glibc extensions and use only libc functions that the standard requires to be in every implementation of libc. Conversely, glibc itself is so highly portable that its requiring glibc would result in greater portability than attempting to write portable versions of its extensions yourself. You should use your judgment.

libc is included as part of the POSIX standard, discussed later this chapter. As with all POSIX functions, glibc extensions to libc are carefully documented. I'll explain how to identify and interpret this documentation later this chapter.

Tips on Writing Portable C Code

The C specification is purposely vague about many details to allow compilers greater liberty in creating the most efficient programs from a given source. Many things are purposely not clearly defined. Just as it is a common problem for people to write code that compiles with a C99 compiler but fails on others, it's a similarly common problem to write code that works on your own machine but fails on others.

Various slight differences between different platforms can cause a wealth of potential incompatibilities. Because you'll likely do all your development on one platform (most Gaim development is done on Linux running on x86 processors), it's hard to detect portability issues. It's rare that an open source developer has access to enough different platforms. Portability issues of this type most often come as the popularity of your project rises and people start using it on platforms you've never even heard of.

Although the variety of platforms your software may run on is endless, the possible portability mistakes are limited and are almost always from assuming everything works the way GCC on x86 processors works.

Most such portability bugs boil down to assuming that your data will be represented in memory a certain way. This includes both word size and endianness. For example, it's common to assume that an int will be stored little-endian in 32 bits. While this is true for x86 processors, it's not true for most other architectures.

■Note A platform's word size is the number of bits allocated to each memory address. Most current systems have 32-bit words, but 64-bit machines are emerging quickly. Endianness was discussed in Chapter 7 and refers to how a machine represents numbers that occupy multiple words. A big-endian system gives the most significant byte to the lowest memory address. A little-endian system gives the most significant byte to the greatest memory address.

Because the C specification makes no rules as to how values are stored in memory, your code cannot make any assumptions as to how values are stored in memory. Don't assume that a char takes 8 bits. On some machines, it takes 9. Even expert programmers will introduce portability errors. They may assume that value >> 1 is equivalent to value / 2, but much faster. While this is often true, it's not *always* true. For the sake of portability, you're best off leaving optimization to the compiler rather than doing it yourself.

When you do come across code that has a very good reason to optimized for a specific machine, or you have code that is inherently nonportable, it's best to localize it within a single source file. Gaim, for instance, requires a lot of source code specific to Windows. Rather than including it throughout Gaim, Windows-specific source is found in the win32 subdirectory of src/ and in win_gaim.c.

Another important step to increasing portability is to minimize the number of external dependencies your project requires. Every library you depend on must be portable, and each can be a limiting factor in what platforms your code can run on. Gaim has relatively few dependencies (although it can be linked against several other libraries optionally), and this allows it to be extremely portable compared to many other open source projects. While Gaim would benefit from introducing particular additional library dependencies, it avoids doing so in the interest of portability.

Having perfectly valid C code that runs perfectly on every hardware configuration is not enough for portability. Your code must also interact properly with the operating system. There is a huge variety of operating systems in existence, and, while the compiler will compile valid code for each operating system it targets, how can you be sure it will run properly on each OS? The answer lies in POSIX, a standard for operating systems.

POSIX

As UNIX was ported to various hardware configurations, changes were made to each port, causing incompatibilities. A program that compiled and ran correctly on one machine might not compile or run on another. The two main UNIX variants at this time (the late 1980s) were known as BSD and System V. The two diverged greatly.

This divergence in incompatible UNIX operating systems allowed other operating systems, particularly Microsoft Windows NT, to gain a foothold. The UNIX community responded by creating the Single UNIX Specification, commonly called POSIX, for Portable Operating System Interface, where the X indicates its UNIX origin.

POSIX specifies what every UNIX system is required to have. It describes the shell: what commands it must provide and how it must interact with the user. It provides a list of utilities required on any UNIX system and how those utilities must behave. It provides a list of system calls and header files available to any program running on the system. By adhering to these specifications, an operating system ensures that any application written with POSIX in mind will work flawlessly. Likewise, any application can depend on the interfaces provided by POSIX while remaining portable.

The portability provided by POSIX is a huge success. It's nearly unheard of for a UNIX application not to work universally across all operating system variants, and when it does, it's almost always an error in the application not following the POSIX specification carefully enough. Operating systems such as Linux have been developed from scratch based solely on the POSIX standards. These from-scratch operating systems enjoy the same portability as operating systems deriving from the original UNIX.

Writing POSIX-compliant code isn't hard. As there is little room for confusion—unlike with the conflicting versions of the C specification. If your code works on one operating system, it will probably work on all the others. Also, there are relatively few OS-specific extensions to the parts of POSIX relevant to application development.

The relevant parts of the POSIX standard are the library and system calls available to you. Included in this is the C standard library, so by knowing how to write portable C code, you've also learned a large element of writing POSIX-compliant code. The rest of the POSIX function calls you make are system calls allowing low-level functionalities like syncing the contents of the disk (sync()) or higher-level calls providing such things as sockets, seen in Chapter 7. As you learn about these functions, you will find relevant portability information for in the documentation.

POSIX functions are documented in man pages (as required by POSIX itself). To read a man page for a given function, run man with the function as an argument. For instance, running man select returns the man page for the select() function, which includes portability information such as the following:

On Linux, the function select *modifies* timeout *to reflect the amount of time slept; most other implementations do not do this. This causes problems both when Linux code which reads timeout is ported to other operating systems, and when code is ported to Linux that reuses a struct timeval for multiple selects in a loop without initializing it. Consider timeout to be undefined after select returns.*

This sort of message is typical of a man page. It explains the problem (Linux handles this function differently from other operating systems), what causes it (reading or reusing the timeout argument after the function returns), and how to avoid it (consider timeout to be undefined after select() returns). Reading the man page for select() should let you fully understand how to use it portably.

By carefully adhering to the POSIX standard and avoiding any implementation-specific extensions, your application is guaranteed to work correctly on any UNIX system, including Linux, Solaris, BSD, and Mac OS X. The very vast majority of potential users for your desktop application, however, do not use a POSIX-compliant operating system; Windows is, by far, the most popular desktop operating system. For Gaim, MinGW solves the problem of getting UNIX programs to compile on Windows.

Porting to Windows with MinGW

MinGW (Minimalist GNU for Windows) ports the GCC compiler to Windows. Although it doesn't provide any POSIX compatibility itself, it compiles C code (and other languages supported by GCC) to native Windows applications.

It comes with its own version of Microsoft's API header files and links against the standard libraries found in a Windows application. Most anything you can do in C with Microsoft's own C compiler can be done with MinGW. This allows us to add Windows-specific functions to Gaim. We allow our buddy list to be "docked," for instance.

If you're a Windows user, you installed MinGW in Chapter 1 and have been using it since. Because it's merely a port of GCC, it handles source code the same way as GCC. What you learned in Chapter 3 about GCC is also true for MinGW, including preprocessor directives.

GCC provides preprocessor directives based on the system it's compiling for. For portability to Windows, the most important is the _WIN32 macro. This macro will be defined if GCC is compiling for Windows. Many of the otherwise-unavoidable differences between the two platforms are managed with this _WIN32 macro and #ifdef statements.

For instance, POSIX requires that the slash character, /, be used to separate directories and files in the file system. Windows uses the backslash, \. To avoid this problem, code will generally avoid using either specifically, but rather use a macro such as DIR_SEPARATOR, which is defined differently for each system:

```
#ifdef _WIN32
#define G_DIR_SEPARATOR '\'
#else
#define G_DIR_SEPARATOR '/'
#endif
```

What makes MinGW possible is the MinGW runtime, which is included in every application compiled by MinGW. This runtime is a "glue" attaching MinGW-compiled applications to the Windows operating system. It allows for programs that use the Windows operating system natively, but by itself it does not provide POSIX compatibility; instead, it provides the ability to make system calls that can be wrapped to provide equivalent functionality for much of POSIX.

Cygwin

Due to the vastly different natures of Windows and UNIX, complete POSIX compatibility is impossible without essentially emulating a UNIX environment. This is the approach that Cygwin takes. Gaim's Windows port is developed in this emulated environment. An application developed against Cygwin can expect the system to behave exactly like a UNIX system.

Cygwin does things like implement its own UNIX-like file system in a directory within the Windows native file system. This allows for nearly complete POSIX compatibility, but slows down the system and limits how well it can access the underlying Windows environment.

■Note Cygwin allows you to run UNIX applications on Windows. The opposite of this, running Windows applications on UNIX, is achieved by the Wine project. Considering that Windows lacks formal standardization along the lines of POSIX, Wine works very well. Just as Cygwin offers libraries to easily port your UNIX code to Windows, Wine makes it easy to port Windows code to UNIX. However, because Windows is not clearly standardized and the Wine project is based on a lot of guesswork and reverse engineering, attempts to port UNIX applications to Windows tend to be more successful.

Cygwin is a popular environment from which to run the GNU development tools, such as make and GCC, because they expect to run on a POSIX-compliant machine. For developing Windows applications, however, it's a poor choice. It's usually better to isolate your POSIX-specific code from Windows code that does the same thing than it is to develop for an emulated UNIX environment.

Windows Compatibility Libraries

Fortunately for us, it's in Microsoft's best interest to make it easy for developers to port their UNIX applications to Windows. As such, large parts of POSIX are already available natively on Windows. The C standard library, for instance, is present, as required by the C specification. MinGW has no trouble using it. Similarly, Windows provides the Winsock API, which is nearly identical to BSD sockets.

However, some aspects of Windows are simply too different to be easily made POSIX-compliant. These aspects include threading, managing files, and loading dynamic libraries, such as plug-ins. Cross-platform desktop applications typically use compatibility libraries that provide the same interface for these tasks, regardless of what system they run on.

What these libraries essentially amount to is a two or more sets of functions with identical interfaces, separated by `#ifdef _WIN32` as seen earlier. That example, in fact, comes from GLib, which provides this functionality to Gaim.

GLib

The next layer of portability is provided by GLib, one of GTK+'s support libraries. I've already presented GLib in Chapters 4 and 5 in explaining how it provides object-oriented facilities to GTK+, how it provides a main loop and allows input from the network or from the user to trigger callbacks from it, and how it provides useful data types and utilities to make programming in C easier. It is these utility functions that lend portability to applications that use it.

GLib attempts to bridge the gap between the Windows API and that provided by POSIX. The result is that, instead of your code depending on functions available in POSIX, it depends on the GLib equivalents. This is why GTK+ code rarely uses standard system calls, libc calls, or even data types. Instead of using char, it uses gchar. Instead of malloc() it uses g_malloc().

Some of these measures are a bit extreme, especially given the previous portability efforts. You already know that you can't trust the size of an int, and won't write code that depends on it; you don't need a gint type. In fact, some of the GLib equivalents don't even add anything portability-wise, and exist only for conformity. However, even these functions can be useful. If tomorrow a brand-new operating system sprung up with its own set of unique compatibilities, your GLib application wouldn't need a single change to support it once GLib were upgraded. Using GLib's portability functionality is a good habit to learn, despite Gaim using it only irregularly.

Gaim typically uses the standard C data types, char, int, etc., and only infrequently uses types such as gchar, or gint. When it does, it's usually within GTK+ implementation widgets or other GTK+-intensive code in order to add consistency with GTK+'s own API. Portable utility macros and functions, on the other hand, are entirely necessary for Gaim to run on Windows.

■**Note** GLib's data types are perfectly compatible with C's standard data types. Any function that expects a char can be passed a gchar, and vice versa, without as much as a compiler warning.

Portable Macros

GLib provides a few common macros that provide platform-neutral functionality. I've already discussed one such macro, G_DIR_SEPARATOR, which returns the directory separator character depending on the operating system. A similar macro is G_DIR_SEPARATOR_S, which returns the separator as a string rather than a char. This is useful when dealing with functions that take strings, such as g_strdup_printf().

■**Tip** Because two string literals (strings specified in source code within quotation marks) back-to-back is equivalent to the two strings concatenated together, code like G_DIR_SEPARATOR_S "directory" G_DIR_SEPARATOR "file" is perfectly valid syntax. It's also a lot neater than piecing together the path with library calls.

Another useful pair of macros allows you to convert between integers and pointers. Recall that every callback function in GTK+ accepts a void pointer specified when the callback was attached. It's often useful to attach only an integer, but inconvenient to allocate room for one, send a pointer to it, and free it later.

Of course, pointers are just numbers anyway, so you should be able to send the number you want, however meaningless it is as a memory address, to the callback, disguised as a pointer:

```
g_signal_attach(object, "signal", callback, (void*)5);
```

However, this makes the assumption that you can safely store an integer in memory reserved for a pointer. As I explained earlier, most nonportable C comes from making invalid assumptions like this. In particular, this code is likely to fail on 64-bit architectures, which are likely to handle the two types differently.

GINT_TO_POINTER() and GPOINTER_TO_INT() safely handle the conversion from integer to pointer and from pointer to integer, respectively. It allows you to send your integer values to callback functions. You may not, however, use this for the opposite reason: attempting to store pointers in ints is just not possible in C.

Utility Functions

In addition to macros, GLib provides a large number of portable utility functions that replace or enhance those in POSIX. Because different implementations of POSIX—including the parts implemented in Windows—differ where behaviors are not clearly defined, it's easy to introduce portability problems when dealing with these ambiguous functions. By using their GLib equivalents, you ensure your code will work the same way, regardless of where it runs.

These functions include many of the string utilities in Chapter 8. The names of these functions are typically the name of the POSIX function, prefixed with g_. These functions include g_strdup(), g_strstr(), and g_printf(). These functions behave as you would expect them to if you're familiar with C programming (their documentation appears at http://developer. gnome.org/doc/API/2.0/glib/glib-String-Utility-Functions.html). The string utilities do the same thing regardless of what platform they run on. Any platform that runs C represents strings the same way, and GLib can modify these strings directly. GLib also provides functions that may do vastly different things on UNIX than on Windows, but to the same effect. These functions tend to focus on environment variables and file paths.

Environment variables are variables set at the shell before running a program. That program can then request the value of any environment variable by name. Environment variables are a way of creating system-wide preferences. They're similar to command-line variables, except they're used for all applications. On UNIX, they provide a lot of information to the user: the username, the current directory, and the preferred language to use, for example. Windows uses them to a lesser extent, but they still exist.

You can portably read an environment variable from either operating system with GLib's g_getenv() function. However, UNIX programmers used to getting certain information about the user from his environment variable—suppose the username, stored in $HOME—must realize this cannot be done portably as Windows does not set the $USER variable. For this reason, GLib provides portable methods of fetching information about the environment.

Caution Although on Windows, the result of g_getenv() and of any other function that returns information about the environment is guaranteed to be UTF-8, the encoding used on UNIX is undefined and there's no good way of figuring it out. Fortunately, the recent trend in Linux distributions is to use UTF-8 encoding; if you have no way of knowing, you're best assuming UTF-8.

---

g_get_user_name() will return the username on either system. On UNIX, it will return the result of g_getenv("USER"); (technically, it fetches the username from the passwd file, which contains this information); on Windows, it calls the GetUserNameW() function from the Win32 API. The same feature is implemented in entirely different ways, but provides the programmer an identical interface to access the username. Similar functions provide ways of learning which directories should be used for storing various data or settings. The user's data directory, for instance, comes from the XDG_DATA_HOME variable on UNIX and from the Windows CSIDL_PERSONAL "special folder." The correct path can always be returned with g_get_user_data_dir(). Once you have this path, GLib provides a convenient way of working with it and creating filenames within it.

I've already mentioned the G_DIR_SEPARATOR macro that you must use to portably create paths. In actuality, though, this macro is almost never needed, as GLib provides utility functions to parse and create file paths using the correct directory separator.

Perhaps the most useful of these is g_build_path(). This function takes as arguments a NULL-terminated list of string and returns a string containing a valid path with the given strings separated by the proper directory separator. To retrieve the directory Gaim uses for storing logs, for instance, one might call

```
gchar *log_dir = g_build_path(g_get_user_data_dir(), ".gaim", "logs", NULL);
```

Note g_get_user_data_dir() was added to GLib in version 2.6. Because Gaim needs to compile against GLib 2.0, it does not actually use this function.

As stated earlier, some of these utility functions—particularly the string utilities—currently have no inherent portability advantages. They exist for consistency as not to require the programmer to remember which POSIX functions are in GLib and which aren't. In these cases, you can safely swap between the standard C functions and GLib functions. The same is not the case with GLib's memory-allocation functions.

Memory Allocation

Although GLib's memory allocation API is not much more than C's API with the g_ prefix, the functions do not behave exactly the same. The implication is that, in an application using GLib, you should always use g_malloc() and g_free(), as swapping between the two can lead to failure.

The reason for this is that GLib allows the programmer to specify which functions to use for allocating and freeing memory. By default, GLib will use plain malloc() and free(), but it provides one particular set of functions itself that is useful for debugging.

The group of functions that GLib uses for memory allocation is called GMemVTable. You tell GLib which to use with the function g_mem_set_vtable(). This function *must* be called before any other GLib function call (otherwise you may wind up with memory allocated with the default GMemVTable, then later freed with the new one). For GTK+ applications, this implies including it before any GTK+ function calls also. Right before gtk_main() is probably a good place:

```
g_mem_set_vtable(glib_mem_profiler_table);
```

glib_mem_profiler_table is a GMemVTable that tracks statistics about how much memory is being allocated and freed. By calling g_mem_profile(), you cause the program to print these statistics to the console. Changing the GMemVTable shouldn't be done typically as it's considerably slower, but it may be useful for debugging memory problems. Naturally, using the profiling allocator and then freeing that memory with free() would throw off the statistics. If some other GMemVTable were used, the consequences could be worse. Don't ever attempt to mix the two in the same code. Because GTK+ and its support libraries use GLib for all their memory allocation, you should, too.

File Management

GLib also wraps libc's standard file I/O functions. It does this to allow better portability to Windows, especially with respect to internationalization.

Windows has no support for internationalized filenames from its implementation of libc. Therefore, in order to create a non-English file name, it's necessary to use its Win32 API, which provides functions specifically for dealing with foreign filenames.

These functions, as you could have guessed, are identical in name to libc's file I/O functions. They include g_open(), g_close(), g_write(), and g_read(). However, GLib's API also provides convenience utilities, such as g_file_get_contents(), which allocates memory and reads the entire contents of a file into it. Anyone who's ever done file I/O in C recognizes how useful this is.

■Tip When opening files with open() (or g_open()), the final agument is the mode in which you specify if you're reading, writing, or appending with r, w, or a, respectively. For portability concerns, UNIX programmers need to keep in mind the b mode, which specifies binary files. If that mode isn't set, UNIX-style newlines ("\n") will be replaced with Windows-style newlines ("\r\n") on Windows machines. This can have numerous consequences and you definitely need to stay aware of it.

Plug-Ins

Shared objects are binary files containing code that isn't linked to an application until runtime. These are very useful for many reasons: most libraries are installed as shared objects, allowing you to maintain libraries independently from the programs that use them. Shared objects are also useful to many applications as plug-ins—bits of code linked to the application at the request of the user, implementing functionality not normally found in the application.

No system for loading plug-ins or other shared objects was specified by POSIX until 2003. Plenty of older machines are still running, each with its own mechanism for dynamic library loading. Therefore, even if you limit your application to UNIX, you cannot depend on any single interface. Windows has its own interface of accessing its plug-ins, known as Dynamically Linked Libraries (DLLs). GLib wraps three of these mechanisms—that used by Sun and Linux, that used by HP-UX, and that used by Windows—into a single API called GModule.

Adding plug-in support to your application is simple with GModule. The first thing you must do is to make sure the platform you're running on supports GModule by calling g_module_supported():

```
if (!g_module_supported()) return;
```

Once you've ensured GModule is supported, you can start loading plug-ins. If you want to portably store a list of plug-ins to load—in a configuration file, perhaps—you can store only the base name of the file, minus the extension. For instance, Gaim's history plug-in (which inserts the last conversation you had with someone in any new conversation window with that person) is located on my machine at `/usr/local/lib/gaim/history.so`. On a Windows machine, it's stored at `C:\Program Files\Gaim\plugins\history.dll`. I can store merely "history" and use `g_module_build_path()` to construct the full filename, portable on any machine:

```
gchar *plugin_path = g_module_build_path(LIBDIR, "history");
```

This function is similar to `g_build_path()`, but takes only two arguments: a directory and a filename. `LIBDIR` is a macro included in Gaim that returns the correct directory for storing plug-ins, depending on the system. GLib concatenates the two and appends the appropriate extension. Now that you have a valid path to this plug-in, you can load it with a single function call.

■Note Because Gaim has multiple directories from which plug-ins can be loaded, it cannot safely use the technique described here. There could be a `history.so` in every directory where plug-ins are stored. Gaim saves the complete path to each plug-in and falls back on using only the base name if the entire path doesn't exist. This still allows people to use the same configuration across platforms.

To load a plug-in, call `g_module_open()`. This function takes two arguments: the path you've created and a bitmask of `GModuleFlags`. These flags specify how the symbols (function names and variables) are bound. `G_MODULE_BIND_LAZY` tells GModule not to look up symbols until they're needed, and `G_MODULE_BIND_LOCAL` causes those symbols not to be accessible outside of GModule. Leaving `flags` as 0 is usually acceptable:

```
GModule *module = g_module_open(plugin_path, 0);
```

While the module is open, you can access all the symbols in it. A symbol is any function or variable name. A dynamic library stores the location of all these by name. So in a Gaim plug-in, which is required to have a `gaim_init_plugin()` function, the plug-in stores the location of that function and can return it when asked. To retrieve the location of a symbol, call `g_module_symbol()`:

```
gboolean (*init_function)(GaimPlugin*);
if (!g_module_symbol(module, "gaim_init_plugin", &init_function)) return;
```

The first argument to `g_module_symbol()` is the opened `GModule` object. The second argument is the symbol name, and the third is a pointer in which to store its address. In this case, `gaim_init_plugin()` is a function taking a `GaimPlugin`, and returns a `gboolean`. A function pointer of this type is what we give to `g_module_symbol()`. Note that there is no type-checking. If this library contains an `int` called `gaim_init_plugin`, it will return that. This would cause a crash when the function runs, which would be considered the plug-in's fault. There's nothing GModule can do to prevent that. `g_module_symbol()` returns a `gboolean`, which will be `TRUE` if the symbol was found and correctly resolved.

■**Note** Windows won't let you resolve a function within a DLL unless it's explicitly defined to be made available. To do this, include G_MODULE_EXPORT before the function name (e.g., G_MODULE_EXPORT gboolean gaim_init_plugin(GaimPlugin *plugin)) to cause the compiler to make the symbol externally available. Similarly, plug-ins can use global variables in your main program only if they're marked with G_MODULE_IMPORT, although this isn't necessary for functions.

If the symbol is successfully resolved, you can call it just like any other function pointer:

```
gboolean ret = init_function(plugin);
```

You can design your plug-in API however you which. Gaim prefers to load a single function pointer, gaim_init_plugin(), which returns function pointers to all the other functions the Gaim core may need to call. You can design your plug-in API with many different function names exported, each called at a different time. Do whatever you think is best for your application.

When you're finished with the plug-in, unload it with g_module_close():

```
g_module_close(module);
```

The plug-in will be unloaded and any symbols you resolved from it will be invalid; be sure not to attempt to use them afterwards.

GLib provides portable interfaces for managing the system on a low level. The GUI layer is one layer higher. There are several disparate user interface systems, all completely different from one another. GDK allows the same GTK+ code to work on all of them.

GDK

I introduced GDK in Chapter 8 and explained that it abstracted away the details of how interacting with the user with a GUI is accomplished, allowing GTK+ to run on any machine that GDK supports.

GDK is strongly influenced, though, by its initial target, X11, the most commonly used graphical interface on UNIX. Porting GDK to a new platform is largely a matter of applying the principles of X to whatever system you're targeting.

X11

X11 (or X; 11 is the protocol version) is actually a portability layer itself. Because it's based on a network protocol rather than a library (although most X11 development, including GDK, uses a library, Xlib, which is very portable itself), the same exact code will work on any machine with a compliant X server. In fact, the server doesn't even need to be on the same machine and your code, and it will still interact perfectly. This is known as *network transparency*.

This is another good example of abstraction providing portability. You needn't know anything about how the X server works, provided you follow the protocol. To get X to work on a new machine, you just need to write an X server that follows the protocol; you don't even need to recompile your applications. Most UNIX machines run X; you can even run X on your

Windows machine, as shown in Figure 10-2. The Windows X server is implemented by making calls to the Windows GUI system, the Win32 API.

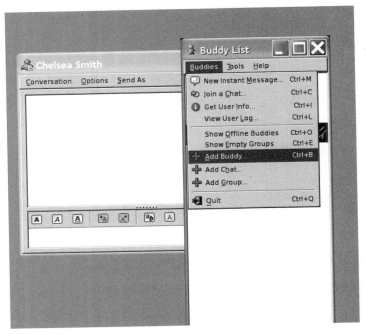

Figure 10-2. *Using network transparency, I can run Gaim from my Linux machine on any system with an X server, including this Windows machine.*

Win32

The Win32 API is what makes interacting via a GUI possible on Windows. To get GTK+ applications to run on Windows, GDK was ported to use the Win32 API. Unlike X11, Win32 is not a protocol, but a set of system calls, many of which are undocumented. Therefore, it's not easy to port Win32 code to other platforms. The best effort is the Wine project, which supports enough of Win32 to run many applications.

Many projects, however, allow you to run GUIs on both X and Win32 by providing a higher-level API that abstracts the details away. Trolltech's Qt (used by the KDE project), wxWidgets, and Mozilla's XUL are all capable of drawing on any platform, as well as GDK.

GDK also allows portability while still allowing you access to the underlying system. For example, if kept inside a `#ifdef _WIN32` or whatever is appropriate, you can access the underlying Win32 data and manipulate GTK+ windows like any other Win32 window. This allows you to do more powerful things that aren't abstracted by GDK. For instance, Gaim flashes conversations in the Windows taskbar when new messages are received.

This ability is accessed via the `window` member of a `GdkWindow` object. On X11, this points to a `Window`, an Xlib data type. On Windows, it points to an `HWND`. Either can be used anywhere a window is called for in Xlib or Win32, respectively. One especially interesting application of using the underlying windowing system in X11 code is the GTK-WIMP theme.

WIMP

An important part of a portable user interface is that the user interface's look and feel match that of the system it's running on. If the application looks clearly out of place, it's obvious that it's not a native application and the user experience suffers. Some projects, such as wxWidgets, actually use Windows widgets natively. Because of its strong hierarchy, including the ability to create your own custom widgets, and its powerful theming system, GTK+ is unable to provide Windows widgets natively. That theming system, however, allows you to draw the elements of your application any way you want. You can draw your interface to make it *look* like a native Windows application even though it isn't, as seen in Figure 10-3.

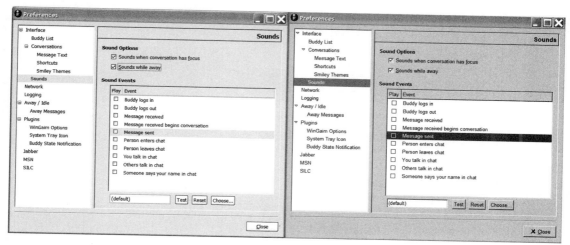

Figure 10-3. *The WIMP theme (left) draws the application to match the Windows theme, resulting in a far better experience than the default theme (right).*

The WIMP theme uses a Windows-style API to draw interface elements. When GTK+ asks the theme to draw a button, the theme in turn asks Windows to do it. It's not actually a Win32 button, but it's drawn just like one. The WIMP theme goes even further and does things such as removing icons from standard buttons like OK (Windows doesn't typically have icons in buttons, but GTK+ applications do) and adding keyboard shortcuts familiar to most Windows users (such as pushing the Escape key to close a dialog).

Using GTK+'s WIMP theme allows your GTK+ applications to have a consistent look across numerous platforms. This is the ideal case for a portable desktop application.

Summary

You now know about the various technologies that combine to provide portability to Gaim. You can use these same technologies in your own applications, and those applications will run on almost any computer imaginable. You understand what precautions to take when using these technologies and should be able to write truly portable code.

You can apply the knowledge you've learned throughout this book—such as networking and GUI coding, as well as the various development tools commonly used in open source software—to create your own networked, cross-platform desktop applications for instant messaging or for whatever you desire. Good luck, and happy hacking.

Index

forums.apress.com
FOR PROFESSIONALS BY PROFESSIONALS™

JOIN THE APRESS FORUMS AND BE PART OF OUR COMMUNITY. You'll find discussions that cover topics of interest to IT professionals, programmers, and enthusiasts just like you. If you post a query to one of our forums, you can expect that some of the best minds in the business—especially Apress authors, who all write with *The Expert's Voice*™—will chime in to help you. Why not aim to become one of our most valuable participants (MVPs) and win cool stuff? Here's a sampling of what you'll find:

DATABASES
Data drives everything.

Share information, exchange ideas, and discuss any database programming or administration issues.

INTERNET TECHNOLOGIES AND NETWORKING
Try living without plumbing (and eventually IPv6).

Talk about networking topics including protocols, design, administration, wireless, wired, storage, backup, certifications, trends, and new technologies.

JAVA
We've come a long way from the old Oak tree.

Hang out and discuss Java in whatever flavor you choose: J2SE, J2EE, J2ME, Jakarta, and so on.

MAC OS X
All about the Zen of OS X.

OS X is both the present and the future for Mac apps. Make suggestions, offer up ideas, or boast about your new hardware.

OPEN SOURCE
Source code is good; understanding (open) source is better.

Discuss open source technologies and related topics such as PHP, MySQL, Linux, Perl, Apache, Python, and more.

PROGRAMMING/BUSINESS
Unfortunately, it is.

Talk about the Apress line of books that cover software methodology, best practices, and how programmers interact with the "suits."

WEB DEVELOPMENT/DESIGN
Ugly doesn't cut it anymore, and CGI is absurd.

Help is in sight for your site. Find design solutions for your projects and get ideas for building an interactive Web site.

SECURITY
Lots of bad guys out there—the good guys need help.

Discuss computer and network security issues here. Just don't let anyone else know the answers!

TECHNOLOGY IN ACTION
Cool things. Fun things.

It's after hours. It's time to play. Whether you're into LEGO® MINDSTORMS™ or turning an old PC into a DVR, this is where technology turns into fun.

WINDOWS
No defenestration here.

Ask questions about all aspects of Windows programming, get help on Microsoft technologies covered in Apress books, or provide feedback on any Apress Windows book.

HOW TO PARTICIPATE:
Go to the Apress Forums site at **http://forums.apress.com/**.
Click the New User link.